THE
GREAT
HOUSE
OF
GOD

THE GREAT HOUSE OF GOD

A Home for Your Heart

MAX LUCADO

WORD PUBLISHING
Dallas • London • Vancouver • Melbourne

WORD PUBLISHING
1997

Unless otherwise indicated, Scripture quotations used in this
book are from the Holy Bible, New Century Version, copyright © 1987,
1988, 1991 by Word Publishing, Dallas, Texas 75234. Used by permission.

Other Scripture references are from the following sources: The Holy Bible,
New International Version (NIV). Copyright © 1973, 1978, 1984, International
Bible Society. Used by permission of Zondervan Bible Publishers.
The King James Version of the Bible (KJV). The Living Bible (TLB),
copyright 1971 by Tyndale House Publishers, Wheaton, IL. Used by permission.
The Message (MSG), copyright © 1993. Used by permission of
NavPress Publishing Group. The New King James Version (NKJV),
copyright © 1979, 1980, 1982, 1992, Thomas Nelson, Inc., Publisher.
J. B. Phillips: The New Testament in Modern English, Revised Edition (PHILLIPS).
Copyright © J. B. Phillips 1958, 1960, 1972. Used by permission of Macmillan
Publishing Co., Inc. The Revised Standard Version of the Bible (RSV).
Copyright © 1946, 1952, 1971, 1973 by the Division of Christian Education of the
National Council of the Churches of Christ in the USA.
Used by permission. The Jerusalem Bible (TJB). Copyright © 1968 by Darton,
Longman, & Todd, Ltd., and Doubleday & Co., Inc. The New
English Bible (NEB). Copyright © 1961, 1970 by the delegates of the Oxford
University Press and the Syndics of the Cambridge University Press.
Reprinted by permission.

LIBRARY OF CONGRESS CATALOGING-IN-PUBLICATION DATA
The great house of God : a home for your heart / Max Lucado.
p. cm.
Includes bibliographical references
ISBN 0-8499-1295-4
1. Lord's prayer. I. Title
BV230.L73 1997
226.9'606—DC21   97-22821
CIP

Printed in the United States of America
0 1 2 3 4   BVG 9 8 7

I gladly dedicate this book to my assistant, Karen Hill.
Thank you for thousands of hours of selfless service.

Contents

Acknowledgments

I appreciate the following friends for helping, tolerating, resuscitating and/or indulging me during the writing of this book:

Liz Heaney—yet another book, yet another year
and still no regrets.

The Oak Hills Church leadership and staff—
I'm out of hibernation! Thanks for covering for me.

The Oak Hills Church—Thanks for ten years (!) of joy.

Steve and Cheryl Green—I don't know what I did to
deserve friends like you, but I'm sure glad I did it.

All my friends at Word/Thomas Nelson—
A hearty thanks for a job well done.

To all my minister friends who use my stuff for sermon ideas—
Power to you! You deserve a break.

To Laura Kendall—a tip o' the hat for your dip o' the quill.
Thanks for your help.

Steve Halliday—for writing the discussion guide.

And to the readers— some of you I'm meeting for the first time,
others for the twelfth. You are so gracious to invite me into your
home. I'll do my best not to overstay my welcome.

And lastly, to my wife Denalyn—
I guess you could say I love you a little.
A little more every minute of every day. (Happy 40th, honey!)

CHAPTER 1

THE
GREAT HOUSE OF GOD

──── *A Home for Your Heart* ────

*I only ask one thing from the LORD.
This is what I want: let me live in the
LORD's house all my life.* —PSALM 27:4

I'D LIKE TO TALK WITH YOU about your house. Let's step through the front door and walk around a bit. Every so often it's wise to do a home inspection, you know—check the roof for leaks and examine the walls for bows and the foundation for cracks. We'll see if your kitchen cupboards are full and glance at the books on the shelves in your study.

What's that? You think it odd that I want to look at your house? You thought this was a book on spiritual matters? It is. Forgive me, I should have been clearer. I'm not talking about your visible house of stone or sticks, wood or straw, but your invisible one of thoughts and truths and convictions and hopes. I'm talking about your spiritual house.

1

You have one, you know. And it's no typical house. Conjure up your fondest notions and this house exceeds them all. A grand castle has been built for your heart. Just as a physical house exists to care for the body, so the spiritual house exists to care for your soul.

You've never seen a house more solid:

the roof never leaks,

the walls never crack,

and the foundation never trembles.

You've never seen a castle more splendid:

the observatory will stretch you,

the chapel will humble you,

the study will direct you,

and the kitchen will nourish you.

Ever lived in a house like this? Chances are you haven't. Chances are you've given little thought to housing your soul. We create elaborate houses for our bodies, but our souls are relegated to a hillside shanty where the night winds chill us and the rain soaks us. Is it any wonder the world is so full of cold hearts?

Doesn't have to be this way. We don't have to live outside. It's not God's plan for your heart to roam as a Bedouin. God wants you to move in out of the cold and live . . . with him. Under his roof there is space available. At his table a plate is set. In his living room a wingback chair is reserved just for you. And he'd like you to take up residence in his house. Why would he want you to share his home?

Simple, he's your Father.

You were intended to live in your Father's house. Any place less than his is insufficient. Any place far from his is dangerous. Only the home built for your heart can protect your heart. And your Father wants you to dwell *in* him.

No, you didn't misread the sentence and I didn't miswrite it. Your Father doesn't just ask you to live *with* him, he asks you to live *in* him. As Paul wrote, "For in him we live and move and have our being" (Acts 17:28 NIV).

Don't think you are separated from God, he at the top end of a great ladder, you at the other. Dismiss any thought that God is on Venus while you are on earth. Since God is Spirit (John 4:23), he is next to you: God himself is our roof. God himself is our wall. And God himself is our foundation.

Moses knew this. "LORD," he prayed, "you have been our home since the beginning" (Ps. 90:1). What a powerful thought: God as your home. Your home is the place where you can kick off your shoes and eat pickles and crackers and not worry about what people think when they see you in your bathrobe.

Your home is familiar to you. No one has to tell you how to locate your bedroom; you don't need directions to the kitchen. After a hard day scrambling to find your way around in the world, it's assuring to come home to a place you know. God can be equally familiar to you. With time you can learn where to go for nourishment, where to hide for protection, where to turn for guidance. Just as your earthly house is a place of refuge, so God's house is a place of peace. God's house has never been plundered, his walls have never been breached.

God can be your dwelling place.

God *wants* to be your dwelling place. He has no interest in being a weekend getaway or a Sunday bungalow or a summer cottage. Don't consider using God as a vacation cabin or an eventual retirement home. He wants you under his roof now and always. He wants to be your mailing address, your point of reference; he wants to be your home. Listen to the promise of his Son, "If my people love me they will obey my teaching. My father will love them and we will come to them and make our home with them" (John 14:23).

For many this is a new thought. We think of God as a deity to discuss, not a place to dwell. We think of God as a mysterious miracle worker, not a house to live in. We think of God as a creator to call on, not a home to reside in. But our Father wants to be much more. He wants to be the one in whom "we live and move and have our being" (Acts 17:28 NIV).

When Jehovah led the children of Israel through the wilderness, he didn't just appear once a day and then abandon them. The pillar of fire was present all night; the cloud was present all day. Our God never leaves us. "I will be with you always," he promised (Matt. 28:20). Our faith takes a quantum leap when we understand the perpetual presence of the Father. Our Jehovah is the fire of our night and the cloud of our day. He never leaves us.

Heaven knows no difference between Sunday morning and Wednesday afternoon. God longs to speak as clearly in the workplace as he does in the sanctuary. He longs to be worshiped when we sit at the dinner table and not just when we come to his communion table. You may go days without thinking of him, but there's never a moment when he's not thinking of you.

Knowing this, we understand Paul's rigorous goal: "We capture every thought and make it give up and obey Christ" (2 Cor. 10:5). We can fathom why he urges us to "pray without ceasing" (1 Thess. 5:17), "be constant in prayer" (Rom. 12:12), "pray in the Spirit at all times" (Eph. 6:18), "continually offer a sacrifice of praise to God" (Heb. 13:15), and "let heaven fill your thoughts" (Col 4:2 TLB).

David, the man after God's own heart, said: "I'm asking Yahweh for one thing, only one thing: to live with him in his house my whole life long. I'll contemplate his beauty, I'll study at his feet. That's the only quiet secure place in a noisy world" (Ps. 27:4–5 MSG). What is this house of God which David seeks? Is David describing a physical structure? Does he long for a building with four walls and a door through which he can enter but never exit? No. "Our LORD does not live in temples built by human hands" (Acts 17:24). When David says, "I will live in the house of the LORD forever" (Ps. 23:6), he's not saying he wants to get away from people. He's saying that he yearns to be in God's presence, wherever he is.

David longs to be in God's house.

I know what you're thinking: *Sure, Max, but he was David. He was the poet and the prince and giant-killer. He didn't have carpools and diapers and a boss who breathes deadlines like a dragon breathes fire. I'd love to live in God's house, too, but for the time being, I'm stuck in the* real *world.*

Forgive me, but I beg to differ. You aren't stuck in the real world. Just the opposite, you are one step away from the house of God. Wherever you are. Whatever time it is. Whether in the office on Thursday or at soccer practice on Saturday, you are only a decision away from the presence of your Father. You need never leave the house of God. You don't need to change your zip code or your neighborhood; all you need to change is your perception.

When your car is stuck in traffic, you can step into the chapel. When the gust of temptation unbalances your stride, step behind the wall of his strength. When the employees belittle you, take a seat in the porch swing next to your Father; he'll comfort you. Remember, this is no house of stone. You won't find it on a map. You won't find it described in a realtor journal.

But you will find it in your Bible. You've seen the blueprint before. You've read the names of the rooms and recited the layout. You're familiar with the design. But chances are you never considered it to be a house plan. You viewed the verses as a prayer.

Indeed they are. The Lord's Prayer. It would be difficult to find someone who hasn't quoted the prayer or read the words:

Our Father who art in heaven,
Hallowed be thy name.
Thy kingdom come,
Thy will be done,
On earth as it is in heaven.
Give us this day our daily bread;
And forgive us our debts,
As we have forgiven our debtors;
And lead us not into temptation,
But deliver us from evil.
For thine is the kingdom and the power and the glory forever.
Amen.

MATTHEW 6:9–13 RSV

Children memorize it. Parishioners recite it. Students study it . . . but I want to challenge us to do something different. I want us to live in it . . . to view it as the floor plan to our spiritual house. In these verses Christ has provided more than a model for prayer, he has provided a model for living. These words do more than tell us what to say to God; they tell us how to exist with God. These words describe a grand house in which God's children were intended to live . . . with him, forever.

Would you like to take a look around? Me, too. I know the perfect place to begin. In the living room a painting hangs over the mantle. The owner of the house treasures it. He invites all who enter to begin their journey gazing at the picture and learning the truth about our Father.

CHAPTER 2

THE
LIVING ROOM

—│ *When Your Heart Needs a Father* │—

Our Father . . .

O UR FATHER who is in heaven . . ." With these words Jesus escorts us into the Great House of God. Shall we follow him? There is so much to see. Every room reveals his heart, every stop will soothe your soul. And no room is as essential as this one we enter first. Walk behind him as he leads us into God's living room.

Sit in the chair that was made for you and warm your hands by the fire which never fades. Take time to look at the framed photos and find yours. Be sure to pick up the scrapbook and find the story of your life. But please, before any of that, stand at the mantle and study the painting which hangs above it.

Your Father treasures the portrait. He has hung it where all can see.

Stand before it a thousand times and each gaze is as fresh as the first. Let a million look at the canvas and each one will see himself. And each will be right.

Captured in the portrait is a tender scene of a father and a son. Behind them is a great house on a hill. Beneath their feet is a narrow path. Down from the house the father has run. Up the trail the son has trudged. The two have met, here, at the gate.

We can't see the face of the son; it's buried in the chest of his father. No, we can't see his face, but we can see his tattered robe and stringy hair. We can see the mud on the back of his legs, the filth on his shoulders and the empty purse on the ground. At one time the purse was full of money. At one time the boy was full of pride. But that was a dozen taverns ago. Now both the purse and the pride are depleted. The prodigal offers no gift or explanation. All he offers is the smell of pigs and a rehearsed apology: "Father, I have sinned against God and done wrong to you. I am no longer worthy to be called your son" (Luke 15:21).

He feels unworthy of his birthright. "Demote me. Punish me. Take my name off the mailbox and my initials off the family tree. I am willing to give up my place at your table." The boy is content to be a hired hand. There is only one problem. Though the boy is willing to stop being a son, the father is not willing to stop being a father.

Though we can't see the boy's face in the painting, we can't miss the father's. Look at the tears glistening on the leathered cheeks, the smile shining through the silver beard. One arm holds the boy up so he won't fall, the other holds the boy close so he won't doubt.

"Hurry!" he shouts. "Bring the best clothes and put them on him. Also, put a ring on his finger and sandals on his feet. And get our fat calf and kill it so we can have a feast and celebrate. My son was dead, but now he is alive again! He was lost but now he is found!" (Luke 15:22–24).

How these words must have stunned the young man, "*My son* was dead . . ." He thought he'd lost his place in the home. After all, didn't he abandon his father? Didn't he waste his inheritance? The boy assumed he had forfeited his privilege to sonship. The father, however, doesn't give up that easily. In his mind, his son is still a son. The child may have been out of the house, but he was never out of his father's heart. He may have left the table, but he never left the family. Don't miss the message here. You may be willing to stop being God's child. But God is not willing to stop being your Father.

OUR *ABBA*

Of all his names, *Father* is God's favorite. We know he loves this name most because this is the one he used most. While on earth, Jesus called God "Father" over two hundred times. In his first recorded words Jesus explained, "Didn't you know that I must be in my Father's house?" (Luke 2:49). In his final triumphant prayer he proclaims, "Father, I give you my life" (Luke 23:46). In the Gospel of John alone, Jesus repeats this name 156 times. God loves to be called Father. After all, didn't Jesus teach us to begin our prayer with the phrase, "Our *Abba*"?

It is difficult for us to understand how revolutionary it was for Jesus to call Jehovah *"Abba."* What is a common practice today was unheard of in Jesus' day. New Testament scholar Joachim Jeremias describes how rarely the term was used:

> With the help of my assistants, I have examined the prayer literature of ancient Judaism. . . . The result of this examination was, that in no place in this immense literature is this invocation of God as *"Abba*, Father" to be found. *Abba* was an everyday word. It was a homely family-word. No Jew would have dared to address God in this manner, yet Jesus did it always in all his prayers which are handed down to us, with one single exception: the cry from the cross, "My God, my God, why have you forsaken me?" In the Lord's prayer, Jesus authorizes his disciples to repeat the word *Abba* after him. He gives them a share in his sonship. He empowers his disciples to speak with their heavenly father in such a familiar and trusting way.[1]

The first two words of the Lord's Prayer are affluent in significance: *"Our Father"* reminds us we are welcome in God's house because we have been adopted by the owner.

GOD'S MISSION: ADOPTION

When we come to Christ, God not only forgives us, he also adopts us. Through a dramatic series of events, we go from condemned orphans with no hope to adopted children with no fear. Here is how it happens. You come before the judgment seat of God full of rebellion and mistakes. Because of his justice he cannot dismiss your sin, but because of his love he cannot dismiss you. So, in an act which stunned the heavens, he punished himself on the cross for your sins. God's justice and love are equally honored. And you, God's creation, are forgiven. But the story doesn't end with God's forgiveness.

> For you have not received a spirit of slavery leading to fear again, but you have received a spirit of adoption as sons by which we cry out "Abba! Father!" The Spirit himself bears witness with our Spirit that we are children of God (Rom. 8:15–16 NASB).

> But when the fullness of time came, God sent forth His Son, born of a woman, born under the Law, in order that He might redeem those who were under the Law, that we might receive the adoption as sons (Gal. 4:4–5 NASB).

It would be enough if God just cleansed your name, but he does more. He gives you *his* name. It would be enough if God just set you free, but he does more. He takes you home. He takes you home to the Great House of God.

Adoptive parents understand this more than anyone. I certainly don't mean to offend any biological parents—I'm one myself. We biological parents know well the earnest longing to have a child. But in many cases our cribs were filled easily. We decided to have a child and a child came. In fact, sometimes the child came with no decision. I've heard of unplanned pregnancies, but I've never heard of an unplanned adoption.

That's why adoptive parents understand God's passion to adopt us. They know what it means to feel an empty space inside. They know what it means to hunt, to set out on a mission, and take responsibility for a child with a spotted past and a dubious future. If anybody understands God's ardor for his children, it's someone who has rescued an orphan from despair, for that is what God has done for us.

God has adopted you. God sought you, found you, signed the papers and took you home.

GOD'S MOTIVE: DEVOTION

As a minister I have had the privilege of witnessing—up close—the emotion of adoption. On one occasion a lady in another state who had heard me speak called and asked if I knew any prospective adoptive parents. Her pregnant daughter was seeking a home for her unborn child. I put her in touch with a family from our congregation and took a front row seat as the drama unfolded.

I saw the joy at the possibility and the heartbreak at the road-blocks. I watched the resolve in the eyes of the father and the determination in the eyes of the mother. They would travel as far as it took and spend every penny they had. They wanted to adopt that child. And they did. Only moments after his birth, the infant was placed in their arms. And this is no exaggeration: They smiled for a month after they brought their son home. I'd see them in the church hallway; they'd be smiling. I'd see them in the parking lot, smiling. From the pulpit I could see them in the congregation, cradling the baby and smiling. I think if I'd preached a sermon on the agony of hell, they would have smiled through every sentence. Why? Because the child they had longed for had come into their home.

Let me ask you, why did this couple adopt that child? They had a happy marriage. They were financially secure and gain-fully employed. What did they hope to gain? Did they adopt the baby so they might have a little extra cash or sleep? You know better. Their supply of both diminished the minute they brought the child home. Then why? Why do people adopt children? As you are thinking, let me tell you why God does.

Delight in these words:

> Long ago, before God made the world, God chose us to be his very own, through what Christ would do for us; he decided then to make us holy in his eyes, without a single fault we who stand before him covered in his love. His unchanging plan has always been to adopt us into his own family by sending Jesus Christ to die for us. *And he did this because he wanted to* (Eph. 1:3–5 TLB, emphasis mine).

And you thought God adopted you because you were good-looking. You thought he needed your money or your wisdom. Sorry. God adopted you simply because he wanted to. You were in his good will and pleasure. Knowing full well the trouble you would be and the price he would pay, he signed his name next to yours and changed your name to his and took you home. Your *Abba* adopted you and became your Father.

May I pause here for just a second? Most of you are with me . . . but a couple of you are shaking your heads. I see those squinty eyes. You don't believe me, do you? You're waiting for the fine print. There's got to be a gimmick. You know life has no free lunch, so you're waiting for the check.

Your discomfort is obvious. Even here in God's living room, you never unwind. Others put on slippers, you put on a front. Others relax, you stiffen. Always on your best behavior, ever anxious that you'll slip up and God will notice and out you'll go.

I understand your anxiety. Our experience with people has taught us that what is promised and what is presented aren't always the same. And for some, the thought of trusting a heavenly Father is doubly difficult because your earthly father disappointed or mistreated you.

If such is the case, I urge you: Don't confuse your heavenly Father with the fathers you've seen on earth. Your Father in heaven isn't prone to headaches and temper tantrums. He doesn't hold you one day and hit you the next. The man who fathered you may play such games, but the God who loves you never will. May I prove my point?

GOD'S METHOD: REDEMPTION

Let's return to the verses that describe your adoption. Read them a second time and see if you can find the verb which precedes the word *adoption* in both verses.

> For you have not received a spirit of slavery leading to fear again, but you have received a spirit of adoption as sons by which we cry out "Abba! Father!" The Spirit himself bears witness with our Spirit that we are children of God (Rom. 8:15–16 NASB).

> But when the fullness of time came, God sent forth His Son, born of a woman, born under the Law, in order that He might redeem those who were under the Law, that we might receive the adoption as sons (Gal. 4:4–5 NASB).

Find it? Not too hard to see, is it? Before the word *adoption* is the word *receive*.

Could Paul have used another phrase? Could he have said, "You have earned the spirit of adoption"? Or "that we might earn our adoption as sons"? I suppose he could have, but we wouldn't have bought it. You and I both know that an adoption is not something we earn; it's something we receive. To be adopted into a family is not a feat one achieves, but rather a gift one accepts.

The parents are the active ones. Adoption agencies don't train children to recruit parents; they seek parents to adopt children. The parents make the call and fill out the papers and endure the interviews and pay the fee and wait the wait. Can you imagine prospective parents saying, "We'd like to adopt Johnny, but first we want to know a few things. Does he have a house to live in? Does he have money for tuition? Does he have a ride to school every morning and clothes to wear every day? Can he prepare his own meals and mend his own clothes?"

No agency would stand for such talk. Its representative would lift her hand and say, "Wait a minute. You don't understand. You don't adopt Johnny because of what he has; you adopt him because of what he needs. He needs a home."

The same is true with God. He doesn't adopt us because of what we have. He doesn't give us his name because of our wit or wallet or good attitude. Paul states it twice because he is doubly concerned that we understand that adoption is something we receive, not something we earn.

Which is *so good* to know. Why? Think carefully about this. If we can't earn our adoption by our stellar performance, can we lose it through our poor performance?

When I was seven years old, I ran away from home. I'd had enough of my father's rules and decided I could make it on my own, thank you very much. With my clothes in a paper bag, I stormed out the back gate and marched down the alley. Like the prodigal son, I decided I needed no father. Unlike the prodigal son, I didn't go far. I got to the end of the alley and remembered I was hungry, so I went back home.

But though the rebellion was brief, it was rebellion nonetheless. And had you stopped me on that prodigal path between the fences and asked me who my father was, I just might have told you how I felt. I just might have said, "I don't need a father. I'm too big for the rules of my family. It's just me, myself and my paper bag." I don't remember saying that to anyone, but I remember thinking it. And I also remember rather sheepishly stepping in the back door and taking my seat at the supper table across from the very father I had, only moments before, disowned.

Did he know of my insurrection? I suspect he did. Did he know of my denial? Dads usually do. Was I still his son? Apparently so. (No one else was sitting in my place.) Had you gone to my father after you had spoken to me and asked, "Mr. Lucado, your son says he has no need of a father. Do you still consider him your son?" what would my dad have said?

I don't have to guess at his answer. He called himself my father even when I didn't call myself his son. His commitment to me was greater than my commitment to him.

I didn't hear the rooster crow like Peter did. I didn't feel the fish belch like Jonah did. I didn't get a robe and a ring and sandals like the prodigal did. But I learned from my father on earth what those three learned from their Father in heaven. Our God is no fair-weather Father. He's not into this love-'em-and-leave-'em-stuff. I can count on him to be in my corner no matter how I perform. You can, too.

May I show you something? Look at the bottom of the painting. See the words etched in gold? The Apostle Paul penned them, but your Father inspired them.

Neither death, nor life, nor angels, nor ruling spirits, nothing now, nothing in the future, no powers, nothing above us, nothing below us, nor anything else in the world will ever be able to separate us from the love of God that is in Christ Jesus our Lord (Rom. 8:38–39).

Your Father will never turn you away. The doors of this room are never closed. Learn to linger in the living room of God's house. When the words of others hurt you or your own failures distress you, step in here. Gaze at this painting and be reminded of your God: It is right to call him Holy; we speak truth when we call him King. But if you want to touch his heart, use the name he loves to hear. Call him *Father*.

CHAPTER 3

THE
FOUNDATION

———┤ *Where Trust Begins* ├———

Our Father who is . . .

THE MOST ESSENTIAL WORD in the Lord's prayer is also the shortest. Be careful you don't miss it. A lot of people do. The word is so brief, it'll sneak right past you if you aren't careful.

Without it, the Great House of God cannot stand. Remove it and the house tumbles to the ground.

What is the word? I'll give you a hint. You just read it.

Where is it? You just read it.

Is it in this sentence? It is. It's also in the answer I just gave.

Come on, Max, is this a joke?

Would I kid you? (By the way, the word was in your question. See it?)

Is. "Our Father who *is* in heaven."

God is. Not God *was*. Not God *will be*. Not God *could be* or *should be*, but God *is*. He is the God of the present tense. And he is the foundation of his own house.

THE MORTAR OF FAITH

I write these words on an airplane. A late airplane. An airplane different from the one I was originally assigned. My first flight was canceled due to a mechanical difficulty. A few dozen not-so-happy campers and I were transferred to another plane. As we checked in for the new flight, I heard many of my fellow passengers ask the attendant, "Is this plane okay? Any mechanical flaws with this 747?" We were full of questions about the plane's ability to fly, but the ticket agent had no questions about our ability to do the same.

Not once were we asked, "How about you? Can you fly? Can you flap your arms and get airborne?" Of course, these are bizarre questions. My ability to fly is not important. My strength is immaterial. I'm counting on the plane to get me home.

Need I make the connection? Your achievements, however noble they may be, are not important. Your credentials, as starry as they may be, are of no concern. God is the foundation of this house. The key question in life is not "How strong am I?" but rather "How strong is God?" Focus on his strength, not yours. Occupy yourself with the nature of God, not the size of your biceps.

That's what Moses did. Or at least that's what God told Moses to do. Remember the conversation at the burning bush? The tone was set in the first sentence. "Take off your sandals because you are standing on holy ground" (Exod. 3:5). With these eleven words Moses is enrolled in a class on God. Immediately the roles are defined. God is holy. Approaching him on even a quarter-inch of leather is too pompous. And as we read further we discover that no time is spent convincing Moses what Moses can do, but much time is spent explaining to Moses what God can do.

You and I tend to do the opposite. We would explain to Moses how he is ideally suited to return to Egypt. (Who better understands the culture than a former prince?) Then we'd remind Moses how perfect he is for wilderness travel. (Who knows the desert better than a shepherd?) We'd spend time reviewing with Moses his resumé and strengths. (Come on Moses, you can do it. Give it a try.)

But God doesn't. The strength of Moses is never considered. No pep talk is given, no pats on the backs are offered. Not one word is spoken to recruit Moses. But many words are used to reveal God. The strength of Moses is not the issue; the strength of God is.

Shall we pause for application? Let's repeat that last sentence and let you fill in a blank. Replace the name of Moses with your name.

> The strength of _____ is not the issue; the strength of God is.

You aren't the force behind the plane nor the mortar within the foundation; God is. I know you know that in your head, but do you know that in your heart? Would you like to? Let me show you some of the boulders which support this mighty house. Let me buttress your confidence in God's house by sharing with you some of his names.

WHAT'S IN A NAME?

Understanding the names of God is no quick study—after all, there are more than eighty names for God in the Old Testament alone. But if you want a place to begin, let me entice you with a few of the compound names given God by some of the heroes of the faith. Each of them reveals a different rock of God's character.

Maybe you are wondering how a study of the names of God can help you understand him. Let me explain. Imagine that you and I are having a conversation in 1978. You approach me on the college campus where I was a student and ask, "Do you know Denalyn Preston?" I would have answered, "Let me think. Oh, I know Denalyn. She's an acquaintance of mine. She's that cute girl who likes to ride bikes and wear overalls to class." That's all I knew about her.

But go forward a year. Now we are in Miami, Florida, where I am a minister and Denalyn is a school teacher. "Do you know Denalyn Preston?" "Of course, I do. She's a friend. I see her every Sunday."

Ask me again a year later, "Denalyn Preston? Sure I know her. She can't take her eyes off of me." (Just kidding, honey.)

Fast forward twelve months. "Who doesn't know Denalyn Preston?" I would answer. "You think she might be willing to go out on a date with me?"

Six months later, "Of course I know her—I can't quit thinking about her. We're going out again next week."

Two months later, "Do I know Denalyn Preston? I'm going to marry her next August!"

Now it's August of 1981. "Do I know Denalyn Preston? No,

but I know Denalyn *Lucado*. She's my wife, and quit bugging us—we're on our honeymoon."

In three years my relationship with Denalyn evolved. And with each change came a new name. She went from *acquaintance* to *friend* to *eye-popping beauty* to *date* to *fiancée* and *wife*. Of course the names have only continued. Now she is *confidante*, *mother of my children, life-long partner, boss* (just kidding, again). The more I know her the more names I give her.

And the more God's people came to know him, the more names they gave him. Initially, God was known as *Elohim*. "In the beginning God [*Elohim*] created" (Gen. 1:1). The Hebrew word *Elohim* carries with it the meaning "strong one or creator" and appears thirty-one times in the first chapter of Genesis, where we see his creative power.[1]

As God revealed himself to his children, however, they saw him as more than a mighty force. They saw him as a loving Father who met them at every crossroad of their lives.

Jacob, for example, came to see God as *Jehovah-raah*, a caring shepherd. "Like a shepherd," Jacob told his family, "God has led me all my life" (Gen. 48:15).

The phrase was surely a compliment to God, for Jacob was a less-than-cooperative sheep. Twice he tricked his brother, at least once he suckered his blind father. He out-crossed his double-crossing father-in-law by conning him out of his livestock and then, when the fellow wasn't looking, made like a Colt out of Baltimore in the middle of the night, sneaking off with anything that wasn't nailed down.

Jacob was never a candidate for the most well-behaved sheep award, but God never forgot him. He gave him food in the famine, forgiveness in his failures, and faith in his final years. Ask Jacob to describe God in a word, and his word would be *Jehovah-raah,* the caring shepherd.

Abraham had a different name for God: *Jehovah-jireh,* the Lord who provides. It's ironic that Abraham would call God "provider," since Abraham was well provided for already. He lived in a split-level tent with a four-camel garage. Life was good in Ur. "But life will be better in Canaan," he told his family. So off they went. When they asked, "Where will we live?" Abraham answered, "God will provide." And God did. When they got caught in an Egyptian scandal, the people wondered, "How will we get out?" Abraham assured them, "God will provide." And he did. When they split up the land and nephew Lot took the grassland and left Uncle Abraham with the rocks, the people wondered, "How will we survive?" Abraham knew the answer: "God will provide." And he did. And when Abraham and Sarah stood next to the empty crib and she wondered how he'd ever be the father of thousands, he'd put his arm around her, whispering, "The Lord will provide."

And God did. And Abraham bounced his firstborn on his hundred-year-old bony knees. Abraham learned that God provides. But even Abraham must have shook his head when God asked him to sacrifice his own son on Mt. Moriah.

Up the mountain they went. "Where is the lamb we will burn as a sacrifice?" his son asked (Gen. 22:7). One wonders how the answer made it past the lump in Abraham's throat: "God will give us the lamb for the sacrifice, my son" (v. 8). *Jehovah-jireh,* the Lord will provide. Abraham tied up his son and placed him on the altar and raised the knife, and the angel stayed his hand. Abraham had proven his faith. He heard a rustling in the thicket and saw a ram caught by his horns in a bush. He offered it as a sacrifice and gave the mountain a name, *Jehovah-jireh,* the Lord provides.

And then there is Gideon. The Lord came to Gideon and told him he was to lead his people in victory over the Midianites. That's like God telling a housewife to stand up to her abusive husband or a high school student to take on drug peddlers or a preacher to preach the truth to a congregation of Pharisees. "Y-y-you b-b-better get somebody else," we stammer. But then God reminds us that he knows we can't, but he can, and to prove it he gives a wonderful gift. He brings a spirit of peace. A peace before the storm. A peace beyond logic, or as Paul described it, "A peace which passes understanding" (Phil. 4:7). He gave it to David after he showed him Goliath; he gave it to Saul after he showed him the gospel; he gave it to Jesus after he showed him the cross. And he gave it to Gideon. So Gideon, in turn, gave the name to God. He built an altar and named it *Jehovah-shalom,* the Lord is peace (Judges 6:24).

At least a couple of the boulders beneath the house knew the chisel of Moses. On one he carved the name *Jehovah-rophe.* You'll find the English translation in Exodus 15:26: "I am the Lord who heals you." Here is the setting. Over a million Israelites have been liberated from captivity and follow Moses into the desert. Their jubilation over liberation soon becomes frustration over dehydration. (Don't groan. I worked ten minutes on that sentence and fought two editors to keep it in.) They walked three days through a land void of shade, streams, houses, and greenery. Their only neighbors were the sun and serpents.

They finally came upon a lake, but the water was brackish, bitter, and dangerous. I'm sure it wasn't funny at the time, but you've got to chuckle about what happens next. "So Moses cried out to the LORD and the LORD showed him a tree" (Exod. 15:25). Moses is begging for water and God gives him wood?

Let's pause and total the damage. Three days in the desert sun. Hopes raised at the sight of a lake. Hopes dashed at the taste of the water. Moses, cotton-mouthed and parched-lipped, asks for relief . . . and God shows him a tree?

Moses responds by throwing the tree into the lake. Maybe he did it out of aggravation: "Here is what I think of this tree stuff." Or maybe out of inspiration: "You're in charge, God." Whatever the reason, the water is purified, the Israelites' thirst is satisfied, and God is glorified. (That sentence only took five minutes.) In this case, God himself reveals his name: "I am the LORD who heals you" (Exod. 15:26).

The operative word here is *I*. God is the one who heals. He may use a branch of medicine and a branch of a hospital or a branch of a live oak tree, but he is the one who takes the poison out of the system. He is *Jehovah-rophe.*

He is also *Jehovah-nissi,* the Lord my banner. In the heat of battle, soldiers feared getting separated from their army. For that reason a banner was carried into the conflict, and if a fighter found himself alone, the raised flag would signal safety. When the Amalekites (the big bad guys) attacked the Israelites (the little good guys), Moses went up on the mountain and prayed. As long as his hands were up, the Israelites prevailed. But when his hands were down, the Amalekites won. Moses was no dummy—he kept his hands up. The Israelites won, the Amalekites ran, and Moses built an altar for God and chiseled a new name on a stone—*Jehovah-nissi*—the Lord my banner (see Exod. 17:8–16).

These are just a few of the names of God which describe his

character. Study them, for in a given day, you may need each one of them. Let me show you what I mean.

When you are confused about the future, go to your *Jehovah-raah*, your caring shepherd. When you are anxious about provision, talk to *Jehovah-jireh*, the Lord who provides. Are your challenges too great? Seek the help of *Jehovah-shalom*, the Lord is peace. Is your body sick? Are your emotions weak? *Jehovah-rophe*, the Lord who heals you, will see you now. Do you feel like a soldier stranded behind enemy lines? Take refuge in *Jehovah-nissi*, the Lord my banner.

Meditating on the names of God reminds you of the character of God. Take these names and bury them in your heart.

God is

    the shepherd who guides,

        the Lord who provides,

            the voice who brings peace in the storm,

                the physician who heals the sick, and

                    the banner that guides the soldier.

And most of all, he . . . is.

CHAPTER 4

THE
OBSERVATORY

Our Father who is in heaven . . .

FEW MORNINGS BACK I was jogging through my neighborhood. I've been known to miss some important dates, but even I could not miss the significance of that day. It was the first day of school. Reminders were everywhere: newscast interviews, stores packed with parents, yellow buses awakened from summer slumber and rumbling down the streets. My own family had spent the previous evening packing backpacks and preparing lunches.

It was no surprise to me, then, to see a pretty little girl step out of her house wearing new clothes and a backpack. She couldn't have been over five or six years of age and was walking toward the curb to wait for her bus. "Have a great first day of school," I greeted as I jogged past.

She stopped and looked at me as if I'd pulled a rabbit out of a hat. "How did you know?!"

She was stunned. From her perspective, I was a genius. Somehow I had miraculously discerned why she was up so early and where she was going. And she was impressed.

"Oh, I just know those kind of things," I shouted back to her. (No need to burst her bubble.)

You, on the other hand, are not so easily impressed. You know how I knew. You understand the difference between a child and a grownup. Adults live in a different world than children. Remember how your parents amazed you? Remember how your dad could identify any car that passed? Weren't you impressed at your mom's ability to turn flour and milk and eggs into a cake? As my parents discussed the Sunday sermon, I can remember thinking, *I didn't understand a word the guy said.*

What's the difference? Simple. By virtue of training and study and experience, adults occupy a different domain. How much more is this true of God. Take the difference between the girl and me, amplify it a million times over, and we begin to see the contrast between us and our Father. Who among us can ponder God without asking the same question the girl did: How did you know?

We ask for grace, only to find forgiveness already offered. (How did you know I would sin?)

We ask for food, only to find provision already made. (How did you know I would be hungry?)

We ask for guidance, only to find answers in God's ancient story. (How did you know what I would ask?)

God dwells in a different realm. "The foolishness of God is higher than human wisdom, and the weakness of God is stronger than human strength" (1 Cor. 1:25). He occupies another dimension. "My thoughts are not like your thoughts. Your ways are not like my ways. Just as the heavens are higher than the earth, so are my ways higher than your ways and my thoughts higher than your thoughts" (Isa. 55:8–9).

Make special note of the word *like*. God's thoughts are not our thoughts, nor are they even *like* ours. We aren't even in the same neighborhood. We're thinking, *Preserve the body;* he's thinking, *Save the soul.* We dream of a pay raise. He dreams of raising the dead. We avoid pain and seek peace. God uses pain to bring peace. "I'm going to live before I die," we resolve. "Die, so you can live," he instructs. We love what rusts. He loves what endures. We rejoice at our successes. He rejoices at our confessions. We show our children the Nike star with the million-dollar smile and say, "Be like Mike." God points to the crucified carpenter with bloody lips and a torn side and says, "Be like Christ."

Our thoughts are not like God's thoughts. Our ways are not like his ways. He has a different agenda. He dwells in a different dimension. He lives on another plane. And that plane is named in the first phrase of the Lord's prayer, *"Our Father who is in heaven."*

THE OBSERVATORY

Having comforted us in the living room and assured us with the foundation, Jesus now leads us upstairs. We ascend to the highest level of the house, stand before a heavy wooden door, and accept God's invitation to enter his observatory.

No telescope is needed in this room. The glass ceiling magnifies the universe until you feel all of the sky is falling around you. Elevated instantly through the atmosphere, you are encircled by the heavens. Stars cascade past until you are dizzy with their number. Had you the ability to spend a minute on each planet and star, one lifetime would scarcely be enough to begin.

Jesus waits until you are caught up in the splendor of it all, and then he reminds you softly, "Your Father is in heaven."

I can remember as a youngster knowing some kids whose fathers were quite successful. One was a judge. The other a prominent physician. I attended church with the son of the mayor. In Andrews, Texas, that's not much to boast about. Nevertheless the kid had clout that most of us didn't. "My father has an office at the courthouse," he could claim.

Guess what you can claim? "My Father rules the universe."

> The heavens tell the glory of God and the skies announce what his hands have made. Day after day they tell the story; night after night they tell it again. They have no speech or words; they have no voice to be heard. But their message goes out through all the world; their words go everywhere on earth" (Ps. 19:1–5).

Nature is God's workshop. The sky is his resume. The universe is his calling card. You want to know who God is? See what he has done. You want to know his power? Take a look at his creation. Curious about his strength? Pay a visit to his home address: 1 Billion Starry Sky Avenue. Want to know his size? Step out into the night and stare at starlight emitted one million years ago and then read 2 Chronicles 2:6, "No one can really build a house for our God. Not even the highest of heavens can hold him."

He is untainted by the atmosphere of sin,

unbridled by the time line of history,

unhindered by the weariness of the body.

What controls you doesn't control him. What troubles you doesn't trouble him. What fatigues you doesn't fatigue him. Is an eagle disturbed by traffic? No, he rises above it. Is the whale perturbed by a hurricane? Of course not, he plunges beneath it. Is the lion flustered by the mouse standing directly in his way? No, he steps over it.

How much more is God able to soar above, plunge beneath, and step over the troubles of the earth! "What is impossible with man is possible with God" (Matt. 19:26). Our questions betray our lack of understanding:

How can God be everywhere at one time? (Who says God is bound by a body?)

How can God hear all the prayers which come to him? (Perhaps his ears are different from yours.)

How can God be the Father, the Son, and the Holy Spirit? (Could it be that heaven has a different set of physics than earth?)

If people down here won't forgive me, how much more am I guilty before a holy God? (Oh, just the opposite. God is always able to give grace when we humans can't—he invented it.)

How vital that we pray, armed with the knowledge that God is in heaven. Pray with any lesser conviction and your prayers are timid, shallow, and hollow. But spend some time walking in the workshop of the heavens, seeing what God has done, and watch how your prayers are energized.

Speaking of the Father's workshop, let me tell you about a visit I paid to one as an eight-year-old.

GOD'S WORKSHOP

The highlight of my Cub Scout career was the Soap Box Derby. You've heard of people standing on their soap boxes to make a point? We got *inside* our soap boxes to win a trophy. The competition was simple. Construct a motorless wooden go-cart and enter it in a downhill race. Some of the creations were fancy, complete with steering wheel and painted casing. Others were nothing more than a seat on a wooden chassis with four wheels and a rope for steering. My plan was to construct a genuine red roadster like the one in the Scout manual. Armed with a saw and hammer, a stack of lumber, and high ambition, I set out to be the Henry Ford of Troop 169.

I don't know how long my dad watched me before he interrupted my work. Probably not long, since my efforts weren't a pretty sight. The saw kept jamming and the wood kept buckling. The nails tended to bend and the panels didn't fit. At some point Dad mercifully intervened, tapped me on the shoulder, and told me to follow him into his workshop.

The small white frame house on the back of our lot was my dad's domain. I'd never really paid attention to what he did in there. All I knew was what I heard: buzzing saws, pounding hammers, and the whistle of a happy worker. I kept my bike in there, but I never noticed the tools. But then again, I'd never tried to build anything before. Over the next couple of hours that day, he introduced me to the magical world of sawhorses, squares, tape measures, and drills. He showed me how to draw a plan and measure the wood. He explained why it was wiser to hammer first and paint later. I was amazed. What was impossible for me was simple for him. Within an afternoon, we had constructed a pretty decent vehicle. And though I didn't leave the race with a trophy, I did leave with a greater admiration for my father. Why? I'd spent some time in his workshop.

You're following me on this one, aren't you? By showing us the heavens, Jesus is showing us his Father's workshop. He lets us hammer our thumbs just enough times and then taps us on the shoulder and says, "Your Father can handle that for you." And to prove it, he takes us into the Father's workshop. With a sweep of the hands he proudly proclaims: "Our Father is in heaven!"

Behold the sun! Every square yard of the sun is constantly emitting 130,000 horse power, or the equivalent of 450 eight-cylinder automobile engines. And yet our sun, as powerful as it is, is but one minor star in the 100 billion orbs which make up our Milky Way Galaxy. Hold a dime in your fingers and extend it arm's length toward the sky, allowing it to eclipse your vision, and you will block out fifteen million stars from your view.

Consider the earth! Our globe's weight has been estimated at six sextillion tons (a six with twenty-one zeroes). Yet it is precisely tilted at twenty-three degrees; any more or any less and our seasons would be lost in a melted polar flood. Though our globe revolves at the rate of one-thousand miles per hour or twenty-five thousand miles per day or nine million miles per year, none of us tumbles into orbit. Our God who "stretches the northern sky out over the empty space and hangs the earth upon nothing" (Job 26:7) also created an invisible band of gravity to hold us secure.[1]

Now as you stand in the observatory viewing God's workshop, let me pose a few questions. If he is able to place the stars in their sockets and suspend the sky like a curtain, do you think it remotely possible that God is able to guide your life? If your God is mighty enough to ignite the sun, could it be that he is mighty enough to light your path? If he cares enough about the planet Saturn to give it rings or Venus to make it sparkle, is there an outside chance that he cares enough about you to meet your needs? Or, as Jesus says,

> Look at the birds in the air. They don't plant or harvest or store into barns, but your heavenly Father feeds them. And you know you are worth much more than the birds. . . . Why do you worry about clothes? Look at how the lilies in the field grow. They don't work or make clothes for themselves. But I tell you that even Solomon with his riches was not dressed as beautifully as one of these flowers. God clothes the grass in the field, which is alive today but tomorrow is thrown into the fire. So you can even be sure that God will clothe you. Don't have so little faith! (Matt. 6:25–30)

Why did he do it? A shack would have sufficed, but he gave us a mansion. Did he have to give the birds a song and the mountains a peak? Was he required to put stripes on the zebra and the hump on the camel? Would we have known the difference had he made the sunsets gray instead of orange? Why do stars have twinkles and the waves snowy crests? Why dash the cardinal in red and drape the beluga whale in white? Why wrap creation in such splendor? Why go to such trouble to give such gifts?

Why do you? You do the same. I've seen you searching for a gift. I've seen you stalking the malls and walking the aisles. I'm not talking about the obligatory gifts. I'm not describing the last-minute purchase of drugstore perfume on the way to the birthday party. Forget blue-light specials and discount purchases; I'm talking about that extra-special person and that extra-special gift. I'm talking about stashing away a few dollars a month out of the grocery money to buy him some lizard-skin boots; staring at a thousand rings to find her the best diamond; staying up all night Christmas Eve, assembling the new bicycle. Why do you do it? You do it so the eyes will pop. You do it so the heart will stop. You do it so the jaw will drop. You do it to hear those words of disbelief, "You did this for *me*?"

That's why you do it. And that is why God did it. Next time a sunrise steals your breath or a meadow of flowers leaves you speechless, remain that way. Say nothing and listen as heaven whispers, "Do you like it? I did it just for you."

I'm about to tell you something you may find hard to believe. You're about to hear an opinion that may stretch your imagination. You don't have to agree with me, but I would like you to consider it with me. You don't have to buy it, but at least think about it. Here it is: *If you were the only person on earth, the earth would look exactly the same.* The Himalayas would still have their drama and the Caribbean would still have its charm. The sun would still nestle behind the Rockies in the evenings and spray light on the desert in the mornings. If you were the sole pilgrim on this globe, God would not diminish its beauty one degree.

Because he did it all for you . . . and he's waiting for you to discover his gift. He's waiting for you to stumble into the den, rub the sleep from your eyes, and see the bright red bike he assembled, just for you. He's waiting for your eyes to pop and your heart to stop. He's waiting for the moment between the dropping of the jaw and the leap of the heart. For in that silence he leans forward and whispers: *I did it just for you.*

Find such love hard to believe? That's okay. Remember the little girl who couldn't imagine how I knew she was going to school? Just because she couldn't comprehend it didn't mean I didn't know it. And just because we can't imagine God's giving us sunsets, don't think God doesn't do it. God's thoughts are higher than ours. God's ways are greater than ours. And sometimes, out of his great wisdom, our Father in heaven gives us a piece of heaven just to show he cares.

CHAPTER 5

THE
CHAPEL

Where Man Covers His Mouth

Hallowed be thy name . . .

HEN I LIVED in Brazil I took my mom and her friend to see Iguacu Falls, the largest waterfalls in the world. Some weeks earlier I'd become an expert on the cataracts by reading an article in *National Geographic* magazine. Surely, I thought, my guests would appreciate their good fortune in having me as a guide.

To reach the lookout point, tourists must walk a winding trail that leads them through a forest. I took advantage of the hike to give an Iguacu nature report to my mom and her friend. So full of information I was, I chattered the entire time. After some minutes, however, I caught myself speaking louder and louder. A sound in the distance forced me to raise my voice. With each turn in the trail, my volume increased. Finally, I was shouting above a roar which was proving to be quite irritating. *Whatever that noise is, I wish they'd shut it off so I could complete my lecture.*

Only after reaching the clearing did I realize that the noise we heard was the waterfalls. My words were drowned out by the force and fury of what I was trying to describe. I could no longer be heard. Even if I could, I no longer had an audience. Even my mother would rather see the splendor than hear my description. I shut my mouth.

There are times when to speak is to violate the moment . . . when silence represents the highest respect. The word for such times is reverence. The prayer for such times is "Hallowed be thy name." And the place for this prayer is the chapel.

If there are walls, you won't notice them. If there is a pew, you won't need it. Your eyes will be fixed on God, and your knees will be on the floor. In the center of the room is a throne, and before the throne is a bench on which to kneel. Only you and God are here, and you can surmise who occupies the throne.

Don't worry about having the right words; worry more about having the right heart. It's not eloquence he seeks, just honesty.

A TIME TO BE SILENT

This was a lesson Job learned. If he had a fault, it was his tongue. He talked too much.

Not that anyone could blame him. Calamity had pounced on the man like a lioness on a herd of gazelles, and by the time the rampage passed, there was hardly a wall standing or a loved one living. Enemies had slaughtered Job's cattle, and lightning had destroyed his sheep. Strong winds had left his partying kids buried in wreckage.

And that was just the first day.

Job hadn't even had time to call Allstate before he saw the leprosy on his hands and the boils on his skin. His wife, compassionate soul that she was, told him to "curse God and die." His four friends came with the bedside manner of drill sergeants, telling him that God is fair and pain is the result of evil, and as sure as two-plus-two equals four, Job must have some criminal record in his past to suffer so.

Each had his own interpretation of God and each spoke long and loud about who God is and why God did what he did. They weren't the only ones talking about God. When his accusers paused, Job gave his response. Back and forth they went . . .

> Job cried out . . . (3:1).
>
> Then Eliphaz the Temanite answered . . . (4:1).
>
> Then Job answered . . . (6:1).
>
> Then Bildad the Shuhite answered . . . (8:1).
>
> Then Job answered . . . (9:1).
>
> Then Zophath the Naamathite answered . . . (11:1).

This verbal ping-pong continues for twenty-three chapters. Finally Job has enough of this "answering." No more discussion-group chit-chat. It's time for the keynote address. He grips the microphone with one hand and the pulpit with the other and launches forth. For six chapters Job gives his opinions on God. This time the chapter headings read: "And Job continued," "And Job continued," "And Job continued." He defines God, explains

God, and reviews God. One gets the impression that Job knows more about God than God does!

We are thirty-seven chapters into the book before God clears his throat to speak. Chapter thirty-eight begins with these words: "Then the LORD answered Job."

If your Bible is like mine, there is a mistake in this verse. The words are fine but the printer uses the wrong size type. The words should look like this:

THEN THE LORD ANSWERED JOB!

God speaks. Faces turn toward the sky. Winds bend the trees. Neighbors plunge into the storm shelters. Cats scurry up the trees and dogs duck into the bushes. "Somethin's a-blowin' in, honey. Best get them sheets off the line." God has no more than opened his mouth before Job knows he should have kept his sore one shut.

> I will ask you questions and you must answer me. Where were you when I made the earth's foundation? Tell me if you understand. Who marked off how big it should be? Surely you know! Who stretched a ruler across it? What were the earth's foundations set on, or who put its cornerstone in place while the morning stars sang together and all the angels shouted with joy? (38:3–6)

God floods the sky with queries, and Job cannot help but get the point: Only God defines God. You've got to know the alphabet before you can read, and God tells Job, "You don't even know the ABC's of heaven, much less the vocabulary." For the first time, Job is quiet. Silenced by a torrent of questions.

> Have you ever gone to where the sea begins or walked the valleys under the sea? . . . Have you ever gone to the storehouse for snow or seen the storehouses for hail. . . ? Are you the one who gives the horse his strength or puts the flowing mane on its neck? Do you make the horse jump like a locust? Is it through your wisdom that the hawk flies and spreads its wings toward the south? (38:16, 22; 39:19–20, 26)

Job barely has time to shake his head at one question before he is asked another. The Father's implication is clear: "As soon as you are able to handle these simple matters of storing stars and stretching the neck of the ostrich, then we'll have a talk about pain and suffering. But until then, we can do without your commentary."

Does Job get the message? I think so. Listen to his response. "I am not worthy; I cannot answer you anything, so I will put my hand over my mouth" (40:4).

Notice the change. Before he heard God, Job couldn't speak enough. After he heard God, he couldn't speak at all.

Silence was the only proper response. There was a time in the life of Thomas à Kempis when he, too, covered his mouth. He had written profusely about the character of God. But one day God confronted him with such holy grace that, from that moment on, all à Kempis's words "seemed like straw." He put down his pen and never wrote another line. He put his hand over his mouth.

The word for such moments is reverence.

The room for such moments is the chapel.

The phrase for the chapel is "Hallowed be thy name."

A CUT ABOVE

This phrase is a petition, not a proclamation. A request, not an announcement. Hallowed *be* your name. We enter the chapel and beseech, "Be hallowed, Lord." Do whatever it takes to be holy in my life. Take your rightful place on the throne. Exalt yourself. Magnify yourself. Glorify yourself. You be Lord, and I'll be quiet.

The word *hallowed* comes from the word *holy,* and the word *holy* means "to separate." The ancestry of the term can be traced back to an ancient word which means "to cut." To be holy, then, is to be a cut above the norm, superior, extraordinary. Remember what we learned in the observatory? The Holy One dwells on a different level from the rest of us. What frightens us does not frighten him. What troubles us does not trouble him.

I'm more a landlubber than a sailor, but I've puttered around in a bass boat enough to know the secret for finding land in a storm . . . You don't aim at another boat. You certainly don't stare at the waves. You set your sights on an object unaffected by the wind—a light on the shore—and go straight toward it. The light is unaffected by the storm.

By seeking God in the chapel, you do the same. When you set your sights on our God, you focus on one "a cut above" any storm life may bring.

Like Job, you find peace in the pain.

Like Job, you cover your mouth and sit still.

"Be still, and know that I am God" (Ps. 46:10). This verse contains a command with a promise.

The command?

Be still.

Cover your mouth.

Bend your knees.

The promise? You will *know that I am God.*

The vessel of faith journeys on soft waters. Belief rides on the wings of waiting.

Linger in the chapel. Linger often in the chapel. In the midst of your daily storms, make it a point to be still and set your sights on him. Let God be God. Let him bathe you in his glory so that both your breath and your troubles are sucked from your soul. Be still. Be quiet. Be open and willing. Then you will know that God is God, and you can't help but confess, "Hallowed be thy name."

CHAPTER 6

THE
THRONE

— | *Touching the King's Heart* | —

Thy kingdom come . . .

OUR FAMILY went desk hunting recently. I needed a new one for the office, and we'd promised Andrea and Sara desks for their rooms. Sara was especially enthused. When she comes home from school, guess what she does? She plays school! I never did that as a kid. I tried to forget the classroom activities, not rehearse them. Denalyn assures me not to worry, that this is one of those attention-span differences between genders. So off to the furniture store we went.

When Denalyn buys furniture she prefers one of two extremes—so antique it's fragile or so new it's unpainted. This time we opted for the latter and entered a store of in-the-buff furniture.

Andrea and Sara succeeded quickly in making their selections, and I set out to do the same. Somewhere in the process Sara learned we weren't taking the desks home that day, and this news disturbed her deeply. I explained that the piece had to be painted and they would deliver the desk in about four weeks. I might as well have said four millennia.

Her eyes filled with tears, "But, Daddy, I wanted to take it home today."

Much to her credit she didn't stomp her feet and demand her way. She did, however, set out on an urgent course to change her father's mind. Every time I turned a corner she was waiting on me.

"Daddy, don't you think we could paint it ourselves?"

"Daddy, I just want to draw some pictures on my new desk."

"Daddy, please let's take it home today."

After a bit she disappeared, only to return, arms open wide and bubbling with a discovery. "Guess what, Daddy. It'll fit in the back of the car!"

You and I know that a seven-year-old has no clue what will or won't fit in a vehicle, but the fact that she had measured the trunk with her arms softened my heart. The clincher, though, was the name she called me: "Daddy, can't we please take it home?"

The Lucado family took a desk home that day.

I heard Sara's request for the same reason God hears ours. Her desire was for her own good. What dad wouldn't want his child to spend more time writing and drawing? Sara wanted what I wanted for her, she only wanted it sooner. When we agree with what God wants, he hears us, as well. (See 1 John 5:14.)

Sara's request was heartfelt. God, too, is moved by our sincerity. The "earnest prayer of a righteous man has great power" (James 5:16 TLB).

But most of all, I was moved to respond because Sara called me "Daddy." Because she is my child, I heard her request. Because we are his children, God hears ours. The king of creation gives special heed to the voice of his family. He is not only willing to hear us, he loves to hear us. He even tells us what to ask him.

"Thy kingdom come."

THY KINGDOM COME

We're often content to ask for less. We entered the Great House of God with a satchel full of requests—promotions desired, pay raises wanted, transmission repairs needed, and tuitions due. We'd typically say our prayers as casually as we'd order a burger at the drive-through: "I'll have one solved problem and two blessings, cut the hassles, please."

But such complacency seems inappropriate in the chapel of worship. Here we are before the King of kings. We've just covered our mouths out of reverence for his holiness, now do we open them with the topic of transmissions? Not that our needs don't matter to him, mind you. It's just that what seemed so urgent outside the house seems less significant in here. The pay raise is still needed and the promotion is still desired, but is that where we start?

Jesus tells how to begin. "When you pray, pray like this. 'Our Father who is in heaven, hallowed be thy name. Thy kingdom come.'"

When you say, "Thy kingdom come," you are inviting the Messiah himself to walk into your world. "Come, my King! Take your throne in our land. Be present in my heart. Be present in my office. Come into my marriage. Be Lord of my family, my fears, and my doubts." This is no feeble request; it's a bold appeal for God to occupy every corner of your life.

Who are you to ask such a thing? Who are you to ask God to take control of your world? You are his child, for heaven's sake! And so you ask boldly. "So let us come boldly to the very throne of God and stay there to receive his mercy and to find grace to help us in our times of need" (Heb. 4:16).

A SPIRITUAL DRAMA

A wonderful illustration of this kind of boldness is in the story of Hadassah. Though her language and culture are an atlas apart from ours, she can tell you about the power of a prayer to a king. There are a couple of differences, though. Her request was not to her father, but to her husband, the king. Her prayer wasn't for a desk, but for the delivery of her people. And because she entered the throne room, because she opened her heart to the king, he changed his plans and millions of people in 127 different countries were saved.

Oh, how I'd love for you to meet Hadassah. But since she lived in the fifth century BC, such an encounter is not likely. We'll have to be content with reading about her in the book which bears her name—her other name—the book of Esther.

And what a book it is! Hollywood would have a challenge matching the drama of this story . . . the evil Haman who demanded that all pay him homage . . . the gutsy Mordecai who refused to bow before Haman . . . Mordecai's great words to Esther that she may have been chosen queen for "such a time as this" . . . and Esther's conviction to save her people. "If I perish, I perish," she resolved.

Let's review the central characters.

Xerxes was the king of Persia. He was an absolute monarch over the land from India to Ethiopia. Let Xerxes raise an eyebrow and the destiny of the world would change. In this respect he symbolized the power of God, for our King guides the river of life, and he doesn't even raise an eyebrow.

Haman (whose name sounds like hangman, which you will soon see as more than a curious coincidence) was the right-hand man of Xerxes. Read every word about the man and you'll find nothing good about him. He was an insatiable egotist who wanted the worship of every person in the kingdom. Perturbed by a peculiar minority called the Jews, he decided to exterminate them. He convinced Xerxes that the world would be better with a holocaust and set a date for the genocide of all of Abraham's children.

Haman is a servant of hell and a picture of the devil himself, who has no higher aim than to have every knee bow as he passes. Satan also has no other plan than to persecute the promised people of God. He comes to "steal and kill and destroy" (John 10:10). "He is filled with anger because he knows he does not have much time" (Rev. 12:12). Since the lie in the garden, he has sought to derail God's plan. In this case Satan hopes to destroy the Jews, thereby destroying the lineage of Jesus. For Haman, the massacre is a matter of expediency. For Satan, it is a matter of survival. He will do whatever it takes to impede the presence of Jesus in the world.

That's why he doesn't want you to pray as Jesus taught, "Thy kingdom come."

Esther, Mordecai's adopted daughter, became queen by winning a Miss Persia contest. In one day she went from obscurity to royalty, and in more ways than one she reminds you of you.

Both of you are residents of the palace: Esther, the bride of Xerxes and you, the bride of Christ. Both of you have access to the throne of the king, and you both have a counselor to guide and teach you. Your counselor is the Holy Spirit. Esther's counselor was Mordecai.

It was Mordecai who urged Esther to keep her Jewish nationality a secret. It was also Mordecai who persuaded Esther to talk to Xerxes about the impending massacre. You may wonder why she would need any encouragement. Mordecai must have wondered the same thing. Listen to the message he got from Esther: "No man or woman may go to the king in the inner courtyard without being called. There is only one law about this: Anyone who enters must be put to death unless the king holds out his gold scepter. Then that person may live. And I have not been called to go to the king for thirty days" (Esther 4:11).

As strange as it may sound to us, not even the queen could approach the king without an invitation. To enter his throne room uninvited was to risk a visit to the gallows. But Mordecai convinces her to take the risk. If you wonder why I see Mordecai as a picture of the Holy Spirit, watch how he encourages her to do what is right. "Just because you think you live in the king's palace, don't think that out of all the Jewish people you alone will escape. If you keep quiet at this time, someone else will help and save the Jewish people, but you and your father's family will all die. And who knows, you may have been chosen queen for such a time as this" (Esther 4:13–14).

Watch how Esther responds. "Esther put on her royal robes and stood in the inner courtyard of the king's palace, facing the king's hall" (Esther 5:1).

Can't you see her? Right off the cover of *Mademoiselle* magazine? Can't you see King Xerxes? Flipping through his copy of *Car and Chariot.* On either side of him is a burly-chested guard. Behind him is a chattering eunuch. Ahead of him is a long day of cabinet meetings and royal red tape. He lets out a sigh and sinks down into his throne . . . and out of the corner of his eye, he sees Esther.

"When the king saw Queen Esther standing in the courtyard, he was pleased" (5:2). Let me give you my translation of that verse: "When the king saw Queen Esther standing in the courtyard he said, 'a-hubba-hubba-hubba.'" "He held out to her the gold scepter that was in his hand, so Esther went forward and touched the end of it" (5:2).

What follows is the rapid collapse of Satan's deck of cards. Haman schemes to string up Mordecai, the only man who won't grovel at his feet. Esther plans to throw a couple of banquets for Xerxes and Haman. At the end of the second banquet Xerxes begs Esther to ask for something. Esther looks sort of sheepishly at the floor and says, "Well, now that you mention it, there is one eensy weensy favor I've been wanting to ask." And she proceeds to inform the king about the raging anti-Semite who was hell-bent on killing her friends like rats, which meant that Xerxes was about to lose his bride if he didn't act soon, and you don't want that, do you honey?

Xerxes demands the name of the murderer, and Haman looks for the exits. Esther spills the beans, and Xerxes loses his cool. He storms out the door to take a Prozac only to return and find Haman at the feet of Esther. Haman is begging for mercy, but the king thinks he's making a move on the queen. And before Haman has a chance to explain, he's headed to the same gallows he'd built for Mordecai.

Haman gets Mordecai's rope. Mordecai gets Haman's job. Esther gets a good night's sleep. The Jews live to see another day. And we get a dramatic reminder of what happens when we approach our King.

Like Esther, we have been plucked out of obscurity and given a place in the palace.

Like Esther, we have royal robes; she was dressed in cloth, we are dressed in righteousness.

Like Esther, we have the privilege of making our request.

That's what Sara did. Her request wasn't as dramatic as Esther's, but it changed her father's plans. By the way, the living parable of Sara and her desk didn't stop at the store.

On the way home she realized that my desk was still at the store. "I guess you didn't beg, did you, Daddy?" (We have not because we ask not.)

When we unloaded her desk she invited me to christen it with her by drawing a picture. I made a sign which read, "Sara's desk." She made a sign which read, "I love my Daddy." (Worship is the right response to answered prayer.)

My favorite part of the story is what happened the next day. I shared this account in my Sunday sermon. A couple from our church dropped by and picked the desk up, telling us they would paint it. When they returned it a couple of days later, it was covered with angels. And I was reminded that when we pray for God's kingdom to come, it comes! All the hosts of heaven rush to our aid.

CHAPTER 7

THE
STUDY

— | *How God Reveals His Will* | —

Thy will be done . . .

ERE THE SCENE not so common it would be comical. Two heavy-hearted disciples slouching their way home to Emmaus. By the slump in their shoulders, you'd never know today was Resurrection Sunday. By the looks on their faces, you'd think Jesus was still in the tomb. "We were hoping that he would free Israel," they lament (Luke 24:21).

As if he hasn't! How could you be so close to Christ and miss the point? Jesus has just redeemed the world and they are complaining about Rome? Jesus came to deal with sin and death—and they want him to deal with Caesar and soldiers? Jesus came to set us free from hell—and they want to be set free from taxes?

69

Talk about a miscommunication! They missed the revolution!

I made the same mistake last month. The revolution I missed was nothing like the ones the disciples missed, but I missed it just the same.

The New England colonies were never the same after the Boston Tea Party. Europe was never the same after the Battle of Normandy. The church was never the same after Luther hammered his ninety-five theses on the Wittenburg Door. And my life will never be the same now that e-mail has entered our office.

The avant-garde thinkers on the church staff had been lobbying for this change for months. "Just think," they would say, "just move the cursor and click the mouse and the message is sent."

Easy for them to say. They speak Computer-ese. Not me. Up until recently I thought a *cursor* was a person with foul language and a *mouse* was a rodent you trapped. As far as I knew, *logging-on* was the job of the lumberjack and a *monitor* was the guy who asked you what you were doing roaming the halls during class.

How was I to know that *interface* was a computer term? I thought it was slang for a slam-dunk. (Interface, baby!) Forgive me for lagging behind (or is that "logging behind"?), but a fellow can only handle so much. It happened overnight. I went to sleep in a simple society of sticky-notes and awoke in a paperless culture of e-mail. You can imagine my confusion as everyone started jabbering in this new vocabulary. "I e-mailed you a memo I found at www.confusion.com. Why don't you download your bat.file in my subdirectory and we can interface on the internet?"

What was wrong with, "Did you get my note?"

I miss the old days. I miss the bygone era of pen touching paper and sticky-notes on my door. I long to see handwriting again and to use the "while you were out message" as a coaster for my coffee cup.

But change was inevitable and, digging my heels in the carpet, I was pulled into the netherworld of e-mail. Partly because I was busy but mostly because I was stubborn, I procrastinated learning the system. Every day the computer net mail beeped to alert me about incoming messages. And everyday the number increased. "Max Lucado has 10 unread messages in his box." "Max Lucado has 52 unread messages in his box." "Max Lucado has 93 unread messages in his box."

Finally I gave in. After being carefully tutored and mastering the correct double click of the hamster (I mean the mouse), I found myself gazing inside a room full of information, all waiting for me. There was a letter from Africa, a joke about preachers, a dozen or so announcements about meetings (I had missed—oops!). Within a few minutes I was updated, informed and, I'll admit it, enlightened. As much as I hate to say so, it felt good to get the messages again.

Which is similar to how the two men on the road to Emmaus must have felt. They, too, had missed out on some information. They, too, were confused. They'd missed more than a memo on a committee meeting, however. They'd missed the meaning of the death of Jesus. What should have been a day of joy was to them a day of despair. Why? They didn't know how to understand God's will.

They aren't alone. More than one of us has spent hours staring at the monitor of life wondering what direction to take. We know God has a will for us. "I have good plans for you, not plans to hurt you. I will give you hope and a good future" (Jer. 29:11).

God has a plan and that plan is good. Our question is, how do I access it? Other people seem to receive guidance; how can I? One of the best ways to answer this question is to study the story of these two confused disciples on the road to Emmaus. And I know no better time to answer these questions than now as we enter into the next room in God's Great House and pray, "Thy will be done."

Just down the hall from the chapel is a room uncluttered by televisions, stereos, and e-mail-infected computers. Envision a study with bookshelves lining the walls, a braided rug on the floor and an inviting fire in the hearth. In front of the fire are two high, wing chairs, one for you and one for your Father. Your seat is empty, and your Father motions for you to join him. Come and sit and ask him whatever is on your heart. No question is too small, no riddle too simple. He has all the time in the world. Come and seek the will of God.

To pray, "Thy will be done" is to seek the heart of God. The word *will* means "strong desire." The study is where we learn what God desires. What is his heart? His passion? He wants you to know it.

Shall God hide from us what he is going to do? Apparently not, for he has gone to great lengths to reveal his will to us. Could he have done more than send his Son to lead us? Could he have done more than give his word to teach us? Could he have done more than orchestrate events to awaken us? Could he have done more than send his Holy Spirit to counsel us?

God is not the God of confusion, and wherever he sees sincere seekers with confused hearts, you can bet your sweet December that he will do whatever it takes to help them see his will. That's what he was doing on the road to Emmaus.

Everybody else was on-line, and they were on foot. They saw the death of Jesus as the death of the movement, and they packed their bags and headed home. And that is where they were going when Jesus appeared to them. How sweet is the appearance of Jesus on the road. Let a lamb take the wrong turn and miss the pasture and our Shepherd, unwilling to let him wander too far, comes to guide him home. How does he do this? How does he reveal his will to us? You might be surprised at the simplicity of the process.

THROUGH THE PEOPLE OF GOD

The first mistake of the duo was to disregard the words of their fellow disciples. God reveals his will through a community of believers. On the first Easter, he spoke through women who spoke to the others. "Today some women among us amazed us. Early this morning they went to the tomb, but they did not find his body there. They came and told us that they had seen a vision of angels who said Jesus was alive" (Luke 24: 22–23).

His plan hasn't changed. Jesus still speaks to believers through believers. "The whole body depends on Christ, and all the parts of the body are joined and held together. Each part does its own work to make the whole body grow and be strong with love" (Eph. 4:15).

While I was driving to my office this morning, my eye saw a traffic light. The sensors within my eye perceived that the color of the light was red. My brain checked my memory bank and announced the meaning of a red light to my right foot. My right foot responded by leaving the accelerator and pressing the brake.

Now what if my body hadn't functioned properly? What if my eye had decided not to be a part of the body because the nose had hurt its feelings? Or what if the foot was tired of being bossed around and decided to press the gas pedal instead of the brake? Or what if the right foot was in pain, but too proud to tell the left foot, so the left foot didn't know to step in and help? In all instances, a wreck would occur.

God has given each part of the body of Christ an assignment. One way God reveals his will to you is through the church. He speaks to one member of his body through another member. It could happen in a Bible class, a small group, during communion, or during dessert. God has as many methods as he has people.

That, by the way, is why Satan doesn't want you in church. You've noticed, haven't you, that when you're in a spiritual slump, you head out to Emmaus, too. You don't want to be with believers. Or if you do, you sneak in and sneak out of the service, making excuses about meals to prepare or work to do. The truth is, Satan doesn't want you hearing God's will. And since God reveals his will to his children through other children, he doesn't want you in a church. Nor does he want you reading your Bible. Which takes us to another way God reveals his will.

THROUGH THE WORD OF GOD

The disciples disregarded the Word of God. That was their second mistake. Rather than consult the Scriptures, they listened to their fears. Jesus corrects this by appearing to them and conducting a Bible study. We'd expect something a bit more dramatic from one who had just defeated death—turn a tree into a dog or suspend the disciples a few feet in the air. But Jesus sees no need to do more than reacquaint his followers with Scripture.

> "You are foolish and slow to believe everything the prophets said. They said that the Christ must suffer these things before he enters his glory." Then starting with what Moses and the prophets had said about him, Jesus began to explain everything that had been written about himself in the Scriptures. (Luke 24:25–27)

Through the words of the prophets, he used Scripture to reveal his will. Doesn't he do the same today? Open the Word of God and you'll find his will.

> This is God's will, that I should raise up those he has given me. (John 6:39)

> It is God's will that you be born again, that you be "born not of the will of flesh nor of the will of man but of God." (John 1:13)

> It is not God's will that one little one perish. (Matt. 18:14)

> It is my Father's will that everyone who sees the Son and believes on him should have eternal life—that I should raise him at the Last Day. (John. 6:40)

It is his will that the world be saved. Knowing that, then, my task is to align myself with his will. Anytime I find myself choosing between two roads I must ask, "Which road will contribute more to the kingdom of God?"

Sometimes it's obvious. There is no way, for example, that pornography advances the cause of God. It's beyond reason to think that embezzlement enhances the kingdom (even if you tithe on your take). I would take issue with the person who justifies her drug addiction as a way to draw nearer to the mystical side of God.

Other times it's not as clear, but the question is still helpful. Forced to choose between two professions? Will one allow you to have a greater impact for the kingdom? Torn between two churches to attend? Will one afford you a greater chance to glorify God? You wonder if this person is the spouse for you? Ask yourself, Will he or she help me bring glory to God?

His *general* will provides us with guidelines which help us understand his *specific* will for our individual lives.

THROUGH A WALK WITH GOD

> They begged him, "Stay with us; . . . it is almost night."
> So he went in to stay with them. (Luke 24: 29)

We also learn God's will by spending time in his presence. The key to knowing God's heart is having a relationship with him. A *personal* relationship. God will speak to you differently than he will speak to others. Just because God spoke to Moses through a burning bush, that doesn't mean we should all sit next to a bush waiting for God to speak. God used a fish to convict Jonah. Does that mean we should have worship services at Sea World? No. God reveals his heart personally to each person.

For that reason, your walk with God is essential. His heart is not seen in an occasional chat or weekly visit. We learn his will as we take up residence in his house every single day.

If you were to take a name at random out of the phone book and ask me, "Max, how does Chester Whomever feel about adultery?" I couldn't answer. I don't know Chester Whomever. But if you were to ask me, "Max, how does Denalyn Lucado feel about adultery?" I wouldn't even have to call her. I know. She's my wife. We have walked together long enough that I know what she thinks.

The same is true with God. Walk with him long enough and you come to know his heart. When you spend time with him in his study, you see his passion. Welcome him to enter the gateway of your soul and you'll perceive his will. By the way, did you notice that curious action of Jesus found in verse 28? "They came near the town of Emmaus and Jesus acted as if he were going farther."

Doesn't Jesus want to be with the disciples? Of course he does. But he doesn't want to be where he's not invited. Ever the gentleman, our Lord awaits our invitation. Please note, it was after they gave this invitation that they were "allowed to recognize Jesus" (v. 31).

There is one final way God reveals his will.

THROUGH THE FIRE OF GOD

When they saw who he was, he disappeared. They said to each other, "It felt like a fire burning in us when Jesus talked to us on the road and explained the Scriptures to us." (vv. 31–32)

Don't you love that verse? They knew they had been with Jesus because of the fire within them. God reveals his will by setting a torch to your soul. He gave Jeremiah a fire for hard hearts. He gave Nehemiah a fire for a forgotten city. He set Abraham on fire for a land he'd never seen. He set Isaiah on fire with a vision he couldn't resist. Forty years of fruitless preaching didn't extinguish the fire of Noah. Forty years of wilderness wandering didn't douse the passion of Moses. Jericho couldn't slow Joshua, and Goliath didn't deter David. There was a fire within them.

And isn't there one within you? Want to know God's will for your life? Then answer this question: What ignites your heart? Forgotten orphans? Untouched nations? The inner city? The outer limits?

Heed the fire within!

Do you have a passion to sing? Then sing!

Are you stirred to manage? Then manage!

Do you ache for the ill? Then treat them!

Do you hurt for the lost? Then teach them!

As a young man I felt the call to preach. Unsure if I was correct in my reading of God's will for me, I sought the counsel of a minister I admired. His counsel still rings true. "Don't preach," he said, "unless you have to."

As I pondered his words I found my answer: "I *have* to. If I don't, the fire will consume me."

What is the fire that consumes you?

Mark it down: Jesus comes to set you on fire! He walks as a torch from heart to heart, warming the cold and thawing the chilled and stirring the ashes. He is at once a Galilean wildfire and a welcome candle. He comes to purge infection and illuminate your direction.

The fire of your heart is the light of your path. Disregard it at your own expense. Fan it at your own delight. Blow it. Stir it. Nourish it. Cynics will doubt it. Those without it will mock it. But those who know it—those who know *him*—will understand it.

To meet the Savior is to be set aflame.

To discover the flame is to discover his will.

And to discover his will is to access a world like none you've ever seen.

CHAPTER 8

THE
FURNACE

On earth as it is in heaven . . .

I'D LIKE YOU TO THINK about someone. His name is not important. His looks are immaterial. His gender is of no concern. His title is irrelevant. He is important not because of who he is, but because of what he did.

He went to Jesus on behalf of a friend. His friend was sick, and Jesus could help, and someone needed to go to Jesus, so someone went. Others cared for the sick man in other ways. Some brought food, others provided treatment, still others comforted the family. Each role was crucial. Each person was helpful, but none was more vital than the one who went to Jesus.

He went because he was asked to go. An earnest appeal came from the family of the afflicted. "We need someone who will tell

Jesus that my brother is sick. We need someone to ask him to come. Will you go?"

The question came from two sisters. They would have gone themselves, but they couldn't leave their brother's bedside. They needed someone else to go for them. Not just anyone, mind you, for not just anyone could. Some were too busy, others didn't know the way. Some fatigued too quickly, others were inexperienced on the path. Not everyone could go.

And not everyone would go. This was no small request the sisters were making. They needed a diligent ambassador, someone who knew how to find Jesus. Someone who wouldn't quit mid-journey. Someone who would make sure the message was delivered. Someone who was as convinced as they were that Jesus *must* know what had happened.

They knew of a trustworthy person, and to that person they went. They entrusted their needs to someone, and that someone took those needs to Christ.

"So Mary and Martha sent *someone* to tell Jesus, 'Lord, the one you love is sick'" (John 11:3, emphasis mine).

Someone carried the request. Someone walked the trail. Someone went to Jesus on behalf of Lazarus. And because someone went, Jesus responded.

Let me ask you, how important was this person in the healing of Lazarus? How essential was his role? Some might regard it as secondary. After all, didn't Jesus know everything? Certainly he knew that Lazarus was sick. Granted, but he didn't respond to the need until someone came to him with the message. "When Jesus heard this, he said, 'This sickness will not end in death. It is for the glory of God to bring glory to the son of God'" (v. 4).

When was Lazarus healed? After *someone* made the request. Oh, I know the healing wouldn't unfold for several days, but the timer was set when the appeal was made. All that was needed was the passage of time.

Would Jesus have responded if the messenger had not spoken? Perhaps, but we have no guarantee. We do, however, have an example: The power of God was triggered by prayer. Jesus looked down the very throat of death's cavern and called Lazarus back to life . . . all because someone prayed.

THE FURNACE

In the Great House of God there is a furnace. This furnace affects the whole house, and your prayers fuel the furnace. Your intercession is coal on the fire. Your pleadings are kindling to the flames. The furnace is sturdy, the vents are ready; all that is needed is your prayer.

> Prayer is essential in this ongoing warfare. Pray long
> and hard. Pray for your brothers and your sisters.
> (Eph. 6:18 MSG)

In the economy of heaven, the prayers of saints are a valued commodity. John, the apostle, would agree. He wrote the story of Lazarus and was careful to show the sequence: The healing began when the request was made.

This wouldn't be the last time John would make the same point. Read these words, penned later by John. "On the Lord's Day I was in the Spirit and I heard a loud voice behind me that sounded like a trumpet" (Rev. 1:10).

IN THE SPIRIT ON THE LORD'S DAY

We've just moved six decades into the future. John is old now. He's the silver-haired figure stepping through the jagged rocks on a beach. He's looking for a flat place where he can kneel. It is the Lord's day. And John has come to see his Lord.

We don't know who first called this day the Lord's day, but we know why. It was and is his day. It belongs to him. He left his imprint on hell itself that morning. Friday's trial became Sunday's trumpet. This is the Lord's day.

This is also John's spiritual birthday. Decades earlier, on the first Lord's day, John was shaken from his sorrow and sleep by the announcement, "They have taken the Lord out of the tomb and we don't know where they have put him" (John 20:2). On legs much younger and stronger, John sprinted to the empty tomb and the fulfilled promise. Speaking of himself, he later confided, "The other follower, who had reached the tomb first, also went in. He saw and believed" (John 20:8).

After the resurrection came persecution, and the Father scattered his disciples over society like a spring wind scatters dandelions. John, the eyewitness, was placed in Ephesus. There is good reason to believe he spent every Lord's day in the same way he spent the first, leading a friend into the empty tomb of Jesus.

But on this Sunday he has no friend to take to the tomb. He is exiled, banished from his friends. Alone on Patmos. Cut off. With the stroke of a magistrate's pen he was sentenced to pass his days with no companion, with no church.

Rome had stilled the tongue of Peter and silenced the pen of Paul. Now she would break the shepherd's staff of John. No doubt she felt smug in her proscription. One by one, the iron fist of Caesar would crush the fragile work of the Galilean.

If only she had known. But she had no idea. No clue. No concept. For what Rome intended as isolation, heaven ordained as revelation. Rome placed John on Patmos for punishment. Heaven placed John on Patmos for privilege. The same apostle who saw the open grave of Christ was now to glimpse the open door of heaven.

It was the Lord's day, you see. Nothing Rome could do could change that fact. It was the Lord's day in Rome and in Jerusalem. It was the Lord's Day in Egypt and Ethiopia and even along the barren stretches of Patmos. It was the Lord's day. And John was, in his words, "in the Spirit" on the Lord's day. Though he was cut off from man, he was in the very presence of God. Though he was far from friends, he was face-to-face with his Friend. He was praying.

And as he prayed, he again was met by an angel. He again saw what no man had ever seen. The same eyes that saw the resurrected Lord now saw heaven open. And for the next few seconds, minutes, or days, John was caught up in the fury and passion of living in the end of times and in the presence of God.

AND HEAVEN WAS SILENT

Though much could be said about what he saw, let's focus on what he heard. Before John speaks of what he saw, he speaks of what he heard, and what he heard was stunning. "On the Lord's day I was in the Spirit and I heard a voice behind me that sounded like a trumpet" (Rev. 1:10). I can imagine a voice and I can imagine a trumpet, but to imagine the silver-toned trumpet-voice is beyond me. And so we are welcomed to the world of Revelation, a realm where what can't happen on earth always happens in heaven.

For eight chapters we read about the noises of heaven John's ears hear—the glorious, loud, rambunctious, soft, holy sounds of heaven. The angels speak. The thunder booms. The living creatures chant, "Holy, holy, holy," and the elders worship, "You are worthy our Lord and our God to receive glory and honor and power, because you made all things" (4:10). The souls of the martyrs call out, "How long?" (6:10). The earth quakes, and the stars fall like figs in a windstorm. One hundred forty-four thousand people from every nation, tribe, people and language of the earth shout in a loud voice, "Salvation belongs to our God, who sits on the throne and to the lamb" (7:10).

The air is full of sounds—earthquakes, trumpets, proclamations, and declarations. From the first word of the angel there is constant activity and non-stop noise until: "There was silence in heaven for about half an hour . . . " (8:1). Strange this sudden reference to minutes. Nothing else is timed. We are not told the length of the worship or the duration of the songs, but the silence lasted for "about half an hour." "What do you mean, 'about half an hour'?" we want to ask. Did John time it? Why "half an hour"? Why not fifteen minutes or one hour? I don't know. I don't know if John was literal or symbolic. But I do know that, as an orchestra falls silent at the lifting of the conductor's baton, so heaven hushed when the Lamb opened the seventh seal.

As the first six seals revealed how God acts, the seventh revealed how God listens. Look what happens after the seventh seal is opened.

> When the Lamb opened the seventh seal, there was silence in heaven for about half an hour. And I saw the seven angels who stand before God and to whom were given seven trumpets. Another angel came and stood at the altar, holding a golden pan for incense. He was given much incense to offer with the prayers of all God's holy people. The angel put this offering on the golden altar before the throne. The smoke from the incense went up from the angel's hand to God with the prayers of God's holy people. Then the angel filled the incense pan with fire from the altar and threw it on the earth, and there were flashes of lightning, thunder and loud noises, and an earthquake. (8:1–5)

Every song ceased. Every being of the heavenly city hushed. The noise stopped. A sudden stillness fell like a curtain. Why? Why did the Lamb lift his hand for silence? Why did the silver-trumpet voices hush? Because someone was praying. Heaven paused, and Heaven pauses to hear the prayers of . . . someone. A mother for her child. A pastor for a church. A doctor for the diseased. A counselor for the confused. Someone steps up to the furnace with a burden and prays, "Lord, the one you love is sick."

WHEN JESUS HEARD THIS

The phrase the friend of Lazarus used is worth noting. When he told Jesus of the illness he said, "Lord, the one you love is sick." He doesn't base his appeal on the imperfect love of the one in need, but on the perfect love of the Savior. He doesn't say, "The one *who loves you* is sick." He says, "The one *you love* is sick." The power of the prayer, in other words, does not depend on the one who makes the prayer, but on the one who hears the prayer.

We can and must repeat the phrase in manifold ways. "The one you love is tired, sad, hungry, lonely, fearful, depressed." The words of the prayer vary, but the response never changes. The Savior hears the prayer. He silences heaven, so he won't miss a word. He hears the prayer. Remember the phrase from John's gospel? "When Jesus *heard* this, he said, 'This sickness will not end in death'" (John 10:4 emphasis mine).

The Master heard the request. Jesus stopped whatever he was doing and took note of the man's words. This anonymous courier was heard by God.

You and I live in a loud world. To get someone's attention is no easy task. He must be willing to set everything aside to listen: turn down the radio, turn away from the monitor, turn the corner of the page and set down the book. When someone is willing to silence everything else so he can hear us clearly, it is a privilege. A rare privilege, indeed.

So John's message is critical. You can talk to God because God listens. Your voice matters in heaven. He takes you very seriously. When you enter his presence, the attendants turn to you to hear your voice. No need to fear that you will be ignored. Even if you stammer or stumble, even if what you have to say impresses no one, it impresses God—and he listens. He listens to the painful plea of the elderly in the rest home. He listens to the gruff confession of the death-row inmate. When the alcoholic begs for mercy, when the spouse seeks guidance, when the businessman steps off the street into the chapel, God listens.

Intently. Carefully. The prayers are honored as precious jewels. Purified and empowered, the words rise in a delightful fragrance to our Lord. "The smoke from the incense went up from the angel's hand to God." Incredible. Your words do not stop until they reach the very throne of God.

Then, the angel "filled the incense pan with fire from the altar and threw it on the earth" (Rev. 8:5). One call and Heaven's fleet appears. Your prayer on earth activates God's power in heaven, and "God's will is done on earth as it is in heaven."

You are the someone of God's kingdom. You have access to God's furnace. Your prayers move God to change the world. You may not understand the mystery of prayer. You don't need to. But this much is clear: Actions in heaven begin when someone prays on earth. What an amazing thought!

When you speak, Jesus hears.

And when Jesus hears, thunder falls.

And when thunder falls, the world is changed.

All because someone prayed.

CHAPTER 9

THE KITCHEN

—| *God's Abundant Table* |—

Give us this day our daily bread . . .

I DID A BIT OF RESEARCH on the culture of the kitchen this week. Here is what I learned: People love to talk about food. If you're ever in need of a conversation prompter, try this one: "Do you know any curious dining practices?" There'll be no shortage of stories. The kitchen seems to be one place where all of us have some experience. In fact, you might say that some people are (ahem) heavyweights in this area. Ask people to relate curious eating habits and they'll give you a mouthful.

Like the uncle who pours syrup on everything he eats. ("Everything?" I asked the same question. *Everything*, I was assured.)

Like the father who puts gravy on his cake and the other father who eats his pie crust first. (Says he likes to save the point till last.)

Like the dad (mine) who crumbled his cornbread in butter-milk.

One remembered a verse:

> I eat my peas with honey.
> I've done it all my life.
> It makes them taste funny.
> But it keeps them on my knife.[1]

Another remembered an old wives' tale about eating ice cream with the spoon upside down to prevent headaches. More than one person was taught to eat bread after fish and never to drink milk with fish.

I was surprised how many hate to intermingle their servings. "First, I eat all my beans. Then all my corn. Then all my meat." (Correct me if I'm wrong, but aren't they about to be mixed anyway?) One fellow carries this to an extreme. Whereas many segregate their foods so they don't touch while on the plate, he puts each portion on its own saucer.

A history buff reminded me that kitchens in colonial America had a trough in the floor into which the bones would be tossed and near which the dogs would wait. Speaking of dogs, more than one person remembered the childhood days of smuggling un-wanted food to their pet and then smiling innocently as mom applauded the clean plate.

Burps are welcome in China. And an empty plate among some Latin cultures only assures your host that you're still hungry. The practice of intersecting the fork and knife on a finished plate was begun by Italian nobility who saw the cross as an act of thanksgiving.[2]

Emily Post would have groaned at some of the earliest writings on etiquette. One written in the 1530s stated: "If you can't swallow a piece of food, turn around discreetly and throw it somewhere."[3]

My favorite table morsel was the story of the man with nine sons. The rule of his kitchen was simple: Dad gets the last piece of chicken. If he doesn't want it, the fastest fork wins. One night, as all ten eyed the final piece on the plate, a thunderstorm caused an electrical blackout. There was a scream in the dark, and when the lights returned, the dad's hand was on the chicken platter with nine forks sticking in it.

Everybody has a kitchen story because everybody has a history in the kitchen. Whether yours was a campfire in the jungle or a culinary castle in Manhattan, you learned early that in this room your basic needs were supplied. A garage is optional. A living room is negotiable. An office is a luxury. But a kitchen? Absolutely essential. Every house has one. Even the Great House of God.

KITCHEN RULES

Or perhaps we should say *especially* the Great House of God. For who is more concerned with your basic needs than your Father in heaven? God is not a mountain guru only involved in the mystical and spiritual. The same hand that guides your soul gives food for your body. The one who clothes you in goodness is the same one who clothes you in cloth. In the school of life, God is both the teacher and the cook. He provides fire for the heart and food for the stomach. Your eternal salvation and your evening meal come from the same hand. There is a kitchen in

God's Great House; let's journey downstairs and enjoy its warmth.

The table is long. The chairs are many and the food ample. On the wall hangs a simple prayer: *"Give us this day our daily bread."* The words, though they be brief, raise some good questions. For example, where is the "please"? Dare we saunter into the presence of God and say, "Give us"? Another question concerns the paucity of the prayer. Just bread? Any chance for some spaghetti? And what about tomorrow? Why are we to pray for today's provisions and not those of the future?

Perhaps the best way to answer these questions is to look again at the wall of the kitchen. Beneath the prayer, "Give us this day our daily bread," I can envision two statements. You might call them rules of the kitchen. You've seen such rules before. "No singing at the table." "Wash before you eat." "Carry your plate to the sink." "Max gets double portions of dessert." (I wish!)

God's kitchen has a couple of rules as well. The first is a rule of dependence:

RULE #1: DON'T BE SHY, ASK

The first word in the phrase, "Give us this day our daily bread," seems abrupt. Sounds terse, doesn't it? Too demanding. Wouldn't an "If you don't mind" be more appropriate? Perhaps a "Pardon me, but could I ask you to give . . ." would be better? Am I not being irreverent if I simply say, "Give us this day our daily bread"? Well, you are if this is where you begin. But it isn't. If you have followed Christ's model for prayer, your preoccupation has been his wonder rather than your stomach. The first three petitions are God-centered, not self-centered. "Hallowed be your name . . . your kingdom come . . . your will be done."

Your first step into the house of God was not to the kitchen but to the living room, where you were reminded of your adoption. "Our *Father* who is in heaven." You then studied the foundation of the house, where you pondered his permanence. "Our Father *who is* in heaven." Next you entered the observatory and marveled at his handiwork: "Our Father who is in *heaven*." In the chapel, you worshiped his holiness: "Hallowed be thy name." In the throne room, you touched the lowered scepter and prayed the greatest prayer, "Thy kingdom come." In the study, you submitted your desires to his and prayed, "Thy will be done." And all of heaven was silent as you placed your prayer in the furnace, saying, "on earth as it is in heaven."

Proper prayer follows such a path, revealing God to us before revealing our needs to God. (You might reread that one.) The purpose of prayer is not to change God, but to change us, and by the time we reach God's kitchen, we are changed people. Wasn't our heart warmed when we called him Father? Weren't our fears stilled when we contemplated his constancy? Weren't we amazed as we stared at the heavens?

Seeing his holiness caused us to confess our sin. Inviting his kingdom to come reminded us to stop building our own. Asking God for his will to be done placed our will in second place to his. And realizing that heaven pauses when we pray left us breathless in his presence.

By the time we step into the kitchen, we're renewed people! We've been comforted by our father, conformed by his nature, consumed by our creator, convicted by his character, constrained by his power, commissioned by our teacher, and compelled by his attention to our prayers.

The prayer's next three petitions encompass all of the concerns of our life. "This daily bread" addresses the present. "Forgive our sins" addresses the past. "Lead us not into temptation" speaks to the future. (The wonder of God's wisdom: how he can reduce all our needs to three simple statements.)

First he addresses our need for bread. The term means all of a person's physical needs. Martin Luther defined bread as "Everything necessary for the preservation of this life, including food, a healthy body, house, home, wife and children." This verse urges us to talk to God about the necessities of life. He may also give us the luxuries of life, but he certainly will grant the necessities.

Any fear that God wouldn't meet our needs was left in the observatory. Would he give the stars their glitter and not give us our food? Of course not. He has committed to care for us. We aren't wrestling crumbs out of a reluctant hand, but rather confessing the bounty of a generous hand. The essence of the prayer is really an affirmation of the Father's care. Our provision is his priority.

Turn your attention to Psalm 37.

> Trust in the Lord and do good. Live in the land and feed on truth. Enjoy serving the Lord and he will give you what you want. Depend on the Lord; trust him and he will take care of you. (vv. 3–4)

God is committed to caring for our needs. Paul tells us that a man who won't feed his own family is worse than an unbeliever (1 Tim. 5:8). How much more will a holy God care for his children? After all, how can we fulfill his mission unless our needs are met? How can we teach or minister or influence unless we have our basic needs satisfied? Will God enlist us in his army and not provide a commissary? Of course not.

"I pray that the God of peace will give you everything you need so you can do what he wants" (Heb. 13:20). Hasn't that prayer been answered in our life? We may not have had a feast, but haven't we always had food? Perhaps there was no banquet, but at least there was bread. And many times there was a banquet.

In fact, many of us in the United States have trouble relating to the phrase "Give us this day our daily bread" because our pantries are so packed and our bellies so full we seldom ask for food. We ask for self-control. We don't say, "God let me eat." We say, "God, help me not to eat so much." You won't find books in our stores on surviving starvation, but you'll find shelves loaded with books on losing weight. This doesn't negate the importance of this phrase, however. Just the opposite. For us, the blessed of belly, this prayer has double meaning.

We pray, only to find our prayer already answered! We are like the high school senior who decides to go to college and then learns the cost of tuition. He runs to his father and pleads, "I'm sorry to ask so much, Dad, but I have nowhere else to go. I want to go to college and I don't have a penny." The father puts his arms around the son and smiles and says, "Don't worry, son. The day you were born I began saving for your education. I've already provided for your tuition."

The boy made the request only to find the father had already met it. The same happens to you. At some point in your life it occurs to you that someone is providing for your needs. You take a giant step in maturity when you agree with David's words in 1 Chronicles 29:14: "Everything we have has come from you, and we only give you what is yours already" (TLB). You may be writing a check and stirring the soup, but there's more to putting food on the table than that. What about the ancient symbiosis of the seed and the soil and the sun and the rain? Who created animals for food and minerals for metal? Long before you knew you needed someone to provide for your needs, God already had.

So the first rule in the kitchen is one of dependence. Ask God for whatever you need. He is committed to you. God lives with the self-assigned task of providing for his own, and so far, you've got to admit, he's done pretty well at the job.

The second rule is one of trust.

RULE #2: TRUST THE COOK

My informal survey on eating habits reminded me of the time I pigged out on a Pillsbury Dough tube. When I was a youngster my mom would let me lick the bowl after she used it to stir the cookie dough. I remember thinking how great it would be to make a meal out of the gooey stuff. In college my dream came true.

Four of us friends went to a weekend retreat at a farm. On the way we stopped at a grocery store. As you can imagine, we were careful to select proper vegetables, skim milk, no-fat yogurt— and we stayed away from the sweets. We also drove by the White House and picked up the President and the First Lady to do our laundry. Are you kidding? We filled our basket with nothing but fantasy. And for me, my fantasy was cookie dough! This was going to be a Pillsbury Dough Boy weekend. That night I peeled the plastic off the dough like the peeling off a banana and took a big bite . . . then another . . . then anothuuuther . . . then uhhh-nuuuther. Then . . . yuck. I'd had enough.

That usually happens when we make our own menu. You'll notice this is the first time we've used the word *menu*. The kitchen in God's house is no restaurant. It's not owned by a stranger, it's run by your Father. It's not a place you visit and leave; it's a place to linger and chat. It's not open one hour and closed the next; the kitchen is ever available. You don't eat and then pay; you eat and say thanks. But perhaps the most important difference between a kitchen and a restaurant is the menu. A kitchen doesn't have one.

God's kitchen doesn't need one. Things may be different in your house, but in the house of God, the one who provides the food is the one who prepares the meal. We don't swagger into his presence and demand delicacies. Nor do we sit outside the door and hope for crumbs. We simply take our place at the table and gladly trust him to "Give us this day our daily bread."

What a statement of trust! Whatever you want me to have is all I want. In his book *Victorious Praying*, Alan Redpath translates the phrase, "Give us this day bread suited to our need."[4] Some days the plate runs over. God keeps bringing out more food and we keep loosening our belt. A promotion. A privilege. A friendship. A gift. A lifetime of grace. An eternity of joy. There are times when we literally push ourselves back from the table, amazed at God's kindness. "You serve me a six-course dinner right in front of my enemies. You revive my drooping head; my cup fills with blessing" (Ps. 23:5 MSG).

And then there are those days when, well, when we have to eat our broccoli. Our daily bread could be tears or sorrow or discipline. Our portion may include adversity as well as opportunity.

This verse was on my mind last night during family devotions. I called my daughters to the table and set a plate in front of each. In the center of the table I placed a collection of food: some fruit, some raw vegetables and some Oreo cookies. "Every day," I explained, "God prepares for us a plate of experiences. What kind of plate do you most enjoy?"

The answer was easy. Sara put three cookies on her plate. Some days are like that, aren't they? Some days are "three cookie days." Many are not. Sometimes our plate has nothing but vegetables—twenty-four hours of celery, carrots, and squash. Apparently God knows we need some strength, and though the portion may be hard to swallow, isn't it for our own good? Most days, however, have a bit of it all. Vegetables, which are healthy but dull. Fruit, which tastes better and we enjoy. And even an Oreo, which does little for our nutrition, but a lot for our attitude.

All are important and all are from God. "We know that in everything God works for the good of those who love him" (Rom. 8:28). We, like Paul, must learn the "secret of being happy at anytime in everything that happens, when I have enough to eat and when I go hungry, when I have more than I need and when I do not have enough. I can do all things through Christ, because he gives me strength" (Phil. 4:12).

Perhaps the heart of the prayer is found in the book of Proverbs.

> Give me enough food to live on, neither too much nor too little. If I'm too full, I might get independent, saying, "God, Who needs him?" If I'm poor, I might steal and dishonor the name of my God. (Prov. 30:8–9)

The next time your plate has more broccoli than apple pie, remember who prepared the meal. And the next time your plate has a portion you find hard to swallow, talk to God about it. Jesus did. In the garden of Gethsemane his Father handed him a cup of suffering so sour, so vile, that Jesus handed it back to heaven. "My Father," he prayed, "if it is possible may this cup be taken from me. Yet not as I will, but as you will" (Matt. 26:39).

Even Jesus was given a portion he found hard to swallow. But with God's help, he did. And with God's help, you can too.

CHAPTER 10

THE
ROOF

─┤ *Beneath God's Grace* ├─

Forgive us our debts . . .

FORGIVE ME for broaching the issue, but I must.

I realize the topic is personal, but it's time we went public.

I need to talk to you about being overdrawn at the bank.

Your paycheck was late. Your landlord cashed your rent check too quickly. You were going to make a deposit, but your aunt called from Minnesota and by the time you got to the bank it was closed and you didn't know how to make a night deposit.

Regardless of the reason, the result is the same: INSUFFICIENT FUNDS. What an ominous phrase. In the great gallery of famous phrases, "insufficient funds" hangs in the same hallway with "The IRS will audit your account," "A root canal is necessary," and "Let's stop dating and just be friends." INSUFFICIENT FUNDS. (To get the full impact of the phrase, imagine hearing the words spoken by a man with fangs, black cape and a deep voice in a Transylvania castle. "You have insufficient funds.")

You are overdrawn. You gave more than you had to give. You spent more than you had to spend. And guess who has to cough up some cash? Not the bank; they didn't write the check. Not the store; they didn't make the purchase. Not your aunt in Minnesota, unless she's got a soft spot in her heart for you. In the grand scheme of things, you can make all the excuses you want, but a bounced check lands in the lap of the one who wrote it.

What do you do if you don't have any money? What do you do if you have nothing to deposit but an honest apology and good intentions? You pray that some wealthy soul will make a huge deposit in your account. If you're talking about your financial debt, that's not likely to happen. If you're talking about your spiritual debt, however, it already has.

Your Father has covered your shortfall. In God's house you are covered by the roof of his grace.

THE ROOF OF PROTECTION

The roof of a house is seldom noticed. How often do your guests enter your doorway saying, "You have one of the finest roofs I've ever seen!" We've had hundreds of people in and out of our home through the years, and I honestly can't remember one comment about the roof. They might remind me to cut the grass or clean my sidewalk, but compliment my roof? Not yet.

Such disregard is no fault of the builder. He and his crew labored hours, balancing beams and nailing shingles. Yet, in spite of their effort, most people would notice a two-dollar lamp before they would notice the roof.

Let's not make the same mistake. As God covered his Great House, he spared no expense. In fact, his roof was the most costly section of the structure. It cost him the life of his Son. He invites us to study his work by virtue of three words in the center of the prayer. "Forgive our debts."

WE OWE A DEBT WE CANNOT PAY

Debt. The Greek word for debt has no mystery. It simply means "to owe someone something." If to be in debt is to owe someone something, isn't it appropriate for us speak of debt in our prayer, for aren't we all in debt to God?

Aren't we in God's debt when we disobey his commands? He tells us to go south and we go north. He tells us to turn right and we turn left. Rather than love our neighbor, we hurt our neighbor. Instead of seeking his will, we seek our will. We're told to forgive our enemies, but we attack our enemies. We disobey God.

Aren't we in God's debt when we disregard him? He makes the universe and we applaud science. He heals the sick and we applaud medicine. He grants beauty and we credit Mother Nature. He gives us possessions and we salute human ingenuity.

Don't we go into debt when we disrespect God's children? What if I did to you what we do to God? What if I shouted at your child in your presence? What if I called him names or struck him? You wouldn't tolerate it. But don't we do the same? How does God feel when we mistreat one of his children? When we curse at his offspring? When we criticize a co-worker, or gossip about a relative, or speak about someone before we speak to them? Aren't we in God's debt when we mistreat a neighbor?

"Wait a second, Max. You mean every time I do one of these things, I'm writing a check on my heavenly bank account?"

That's exactly what I'm saying. I'm also saying that if Christ had not covered us with his grace, each of us would be overdrawn on that account. When it comes to goodness we would have insufficient funds. Inadequate holiness. God requires a certain balance of virtue in our account, and it's more than any of us has alone. Our holiness account shows insufficient funds, and only the holy will see the Lord; what can we do?

We could try making a few deposits. Maybe if I wave at my neighbor or compliment my husband or go to church next Sunday, I'll get caught up. But how do you know when you've made enough? How many trips do I need to make to the bank? How much credit do I need? When can I relax?

That's the problem. You never can. "People cannot do any work that will make them right with God" (Rom. 4:5). If you are trying to justify your own statement, forget ever having peace. You're going to spend the rest of your days huffing and puffing to get to the drive-through window before the bank closes. You are trying to justify an account you can't justify. May I remind you of the roof of grace which covers you?

"It is God who justifies" (8:33).

GOD PAID A DEBT HE DID NOT OWE

God assigned himself the task of balancing your account. You cannot deal with your own sins. "Only God can take away sins"

(Mark 2:7). Jesus is "The Lamb of God, who takes away the sin of the world." It's not you! (John 1:29).

How did God deal with your debt?

Did he overlook it? He could have. He could have burned the statement. He could have ignored your bounced checks. But would a holy God do that? *Could* a holy God do that? No. Else he wouldn't be holy. Besides, is that how we want God to run his world—ignoring our sin and thereby endorsing our rebellion?

Did he punish you for your sins? Again, he could have. He could have crossed your name out of the book and wiped you off the face of the earth. But would a loving God do that? *Could* a loving God do that? He loves you with an everlasting love. Nothing can separate you from his love.

So what did he do? "God put the world square with himself through the Messiah, giving the world a fresh start by offering the forgiveness of sins. . . . How, you say? In Christ. God put on him the wrong who never did anything wrong, so you could be put right with God" (2 Cor. 5:19–21 MSG).

Don't miss what happened. He took your statement flowing with red ink and bad checks and put his name at the top. He took his statement, which listed a million deposits and not one withdrawal, and put your name at the top. He assumed your debt. You assumed his fortune. And that's not all he did.

He also paid your penalty. If you are overdrawn at a bank, a fine must be paid. If you are overdrawn with God, a penalty must be paid as well. The fine at the bank is a hassle. But the penalty from God is hell. Jesus not only balanced your account, he paid your penalty. He took your place and paid the price for your sins. "He changed places with us and put himself under that curse" (Gal. 3:13).

That's what Christ did definitively: suffered because of others' sins, the Righteous one for the unrighteous ones. He went through it all— was put to death and then made alive— to bring us to God. (1 Pet. 3:18 MSG)

But he was wounded for the wrong we did; he was crushed for the evil we did. The punishment, which made us well, was given to him, and we are healed because of his wounds. (Isa. 53:5)

"With one sacrifice, Jesus made perfect forever those who are being made holy" (Heb. 10:14). No more sacrifice needs to be made. No more deposits are necessary. So complete was the payment that Jesus used a banking term to proclaim your salvation. "It is finished!" (John 19:30). *Tetelestai* was a financial term used to announce the final installment, the ultimate payment.

Now, if the task is finished, is anything else required of you? Of course not. If the account is full, what more could you add? Even saying the phrase "forgive our debts" does not earn grace. We repeat the words to remind us of the forgiveness we have, not to attain a forgiveness we need. I'll say more about that in the next chapter, but before moving on may we talk frankly?

For some of you these thoughts about bounced checks and God's grace aren't new, but aren't they precious? Honestly, have you ever been given a gift which compares to God's grace? Finding this treasure of mercy makes the poorest beggar a prince. Missing this gift makes the wealthiest man a pauper.

Again, many of you knew that. I pray the reminder encourages you.

But for others, this is more than good news . . . it is *new* news. You never knew there was a roof of grace. And what a grand roof it is. The tiles are thick and the beams are sturdy. Under it you are shielded from the storms of guilt and shame. Beneath the covering of Christ, no accuser can touch you and no act can condemn you.

Isn't it good to know you don't have to stand outside in the storm anymore?

"But is it big enough for me?" you ask. Well, it was big enough for one who denied Christ (Peter). One who mocked Christ (the thief on the cross). One who persecuted Christ (Paul). Yes, it's big enough for you. Though you've spent a lifetime writing insufficient checks, God has stamped these words on your statement: MY GRACE IS SUFFICIENT FOR YOU.

Picture, if you will, a blank check. The amount of the check is "sufficient grace." The signer of the check is Jesus. The only blank line is for the payee. That part is for you. May I urge you to spend a few moments with your Savior receiving this check? Reflect on the work of his grace. Look toward the roof. Its beams are from Calvary and the nails once held a Savior to the cross. His sacrifice was for you.

Express your thanks for his grace. Whether for the first time or the thousandth, let him hear you whisper, "Forgive us our debts." And let him answer your prayer as you imagine writing your name on the check.

Perhaps I best slip out now and leave the two of you to talk. I'll be waiting in the hallway of the Great House of God.

CHAPTER II

THE
HALLWAY

——| *Grace Received, Grace Given* |——

Forgive us our debts as we also have forgiven our debtors . . .
For if you forgive men when they sin against you,
your heavenly Father will also forgive you.
But if you do not forgive men their sins, your
Father will not forgive your sins . . .

I'D LIKE TO TALK to you about bounty hunters, nitro around the neck, one of the greatest principles in the Bible, and okra and anchovy sandwiches. But before I do, let's start with a thought about hit men.

Living in the cross hairs of a hit man is no treat. I should know. I had one after me for three months. He wasn't a Mafia member, nor was he a gang member. He didn't carry a gun with a scope; his weapons were even deadlier. He had a phone number and a commission—track me down and make me pay.

His job? Collect past-due payments for a credit card company.

I hope you'll believe me when I say I had paid my bill. He certainly didn't believe me. I knew I'd paid the bill—I had the canceled check to prove it. The only problem was that the check was on a boat with all our other belongings somewhere between Miami and Rio. We had just moved to Brazil and our possessions were in transit. I wouldn't have access to my bank statement for three months. He wasn't about to wait that long.

He threatened to ruin my credit, sue the travel agency and call the police; he even said he would tell my mother (the big tattletale). After weeks of calling me collect, he suddenly quit bugging me. No explanation. All I can figure is that he traced the error to north of the equator rather than south, and he left me alone. He also left me amazed. I remember asking Denalyn, "What kind of person would enjoy such a job? His profession is aggravation."

A good day for him means a bad day for everyone he contacts. Don't get me wrong, I understand why such an occupation is necessary. I just wonder what kind of person would want such a job? Who wants to be a missionary of misery? Collectors spend the day making people feel bad. No one wants to take their calls. No one is happy to see them at the door. No one wants to read their letters. Can you imagine what their spouse says as they go to work? "Make 'em squirm, honey." Do their bosses motivate them with the "blood out of a turnip" award? Who is their hero? Godzilla? What a job. Their payday is in your paycheck, and they are out to get it. Can you imagine spending your days like that?

Perhaps you can. Perhaps all of us can. Even the best among us spend time demanding payment. Doesn't someone owe you something? An apology? A second chance? A fresh start? An explanation? A thank you? A childhood? A marriage? Stop and think about it (which I don't encourage you to do for long), and you can make a list of a lot of folks who are in your debt. Your parents should have been more protective. Your children should have been more appreciative. Your spouse should be more sensitive. Your preacher should have been more attentive.

What are you going to do with those in your debt? People in your past have dipped their hands in your purse and taken what was yours. What are you going to do? Few questions are more important. Dealing with debt is at the heart of your happiness. It's also at the heart of the Lord's prayer.

Having reminded us of the grace we have received, Jesus now speaks of the grace we should share.

> Forgive us our debts as we also have forgiven our debtors. . . . For if you forgive men when they sin against you, your heavenly Father will also forgive you. But if you do not forgive men their sins, your Father will not forgive your sins. (Matt. 6:12,14–15 NIV)

Through the center of the Great House of God runs a large hallway. You can't get from one room to another without using it. Want to leave the kitchen and go to the study? Use the corridor. Want to take the stairs to the chapel? Use the corridor. You can't go anywhere without walking the hallway. And you can't walk the hallway without bumping into people.

Jesus does not question the reality of your wounds. He does not doubt that you have been sinned against. The issue is not the existence of pain, the issue is the treatment of pain. What are you going to do with your debts?

Dale Carnegie tells about a visit to Yellowstone Park where he saw a grizzly bear. The huge animal was in the center of a clearing, feeding on some discarded camp food. For several minutes he feasted alone; no other creature dared draw near. After a few moments a skunk walked through the meadow toward the food and took his place next to the grizzly. The bear didn't object and Carnegie knew why. "The grizzly," said, "knew the high cost of getting even."[1]

We'd be wise to learn the same. Settling the score is done at great expense.

THE HIGH COST OF GETTING EVEN

For one thing, you pay a price relationally.

Have you ever noticed in the western movies how the bounty hunter travels alone? It's not hard to see why. Who wants to hang out with a guy who settles scores for a living? Who wants to risk getting on his bad side? More than once I've heard a person spew his anger. He thought I was listening, when really I was thinking, *I hope I never get on his list.* Cantankerous sorts, these bounty hunters. Best leave them alone. Hang out with the angry and you might catch a stray bullet. Debt-settling is a lonely occupation. It's also an unhealthy occupation.

You pay a high price physically.

The Bible says it best. "Resentment kills a fool" (Job 5:2 NIV). It reminds me of an old Amos and Andy routine. Amos asks Andy what that little bottle is he's wearing around his neck. "Nitroglycerine," he answers. Amos is stunned that Andy would be wearing a necklace of nitro, so he asks for an explanation. Andy tells him about a fellow who has a bad habit of poking people in the chest while he's speaking. "It drives me crazy," Andy says. "I'm wearing this nitro so the next time he pokes me, I'll blow his finger off."

Andy's not the first to forget that when you try to get even, you get hurt. Job was right when he said, "You tear yourself to pieces in your anger" (Job 18:4). Ever notice that we describe the people who bug us as a "pain in the neck"? Whose neck are we referring to? Certainly not theirs. We are the ones who suffer.

Sometime ago I was speaking about anger at a men's gathering. I described resentment as a prison and pointed out that when we put someone in our jail cell of hatred, we are stuck guarding the door. After the message a man introduced himself as a former prison inmate. He described how the guard at the gate of a prison is even more confined than a prisoner. The guard spends his day in a four-by-five-foot house. The prisoner has a ten-by-twelve-foot cell. The guard can't leave, the prisoner gets to walk around. The prisoner can relax, but the guard has to be constantly alert. You might object and say, "Yes, but the guard of the prison gets to go home at night." True, but the guard of the prison of resentment doesn't.

If you're out to settle the score, you'll never rest. How can you? For one thing, your enemy may never pay up. As much as you think you deserve an apology, your debtor may not agree. The racist may never repent. The chauvinist may never change. As justified as you are in your quest for vengeance, you may never get a penny's worth of justice. And if you do, will it be enough?

Let's really think about this one. How much justice is enough? Picture your enemy for a moment. Picture him tied to the whipping post. The strong-armed man with the whip turns to you and asks, "How many lashes?" And you give a number. The whip cracks and the blood flows and the punishment is inflicted. Your foe slumps to the ground and you walk away.

Are you happy now? Do you feel better? Are you at peace? Perhaps for a while, but soon another memory will surface and another lash will be needed and . . . when does it all stop?

It stops when you take seriously the words of Jesus. Read them again: "Forgive us our debts as we also have forgiven our debtors. . . . For if you forgive men when they sin against you, your heavenly Father will also forgive you. But if you do not forgive their sins, your Father will not forgive your sins."

Through this verse we learn the greatest cost of getting even. I've suggested that you pay a high price relationally and physically, but Jesus has a far more important reason for you to forgive. If you don't, you pay a high price spiritually.

Before we discuss what these verses mean, it would be wise to point out what they do not mean. The text does not suggest that we earn God's grace by giving grace. At first blush, the phrase appears to present a type of triangular peace treaty. "If I forgive my enemy, then God will forgive me." A casual reading suggests we earn our forgiveness by offering forgiveness to others. Mercy is a merit which saves me. Such an interpretation is impossible for the simple reason that it conflicts with the rest of Scripture. If we can attain forgiveness by forgiving others (or any other good work), then why do we need a Savior? If we can pay for our sins through our mercy, why did Jesus die for our sins? If salvation is a result of our effort, then why did Paul insist, "You have been saved by grace through believing. You did not save yourselves. It was a gift from God" (Eph. 2:8).

Salvation is a free gift.

The question from the last chapter surfaces again. If we are already forgiven, then why does Jesus teach us to pray, "Forgive us our debts"?

The very reason you would want your children to do the same. If my children violate one of my standards or disobey a rule, I don't disown them. I don't kick them out of the house or tell them to change their last name. But I do expect them to be honest and apologize. And until they do, the tenderness of our relationship will suffer. The nature of the relationship won't be altered, but the intimacy will.

The same happens in our walk with God. Confession does not create a relationship with God, it simply nourishes it. If you are a believer, admission of sins does not alter your position before God, but it does enhance your peace with God. When you confess, you agree; you quit arguing with God and agree with him about your sin. Unconfessed sin leads to a state of disagreement. You may be God's child, but you don't want to talk to him. He still loves you, but until you admit what you've done, there's going to be tension in the house.

But just as unconfessed sin hinders joy, confessed sin releases it. When we admit sin we are like a first grader standing before the teacher with a messy paper. "I colored outside the lines too many times. Could I start over on a clean sheet?" "Of course," says the teacher. Happy is the first grader who gets a second chance, or as David wrote, "Happy is the person whose sin is forgiven, whose wrongs are pardoned" (Ps. 32:1). So we dash back to our seat and start over.

Would there ever be a case when the teacher would leave you to draw on your soiled paper? There might be. I can think of one example when the teacher might refuse to give you a second chance. Suppose she witnesses your mistreatment of the kid in the next desk. A few minutes earlier she saw him ask you for a piece of paper out of your tablet, and you refused. Though you had plenty to give, you clutched your Big Chief with both hands and refused to share. And now here you are making the same request of her?

Who would blame her if she said, "I tell you what, I'm going to grant you the same kindness you gave your classmate. The way you treat Harry is the way I'll treat you. You're still my student, and I'm still your teacher. I'm not kicking you out of class, but I am going to give you a chance to learn a lesson." Now we're getting down to the nitty-gritty of the verse, for this is exactly what the phrase means: "Forgive us our debts as we have forgiven our debtors."

ONE OF THE GREATEST PRINCIPLES IN THE BIBLE

"Treat me as I treat my neighbor." Are you aware that this is what you are saying to your Father? Give me what I give them. Grant me the same peace I grant others. Let me enjoy the same tolerance I offer. God will treat you the way you treat others.

In any given Christian community there are two groups: those who are contagious in their joy and those who are cranky in their faith. They've accepted Christ and are seeking him, but their balloon has no helium. One is grateful, the other is grumpy. Both are saved. Both are heaven bound. But one sees the rainbow and the other sees the rain.

Could this principle explain the difference? Could it be that they are experiencing the same joy they have given their offenders? One says, "I forgive you," and feels forgiven. The other says, "I'm ticked off," and lives ticked off at the world.

Elsewhere Jesus said:

Don't judge other people, and you will not be judged. Don't accuse others of being guilty, and you will not be accused of being guilty. *Forgive, and you will be forgiven. Give, and you will receive.* You will be given much. Pressed down, shaken together, and running over, it will spill into your lap. The way you give to others is the way God will give to you. (Luke 6:37–38, emphasis mine)

It's as if God sends you to the market to purchase your neighbor's groceries saying, "Whatever you get your neighbor, get also for yourself. For whatever you give him is what you receive."

Pretty simple system. I'm not too bright, but I can figure this one out. I love thick, juicy hamburger meat, so I buy my neighbor thick, juicy hamburger meat. I'm crazy about double-chocolate ice cream, so I buy my neighbor double-chocolate ice cream. And when I drink milk, I don't want the skimpy skim stuff that Denalyn makes me drink. I want Christian milk, just like God made it. So what do I buy my neighbor? Christian milk, just like God made it.

Let's take this a step further. Suppose your neighbor's trash blows into your yard. You mention the mess to him, and he says he'll get to it sometime next week. You inform him that you've got company coming and couldn't he get out of that chair and do some work? He tells you not to be so picky, that the garbage fertilizes your garden. You're just about to walk across the lawn to have a talk when God reminds you, "Time to go to the market and buy your neighbor's groceries." So you grumble and mumble your way to the store, and then it hits you, "I'll get even with the old bum." You go straight to the skim milk. Then you make a beeline to the anchovies and sardines. You march right past the double-chocolate ice cream and head toward the okra and rice. You make a final stop in the day-old bread section and pick up a crusty loaf with green spots on the edge.

Chuckling, you drive back to the house and drop the sack in the lap of your lazy, good-for-nothing neighbor. "Have a good dinner." And you walk away.

All your brilliant scheming left you hungry, so you go to your refrigerator to fix a sandwich, but guess what you find. Your pantry is full of what you gave your enemy. All you have to eat is exactly what you just bought. We get what we give.

Some of you have been eating sardines for a long time. Your diet ain't gonna change until you change. You look around at other Christians. They aren't as sour as you are. They're enjoying the delicacies of God, and you're stuck with okra and anchovies on moldy bread. You've always wondered why they look so happy and you feel so cranky. Maybe now you know. Could it be God is giving you exactly what you're giving someone else?

Would you like a change of menu? Earlier I referred to a men's conference where I spoke on the topic of anger. A couple of weeks after I returned home I received this letter from a man named Harold Staub.

Max,

Thank you so much for speaking on forgiveness at Promise Keepers in Syracuse, NY, on June 7 and 8. I was there. Just want you to know I went home, talked to my wife on many subjects about forgiveness—the best two weeks of my life. You see, she went home to be with the Lord on June 24, totally forgiven. How wonderful is his love. Thank you so very much.[2]

When we called Harold to ask his permission to print his letter, he shared the touching details of his final days with his wife. He didn't know she was near death, nor did she. He did know, however, that some unresolved issues lay between them. Upon arriving home, he went to her, knelt before her and asked forgiveness for anything he'd ever done. The gesture opened a floodgate of emotions and the two talked late into the night. The initial effort at reconciliation continued for two weeks. The marriage enjoyed a depth not yet known. When Harold's wife died suddenly of an embolism, he was shocked. But he was ready and now he is at peace.

What about you? Would you like some peace? Then quit giving your neighbor such a hassle. Want to enjoy God's generosity? Then let others enjoy yours. Would you like assurance that God forgives you? I think you know what you need to do.

So, what will you be eating? Chocolate ice cream or okra? It's up to you.

CHAPTER 12

THE
FAMILY ROOM

—| *Learning to Live Together* |—

Our . . .

W E ARE MUCH LIKE Ruth and Verena Cady. Since their birth in 1984 they have shared much. Just like any twins, they have shared a bike, a bed, a room, and toys. They've shared meals and stories and TV shows and birthdays. They shared the same womb before they were born and the same room after they were born. But the bond between Ruthie and Verena goes even further. They share more than toys and treats; they share the same heart.

Their bodies are fused together from the sternum to the waist. Though they have separate nervous systems and distinct personalities, they are sustained by the same, singular three-chambered heart. Neither could survive without the other. Since separation is not an option, cooperation becomes an obligation.

They have learned to work together. Take walking, for example. Their mother assumed they would take turns walking forward or backwards. It made sense to her that they would alternate; one facing the front and the other the back. The girls had a better idea. They learned to walk sideways, almost like dancing. And they dance in the same direction.

They've learned to make up for each other's weaknesses. Verena loves to eat, but Ruthie finds sitting at the table too dull. Ruthie may eat only a half cup of fruit a day. No problem, her sister will eat enough for both. It's not unusual for her to have three bowls of cereal, two yogurts and two pieces of toast for breakfast. Ruthie tends to get restless while her sister eats and has been known to throw a bowl of ice cream across the room. This could lead to discipline for her, but also has consequences for her sister.[1]

When one has to sit in the corner, so does the other. The innocent party doesn't complain; both learned early that they are stuck together for the good and the bad. Which is just one of the many lessons these girls can teach those of us who live in God's Great House.

Don't we share the same kitchen? Aren't we covered by the same roof and protected by the same walls? We don't sleep in the same bed, but we sleep under the same sky. We aren't sharing one heart . . . but then again maybe we are; for don't we share the same hope for eternity, the same hurt from rejection, and the same hunger to be loved? Like the Cady twins, don't we have the same Father?

We don't pray to *my* Father or ask for *my* daily bread or ask

God to forgive *my* sins. In God's house we speak the language of plurality: "*our* Father," "*our* daily bread," "*our* debts," "*our* debtors," "lead *us* not into temptation," and "deliver *us*."

The abundance of plural pronouns escorts us into one of the most colorful rooms in the house, the family room.

THE FAMILY ROOM

If you'd like a reminder of our Father's creativity, you'll find one here. We all call God "Father" and we all call Christ "Savior," but beyond that, things are quite diverse. Take a walk around the room and see what I mean.

Shoot some snooker with the bikers at the pool table.

Pick up a Swahili phrase from the tribesmen.

Eavesdrop on the theologians discussing dispensationalism.

Experience worship with a bagpipe, then cross the room and try the same with the accordion.

Ask the missionary if she ever gets lonely and the Bible translator if he ever gets confused.

Hear the testimony of the murderer and the music of the minstrel.

And if you're wondering how those folks from the other denominations got here, ask them. (They may want to ask you the same question.)

Oh, the diversity of God's family.

We are olive-skinned, curly-haired, blue-eyed and black.
    We come from boarding schools and ghettos, mansions
        and shacks.
We wear turbans, we wear robes. We like tamales. We eat rice.
    We have convictions and opinions, and to agree would be nice,
        but we don't, still we try and this much we know:
        'Tis better inside with each other than outside living alone.

Quite a family, wouldn't you agree? From God's perspective we have much in common. Jesus lists these common denominators in his prayer. They are easy to find. Every time we see the word *our* or *us*, we find a need.

WE ARE CHILDREN IN NEED OF A FATHER

During the writing of this book, my daughter Jenna and I spent several days in the old city of Jerusalem. (I've promised to take each of my daughters to Jerusalem when they're twelve years old. Got the idea from Joseph.) One afternoon, as we were exiting the Jaffa gate, we found ourselves behind an orthodox Jewish family—a father and his three small girls. One of the daughters, perhaps four or five years of age, fell a few steps behind and couldn't see her father. "*Abba!*" she called to him. He stopped and looked. Only then did he realize he was separated from his daughter. "*Abba!*" she called again. He spotted her and immediately extended his hand. She took it and I took mental notes as they continued. I wanted to see the actions of an *abba*.

He held her hand tightly in his as they descended the ramp. When he stopped at a busy street, she stepped off the curb, so he pulled her back. When the signal changed, he led her and her sisters through the intersection. In the middle of the street, he reached down and swung her up into his arms and continued their journey.

Isn't that what we all need? An *abba* who will hear when we call? Who will take our hand when we're weak? Who will guide us through the hectic intersections of life? Don't we all need an *abba* who will swing us up into his arms and carry us home? We all need a father.

WE ARE BEGGARS IN NEED OF BREAD

Not only are we children in need of a father, we are also beggars in need of bread. "Give us this day our daily bread," we pray.

You may not appreciate my using the term *beggar*. You may prefer the word *hungry*. "We are all hungry, in need of bread." Such a phrase certainly has more dignity than the word *beggar*. Who wants to be called a beggar? Didn't you earn the money to buy the bread that sits on your table? Who are you to beg for anything? In fact, you may even find the word *hungry* offensive. To be hungry is to admit a basic need, something we sophisticated people are reluctant to do. Let me think, there must be a better phrase. How about this one? We aren't beggars, nor are we hungry; we are simply "abdominally challenged." There, that's better! "Abdominally challenged, in need of bread." You maintain a sense of independence with that word.

After all, you are ultimately responsible for the food you eat, right? Didn't you create the ground in which the seed was sown?

No? Well, at least you made the seed? You didn't? What about the sun? Did you provide the heat during the day? Or the rain, did you send the clouds? No? Then exactly what did you do? You harvested food you didn't make from an earth you didn't create.

Let me see if I have this straight. Had God not done his part, you would have no food on your table. Hmmm, perhaps we best return to the word *beggar*. We are all beggars, in need of bread.

SINNERS IN NEED OF GRACE

We share one other need: We are sinners in need of grace, strugglers in need of strength. Jesus teaches us to pray, "Forgive our debts . . . and lead us not into temptation."

We've all made mistakes and we'll all make some more. The line that separates the best of us from the worst of us is a narrow one, hence we'd be wise to take seriously Paul's admonition:

> Why do you judge your brothers or sisters in Christ? And why do you think you are better than they? We will all stand before the Lord to be judged, because it is written in the Scriptures: "As surely as I live, says the Lord, everyone will bow before me; everyone will say that I am the Lord." (Rom. 14:10)

Your sister would like me to remind you that she needs grace. Just like you need forgiveness, so does she. There comes a time in every relationship when it's damaging to seek justice, when settling the score only stirs the fire. There comes a time when the best thing you can do is accept your brother and offer him the same grace you've been given.

That's what Jenna did.

Earlier I mentioned our recent trip to Israel. I'll conclude by referring to it one more time. She and I boarded a 1:00 A.M. flight in Tel Aviv which would carry us back to the States. Traveling is always hectic, but that night it was especially bad. The plane was packed and we were delayed because of extra-tight airport security. As we boarded, I realized that our seats weren't together. We were separated by an aisle. With no time to seek help from the front desk, I determined to persuade the fellow sitting next to Jenna to swap seats with me. *Surely he'll understand,* I thought. He didn't. He was already nestled down for the ten-hour flight and wasn't about to move. "Please," I begged, "let me sit by my daughter."

"I'm not moving."

"Come on, sir. Let's trade places."

He leaned up and looked at my seat and leaned back. "No thanks," he declined.

Growl. I took my seat and Jenna took hers next to the thoughtless, heartless scoundrel. As the plane prepared for take-off, I dedicated my mind to drawing a mental sketch of the jerk. Wasn't hard. Only a glance or two in his direction and I had him pegged as a terrorist on his way to assassinate the president of our country. By the time the plane was backing up, I was plotting how I'd trip him if he dared walk to the restroom during the flight. No doubt he'd smuggled a gun on board and it would fall to me to apprehend him.

I turned to intimidate him with a snarl and saw, much to my surprise, Jenna offering him a pretzel. What? My daughter fraternizing with the enemy! And even worse, he took it! As if the pretzel were an olive branch, he accepted her gift and they both leaned their seats back and dozed off.

I eventually dozed myself, but not before I'd learned the lesson God had used my daughter to teach me.

In God's house we occasionally find ourselves next to people we don't like. If we could ask them to leave, we would, but we aren't given the option. All of us are here by grace and, at some point, all of us have to share some grace. So the next time you find yourself next to a questionable character, don't give him a hard time . . . give him a pretzel.

CHAPTER 13

THE
WALLS

And lead us not into temptation,
but deliver us from the evil one . . .

THE SMALL POPULATION of people who saw me play
school athletics have never questioned my decision to
enter the ministry. I have, however, received a letter reminding me of the time I deep-snapped a football over the punter's
head. Another former classmate reminisced with me about the
fly ball that slipped out of my glove and allowed the winning run
to score. And then there was the time my buddy scored a touch-
down on an eighty-yard punt return only to have it called back
because his buddy, yours truly, got penalized for clipping. Oh,
the pain of such memories. They hurt, not just because I messed
up, but because I helped the other team. It's bad to lose; it's worse
still to help your opponent win!

My most blatant experience of aiding the opposition occurred in a sixth-grade basketball tournament. I can't remember the exact score when I finally got to play, but I know it was close. I recall a loose ball, a scramble to grab it and complete surprise when my teammate on the bottom of the pile threw it to me. When I saw that no one was between me and the basket, I took off. With the style of an MVP-to-be, I made a lay-up worthy of air-time on ESPN. My surprise at the ease of the basket was surpassed only by my surprise at the silence of the crowd.

No one applauded! Rather than pat me on the back, my team buried their faces in their hands. That's when I realized what I'd done. I'd made a basket on the wrong end of the court—I'd aided the enemy! I'd helped the wrong team. No wonder no one tried to stop me—I was helping their side.

Can you imagine how silly I felt?

If you can, then you can imagine how silly Satan must feel. Such is the pattern of the devil's day. Every time he sets out to score one for evil, he ends up scoring a point for good. When he schemes to thwart the kingdom, he always advances it. May I offer a few examples from the Bible?

BACKFIRES OF HELL

Remember Abraham's wife, Sara? God promised her a child, but she remained childless for decades. Satan used an empty crib to stir up tension and dissension and doubt. Sara would serve as his *prima facie* evidence as to why you can't trust God. In the end, she modeled just the opposite. The thought of this ninety-year-old in the maternity ward has instructed millions that God saves the best for last.

How about Moses? Satan and his hoard howled with delight the day the young prince was run out of Egypt by the very people he wanted to deliver. They thought they'd derailed God's plan, when actually they'd played into God's hand. God used the defeat to humble his servant and the wilderness to train him. The result stood before Pharaoh forty years later, a seasoned Moses who'd learned to listen to God and survive in the desert.

And what about Daniel? The sight of Jerusalem's best young men being led into captivity appeared to be a victory for Satan. Hell's strategy was to isolate the godly young men. Again, the plan boomeranged. What Satan intended as captivity, God used for royalty. Daniel was soon asked to serve in the king's court. The very man Satan sought to silence spent most of his life praying to the God of Israel and advising the kings of Babylon.

And consider Paul. Satan hoped the prison would silence his pulpit, and it did, but it also unleashed his pen. The letters to the Galatians, Ephesians, Philippians, and Colossians were all written in a jail cell. Can't you just see Satan kicking the dirt and snarling his lips every time a person reads those epistles? He helped write them!

Peter is another example. Satan sought to discredit Jesus by provoking Peter to deny him. But the plan backfired. Rather than be an example of how far a fellow can fall, Peter became an example of how far God's grace extends.

Every time Satan scores a basket, the other team gets the points. He's the Colonel Klink of the Bible. Remember Klink? He was the fall guy for Hogan on the television series, *Hogan's Heroes.* Klink supposedly ran a German POW camp during World War II. Those inside the camp, however, knew better. They knew who *really* ran the camp: the prisoners. They listened to Klink's calls and read his mail. They even gave Klink ideas, all the while using him for their own cause.

Over and over the Bible makes it clear who really runs the earth. Satan may strut and prance, but it's God who calls the shots.

DELIVER US FROM THE EVIL ONE

The next-to-last phrase in the Lord's prayer is a petition for protection from Satan: "And lead us not into temptation, but deliver us from the evil one."

Is such a prayer necessary? Would God ever lead us into temptation? James 1:13 says, "When people are tempted they should not say, 'God is tempting me.' Evil cannot tempt God, and God himself does not tempt anyone." If God does not tempt us, then why pray, "Lead us not into temptation"? These words trouble the most sophisticated theologian.

But they don't trouble a child. And this is a prayer for the child-like heart. This is a prayer for those who look upon God as their *Abba.* This is a prayer for those who have already talked to their Father about provision for today ("Give us our daily bread.") and pardon for yesterday ("Forgive us our debts."). Now the child needs assurance about protection for tomorrow.

The phrase is best understood with a simple illustration. Imagine a father and son walking down an icy street. The father cautions the boy to be careful, but the boy is too excited to slow down. He hits the first patch of ice. Up go the feet and down plops the bottom. Dad comes along and helps him to his feet. The boy apologizes for disregarding the warning and then, tightly holding his father's big hand, he asks, "Keep me from the slippery spots. Don't let me fall again."

The Father is so willing to comply. "The steps of the godly are directed by the Lord. He delights in every detail of their lives. Though they stumble, they will not fall, for the Lord holds them by the hand" (Ps. 37:23–24 TLB). Such is the heart of this petition. It's a tender request of a child to a father. The last few slips have taught us—the walk is too treacherous to make alone. So we place our small hand in his large one and say, "Please, *Abba*, keep me from evil."

THE EVIL ONE

Besides, who else would we trust to deliver us from the Evil One? We have heard of this devil. And what we've heard disturbs us. Twice in Scripture the curtain of time is pulled back and we are granted a glimpse at the most foolish gamble in history. Satan was an angel who was not content to be near God; he had to be above God. Lucifer was not satisfied to give God worship; he wanted to occupy God's throne.

According to Ezekiel both Satan's beauty and evil were unequaled among the angels:

> You were an example of what was perfect, full of wisdom and perfect in beauty. You had a wonderful life, as if you were in Eden, the Garden of God. Every valuable gem was upon you . . . You walked among the gems that shined like fire. Your life was right and good from the day you were created, until evil was found in you. (Ezek. 28:12–15)

The angels, like humans, were made to serve and worship God. The angels, like humans, were given free will. Otherwise how could they worship? Both Isaiah and Ezekiel describe an angel more powerful than any human, more beautiful than any creature, yet more foolish than any being who has ever lived. His pride was his downfall.

Most scholars point to Isaiah 14:13–15 as the description of Lucifer's tumble:

> I will go up to heaven. I will put my throne above God's
> stars. I will sit on the mountains of the gods, on the slopes of
> the sacred mountain. I will go up above the tops of the clouds.
> I will be like God Most High.

You can't miss the cadence of arrogance in the words: "I will . . . I will . . . I will . . . I will . . . I will." Because he sought to be like God, he fell away from God and has spent history trying to convince us to do the same. Isn't that the strategy he used with Eve? "You will be like God," he promised (Gen. 3:5).

He has not changed. He is as self-centered now as he was then. He is as foolish now as he was then. And he is just as limited now as he was then. Even when Lucifer's heart was good, he was inferior to God. All angels are inferior to God. God knows everything, they only know what he reveals. God is everywhere, they can only be in one place. God is all-powerful, angels are only as powerful as God allows them to be. All angels, including Satan, are inferior to God. And this may surprise you: Satan is still a servant to God.

THE DEVIL IS "GOD'S DEVIL"

He doesn't want to be. He doesn't intend to be. He would like nothing more than to build his own kingdom, but he can't. Every time he tries to advance his cause, he ends up advancing God's.

Erwin Lutzer articulates this thought in his book, *The Serpent of Paradise:*

> The devil is just as much God's servant in his rebellion as he was in the days of his sweet obedience. . . . We can't quote Luther too often: The devil is God's devil.
>
> Satan has different roles to play, depending on God's counsel and purposes. He is pressed into service to do God's will in the world; he must do the bidding of the Almighty. We must bear in mind that he does have frightful powers, but knowing that those can only be exercised under God's direction and pleasure gives us hope. Satan is simply not free to wreak havoc on people at will."[1]

Satan doing the bidding of the Almighty? Seeking the permission of God? Does such language strike you as strange? It may. If it does, you can be sure Satan would rather you not hear what I'm about to say to you. He'd much rather you be deceived into thinking of him as an independent force with unlimited power. He doesn't want me to tell you about the walls that surround the Great House of God. Satan cannot climb them, he cannot penetrate them. He has absolutely no power, except that power that God permits.

He'd rather you never hear the words of John, "God's Spirit who is in you, is greater than the devil who is in the world" (1 John 4:4). And he'd certainly rather you never learn how God uses the devil as an instrument to advance the cause of Christ.

How does God use Satan to do the work of heaven? God uses Satan to:

1. *Refine the faithful.* We all have the devil's disease. Even the meekest among us have a tendency to think too highly of ourselves. Apparently Paul did. His resume was impressive: a personal audience with Jesus, a participant in heavenly visions, an apostle chosen by God, an author of the Bible. He healed the sick, traveled the world, and penned some of history's greatest documents. Few could rival his achievements. And maybe he knew it. Perhaps there was a time when Paul began to pat himself on the back. God, who loved Paul and hates pride, protected Paul from the sin. And he used Satan to do it.

> To keep me from becoming conceited because of these surpassingly great revelations, there was given me a thorn in my flesh, a messenger from Satan to torment me. (2 Cor. 12:7)

We aren't told the nature of the thorn, but we are told its purpose—to keep Paul humble. We are also told its origin—a messenger from Satan. The messenger could have been a pain, a problem or a person who was a pain. We don't know. But we do know the messenger was under God's control. Please note verse eight, "Three times I pleaded with the Lord to take it away from me. But he said to me, 'My grace is sufficient for you, my power is made perfect in weakness.' " Satan and his forces were simply a tool in the hand of God to strengthen a servant.

Another example of the devil as God's servant is the temptation of Job. The devil dares to question the stability of Job's faith and God gives him permission to test Job. "All right then," God says, "everything Job has is in your power, but you must not touch Job himself" (Job 1:12). Note that God set both the permission and parameters of the struggle. Job passes the test and Satan complains, stating that Job would have fallen had he been forced to face pain. Again God gives permission and again God gives the parameters. "Job is in your power," he tells Satan, "but you may not take his life" (2:6).

Though the pain and the questions are abundant, in the end Job's faith and health are greater than ever. Again, we may not understand the reason for the test, but we know its source. Read this verse out of the last chapter. The family of Job: "Comforted him and made him feel better about the trouble God *the Lord* had brought on him" (42:11, emphasis mine).

Satan has no power except that which God gives him.

To the first-century church Smyrna, Christ said, "Do not be afraid of what you are about to suffer. I tell you, the devil will put some of you in prison to test you, and you will suffer for ten days. But be faithful, even if you have to die, and I will give you the crown of life" (Rev. 2:10).

Analyze Jesus' words for a minute. Christ informs the church of the persecution, the duration of the persecution (ten days), the reason for the persecution (to test you) and the outcome of the persecution (a crown of life). In other words, Jesus uses Satan to fortify his church.

Colonel Klink blows another one. Satan scores again for the other team. Don't you know that bugs him? Even when he appears to win, he loses. Martin Luther was right on target when he described the devil as God's tool, a hoe used to care for his garden. The hoe never cuts what the gardener intends to save and never saves what the gardener intends to weed. Surely a part of Satan's punishment is the frustration he feels in unwillingly serving as a tool to create a garden for God. Satan is used by God to refine the faithful.

God also uses the devil to:

2. *Awaken the sleeping.* Hundreds of years before Paul, another Jewish leader battled with his ego, but he lost. Saul, the first king of Israel, was consumed with jealousy. He was upstaged by David, the youngest son of a shepherding family. David did everything better than Saul: he sang better, he impressed the women more, he even killed the giants Saul feared. But rather than celebrate David's God-given abilities, Saul grew insanely hostile. God, in an apparent effort to awaken Saul from this fog of jealousy, enlisted the help of his unwilling servant, Satan. "The next day an evil spirit from God rushed upon Saul, and he prophesied in his house" (1 Sam. 18:10).

Observe a solemn principle: There are times when hearts grow so hard and ears so dull that God turns us over to endure the consequence of our choices. In this case, the demon was released to torment Saul. If Saul would not drink from the cup of God's kindness, let him spend some time drinking from the cup of hell's fury. "Let him be driven to despair that he might be driven back into the arms of God."[2]

The New Testament refers to incidents where similar discipline is administered. Paul chastises the church in Corinth for their tolerance of immorality. About an adulterer in the church he says:

> Then hand this man over to Satan. So his sinful self will
> be destroyed, and his spirit will be saved on the day of the
> Lord. (1 Cor. 5:5).

Paul gives comparable instruction to Timothy. The young evangelist was dealing with two disciples who'd made a shipwreck of their faith and had negatively influenced others. His instruction to Timothy? "Hymenaeus and Alexander have done that, and I have given them to Satan so they will learn not to speak against God" (1 Tim. 1:20).

As drastic as it may appear, God will actually allow a person to experience hell on earth, in hopes of awakening his faith. A holy love makes the tough choice to release the child to the consequences of his rebellion.

By the way, doesn't this help explain the rampant evil which exists in the world? If God allows us to endure the consequences of our sin and the world is full of sinners, then the world is going to abound in evil. Isn't this what Paul meant in the first chapter of Romans? After describing those who worship the creation rather than the creator, Paul says, "God left them and let them do the shameful things they wanted to do" (Rom. 1:26). Does God enjoy seeing the heartbreak and addictions of his children? No more than a parent enjoys disciplining a child. But holy love makes tough choices.

Remember, discipline should result in mercy, not misery. Some saints are awakened by a tap on the shoulder while others need a two-by-four to the head. And whenever God needs a two-by-four, Satan gets the call. He also gets the call to:

3. *Teach the church.* Perhaps the clearest illustration of how God uses Satan to achieve his purposes is found in the life of

Peter. Listen to the warning Jesus gives to him: "Simon, Simon, Satan has asked to test all of you as a farmer sifts his wheat. I have prayed that you will not lose your faith! Help your brothers be stronger when you come back to me" (Luke 22:31–32).

Again, notice who is in control. Even though Satan had a plan, he had to get permission. "All authority in heaven and on earth has been given to me," Jesus explained, and this is proof (Matt. 28:18 NIV). The wolf cannot get to the sheep without permission of the Shepherd, and the Shepherd will only permit the attack if, in the long term, the pain is worth the gain.

The purpose of this test is to provide a testimony for the church. Jesus was allowing Peter to experience a trial so he could encourage his brothers. Perhaps God is doing the same with you. God knows that the church needs living testimonies of his power. Your difficulty, your disease, your conflict are preparing you to be a voice of encouragement to your brothers. All you need to remember is that:

> No test or temptation that comes your way is beyond the course of what others have had to face. All you need to remember is that God will never let you down; he'll never let you be pushed beyond your limit; he'll always be there to help you come through it. (1 Cor. 10:13)

> You intended evil against me, but God meant it for good. (Gen. 50:20)

Remember, Satan cannot penetrate the walls of the Great House of God.

Is it still hard to imagine how your struggle could lead to any good? Still hard to conceive how your disease or debt or death could be a tool for anything worthwhile? If so then I've got one final example. While not wanting to minimize your struggle, I must say yours is a cakewalk compared to this one. A sinless Savior was covered with sin. The author of life was placed in the cave of death. Satan's victory appeared sure. Finally, the devil had scored on the right end of the court. And not only had he scored, he'd slam-dunked the MVP and left him lying on the floor. The devil had blown it with everyone from Sara to Peter, but this time he'd done it right. The whole world had seen it. The victory dance had already begun.

But all of a sudden there was a light in the tomb and a rumbling of the rock; then Friday's tragedy emerged as Sunday's Savior, and even Satan knew he'd been had. He'd been a tool in the hand of the gardener. All the time he thought he was defeating heaven, he was helping heaven. God wanted to prove his power over sin and death, and that's exactly what he did. And guess who helped him do it? Once again Satan's lay-up becomes a foul-up. Only this time, he didn't give heaven some points, he gave heaven the championship game.

Jesus emerged as the victor and Satan was left looking like a . . . well, I'll let you figure that out. Take the first letter of each of the ways God uses the devil and see if you can find Satan's true identity.

Refine the faithful.

Awaken the sleeping.

Teach the church.

CHAPTER 14

THE CHAPEL

Relying on God's Power

*For thine is the kingdom and the power
and the glory forever. Amen.*

I CAME ACROSS AN ARTICLE of a lady who reminds me
of us. She went up a mountain she should have avoided.
No one would have blamed her had she stayed behind. At
twelve below zero, even Frosty the Snowman would have opted
for the warm fire. Hardly a day for snow skiing, but her husband insisted and she went.

While waiting in the lift line she realized she was in need of a
restroom, *dire* need of a restroom. Assured there would be one at
the top of the lift, she and her bladder endured the bouncy ride,
only to find there was no facility. She began to panic. Her husband had an idea: Why not go into the woods? Since she was

wearing an all-white outfit, she'd blend in with the snow. And what better powder room than a piney grove?

What choice did she have? She skied past the tree line and arranged her ski suit at half mast. Fortunately, no one could see her. Unfortunately, her husband hadn't told her to remove her skis. Before you could say, "Shine on harvest moon," she was streaking backwards across the slope, revealing more about herself than she ever intended. (After all, hindsight is 20/20.) With arms flailing and skis sailing, she sped under the very lift she'd just ridden and collided with a pylon.

As she scrambled to cover the essentials, she discovered her arm was broken. Fortunately her husband raced to her rescue. He summoned the ski patrol, who transported her to the hospital.

While being treated in the emergency room, a man with a broken leg was carried in and placed next to her. By now she'd regained her composure enough to make small talk. "So, how'd you break your leg?" she asked.

"It was the darndest thing you ever saw," he explained. "I was riding up the ski lift and suddenly I couldn't believe my eyes. There was this crazy woman skiing backwards, at top speed. I leaned over to get a better look and I guess I didn't realize how far I'd moved. I fell out of the lift."

Then he turned to her and asked, "So how'd you break your arm?"[1]

Don't we make the same mistake? We climb mountains we were never intended to climb. We try to go up when we should have stayed down, and as a result, we've taken some nasty spills in full view of a watching world. The tale of the lady (sorry, I couldn't resist) echoes our own story. There are certain mountains we were never made to climb. Ascend them and you'll end up bruised and embarrassed. Stay away from them and you'll sidestep a lot of stress. These mountains are described in the final phrase of the Lord's prayer, "Thine is the kingdom and the power and the glory forever. Amen."

Our Lord's prayer has given us a blueprint for the Great House of God. From the living room of our Father to the family room with our friends, we are learning why David longed to "live in the house of the LORD forever" (Ps. 23:6). In God's house we have everything we need: a solid foundation, an abundant table, sturdy walls, and an impenetrable roof of grace.

And now, having seen every room and explored each corner, we have one final stop. Not to a new room, but to one we have visited earlier. We return to the chapel. We return to the room of worship. The chapel, remember, is where we stand before God and confess, "Hallowed be thy name."

The chapel is the only room in the house of God we visit twice. It's not hard to see why. It does us twice as much good to think about God as it does to think about anyone or anything else. God wants us to begin and end our prayers thinking of him. Jesus is urging us to look at the peak more than we look at the trail. The more we focus up there, the more inspired we are down here.

Some years ago a sociologist accompanied a group of mountain climbers on an expedition. Among other things, he observed a distinct correlation between cloud cover and contentment. When there was no cloud cover and the peak was in view, the climbers were energetic and cooperative. When the gray clouds eclipsed the view of the mountaintop, though, the climbers were sullen and selfish.

The same thing happens to us. As long as our eyes are on his majesty there is a bounce in our step. But let our eyes focus on the dirt beneath us and we will grumble about every rock and crevice we have to cross. For this reason Paul urged, "Don't shuffle along, eyes to the ground, absorbed with the things right in front of you. Look up, and be alert to the things going on around Christ—that's where the action is. See things from his perspective" (Col 3:1–2 MSG).

Paul challenges you to "be alert to the things going on around Christ." The Psalmist reminds you to do the same, only he uses a different phrase. "O magnify the LORD with me and let us exalt his name together" (Ps. 34:3).

Magnify. What a wonderful verb to describe what we do in the chapel. When you magnify an object, you enlarge it so that you can understand it. When we magnify God, we do the same. We enlarge our awareness of him so we can understand him more. This is exactly what happens in the chapel of worship—we take our mind off ourselves and set it on God. The emphasis is on him. "*Thine* is the kingdom and the power and the glory forever."

And this is exactly the purpose of this final phrase in the Lord's prayer. These words magnify the character of God. I love the way this phrase is translated in *The Message:*

You're in charge!

You can do anything you want!

You're ablaze in beauty!

Yes! Yes! Yes!

Could it be any simpler? God is in charge! This concept is not foreign to us. When the restaurant waiter brings you a cold hamburger and a hot soda, you want to know who is in charge. When a young fellow wants to impress his girlfriend, he takes her down to the convenience store where he works and boasts, "Every night from five to ten o'clock, I'm in charge." We know what it means to be in charge of a restaurant or a store, but to be in charge of the universe? This is the claim of Jesus.

> God raised him from the dead and set him on a throne in deep heaven, *in charge* of running the universe, everything from galaxies to governments, no name and no power is exempt from his rule. And not just for the time being but forever. He is *in charge* of it all, has the final word on every-thing. At the center of all this Christ rules the church. (Eph. 1:22–23 MSG, emphasis mine)

There are many examples of Jesus' authority, but I'll just men-tion one of my favorites. Jesus and the disciples are in a boat crossing the sea of Galilee. A storm arises suddenly and what was placid becomes violent—monstrous waves rise out of the sea and slap the boat. Mark describes it clearly: "A furious squall came up, and the waves broke over the boat so that it was nearly swamped" (Mark 4:37 NIV).

It's very important that you get an accurate picture, so I'm going to ask you to imagine yourself in the boat. It's a sturdy vessel, but no match for these ten-foot waves. It plunges nose first into the wall of water. The force of the waves dangerously tips the boat until the bow seems to be pointing straight at the sky, and just when you fear flipping over backwards, the vessel pitches forward into the valley of another wave. A dozen sets of hands join yours in clutching the mast. All your shipmates have wet heads and wide eyes. You tune your ear for a calming voice, but all you hear are screams and prayers. All of a sudden it hits you—someone is missing. Where is Jesus? He's not at the mast. He's not grabbing the edge. Where is he? Then you hear something—a noise . . . a displaced sound . . . like someone is snoring. You turn and look, and there curled in the stern of the boat is Jesus, sleeping!

You don't know whether to be amazed or angry, so you're both. How can he sleep at a time like this? Or as the disciples asked, "Teacher, don't you care if we drown" (Mark 4:38, NIV)?

If you're a parent of a teenager, you've been asked similar questions. The time you refused to mortgage your house so your daughter could buy the latest style tennis shoes, she asked, "Don't you care if I look out of date?"

When you insisted that your son skip the weekend game and attend his grandparents' golden anniversary, he asked, "Don't you care if I have a social life?"

When you limited the ear piercing to one hole per lobe, the accusation came thinly veiled as a question, "Don't you care if I fit in?"

Do the parents care? Of course they do. It's just that they have a different perspective. What the teenager sees as a storm, mom and dad see as a spring shower. They've been around enough to know these things pass.

So had Jesus. The very storm which made the disciples panic made him drowsy. What put fear in their eyes put him to sleep. The boat was a tomb to the followers and a cradle to Christ. How could he sleep through the storm? Simple, he was in charge of it.

The same happens with you and televisions. Ever doze off with the TV on? Of course you have. But put the same television in the grass hut of a primitive Amazonian Indian who has never seen one and, believe me, he won't sleep. How could anyone sleep in the presence of a talking box! As far as he knows, those little people behind the glass wall might climb out of the box and come after him. There is no way he's going to sleep. And there is no way he's going to let you sleep either. If you doze off, he'll wake you up. Don't you care that we're about to be massacred? Rather than argue with him, what do you do? You just point the remote at the screen and turn it off.

Jesus didn't even need a remote. "He got up, rebuked the wind and said to the waves, 'Quiet! Be still!' Then the wind died down and it was completely calm. He said to his disciples, 'Why are you so afraid? Do you still have no faith'" (Mark. 4:39–40, NIV)?

Incredible. He doesn't chant a mantra or wave a wand. No angels are called, no help is needed. The raging water becomes a stilled sea, instantly. Immediate calm. Not a ripple. Not a drop. Not a gust. In a moment the sea goes from a churning torrent to a peaceful pond. The reaction of the disciples? Read it in verse 41: "They were in absolute awe, staggered. 'Who is this anyway?' they asked. 'Wind and sea at his beck and call!'" (MSG).

They'd never met a man like this. The waves were his subjects and the winds were his servants. And that was just the beginning of what his sea mates would witness. Before it was over, they would see fish jump into the boat, demons dive into pigs, cripples turn into dancers, and cadavers turn into living, breathing people. "'He even gives orders to evil spirits and they obey him!'" the people proclaimed (Mark 1:27).

Is it any wonder the disciples were willing to die for Jesus? Never had they seen such power, never had they seen such glory.

It was like, well, like the whole universe was his kingdom. You wouldn't have needed to explain this verse to them; they knew what it meant: "Thine is the kingdom and the power and the glory forever."

In fact, it was two of these rescued fishermen who would declare his authority most clearly. Listen to John: "Greater is he who is in you than he who is in the world" (1 John 4:4). Listen to Peter: "Jesus has gone into heaven and is at God's right hand ruling over angels, authorities and powers" (1 Pet. 3:22).

It's only right that they declare his authority. And it's only right that we do the same. And that is exactly what this phrase is, a declaration. A declaration of the heart. A declaration God deserves to hear. Doesn't he? Doesn't he deserve to hear us proclaim his authority? Isn't it right for us to shout from the bottom of our hearts and at the top of our voice, "Thine is the kingdom and the power and the glory forever!" Isn't it right for us to stare at these mountain peaks of God and worship him?

Of course it is. Not only does God deserve to hear our praise, we need to give it.

MOUNTAINS YOU WEREN'T MADE TO CLIMB

There are certain mountains only God can climb. The names of these mountains? You'll see them as you look from the window of the chapel in the Great House of God. "Thine is the kingdom, and the power and the glory forever." A trio of peaks mantled by the clouds. Admire them, applaud them, but don't climb them.

It's not that you aren't welcome to try, it's just that you aren't able. The pronoun is *thine*, not *mine*; *thine* is the kingdom, not

mine is the kingdom. If the word *Savior* is in your job description, it's because you put it there. Your role is to help the world,
not save it. Mount Messiah is one mountain you weren't made
to climb.

Nor is Mount Self-Sufficient. You aren't able to run the world,
nor are you able to sustain it. Some of you think you can. You
are self-made. You don't bow your knees, you just roll up your
sleeves and put in another twelve-hour day . . . which may be
enough when it comes to making a living or building a business.
But when you face your own grave or your own guilt, your power
will not do the trick.

You were not made to run a kingdom, nor are you expected to
be all-powerful. And you certainly can't handle all the glory.
Mount Applause is the most seductive of the three peaks. The
higher you climb the more people applaud, but the thinner the
air becomes. More than one person has stood at the top and
shouted, "Mine is the glory!" only to lose their balance and fall.

"Thine is the kingdom and the power and the glory forever."
What protection this final phrase affords. As you confess that
God is in charge, you admit that you aren't. As you proclaim that
God has power, you admit that you don't. And as you give God
all the applause, there is none left to dizzy your brain.

Let's let the lady on the slope teach us a lesson: There are
certain mountains we weren't meant to climb. Stay below where
you were made to be, so you won't end up exposing yourself
to trouble.

CHAPTER 15

A Home for Your Heart

MY DAUGHTER Sara had a friend over to spend the night recently. There was no school the next day, so we let the two of them stay up as late as they wanted. A bedtime reprieve for a couple of seven-year-olds is like freeing a convict from death row. The two outlasted me. I was dozing in my chair when I awoke and realized it was nearly midnight and they were still awake. "All right, girls," I informed them, "we better go to bed." Groaning the entire time, they changed clothes, brushed their teeth, and climbed in the sack. That's when our little guest asked to call her mom. At first we declined, but then the chin trembled and the eyes misted, and, knowing we were moments away from an explosion, we gave her the phone.

I could envision what was happening on the other end of the line—a phone ringing in the dark, a mom reaching over the slumbering husband to grab the receiver.

The little girl didn't even say hello. "Mommy, I want to come home." With a teddy bear in one hand and the phone in the other, she pleaded her case. She was afraid of waking up in a strange room. This wasn't her house. She wanted her bed, her pillow and most of all, her mommy.

I can't blame her. When I travel, the hardest part of the trip is going to sleep. The pillow never feels right, the sheets are too . . . too stiff? Besides, who knows who slept here last night. The curtains never block the flashing neon light outside the window. I need to get up early, but can I trust the operator to remember the wake-up call? After all, there was that night in Boise when no one called me and . . . off go my thoughts, covering every issue from Denalyn's doctor visit to tomorrow's flight to next spring's income tax. I'd call home, but it's too late. I'd go for a walk, but I might get mugged. I'd order room service, but I already have. I'd go home but, well, I'm supposed to be a grown man. Finally, I sit up in bed and flip on the TV and watch Sports Center until my eyes burn, then eventually doze off.

I can relate to Sara's friend. When it comes to resting your body, there's no house like your own.

I can also relate to the Psalmist, David. When it comes to resting your soul, there is no place like the Great House of God. "I'm asking Yahweh for one thing," he wrote, "only one thing: to live with him in his house my whole life long. I'll contemplate his beauty, I'll study at his feet. That's the only quiet secure place in a noisy world" (Ps. 27:4–5 MSG).

If you could ask God for one thing, what would you request? David tells us what he would ask. He longs to *live* in the house of God. I emphasize the word live, because it deserves to be emphasized. David doesn't want to chat. He doesn't desire a cup of coffee on the back porch. He doesn't ask for a meal or to spend an evening in God's house. He wants to move in with him . . . forever. He's asking for his own room . . . permanently. He doesn't want to be stationed in God's house, he longs to retire there. He doesn't seek a temporary assignment, but rather lifelong residence.

When David says, "I will live in the house of the Lord forever" (Ps. 23:6), he's saying simply that he never wants to step away from God. He craves to remain in the aura, in the atmosphere, in the awareness that he is in God's house, wherever he is.

The Lord's Prayer is a floor plan of the house of God: a step-by-step description of how God meets our needs when we dwell in him. Everything that occurs in a healthy house is described in this prayer. Protection, instruction, forgiveness, provision . . . all occur under God's roof.

"Then why," you might ask, "don't more people feel protected, forgiven, or instructed?"

My answer is as simple as the question is direct. Most have not learned to dwell in the house. Oh, we visit it. We stop in for the day or even drop by for a meal. But abide here? This is God's desire.

Remember the promise of his Son, "If people love me, they will obey my teaching. My Father will love them and we will come to them and make our home with them" (John 14:23). He wants to be the one in whom "we live and move and have our being" (Acts 17:28 NIV).

Let me conclude with an example of how this prayer can be a home for your heart. I have a long way to go, but I'm trying to learn to dwell in the Great House of God. Over the last seven days I took note of the times I took strength from a part of the house.

On Monday I was tired, physically drained, so I stepped into the chapel and said, "Thine is the power," and the Father reminded me it was okay to rest.

On Tuesday I had more to do than I had hours to do it. Rather than stress out, I stepped into the kitchen and asked for daily bread. He gave me the strength to get everything done.

On Wednesday I was in the kitchen again. Needing some ideas for a children's book, I stepped up to the table and made a request. By bedtime the manuscript was drafted.

We had a strategic staff meeting this week. We began with a half-hour of prayer and worship during which I stepped into the observatory and then into the chapel. I asked the God who made the heavens to make sure the meeting went well, and he did. I asked the Holy God who is above us to guide us, and he did.

On one occasion I was impatient. I went into the hallway to ask for God's grace, only to find it already given. On another I was tempted, yet at just the right time a person entered the room with a word of wisdom, and I was reminded of the thickness of the wall. And then there was the frustration I felt over a person's opinion. Not knowing how to respond, I stepped into the study and opened the word, and 1 Corinthians 13 reminded me, "Love is patient and kind."

I don't want to leave the wrong impression. There were times when I worried rather than worshipped, there were times when I told God what I had to have rather than trust him to fill my plate. But day by day, I'm learning to live in the Great House of God.

I hope you are, too. Take Paul's advice and "pray without ceasing." Make it your aim never to leave God's house. When you're worried about your bills, step into God's kitchen. When you feel bad about a mistake, look up at the roof. When you call on a new client, whisper a prayer as you enter the office: "Thy kingdom come to this place." When you're in a tense meeting, mentally step into the furnace room and pray, "Let the peace of heaven be felt on earth." When it's hard to forgive your spouse, pull out the check of grace God has given you.

My prayer for you is the same as Paul's: "Let your minds be remade and your whole nature thus transformed" (Rom. 12:2 NEB). May the Holy Spirit change your mind. May you grow so at ease in the house of God that you never leave it. And when you find yourself in another house, may you do what Sara's friend did— call home. Tell your Father that you can't rest in anyone's house but his. He won't mind the call. In fact, he'll be waiting by the phone.

POSTSCRIPT

We're Home.

DOESN'T IT FEEL WONDERFUL, knowing we're home where we belong? Here, in the place where our spirit has longed to rest . . . the place where we feel safe and secure.

Could I make a suggestion for your life in God's Great House? Each day, as you awaken in his presence, remember the blueprint. And as you talk to your Father, trace the floor plan in your mind. It's a helpful way to enter his presence. Here's an example of how the Lord's Prayer can guide your prayers:

Our Father
Thank you for adopting me into your family.

who is
Thank you, my Lord,
for being a God of the present tense:
my Jehovah-jireh (the God who provides),
my Jehovah-raah (the caring Shepherd),
my Jehovah-shalom (the Lord is peace),
my Jehovah-rophe (the God who heals),
and my Jehovah-nissi (Lord, my banner).

in heaven,
Your workshop of creation reminds me: If you can make
the skies, you can make sense out of my struggles.

Hallowed be thy name.
Be holy in my heart.
You are a "cut above" all else.
Enable me to set my sights on you.

Thy kingdom come,
Come kingdom!
Be present, Lord Jesus!
Have free reign in every corner of my life.

Thy will be done,
Reveal your heart to me, dear Father.
Show me my role in your passion.
Grant me guidance in the following decisions . . .

On earth as it is in heaven.
Thank you that you silence heaven to hear my prayer.
On my heart are the ones you love.
I pray for . . .

A Home for Your Heart

Give us this day our daily bread.
I accept your portion for my life today.
I surrender the following concerns
regarding my well-being . . .

Forgive us our debts,
I thank you for the roof of grace over my head,
bound together with the timbers and nails of Calvary.
There is nothing I can do to earn or add to your mercy.
I confess my sins to you . . .

As we also have forgiven our debtors;
Treat me, Father, as I treat others.
Have mercy on the following friends
who have wounded me . . .

Lead us not into temptation,
Let my small hand be engulfed in yours.
Hold me, lest I fall.
I ask for special strength regarding . . .

Our Father . . . give us . . . forgive us . . . lead us
Let your kindness be on all your church.
I pray especially for ministers near
and missionaries far away.

Thine—not mine—is the kingdom,
I lay my plans at your feet.

Thine—not mine—is the power,
I come to you for strength.

Thine—not mine—is the glory,
I give you all the credit.

Forever. Amen.
Thine—not mine—is the power. Amen.

Ⲛotes

CHAPTER 2   *The Living Room*
1. Joachim Jeremias, *The Prayers of Jesus* (New York: SCM Press, 1967), p. 57, as quoted in John Stott, "Has Anyone Told You About the Power of Prayer?" audiotape, All Souls Cassettes, No. E42/1A.

CHAPTER 3   *The Foundation*
1. All information on the names of God was taken from: Nathan Stone, *Names of God* (Chicago: Moody Press, 1944).

CHAPTER 4   *The Observatory*
1. Adapted from Brennan Manning, *The Ragamuffin Gospel* (Portland, OR.: Multnomah Press, 1990), pp. 32–33.

CHAPTER 9   *The Kitchen*
1. Source unknown.
2. Charles Panati, *Panati's Extraordinary Origins of Everyday Things,* (New York: Harper and Row, Publisher, 1987), p. 81.
3. Ibid., p. 86.
4. Alan Redpath, *Victorious Praying,* (Grand Rapids, MI: Revell, 1973), p. 74.

CHAPTER 11   *The Hallway*
1. John MacArthur, "The Pardon of Prayer" audio tape, © 1980 John MacArthur (Word of Grace, Panorama City, CA).
2. Thanks to Harold C. Staub for permission to use this letter.

CHAPTER 12   *The Family Room*
1. K. Hubbard, "A Gift of Grace: The Death of Conjoined Twins Ruth and Verena Cady," *People Weekly,* 5 November 1993, Vol. 36, pp. 42–44.

CHAPTER 13   *The Walls*
1. Erwin Lutzer, *The Serpent of Paradise* (Chicago: Moody Press, 1996), 102.
2. Ibid., 111.

CHAPTER 14   *The Chapel*
1. Lois Lambley, " . . . so how'd you break your arm?" Et Cetera, *North Bend Eagle,* 18 January 1995, p. 4.

STUDY GUIDE

WRITTEN BY STEVE HALLIDAY

—| Chapter 1 The Great House of God |—

LET US PONDER

1. God can be your dwelling place.
   A. In what way can God be someone's "dwelling place"?
   B. Is God your dwelling place? Explain.

2. You may go days without thinking of God, but there's never a moment when he's not thinking of you.
   A. How often do you estimate that you think of God? What keeps you from thinking about him? How do you overcome this obstacle?
   B. Do you believe God never stops thinking about you? Explain.

3. You are one step away from the house of God. Wherever you are. Whatever time it is.
   A. What does Max mean by "stepping into the house of God?"
   B. Does this image of the Great House of God help you to grasp and utilize the Lord's prayer? If so, how? If not, why not?

4. Christ has provided more than a model for prayer, he has

provided a model for living. These words do more than tell us what to say to God, they tell us how to exist with God.

A. In what way is the Lord's Prayer a model for living?

B. How does the Lord's Prayer tell us how to exist with God?

C. What part of the Lord's Prayer speaks most powerfully to you? Why?

LET US PREPARE

1. Read through the Lord's Prayer in Matthew 6:9–13.

   A. What part of this prayer most encourages you? Why?

   B. What part most convicts you? Why?

   C. Are there any parts you don't understand? If so, what are they? (Then especially look for Max's comments on that part later in the book.)

   D. If you were to assign parts of a house to each part of this prayer, how would you do it?

2. Read Acts 17:24–28.

   A. What picture of God does this passage portray? How does this picture fit into your concept of prayer? Explain.

   B. Note verse 28. How does the concept mentioned here fit with Max's image of the Great House of God?

3. Read Psalm 90:1–2.

   A. What is significant about that?

   B. What kind of requests does Moses make of God in the rest of this psalm (see especially verses 12–17).

4. Read 1 Thessalonians 5:17–18; Romans 12:12; Ephesians 6:18–20; Hebrews 13:15,18–19; Colossians 4:2–4; Philippians 4:6–7.

   A. What do you learn about prayer in each of the verses above?

5. How does the pattern of prayer laid out in the Lord's Prayer relate to the passages listed above?

LET US PRAY

1. This week read through the Lord's Prayer in Matthew 6:9–13 at least once each day. Read it meditatively to soak in its rich truth. Then take some time to pray about the concerns that touch your life, based on this pattern prayer.

2. Sit down with a piece of paper and a pen and "take apart" the Lord's Prayer phrase by phrase. Divide the prayer into units that make sense to you—"Our Father," for example, or "hallowed be thy name"—and write a paragraph on how that unit is significant to you. Then take a moment to pray through the whole prayer, especially considering what you have written about its various parts.

THE LIVING ROOM

—| *Chapter 2 When Your Heart Needs a Father* |—

1. You may be willing to stop being God's child. But God is not willing to stop being your Father.
   A. Were you ever "willing" to stop being God's child? If so, explain. What would cause anyone to want to stop being his child?
   B. How do we know God is not willing to stop being our Father? How would you try to explain this to someone who thought it was too good to be true?

2. "Our Father" reminds us we are welcome in God's house because we have been adopted by the owner.
   A. Do you feel welcome in God's house? If so, why? If not, why not?
   B. What is significant about becoming a member of God's family through adoption? Why does the Bible use this term "adopted"?

3. God adopted you simply because he wanted to. You were his good will and pleasure.

A. Why do you think God would want to adopt any of us? What does he get out of the deal?

B. In what way are all believers (including you) God's "good will and pleasure"? Why does Max believe this? Do you believe it? Explain.

4. Our God is no fair weather Father. He's not into this love-'em-and-leave-'em stuff. I can count on him to be in my corner no matter how I perform. You can, too.

A. Why is it important to know that God will never leave us? What does this knowledge do for us?

B. Do you always *feel* as though God is always in your corner? What might account for these feelings? Are they true? How can we deal with them?

LET US PREPARE

1. Consider the phrase "Our Father."
   A. What does this phrase communicate to you? How does it make you feel? What pictures does it bring to mind?
   B. In what ways is God like a father?

2. Read Luke 15:11–32.
   A. What picture of a father is being presented in this story? Why do you think Jesus would paint such a picture?
   B. With which character in the story do you most closely identify? Why?
   C. Why is verse 20 an especially good picture of our heavenly Father? How can keeping this picture in mind help our prayer lives?

3. Read Romans 8:15–17; Galatians 4:4–7; Ephesians 1:3–8.
   A. According to these passages, how does someone become a

child of God?

B. What rights and privileges are granted to God's children, according to these verses?

C. How do you think this knowledge is supposed to affect our prayer lives? Does it influence the way you pray? Why or why not?

LET US PRAY

1. Spend at least five minutes alone with God, speaking to him about nothing other than what it means to you to be called his child.

2. Get out a concordance and find several of the more than 200 times God is called "Father" in the New Testament. Choose ten of these texts and "pray through" them, speaking to God about his fatherly characteristics as described in the verses you chose.

THE FOUNDATION

—| *Chapter 3 Where Trust Begins* |—

1. God is the foundation of his own house.
   A. What does it mean that God is the foundation of his own house?
   B. How stable would the house be if God were not its foundation? Explain.
   C. What would happen if God's house were built on the foundation of your own strength? Do we ever act as though this were true? Explain.

2. The key question in life is not "How strong am I?" but rather "How strong is God?"
   A. Why is this the key question in life?
   B. Why is it so easy to reverse the above statements? Do you ever do this? If so, what happens?
   C. This key question depends on your relationship to God. Explain why this is so, and describe how you came into a relationship with him. How would you describe that relationship?

3. Meditating on the names of God reminds you of the character of God. Take these names and bury them in your heart.

   A. Max lists several of God's names. Which one means the most to you? Why?

   B. How does one "bury" the names of God in one's heart? What does this mean? Why is it important? Have you done this? Explain.

LET US PREPARE

1. Consider the phrase "Our Father *who is.*"

   A. What does it mean to you that God "is"?

   B. How would you feel if God "wasn't"?

   C. How does God show you, personally, that he "is"?

2. Read Isaiah 6:1–4 and Revelation 4:6–11.

   A. What attribute of God is most prominent in these two passages? Describe this trait in your own words.

   B. How do those who surround God as described in these passages respond to him? Why do they so respond?

   C. Why is it important to keep these thoughts in mind when we address our heavenly Father in prayer?

3. Consider the following Scriptures that give various names of God. How is each one important? For each one, identify what life circumstances would make that trait especially appealing:

   A. Genesis 1:1, Elohim (God the Creator).

   B. Genesis 48:15, Jehovah-raah (Caring Shepherd).

   C. Genesis 22:7–8, Jehovah-jireh (The Lord who Provides).

   D. Judges 6:24, Jehovah-shalom (The Lord is Peace).

   E. Exodus 15:26, Jehovah-rophe (The Lord who Heals You).

   F. Exodus 17:8–16, Jehovah-nissi (The Lord my Banner).

LET US PRAY

1. Take a few moments to confess to God your weakness. Be specific—for example, confess your short temper or your pride or your devotion to things rather than people. Then take at least twice as long to praise God for his strength and faithfulness to you. Thank him for cleansing you through the blood of his Son and for adopting you into his family.

2. Pick one of the names of God listed above and meditate on that name for an entire day. Write the appropriate verse on a card and refer to it frequently throughout the day. Then, before you retire for the night, praise God for showing that trait to you and thank him for acting according to his name.

THE OBSERVATORY

— | *Chapter 4 A Heavenly Affection* | —

LET US PONDER

1. God dwells in a different realm. He occupies a different dimension.

    A. In what way does God dwell in a different realm and different dimension from us?

    B. If God does not dwell with us, how can he be of help to us?

2. You want to know who God is? See what he has done.

    A. Do you want to know who God is? Why or why not? What difference does it make?

    B. How does seeing what God has done show us who he is? From what you see, who would you say God is? Explain.

3. Spend some time walking in the workshop of the heavens, seeing what God has done, and watch how your prayers are energized.

    A. Why does Max think there is a connection between gazing at the stars and the strength of one's prayer life? Is this connection present in your life? Explain.

B. When was the last time you spent several minutes just observing the heavens? Could you do so tonight?

4. Next time a sunrise steals your breath or a meadow of flowers leaves you speechless, remain that way. Say nothing and listen as heaven whispers, "Do you like it? I did it just for you."

   A. Why is silence often an appropriate response to the feeling of wonder?

   B. Do you think God would have made the world so beautiful if you were the only one on the planet? Explain.

LET US PREPARE

1. Consider the phrase "Our Father who is in heaven."

   A. Does the fact that God is in heaven make him feel distant to you at times? Explain.

   B. What benefits are there in having a God "in heaven"?

2. Read 1 Corinthians 1:25.

   A. What comparison is made in this verse? What is it intended to convey?

   B. How should this verse give us great confidence in prayer?

3. Read Isaiah 55:8–9.

   A. What comparison is made in this verse? What is it intended to convey?

   B. Why should this verse give us great confidence in prayer?

   C. How can this verse help to explain some of our disappointments in prayer?

4. Read Psalm 19:1–6.

   A. How does the universe teach us about God, according to this passage?

5. What did David learn about God from observing the universe? Do you think this knowledge helped or hindered his prayer life? Explain.

LET US PRAY

1. The next cloudless night, take a half hour to do nothing but lie on the ground and gaze up at the sky. What do you see? Try counting the stars. After you have basked in the glory of the heavens for awhile, spend an equal amount of time praising God for what you have just seen. Praise him for his power, for his wisdom, for his grace and his love. Thank him that you have eyes to see his creation and a mind to comprehend some of it. Focus on his glory and majesty and splendor and might. Have a good time of celebrating God Almighty!

2. Take a few minutes to read through Revelation 21–22:6. Remember that the place this passage describes is God's home and is merely a reflection of his majesty and greatness. Then praise him for creating such a beautiful place where we will spend eternity with him. "Pray through" this passage, thanking him for his goodness in providing such a marvelous eternal home for us.

THE CHAPEL

LET US PONDER

1. There are times when to speak is to violate the moment
    . . . when silence represents the highest respect. The word
    for such times is *reverence*. The prayer for such times is "Hal-
    lowed be thy name."

    A. What does "reverence" mean to you? Why is it associ-
    ated with silence?

    B. How does one "hallow" God's name? From the opposite
    viewpoint, how does one profane it? In the last week, did
    you do more of one than the other? Explain.

2. God says to Job, "As soon as you are able to handle these
    simple matters of storing stars and stretching the neck of the
    ostrich, then we'll have a talk about pain and suffering. But
    till then, we can do without your commentary."

    A. If you had been in Job's shoes, do you think you would
    have reacted much as he did? Why or why not?

    B. In times of trouble, do you ever demand answers of God?
    If he were to respond to your questions, what do you think
    he'd say?

3. When you set your sights on God, you focus on one "cut above" any storm life may bring.

   A. How can you set your sights on God? What does this entail?

   B. How does setting one's sights on God help us in the middle of life's storms? Do you have any personal examples of this? If so, describe them.

LET US PREPARE

1. Consider the phrase "hallowed be thy name."

   A. How does a person "hallow" something?

   B. How does the term "hallow" relate to the term "holy"?

2. Read Job 38:3–18.

   A. What is the point of all of God's questions? What lesson does he want Job to learn?

   B. If you were in Job's shoes at this point in the story, how do you think you would react? Why?

   C. What do you learn about God in this passage?

3. Read Job 40:4–5; 42:1–6.

   A. How did Job react to God's speeches? Was this an appropriate response? Why?

   B. What did Job finally learn about God? How did it change his attitude toward his circumstances?

   C. In all of God's speeches, does he answer Job's questions? What is significant about this?

4. Read Psalm 46:10.

   A. What command are we given in this verse? What is the reason for the command?

   B. Is this an easy command for you to obey? Why or why

not? Why is it so crucial? What do we miss when we ignore it?

1. Go for a long, leisurely walk someplace where you can be alone with God to enjoy the work of his hands. Be silent as you marvel at his handiwork and creativity. Notice everything you can around you—the colors, the smells, the shapes, the immensity and the smallness of his creation. Then at the end of your walk, break your silence and thank him both for the beauty of his creation and for the ability to walk and take it all in. Speak to him reverently and lovingly, trying to avoid making any requests during your prayer.

2. Slowly and carefully read through Job 38–41. Try to picture as much as you can of all the mysteries God describes. Then also try to put yourself in Job's place—how would you feel if God should deliver such a power-packed message to you? Spend some time alone with God, in silence, basking in his overwhelming majesty and splendor.

THE THRONE

Chapter 6 Touching the King's Heart

1. When you say, "thy kingdom come," you are inviting the Messiah himself to walk into your world. . . . This is no feeble request; it's a bold appeal for God to occupy every corner of your life.

   A. Have you ever invited the Messiah to walk into your world? If so, how? If not, why not?

   B. Does God "occupy every corner of your life" right now? Explain. If not, would you like him to? Explain.

2. For Haman, the massacre is a matter of expediency. For Satan, it is a matter of survival. He will do whatever it takes to impede the presence of Jesus in the world.

   A. Why was Satan's plan to wipe out the ancient Jews "a matter of survival"? What did he have at stake?

   B. How do you think Satan tries to impede the presence of Jesus in the world today? How does he do it in your own corner of the world?

3. When we pray for God's kingdom to come, it comes! All the hosts of heaven rush to our aid.

A. If God's kingdom were to come into your workplace, what would happen?

B. In what way do the hosts of heaven rush to our aid when we pray for God's kingdom to come? Have you ever prayed for his kingdom to come, and this didn't seem to happen? Explain. What might we conclude from this?

LET US PREPARE

1. Consider the phrase "thy kingdom come."
   A. When you think of God's coming kingdom, what comes to mind?
   B. Why do you think we should pray that God's kingdom would come?

2. Read Esther 3–9.
   A. What was the calamity facing God's people? Who engineered it? How did he engineer it?
   B. How did God take these terrible circumstances and turn them on their heads? How did what was bad turn into what was good?
   C. What part did Esther play in this drama? What part did Mordecai play? What was the role of the king? From the text's point of view, who is the central character?
   D. Choose one key verse for each of these seven chapters. Why do you think the verses you chose are significant? What do they teach you?
   E. Note that Esther is the only book in the Bible which does not mention God by name. Can you see him in this book anyway? Explain.

3. Read Hebrews 4:14–16.

A. What title is Jesus given in this passage? What does this title tell us about his work on our behalf?

B. What reasons does this passage give us for trusting that Jesus can and will help us (see especially verse 15)?

C. What conclusion is made in verse 16, based on what is said in verses 14–15? Do you take advantage of this? Why or why not?

4. Read Hebrews 12:28.

A. What kind of "kingdom" are we to receive? How is this significant?

B. What is to be our response to this promise?

C. How is God described in this verse? Do you often think of him this way? Explain.

LET US PRAY

1. Get a concordance and look up the word "kingdom" in the Gospel of Matthew (there are more than fifty references). Then take your Bible and read through each of these verses, trying to get a "bird's-eye view" of the kingdom of God. As you read, frequently stop to pray about what you are learning. Remember, you are praying to the king of the kingdom!

2. Spend some time asking God to occupy every corner of your life. What "corners" might you still be withholding from him? Finances? Relationships? Work? School? Recreation? Be as honest with yourself as possible and take inventory of your life. Then invite the King to take control in every area.

THE STUDY

LET US PONDER

1. God has a plan and that plan is good. Our question is, how do I access it?
   A. Do you believe God has a plan for you? If so, why? If not, why not?
   B. How do you "access" God's plan for your own life?
2. To pray, "thy will be done" is to seek the heart of God.
   A. Why does praying "thy will be done" indicate that we're seeking the heart of God? How is this prayer to change us?
   B. If you had to describe the "heart of God" to a non-Christian, what would you say?
3. God's *general* will provides us with guidelines that help us understand his *specific* will for our individual lives.
   A. What does Max mean by God's "general" will? What does he mean by God's "specific" will?
   B. How does God's general will help us to discover God's specific will? How do the two "wills" interrelate? Do you think

his specific will ever contradicts or ignores his general will? Explain.

4. Want to know God's will for your life? Then answer this question: "What ignites your heart?" . . . The fire of your heart is the light of your path. Disregard it at your own expense.

   A. Do you want to know God's will for your life? If he were to tell you specifically and audibly right now what his will for you is, would you be willing to do it, no matter what? Explain.

   B. What ignites your own heart? What fills you with enthusiasm? Do you see how that interest can be translated into God's will for your life? Are there any cautions you should observe with this advice? If so, what?

LET US PREPARE

1. Consider the phrase "thy will be done."

   A. What do you already know about the will of God for you? Do you struggle with any part of it? Explain.

   B. Is it easy or hard for you to submit yourself to the will of God? Explain.

2. Max lists four components that work together to help us find God's will:

   • Through the people of God.
   • Through the Word of God.
   • Through our walk with God.
   • Through the fire of God.

   A. In your own words, explain how each of these components "works."

   B. Which of these components do you utilize most frequently? Which do you tend to overlook? What, if anything, needs to change so that all four can work together for you to find God's will?

3. Read Luke 24:13–35.
   A. What were the two men talking about as they walked to Emmaus? How would you describe their demeanor?
   B. How did Jesus approach the men? Why do you think he approached them like this, and not more directly?
   C. How did the men finally recognize Jesus? Is there anything significant about this? If so, what?
   D. How did the men respond to their encounter? In what way is this a model for us?

4. Read Matthew 7:21, 10:29; John 6:40; Acts 18:21; Romans 12:2; Ephesians 5:17–21; 1 Thessalonians 4:3–8, 5:18.
   A. What do you learn about God's will from these passages?
   B. How eager are you to do the will of God he has already revealed to you? Take time to ask him to help you fulfill his will, whatever it may be for you.

LET US PRAY

1. Get out a concordance and look up the word "will," looking especially for those verses that tell us something about the will of God. Make a list of the items that are specially mentioned as being God's will for all of his children. Then spend some time praying about this list, thanking God for helping you to fulfill his will in those areas in which you are doing well, and asking him for his strength in those areas in which you struggle.

2. Many times we do not know exactly what God's will might be for us; we must follow the Lord's example in the Garden of Gethsemane by telling the Lord our request, then concluding our prayer by asking that "nevertheless, not my will, but your will be done." If there is some issue in your life that fits this model, pray about it right now.

The Furnace

Chapter 8 Because Someone Prayed

1. The power of God was triggered by prayer. Jesus looked down the very throat of death's cavern and called Lazarus back to life . . . all because someone prayed.

    A. Why do you think prayer often "triggers" the power of God? Why does this connection exist?

    B. What do you think might have happened in the case of Lazarus had someone not told Jesus about his friend's condition? Explain.

2. The power of prayer does not depend on the one who *makes* the prayer, but on the one who *hears* the prayer.

    A. Do you think Max is right about the statement above? Why or why not?

    B. Does the character of the person who prays have no bearing on the power of the prayer? Explain.

3. One call and heaven's fleet appears. Your prayer on earth activates God's power in heaven, and "God's will is done on earth as it is in heaven."

A. What would your neighborhood look like if God's will were done there as it is in heaven? What would your home look like? What part, if any, do you play in seeing this happen?

B. If it is true that "one call and heaven's fleet appears," then why do you think the Bible so often instructs us to pray "without ceasing"?

4. You are the someone of God's kingdom. You have access to God's furnace. Your prayers move God to change the world.

A. How often do you take advantage of your access to God's furnace? Are you satisfied with this? If not, what would it take for it to change?

B. Take a little time to discuss some of your prayers that helped "change the world," at least in your little corner of the planet.

LET US PREPARE

1. Consider the phrase "on earth as it is in heaven."

A. How is God's will done in heaven? Begrudgingly? Reluctantly? Complainingly? How do the angels do God's will?

B. How do you usually do God's will on earth? Could it be said that you do his will as it is done in heaven? Explain.

2. Read John 11:1–44.

A. Retell the story in your own words.

B. How does Jesus respond when he hears of Lazarus's illness? Is this what you might have expected? Is it what his disciples expected? Explain.

C. How do Mary and Martha respond to Jesus when he finally comes to their town? How does he respond to them?

    D. Why do you think Jesus waited to perform this miracle (see especially verses 15, 40, and 42).

    E. What does this passage teach you about the will of God?

3. Read Revelation 8:1–5.

    A. Describe what is happening in this passage.

    B. Is any reason given for the silence of heaven in this passage? If so, what is it?

    C. What do you learn about prayer in this passage?

LET US PRAY

1. Get out a concordance and look up the word "hear" wherever it appears in the book of Psalms. Note how often the psalmists declare that God hears their prayers and how often they entreat him to hear. Using their prayers as a model, thank God for hearing you and bring to him any requests you may have.

2. Take stock of the areas of your life over which you exercise substantial control. If God's will is not being done in any of those areas as it would be done in heaven, ask God to help you rectify this. If these areas are going well, thank God for enabling you to do his will.

THE KITCHEN

— | *Chapter 9 God's Abundant Table* | —

1. God is not a mountain guru involved only in the mystical and spiritual. The same hand which guides your soul gives food for your body.

   A. Do you know of anyone who thinks of God only as a "mountain guru"? If so, how do they respond to him? What do they do? What don't they do?

   B. Do you ever tend to think that the "mystical and spiritual" is more important (or more godly) than "food for your body"? Explain. What does God say about this?

2. If you have followed Christ's model for prayer, your preoccupation has been his wonder rather than your stomach. The first three petitions are God-centered, not self-centered.

   A. What does it mean to be preoccupied with God's wonder rather than your stomach? How does someone get to this point?

   B. What do you think Jesus was teaching in the Lord's prayer by making the first three petitions God-centered rather than self-centered? Do your own prayers often follow this model? If not, why not?

3. God lives with the self-assigned task of providing for his own, and so far, you've got to admit, he's done pretty well at the job.

    A. How has God provided for you in this past week? In the past month? In the past year? Since you became a Christian?

    B. Does the knowledge that God promises to provide for you make a difference in the way you live? Why or why not?

4. In the house of God, the one who provides the food is the one who prepares the meal.

    A. What does Max mean in the statement above? What difference does it make?

    B. How has God "prepared the meal" for you? Describe at least one example.

LET US PREPARE

1. Consider the phrase "Give us this day our daily bread."

    A. What do you think is included in the idea of "daily bread"?

    B. Why do you think God tells us to ask every day for what we need that day?

2. Review the two rules Max cites for asking God for our daily bread:

    - Don't be shy, ask.

    - Trust the cook.

    A. Are you ever "shy" about asking God for something? If so, why?

    B. Why is it so important to "trust the cook"? How do we show that we sometimes *don't* trust the cook?

3. Read Psalm 37:3–6.
   A. What advice is given here about seeking our daily bread?
   B. What promise is given us here?
4. Read Matthew 6:25–34.
   A. What advice is given here about seeking our daily bread?
   B. What illustrations are given to help us understand God's ways?
   C. What promise is given to us if we will follow God's way?

LET US PRAY

1. What special needs confront you today? List the pressing needs you have right now (not your special desires, but your needs) and spend some unhurried time with your Lord, asking him to meet the specific needs you bring to him. Then thank him for hearing and trust that he will do what he says.
2. Note that the verse talks about "our" daily needs. What are some of the needs of your loved ones, colleagues or close acquaintances? Make a list of these needs, and pray specifically that God would meet each one. When you are through praying, let these people know that you have been praying for them and ask them to let you know when God meets the need you've prayed about.

THE ROOF

LET US PONDER

1. In God's house you are covered by the roof of his grace.
   A. What does the term "grace" mean to you?
   B. How does grace "cover" you? In what way is a roof a good picture of grace? How has it sheltered you in the past week?

2. If Christ had not covered us with his grace, each of us would be overdrawn on that account. When it comes to goodness we would have insufficient funds. Inadequate holiness.
   A. Was there ever a time where you thought you had sufficient funds to cover your spiritual debts? If so, describe that time. What, if anything, convinced you that you were wrong?
   B. How much holiness would we need to come into God's presence? How can we acquire such holiness?

3. God assumed your debt. You assumed his fortune. And that's not all he did. He also paid your penalty.
   A. What does it mean that God "assumed your debt"? How was this done?

B. What does it mean that you "assumed [God's] fortune"? How was this done?

C. How did God pay your penalty?

LET US PREPARE

1. Consider the phrase "Forgive us our debts."

    A. What "debts" have you owed to God? What does this term "debts" include?

    B. Have you asked God to forgive your debts? If so, how? If not, why not?

    C. How is God able to forgive us of our debts?

2. Max develops two primary ideas in this chapter:

    • We owe a debt we cannot pay.

    • God paid a debt he did not owe.

    A. What is the debt we cannot pay? Why can we not pay it?

    B. Why did God pay a debt he did not owe? How did he pay it?

3. Read Isaiah 64:6 and Romans 3:23.

    A. What do these verses tell us about our debt to God?

    B. What is the result of this debt?

4. Read Romans 4:5, 8:33; 2 Corinthians 5:19–21; Galatians 3:13; 1 Peter 3:18.

    A. How did God handle our debt, according to these verses?

    B. What, if anything, do these verses tell us we are required to do to take advantage of what God has done for us?

LET US PRAY

1. Remind yourself of what Christ went through to provide redemption for us by reading the story of his Passion (Matthew

26:36–28:15; Mark 14:32–16:8; Luke 22:39–24:12; John 18:1–20:9). Take some time to thank him for his grace, especially recalling how he saved you from the just penalty of your own sins.

2. Be in prayer for others you know who do not yet know Christ, that they might also come to know the joy of God's forgiveness. Name these people specifically and ask that God might open a door for his children—perhaps you?—to share the gospel effectively with those who don't yet know him.

The Hallway

LET US PONDER

1. Dealing with debt is at the heart of your happiness. It's also at the heart of the Lord's prayer.
    A. Why is dealing with debt at the heart of a person's happiness?
    B. Why does Max say that debt is at the heart of the Lord's prayer?
    C. How do you typically deal with "debts" owed to you?
2. Confession does not create a relationship with God, it simply nourishes it.
    A. Why does confession not create a relationship with God? If it doesn't create such a relationship, what does?
    B. How does confession "nourish" a relationship with God? Is this easy or hard for you to do? Explain.
3. In any given Christian community there are two groups: those who are contagious in their joy and those who are cranky in their faith.

A. Describe someone you know who is contagious in his or her joy.

B. Describe someone you know (without naming the person!) who is cranky in his or her faith.

C. Which type of Christian do you consider yourself? Would others agree?

4. Want to enjoy God's generosity? Then let others enjoy yours.

A. How can you let others enjoy your generosity this week?

B. If someone were to judge God's generosity by observing your own, what would they think?

LET US PREPARE

1. Consider the phrase "Forgive us our debts as we also have forgiven our debtors."

A. This phrase troubles many people; why do you think it does? Does it trouble you? If so, why?

B. Who are your "debtors"? Have you forgiven them? Explain.

2. Max talks about "the high cost of getting even." What do the following texts tell us about this high cost?

A. Matthew 18:21–35.

B. Matthew 6:14–15.

C. Galatians 5:14–15.

3. Read Luke 6:37–38.

A. What does this text tell us to avoid?

B. What does this text tell us to do?

C. What is the result of our obedience? What is the result of our disobedience?

1. Is there anyone in your life whom you have a hard time forgiving? If so, admit this to the Lord. Tell him about your feelings, without trying to justify why you feel that way. Ask him to give you his strength to do what you believe he is asking you to do: to forgive that person. Confess that this is not something you will be able to do on your own strength and that perhaps you even struggle with the desire to grant forgiveness to the person who hurt you. Commit this to the Lord and allow him to bring you to the place you need to be.

2. Is there anyone in your life who may be having a hard time forgiving you for something you have done? If so, ask the Lord to help you ask forgiveness of this person, no matter how hard it might be. After praying for God's strength and direction, approach the person and try to iron out your problems. Strive for peace.

The Family Room

LET US PONDER

1. We don't pray to *my* Father or ask for *my* daily bread or ask God to forgive *my* sins. In God's house we speak the language of plurality: "our Father," "our daily bread," "our debts," "our debtors," "lead us not into temptation," and "deliver us."
   A. Why do you think Jesus stressed "plurality" in his prayer?
   B. Take stock of your own prayer life. Would you say it is more characterized by "me" prayers or "us" prayers? Explain.

2. We all need a father . . . we are all beggars in need of bread . . . we are sinners in need of grace.
   A. What is your most critical need from your Father? Why?
   B. What kind of "bread" do you most need today? Explain.
   C. What form of grace do you most require right now? Why not ask God to supply it even at this moment?

3. In God's house we occasionally find ourselves next to people we don't like.
   A. What kind of people do you find most difficult to get along with? Why? How do you deal with these folks?

B. Describe a time when you asked God to help you get along with someone you didn't like. What happened?

1. Consider the term "our."
    A. Why do you think Jesus taught us to pray in the plural number rather than in the singular?
    B. Do you make it a habit to pray for others as well as for yourself, or is this something you struggle with? Explain.
2. Max says we all need at least three things:
    *   We are children in need of a father.
    *   We are beggars in need of bread.
    *   We are sinners in need of grace.
    A. In what ways has God shown himself to be a father to you?
    B. In what ways do you recognize that you a beggar in need of bread?
    C. How do you show that you are a sinner in need of grace?
3. Read Romans 12:14–21.
    A. What instruction does this text give us for living with others?
    B. What is the hardest thing in this passage for you to do? Why?
4. Read Romans 14:10–13.
    A. What general rule of thumb does Paul give us here for living with other believers? What is the reason behind this rule of thumb?
    B. What motivation does Paul give in verse 11 for obeying his instruction? Is this something you often think about? Should it be? Explain.

LET US PRAY

1. Get together some evening with a few of your closest Christian friends and agree to pray for an hour—with one catch. Agree that each of you will pray for the others, but that you will not pray for yourself.
2. Spend some time alone praying for the people and ministries of your church. Pray for guidance, for protection, for strength, for God's Spirit to lead you all into his love, truth, and service. Try not to pray much about yourself, but instead focus on the people who are growing in Christ with you at your church.

THE WALLS

LET US PONDER

1. Every time Satan sets out to score one for evil, he ends up scoring a point for good. When he schemes to thwart the kingdom he always advances it.

   A. Give a few biblical examples that illustrate the statements above.

   B. Describe a few incidents from your own life that demonstrated the truth of the statements above.

2. Satan may strut and prance, but it's God who calls the shots.

   A. How does Satan "strut and prance"? How does he do this in your own life?

   B. How important is it to know that "God calls the shots"? What practical difference does this make to the way we live?

3. All angels, including Satan, are inferior to God. And, this may surprise you, Satan is still a servant to God.

   A. Why is it important to know that angels are inferior to God? What would happen if they weren't?

B. In what way is Satan a servant to God?

4. The walls which surround the Great House of God—Satan cannot climb them, he cannot penetrate them. He has absolutely no power, except that power which God permits.

A. What are the "walls" which surround the Great House of God? Of what are they made?

B. Why do you think God permits Satan any power at all?

1. Consider the phrase, "and lead us not into temptation, but deliver us from evil."

A. Why should we pray that God would not lead us into temptation? Is there really any danger of that? If not, what is the purpose of this part of the Lord's Prayer?

B. In what ways has God "delivered you from evil" in the past year?

2. Max says that God uses Satan in three primary ways:
   • To refine the faithful
   • To awaken the sleeping
   • To teach the church

A. How does Satan "refine" the faithful? How has he been used to refine you?

B. How does Satan "awaken the sleeping"? Who are the sleeping? And how does he do this in your own experience?

C. Satan seems an unlikely teacher of the church. What does it mean that he can be used to teach the church? What lessons has your own church learned from him?

3. Read Isaiah 14:12–15 and Ezekiel 28:12–17.

A. What do these passages teach us about the transformation of Satan into an angel of darkness?

B. What was Satan's paramount sin, according to Ezekiel? How is this sin still a potent trap for us?

4. Read John 19:1–16.

A. From a human observer's point of view, who seems to be in control of this scene? Who is really in control? How do you know?

B. Note especially Jesus' words in verse 11. What does he tell Pilate? In what way are his words equally applicable to any of God's adopted children?

LET US PRAY

1. What are your biggest temptations in life? How do you handle them? Read 1 Corinthians 10:12–13; then ask God to give you the strength and the wisdom to handle in a godly way the temptations that come into your life. Ask him to help you remember that often the best course of action is to flee (2 Timothy 2:22) and to enable you to do what will bring him the most glory. Thank him for his protection and his watchful keeping over you.

2. Take some time to recall the many ways God has "delivered you from evil" since you became a Christian. Recount as many as you can think of, thanking God for his power and praising him for his strength and goodness. Then ask him to continue to deliver you from the temptations and trials that inevitably come your way.

THE CHAPEL

LET US PONDER

1. The chapel is the only room in the house of God we visit twice. . . . It does us twice as much good to think about God as it does to think about anyone or anything else. God wants us to begin and end our prayers thinking of him.
   A. Why would God have us visit the "chapel," and no other room, twice? What is so special about the chapel?
   B. Do you usually begin and end your prayers by thinking of God? If not, how can you change your normal practice? And why should you?

2. As long as our eyes are on His Majesty, there is a bounce in our step. But let our eyes focus on the dirt beneath us and we will grumble about every rock and crevice we have to cross.
   A. Why is there a "bounce in our step" when we gaze upon His Majesty? Why does this energize us?
   B. What does it mean to "focus on the dirt beneath us"? Why is this so easy to do? How can we prompt ourselves to quit looking at "dirt" and start gazing at God?

3. You were not made to run a kingdom, nor are you expected to be all-powerful. And you certainly can't handle all the glory.
   A. How do we sometimes act as if we were made to run a kingdom? As if we were all-powerful?
   B. Why aren't we equipped to handle all the glory? If we're not, who is? And what makes him so different from us?

4. As you confess that God is in charge, you admit that you aren't.
   A. How easy is it for you to admit that God is in charge and you aren't? Explain.
   B. What are some practical ways to admit we're not in charge and to confess that God is?

LET US PREPARE

1. Consider the phrase "For thine is the kingdom and the power and the glory. Amen."
   A. In what way is this an appropriate ending to the Lord's Prayer?
   B. How do each of the three main terms—"kingdom," "power," and "glory"—focus our attention once more on God? What do each of these terms convey to you?

2. Read Colossians 3:1–4.
   A. On what things are we to set our minds, according to this passage?
   B. What is the reason for doing so?
   C. What promise is given in verse 4?

3. Read Hebrews 12:2–3.
   A. On what are we to fix our eyes, according to this passage? Why?

B. What happens when we don't comply with this command, according to verse 3? Have you ever experienced such consequences? Explain.

4. Read 1 Corinthians 2:9.
   A. What kind of God do we serve, according to this verse?
   B. How do you respond to the greatness of God's love, as expressed in this verse? How does it make you feel? How does it make you act?

LET US PRAY

Regardless of the time of year when you read this, get a copy of Handel's *Messiah* and play the Hallelujah Chorus. Listen carefully to the words and soak in the surging, powerful music. Then spend some time praising God for who he is and thanking him for what he has done for you. Thank him that he will continue to be a powerful, glorious King in your life and that one day his power and glory and kingdom will be apparent for all the universe to see.

THE GREAT HOUSE OF GOD

Chapter 15 *A Home for Your Heart*

1. If you could ask God for one thing, what would you request?
   A. Answer Max's question above. Why would you ask for this thing?
   B. How different would your answer have been ten years ago? Explain.

2. David craves to remain in the aura, in the atmosphere, in the awareness that he is in God's house wherever he is.
   A. Do you share David's craving? If so, how do you express this craving? If not, why not?
   B. Describe the most unusual place you've ever been in God's house. What happened?

3. Day by day, I'm learning to live in the Great House of God.
   A. Do you live more in God's house than you did five years ago? Explain.
   B. What is so important about the "day by day" phrase above? What is important about the "I'm learning" portion of the statement? What do both of these things imply about living in the Great House of God? How should this be an encouragement to us all?

1. In what way is God "a home for your heart"? How does the Lord's Prayer help you to live in that home?

2. Read Psalm 27:1–5.
   A. What claims does David make in this passage?
   B. What does this passage tell you about David's deepest desires?
   C. What can you learn from David's example here?

3. Read John 14:23.
   A. According to this verse, what is required for us to make our "home" with God?
   B. What promise is given here? Have you taken advantage of this promise? Explain.

4. Read Acts 17:28.
   A. What does this verse tell us about having a relationship with God? Do you have this kind of relationship? If so, describe it.
   B. What does it mean to "live" in God? What does it mean to "move" in God? What does it mean to have one's "being" in God? What does it mean to be one of God's "offspring"?
   C. How is this verse a fitting summary of the main point of *The Great House of God*?

LET US PRAY

1. Read through the entire Lord's Prayer one more time (Matthew 6:9–13). As you read, think through the various "rooms" that exist there. Then pray through the prayer, entering each room and relating each one to the events and challenges and triumphs of your life. Begin with praise, end with praise, and in between make your most urgent requests known to God, both for yourself and for others.

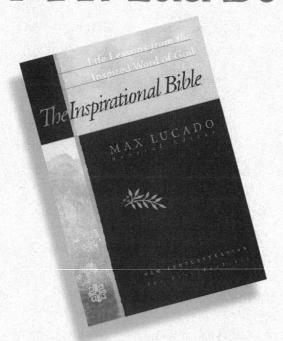

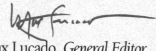

God loves you just the way you are,
but he refuses to leave you that way.
He wants you to be . . .

JUST LIKE JESUS

MAX LUCADO

WORD PUBLISHING

NASHVILLE

A Thomas Nelson Company

Unless otherwise indicated, Scripture quotations used in this book are from the Holy Bible, New Century Version, copyright © 1987, 1988, 1991 by Word Publishing, Dallas, Texas 75234. Used by permission.

Other Scripture references are from the following sources:

The Holy Bible, New International Version (NIV). Copyright © 1973, 1978, 1984, International Bible Society. Used by permission of Zondervan Bible Publishers.

The King James Version of the Bible (KJV).

The Living Bible (TLB), copyright © 1971 by Tyndale House Publishers, Wheaton, Ill. Used by permission.

The Message (MSG), copyright © 1993. Used by permission of NavPress Publishing Group.

The New King James Version (NKJV), copyright © 1979, 1980, 1982, 1992, Thomas Nelson, Inc., Publisher.

J. B. Phillips: The New Testament in Modern English, Revised Edition (PHILLIPS). Copyright © J. B. Phillips 1958, 1960, 1972. Used by permission of Macmillan Publishing Co., Inc.

New American Standard Bible (NASB), © 1960, 1977 by the Lockman Foundation.

The Revised Standard Version of the Bible (RSV). Copyright © 1946, 1952, 1971, 1973 by the Division of Christian Education of the National Council of the Churches of Christ in the USA. Used by permission.

The Jerusalem Bible (TJB). Copyright © 1968 by Darton, Longman, & Todd, Ltd., and Doubleday & Co., Inc.

The New Revised Standard Version Bible (NRSV), © 1989 by the Division of Christian Education of the National Council of the Churches of Christ in the USA.

The Good News Bible: The Bible in Today's English Version (TEV) © 1976 by the American Bible Society.

Library of Congress Cataloging-in-Publication Data

Lucado, Max.
    Just like Jesus : living in the heart of the Savior / by Max Lucado.
      p.   cm.
    Includes bibliographical references.
    ISBN 0-8499-1296-2 (hardcover). — ISBN 0-8499-6285-4 (audio)
    1. Jesus Christ—Example. 2. Spiritual life—Christianity. I. Title.
BT304.2.L83   1998
232.9'04—dc21

                                      98-22587
                                          CIP

Printed in the United States of America
0 1 2 3 4 5 9 BVG 29 28 27 26 25 24 23

To the staff of Oak Hills Church of Christ

*God is fair; he will not forget
the work you did and the love you showed
for him by helping his people.*

HEBREWS 6:10

CONTENTS

My writing room is different. Just a few months ago these walls were white. Now they are green. Once these windows were curtain covered; today they are shielded by shutters. My chair used to sit on a tan carpet, but the tan has been replaced by white. To be candid, I had no problem with the tan carpet. It looked fine to me. Nor did I object to the white walls and curtains. From my perspective the room looked fine.

But not from my wife's perspective. Denalyn loves to decorate. Better stated, she *has* to decorate. She can no more leave a house unchanged than an artist can leave a canvas untouched or a musician a song unsung.

Fortunately she limits her remodeling to what we own. She's never shuffled the furniture in a hotel room or reorganized pictures in the houses of friends. (Though she has been tempted.) She only remodels what we possess. But mark it down: what we possess will be remodeled. For Denalyn, it's not enough to own a house; she has to change the house.

As for me, I'm content with owning the house. My tastes are, shall we say, less sophisticated. In my view a chair and a refrigerator go a long way toward award-winning interior design. For me the herculean task is purchasing the house. Once the transaction is complete and the house is bought, I'm ready to move in and rest.

Not so with Denalyn. As the ink is drying on the deed, she is moving in and remodeling. I wonder if she inherited this trait from her Father, her heavenly Father. You see, the way Denalyn views a house is the way God views a life.

God loves to decorate. God *has* to decorate. Let him live long enough in a heart, and that heart will begin to change. Portraits of hurt will be replaced by landscapes of grace. Walls of anger will be demolished and shaky foundations restored. God can no more leave a life unchanged than a mother can leave her child's tear untouched.

It's not enough for him to own you; he wants to change you. Where you and I might be satisfied with a recliner and refrigerator, he refuses to settle for any dwelling short of a palace. After all, this is his house. No expense is spared. No corners are cut. "Oh, the utter extravagance of his work in us who trust him" (Eph. 1:19 MSG).

This might explain some of the discomfort in your life. Remodeling of the heart is not always pleasant. We don't object when the Carpenter adds a few shelves, but he's been known to gut the entire west wing. He has such high aspirations for you. God envisions a complete restoration. He won't stop until he is finished. And he won't be finished until we have been shaped "along the . . . lines . . . of his Son" (Rom. 8:29 MSG).

Your Creator is remaking you into the image of Christ. He

wants you to be just like Jesus. This is the desire of God and the theme of this book.

Before we go any further, may I stop and say thank you? To spend these moments with you is a high privilege, and I want you to know how grateful I am for the opportunity. My prayer for all who read these words is simple. May God open your eyes so that you can see Jesus. And in seeing Jesus, may you see what you are called to be.

I also would like to introduce you to some of the folks who made this book possible. Here is a salute to some dear friends:

To Liz Heaney and Karen Hill—Few editors cut and paste with such skill and kindness. Thanks again for another valiant work.

To Steve and Cheryl Green—Just having you near simplifies my world. Thank you for all you do.

To the wonderful family of Christians at Oak Hills—Though your taste in a senior minister may be questionable, your love for this one is appreciated. Here is to a decade of work together. May God grant us many more.

To Scott Simpson—What a clutch shot! The timing was perfect for us both. Thanks for the inspiration.

To the skilled team at Word Publishing—Through times of transition, you are reliable and true. I'm honored to be on your roster.

To my daughters Jenna, Andrea, and Sara—If heaven is missing three angels, I know where to find them.

To Kathy, Karl, and Kelly Jordon—The birth of this book coincided with the passing of your husband and father, Kip. He

is sorely missed. On the crowded canvas of publishing, his figure rose high above the others. He will never be replaced, and
he will always be remembered.

And most of all, to Denalyn—What you've done to our
house is nothing compared to what you've done in my heart.
Decorate all you want, honey.

CHAPTER ONE

A HEART LIKE HIS

What if, for one day, Jesus were to become you?

What if, for twenty-four hours, Jesus wakes up in your bed, walks in your shoes, lives in your house, assumes your schedule? Your boss becomes his boss, your mother becomes his mother, your pains become his pains? With one exception, nothing about your life changes. Your health doesn't change. Your circumstances don't change. Your schedule isn't altered. Your problems aren't solved. Only one change occurs.

What if, for one day and one night, Jesus lives your life with his heart? Your heart gets the day off, and your life is led by the heart of Christ. His priorities govern your actions. His passions drive your decisions. His love directs your behavior.

What would you be like? Would people notice a change? Your family—would they see something new? Your coworkers—would they sense a difference? What about the less fortunate?

Would you treat them the same? And your friends? Would they detect more joy? How about your enemies? Would they receive more mercy from Christ's heart than from yours?

And you? How would you feel? What alterations would this transplant have on your stress level? Your mood swings? Your temper? Would you sleep better? Would you see sunsets differently? Death differently? Taxes differently? Any chance you'd need fewer aspirin or sedatives? How about your reaction to traffic delays? (Ouch, that touched a nerve.) Would you still dread what you are dreading? Better yet, would you still do what you are doing?

Would you still do what you had planned to do for the next twenty-four hours? Pause and think about your schedule. Obligations. Engagements. Outings. Appointments. With Jesus taking over your heart, would anything change?

Keep working on this for a moment. Adjust the lens of your imagination until you have a clear picture of Jesus leading your life, then snap the shutter and frame the image. What you see is what God wants. He wants you to "think and act like Christ Jesus" (Phil. 2:5).

God's plan for you is nothing short of a new heart. If you were a car, God would want control of your engine. If you were a computer, God would claim the software and the hard drive. If you were an airplane, he'd take his seat in the cockpit. But you are a person, so God wants to change your heart.

"But you were taught to be made new in your hearts, to become a new person. That new person is made to be like God—made to be truly good and holy" (Eph. 4:23–24).

God wants you to be just like Jesus. He wants you to have a heart like his.

I'm going to risk something here. It's dangerous to sum up grand truths in one statement, but I'm going to try. If a sentence or two could capture God's desire for each of us, it might read like this:

> God loves you just the way you are, but he refuses to leave you that way. He wants you to be just like Jesus.

God loves you just the way you are. If you think his love for you would be stronger if your faith were, you are wrong. If you think his love would be deeper if your thoughts were, wrong again. Don't confuse God's love with the love of people. The love of people often increases with performance and decreases with mistakes. Not so with God's love. He loves you right where you are. To quote my wife's favorite author:

> God's love never ceases. Never. Though we spurn him. Ignore him. Reject him. Despise him. Disobey him. He will not change. Our evil cannot diminish his love. Our goodness cannot increase it. Our faith does not earn it anymore than our stupidity jeopardizes it. God doesn't love us less if we fail or more if we succeed. God's love never ceases.[1]

God loves you just the way you are, but he refuses to leave you that way.

When my daughter Jenna was a toddler, I used to take her to a park not far from our apartment. One day as she was playing in a sandbox, an ice-cream salesman approached us. I purchased her a treat, and when I turned to give it to her, I saw her mouth was full of sand. Where I intended to put a delicacy, she had put dirt.

Did I love her with dirt in her mouth? Absolutely. Was she any less my daughter with dirt in her mouth? Of course not. Was I going to allow her to keep the dirt in her mouth? No way. I loved her right where she was, but I refused to leave her there. I carried her over to the water fountain and washed out her mouth. Why? Because I love her.

God does the same for us. He holds us over the fountain. "Spit out the dirt, honey," our Father urges. "I've got something better for you." And so he cleanses us of filth: immorality, dishonesty, prejudice, bitterness, greed. We don't enjoy the cleansing; sometimes we even opt for the dirt over the ice cream. "I can eat dirt if I want to!" we pout and proclaim. Which is true—we can. But if we do, the loss is ours. God has a better offer. He wants us to be just like Jesus.

Isn't that good news? You aren't stuck with today's personality. You aren't condemned to "grumpydom." You are tweakable. Even if you've worried each day of your life, you needn't worry the rest of your life. So what if you were born a bigot? You don't have to die one.

Where did we get the idea we can't change? From whence come statements such as, "It's just my nature to worry," or, "I'll always be pessimistic. I'm just that way," or, "I have a bad

temper. I can't help the way I react"? Who says? Would we
make similar statements about our bodies? "It's just my nature
to have a broken leg. I can't do anything about it." Of course
not. If our bodies malfunction, we seek help. Shouldn't we do
the same with our hearts? Shouldn't we seek aid for our sour
attitudes? Can't we request treatment for our selfish tirades?
Of course we can. Jesus can change our hearts. He wants us
to have a heart like his.

Can you imagine a better offer?

THE HEART OF CHRIST

The heart of Jesus was pure. The Savior was adored by thousands, yet content to live a simple life. He was cared for by
women (Luke 8:1–3), yet never accused of lustful thoughts;
scorned by his own creation, but willing to forgive them before
they even requested his mercy. Peter, who traveled with Jesus
for three and a half years, described him as a "lamb, unblemished and spotless" (1 Pet. 1:19 NASB). After spending the same
amount of time with Jesus, John concluded, "And in him is no
sin" (1 John 3:5 NIV).

Jesus' heart was peaceful. The disciples fretted over the need
to feed the thousands, but not Jesus. He thanked God for the
problem. The disciples shouted for fear in the storm, but not
Jesus. He slept through it. Peter drew his sword to fight the soldiers, but not Jesus. He lifted his hand to heal. His heart was at
peace. When his disciples abandoned him, did he pout and go
home? When Peter denied him, did Jesus lose his temper? When

the soldiers spit in his face, did he breathe fire in theirs? Far from it. He was at peace. He forgave them. He refused to be guided by vengeance.

He also refused to be guided by anything other than his high call. His heart was purposeful. Most lives aim at nothing in particular and achieve it. Jesus aimed at one goal—to save humanity from its sin. He could summarize his life with one sentence: "The Son of man came to seek and to save the lost" (Luke 19:10 RSV). Jesus was so focused on his task that he knew when to say, "My time has not yet come" (John 2:4) and when to say, "It is finished" (John 19:30). But he was not so focused on his goal that he was unpleasant.

Quite the contrary. How pleasant were his thoughts! Children couldn't resist Jesus. He could find beauty in lilies, joy in worship, and possibilities in problems. He would spend days with multitudes of sick people and still feel sorry for them. He spent over three decades wading through the muck and mire of our sin yet still saw enough beauty in us to die for our mistakes.

But the crowning attribute of Christ was this: his heart was spiritual. His thoughts reflected his intimate relationship with the Father. "I am in the Father and the Father is in me," he stated (John 14:11). His first recorded sermon begins with the words, "The Spirit of the Lord is upon Me" (Luke 4:18 NASB). He was "led by the Spirit" (Matt. 4:1 NIV) and "full of the Holy Spirit" (Luke 4:1 NIV). He returned from the desert "in the power of the Spirit" (Luke 4:14 NIV).

Jesus took his instructions from God. It was his habit to go to worship (Luke 4:16). It was his practice to memorize scripture (Luke 4:4). Luke says Jesus "often slipped away to be alone so he could pray" (Luke 5:16). His times of prayer guided him. He once returned from prayer and announced it was time to move to another city (Mark 1:38). Another time of prayer resulted in the selection of the disciples (Luke 6:12–13). Jesus was led by an unseen hand. "The Son does whatever the Father does" (John 5:19). In the same chapter he stated, "I can do nothing alone. I judge only the way I am told" (John 5:30).

The heart of Jesus was spiritual.

THE HEART OF HUMANITY

Our hearts seem so far from his. He is pure; we are greedy. He is peaceful; we are hassled. He is purposeful; we are distracted. He is pleasant; we are cranky. He is spiritual; we are earthbound. The distance between our hearts and his seems so immense. How could we ever hope to have the heart of Jesus?

Ready for a surprise? You already do. You already have the heart of Christ. Why are you looking at me that way? Would I kid you? If you are in Christ, you already have the heart of Christ. One of the supreme yet unrealized promises of God is simply this: if you have given your life to Jesus, Jesus has given himself to you. He has made your heart his home. It would be hard to say it more succinctly than Paul does: "Christ lives in me" (Gal. 2:20 MSG).

At the risk of repeating myself, let me repeat myself. If you have given your life to Jesus, Jesus has given himself to you. He has moved in and unpacked his bags and is ready to change you "into his likeness from one degree of glory to another" (2 Cor. 3:18 RSV). Paul explains it with these words: "Strange as it seems, we Christians actually do have within us a portion of the very thoughts and mind of Christ" (1 Cor. 2:16 TLB).

Strange is the word! If I have the mind of Jesus, why do I still think so much like me? If I have the heart of Christ, why do I still have the hang-ups of Max? If Jesus dwells within me, why do I still hate traffic jams?

Part of the answer is illustrated in a story about a lady who had a small house on the seashore of Ireland at the turn of the century. She was quite wealthy but also quite frugal. The people were surprised, then, when she decided to be among the first to have electricity in her home.

Several weeks after the installation, a meter reader appeared at her door. He asked if her electricity was working well, and she assured him it was. "I'm wondering if you can explain something to me," he said. "Your meter shows scarcely any usage. Are you using your power?"

"Certainly," she answered. "Each evening when the sun sets, I turn on my lights just long enough to light my candles; then I turn them off."[2]

She's tapped into the power but doesn't use it. Her house is connected but not altered. Don't we make the same mistake? We, too—with our souls saved but our hearts unchanged—are connected but not altered. Trusting Christ for salvation but resisting transformation. We occasionally flip the switch, but most of the time we settle for shadows.

What would happen if we left the light on? What would

happen if we not only flipped the switch but lived in the light? What changes would occur if we set about the task of dwelling in the radiance of Christ?

No doubt about it: God has ambitious plans for us. The same one who saved your soul longs to remake your heart. His plan is nothing short of a total transformation: "He decided from the outset to shape the lives of those who love him along the same lines as the life of his Son" (Rom. 8:29 MSG).

"You have begun to live the new life, in which you are being made new and are becoming like the One who made you. This new life brings you the true knowledge of God" (Col. 3:10).

God is willing to change us into the likeness of the Savior. Shall we accept his offer? Here is my suggestion. Let's imagine what it means to be just like Jesus. Let's look long into the heart of Christ. Let's spend some chapters considering his compassion, reflecting upon his intimacy with the Father, admiring his focus, pondering his endurance. How did he forgive? When did he pray? What made him so pleasant? Why didn't he give up? Let's "fix our eyes on Jesus" (Heb. 12:2 NIV). Perhaps in seeing him, we will see what we can become.

Be gentle and ready to forgive;
never hold grudges. Remember, the Lord
forgave you, so you must forgive others.

COLOSSIANS 3:13 TLB

CHAPTER TWO

LOVING THE PEOPLE
YOU ARE STUCK WITH

A Forgiving Heart

My first pet came in the form of a childhood Christmas Eve gift. Somewhere I have a snapshot of a brown-and-white Chinese pug, small enough to fit in my father's hand, cute enough to steal my eight-year-old heart. We named her Liz.

I carried her all day. Her floppy ears fascinated me, and her flat nose intrigued me. I even took her to bed. So what if she smelled like a dog? I thought the odor was cute. So what if she whined and whimpered? I thought the noise was cute. So what if she did her business on my pillow? Can't say I thought that was cute, but I didn't mind.

Mom and Dad had made it clear in our prenuptial agreement that I was to be Liz's caretaker, and I was happy to oblige. I cleaned her little eating dish and opened her can of puppy food. The minute she lapped up some water, I replenished it. I kept her hair combed and her tail wagging.

Within a few days, however, my feelings changed a bit. Liz was still my dog, and I was still her friend, but I grew weary with her barking, and she seemed hungry an awful lot. More than once my folks had to remind me, "Take care of her. She is your dog."

I didn't like hearing those words—*your dog*. I wouldn't have minded the phrase "your dog to play with" or "your dog when you want her" or even "your dog when she is behaving." But those weren't my parents' words. They said, "Liz is *your dog*." Period. In sickness and in health. For richer, for poorer. In dryness and in wetness.

That's when it occurred to me. *I am stuck with Liz.* The courtship was over, and the honeymoon had ended. We were mutually leashed. Liz went from an option to an obligation, from a pet to a chore, from someone to play with to someone to care for.

Perhaps you can relate. Chances are you know the claustrophobia that comes with commitment. Only instead of being reminded, "She is your dog," you're told, "He is your husband." Or, "She is your wife." Or, "He is your child, parent, employee or boss or roommate" or any other relationship that requires loyalty for survival.

Such permanence can lead to panic—at least it did in me. I had to answer some tough questions. Can I tolerate the same flat-nosed, hairy, hungry face every morning? (You wives know the feeling?) Am I going to be barked at until the day I die? (Any kids connecting here?) Will she ever learn to clean up her own mess? (Did I hear an "amen" from some parents?)

STUCKITITIS

Such are the questions we ask when we feel stuck with someone. There is a word for this condition. Upon consulting the
one-word medical dictionary (which I wrote the day before I
crafted this chapter), I discovered that this condition is a common malady known as *stuckititis*. (*Stuck* meaning "trapped." *Ititis*
being the six letters you tag on to any word you want to sound
impressive. Read it out loud: *stuckititis*.) *Max's Manual of Medical
Terms* has this to say about the condition:

> Attacks of *stuckititis* are limited to people who breathe and
> typically occur somewhere between birth and death.
> *Stuckititis* manifests itself in irritability, short fuses, and a
> mountain range of molehills. The common symptom of
> *stuckititis* victims is the repetition of questions beginning
> with *who, what,* and *why. Who* is this person? *What* was I
> thinking? *Why* didn't I listen to my mother?[1]

This prestigious manual identifies three ways to cope with
stuckititis: flee, fight, or forgive. Some opt to flee: to get out of
the relationship and start again elsewhere, though they are
often surprised when the condition surfaces on the other side
of the fence as well. Others fight. Houses become combat
zones, and offices become boxing rings, and tension becomes a
way of life. A few, however, discover another treatment: forgiveness. My manual has no model for how forgiveness occurs,
but the Bible does.

Jesus himself knew the feeling of being stuck with some-one. For three years he ran with the same crew. By and large, he saw the same dozen or so faces around the table, around the campfire, around the clock. They rode in the same boats and walked the same roads and visited the same houses, and I wonder, how did Jesus stay so devoted to his men? Not only did he have to put up with their visible oddities, he had to endure their invisible foibles. Think about it. He could hear their unspoken thoughts. He knew their private doubts. Not only that, he knew their future doubts. What if you knew every mistake your loved ones had ever made and every mis-take they would ever make? What if you knew every thought they would have about you, every irritation, every dislike, every betrayal?

Was it hard for Jesus to love Peter, knowing Peter would someday curse him? Was it tough to trust Thomas, knowing Thomas would one day question Jesus' resurrection? How did Jesus resist the urge to recruit a new batch of followers? John wanted to destroy one enemy. Peter sliced off the ear of another. Just days before Jesus' death, his disciples were argu-ing about which of them was the best! How was he able to love people who were hard to like?

Few situations stir panic like being trapped in a relationship. It's one thing to be stuck with a puppy but something else entirely to be stuck in a marriage. We may chuckle over goofy terms like *stuckititis,* but for many, this is no laughing matter. For that reason I think it wise that we begin our study of what it means to be just like Jesus by pondering his heart of forgiveness. How was Jesus able to love his disciples? The answer is found in the thirteenth chapter of John.

WITH TOWEL AND BASIN

Of all the times we see the bowing knees of Jesus, none is so precious as when he kneels before his disciples and washes their feet.

It was just before the Passover Feast. Jesus knew that the time had come for him to leave this world and go to the Father. Having loved his own who were in the world, he now showed them the full extent of his love.

> The evening meal was being served, and the devil had already prompted Judas Iscariot, son of Simon, to betray Jesus. Jesus knew that the Father had put all things under his power, and that he had come from God and was returning to God; so he got up from the meal, took off his outer clothing, . . . and began to wash his disciples' feet, drying them with the towel that was wrapped around him. (vv. 1–5 NIV)

It has been a long day. Jerusalem is packed with Passover guests, most of whom clamor for a glimpse of the Teacher. The spring sun is warm. The streets are dry. And the disciples are a long way from home. A splash of cool water would be refreshing.

The disciples enter, one by one, and take their places around the table. On the wall hangs a towel, and on the floor sits a pitcher and a basin. Any one of the disciples could volunteer for the job, but not one does.

After a few moments, Jesus stands and removes his outer garment. He wraps a servant's girdle around his waist, takes up the basin, and kneels before one of the disciples. He unlaces a sandal and gently lifts the foot and places it in the basin, covers it with water, and begins to bathe it. One by one, one grimy foot after another, Jesus works his way down the row.

In Jesus' day the washing of feet was a task reserved not just for servants but for the lowest of servants. Every circle has its pecking order, and the circle of household workers was no exception. The servant at the bottom of the totem pole was expected to be the one on his knees with the towel and basin.

In this case the one with the towel and basin is the king of the universe. Hands that shaped the stars now wash away filth. Fingers that formed mountains now massage toes. And the one before whom all nations will one day kneel now kneels before his disciples. Hours before his own death, Jesus' concern is singular. He wants his disciples to know how much he loves them. More than removing dirt, Jesus is removing doubt.

Jesus knows what will happen to his hands at the crucifixion. Within twenty-four hours they will be pierced and lifeless. Of all the times we'd expect him to ask for the disciples' attention, this would be one. But he doesn't.

You can be sure Jesus knows the future of these feet he is washing. These twenty-four feet will not spend the next day following their master, defending his cause. These feet will dash for cover at the flash of a Roman sword. Only one pair of feet won't abandon him in the garden. One disciple won't desert him at Gethsemane—Judas won't even make it that far! He will abandon Jesus that very night at the table.

I looked for a Bible translation that reads, "Jesus washed all the disciples' feet except the feet of Judas," but I couldn't find one. What a passionate moment when Jesus silently lifts the feet of his betrayer and washes them in the basin! Within hours the feet of Judas, cleansed by the kindness of the one he will betray, will stand in Caiaphas's court.

Behold the gift Jesus gives his followers! He knows what these men are about to do. He knows they are about to perform the vilest act of their lives. By morning they will bury their heads in shame and look down at their feet in disgust. And when they do, he wants them to remember how his knees knelt before them and he washed their feet. He wants them to realize those feet are still clean. "You don't understand now what I am doing, but you will understand later" (John 13:7).

Remarkable. He forgave their sin before they even committed it. He offered mercy before they even sought it.

FROM THE BASIN OF HIS GRACE

Oh, I could never do that, you object. *The hurt is so deep. The wounds are so numerous. Just seeing the person causes me to cringe.* Perhaps that is your problem. Perhaps you are seeing the wrong person or at least too much of the wrong person. Remember, the secret of being just like Jesus is "fixing our eyes" on him. Try shifting your glance away from the one who hurt you and setting your eyes on the one who has saved you.

Note the promise of John, "But if we live in the light, as God is in the light, we can share fellowship with each other. Then the blood of Jesus, God's Son, cleanses us from every sin" (1 John 1:7).

Aside from geography and chronology, our story is the same as the disciples'. We weren't in Jerusalem, and we weren't alive that night. But what Jesus did for them he has done for us. He has cleansed us. He has cleansed our hearts from sin.

Even more, he is still cleansing us! John tells us, "We are *being cleansed* from every sin by the blood of Jesus." In other words, we are *always being cleansed*. The cleansing is not a promise for the future but a reality in the present. Let a speck of dust fall on the soul of a saint, and it is washed away. Let a spot of filth land on the heart of God's child, and the filth is wiped away. Jesus still cleans his disciples' feet. Jesus still washes away stains. Jesus still purifies his people.

Our Savior kneels down and gazes upon the darkest acts of our lives. But rather than recoil in horror, he reaches out in kindness and says, "I can clean that if you want." And from the basin of his grace, he scoops a palm full of mercy and washes away our sin.

But that's not all he does. Because he lives in us, you and I can do the same. Because he has forgiven us, we can forgive others. Because he has a forgiving heart, we can have a forgiving heart. We can have a heart like his.

"If I, your Lord and Teacher, have washed your feet, you also should wash each other's feet. I did this as an example so that you should do as I have done for you" (John 13:14–15).

Jesus washes our feet for two reasons. The first is to give us mercy; the second is to give us a message, and that message is simply this: Jesus offers unconditional grace; we are to offer unconditional grace. The mercy of Christ preceded our mistakes; our mercy must precede the mistakes of others. Those in the circle of Christ had no doubt of his love; those in our circles should have no doubts about ours.

What does it mean to have a heart like his? It means to kneel as Jesus knelt, touching the grimy parts of the people we are stuck with and washing away their unkindnesses with kindness. Or as Paul wrote, "Be kind and loving to each other, and forgive each other just as God forgave you in Christ" (Eph. 4:32).

"But, Max," you are saying, "I've done nothing wrong. I'm not the one who cheated. I'm not the one who lied. I'm not the guilty party here." Perhaps you aren't. But neither was Jesus. Of all the men in that room, only one was worthy of having his feet washed. And he was the one who washed the feet. The one worthy of being served, served others. The genius of Jesus' example is that the burden of bridge-building falls on the strong one, not on the weak one. The one who is innocent is the one who makes the gesture.

And you know what happens? More often than not, if the one in the right volunteers to wash the feet of the one in the wrong, both parties get on their knees. Don't we all think we are right? Hence we wash each other's feet.

Please understand. *Relationships don't thrive because the guilty are punished but because the innocent are merciful.*

THE POWER OF FORGIVENESS

Recently I shared a meal with some friends. A husband and wife wanted to tell me about a storm they were weathering. Through a series of events, she learned of an act of infidelity that had occurred over a decade ago. He had made the mistake of thinking it'd be better not to tell her, so he didn't. But she found out. And as you can imagine, she was deeply hurt.

Through the advice of a counselor, the couple dropped everything and went away for several days. A decision had to be made. Would they flee, fight, or forgive? So they prayed. They talked. They walked. They reflected. In this case the wife was clearly in the right. She could have left. Women have done so for lesser reasons. Or she could have stayed and made his life a living hell. Other women have done that. But she chose a different response.

On the tenth night of their trip, my friend found a card on his pillow. On the card was a printed verse: "I'd rather do nothing with you than something without you." Beneath the verse she had written these words:

I forgive you. I love you. Let's move on.

The card might as well have been a basin. And the pen might as well have been a pitcher of water, for out of it poured pure mercy, and with it she washed her husband's feet.

Certain conflicts can be resolved only with a basin of water. Are any relationships in your world thirsty for mercy? Are there any sitting around your table who need to be assured of your grace? Jesus made sure his disciples had no reason to doubt his love. Why don't you do the same?

*Since you have been chosen by God
who has given you this new kind of life,
and because of his deep love and concern
for you, you should practice tenderhearted
mercy and kindness to others.*

COLOSSIANS 3:12 TLB

CHAPTER THREE

THE TOUCH OF GOD

A Compassionate Heart

May I ask you to look at your hand for a moment? Look at the back, then the palm. Reacquaint yourself with your fingers. Run a thumb over your knuckles.

What if someone were to film a documentary on your hands? What if a producer were to tell your story based on the life of your hands? What would we see? As with all of us, the film would begin with an infant's fist, then a closeup of a tiny hand wrapped around mommy's finger. Then what? Holding on to a chair as you learned to walk? Handling a spoon as you learned to eat?

We aren't too long into the feature before we see your hand being affectionate, stroking daddy's face or petting a puppy. Nor is it too long before we see your hand acting aggressively: pushing big brother or yanking back a toy. All of us learned early that the hand is suited for more than survival—it's a tool of emotional expression. The same hand can help or hurt, extend or clench, lift someone up or shove someone down.

Were you to show the documentary to your friends, you'd be proud of certain moments: your hand extending with a gift, placing a ring on another's finger, doctoring a wound, preparing a meal, or folding in prayer. And then there are other scenes. Shots of accusing fingers, abusive fists. Hands taking more often than giving, demanding instead of offering, wounding rather than loving. Oh, the power of our hands. Leave them unmanaged and they become weapons: clawing for power, strangling for survival, seducing for pleasure. But manage them and our hands become instruments of grace—not just tools in the hands of God, but *God's very hands*. Surrender them and these five-fingered appendages become the hands of heaven.

That's what Jesus did. Our Savior completely surrendered his hands to God. The documentary of his hands has no scenes of greedy grabbing or unfounded finger pointing. It does, however, have one scene after another of people longing for his compassionate touch: parents carrying their children, the poor bringing their fears, the sinful shouldering their sorrow. And each who came was touched. And each one touched was changed. But none was touched or changed more than the unnamed leper of Matthew 8.

> When Jesus came down from the hill, great crowds followed him. Then a man with a skin disease came to Jesus. The man bowed down before him and said, "Lord, you can heal me if you will."

Jesus reached out his hand and touched the man and said, "I will. Be healed!" And immediately the man was healed from his disease. Then Jesus said to him, "Don't tell anyone about this. But go and show yourself to the priest and offer the gift Moses commanded for people who are made well. This will show the people what I have done." (vv. 1–4)

Mark and Luke chose to tell this same story. But with apologies to all three writers, I must say none tell enough. Oh, we know the man's disease and his decision, but as to the rest? We are left with questions. The authors offer no name, no history, no description.

THE ULTIMATE OUTCAST

Sometimes my curiosity gets the best of me, and I wonder out loud. That's what I'm about to do here—wonder out loud about the man who felt Jesus' compassionate touch. He makes one appearance, has one request, and receives one touch. But that one touch changed his life forever. And I wonder if his story went something like this:

For five years no one touched me. No one. Not one person. Not my wife. Not my child. Not my friends. No one touched me. They saw me. They spoke to me. I sensed love in their voices. I saw concern in their eyes. But I didn't feel their touch. There was no touch. Not once. No one touched me.

What is common to you, I coveted. Handshakes. Warm embraces. A tap

on the shoulder to get my attention. A kiss on the lips to steal a heart.
Such moments were taken from my world. No one touched me. No one
bumped into me. What I would have given to be bumped into, to be
caught in a crowd, for my shoulder to brush against another's. But for
five years it has not happened. How could it? I was not allowed on the
streets. Even the rabbis kept their distance from me. I was not permitted
in my synagogue. Not even welcome in my own house.

I was untouchable. I was a leper. And no one touched me. Until today.

I wonder about this man because in New Testament times
leprosy was the most dreaded disease. The condition rendered
the body a mass of ulcers and decay. Fingers would curl and
gnarl. Blotches of skin would discolor and stink. Certain types
of leprosy would numb nerve endings, leading to a loss of fingers, toes, even a whole foot or hand. Leprosy was death by
inches.

The social consequences were as severe as the physical. Considered contagious, the leper was quarantined, banished to a
leper colony.

In Scripture the leper is symbolic of the ultimate outcast:
infected by a condition he did not seek, rejected by those he
knew, avoided by people he did not know, condemned to a
future he could not bear. And in the memory of each outcast
must have been the day he was forced to face the truth: life
would never be the same.

One year during harvest my grip on the scythe seemed weak. The tips
of my fingers numbed. First one finger then another. Within a short time
I could grip the tool but scarcely feel it. By the end of the season, I felt
nothing at all. The hand grasping the handle might as well have

belonged to someone else—the feeling was gone. I said nothing to my wife, but I know she suspected something. How could she not? I carried my hand against my body like a wounded bird.

One afternoon I plunged my hands into a basin of water intending to wash my face. The water reddened. My finger was bleeding, bleeding freely. I didn't even know I was wounded. How did I cut myself? On a knife? Did my hand slide across the sharp edge of metal? It must have, but I didn't feel anything.

"It's on your clothes, too," my wife said softly. She was behind me. Before looking at her, I looked down at the crimson spots on my robe. For the longest time I stood over the basin, staring at my hand. Somehow I knew my life was being forever altered.

"Shall I go with you to tell the priest?" she asked.

"No," I sighed, "I'll go alone."

I turned and looked into her moist eyes. Standing next to her was our three-year-old daughter. Squatting, I gazed into her face and stroked her cheek, saying nothing. What could I say? I stood and looked again at my wife. She touched my shoulder, and with my good hand, I touched hers. It would be our final touch.

Five years have passed, and no one has touched me since, until today.

The priest didn't touch me. He looked at my hand, now wrapped in a rag. He looked at my face, now shadowed in sorrow. I've never faulted him for what he said. He was only doing as he was instructed. He covered his mouth and extended his hand, palm forward. "You are unclean," he told me. With one pronouncement I lost my family, my farm, my future, my friends.

My wife met me at the city gates with a sack of clothing and bread and coins. She didn't speak. By now friends had gathered. What I saw *in their eyes was a precursor to what I've seen in every eye since: fearful pity. As I stepped out, they stepped back. Their horror of my disease was greater than their concern for my heart—so they, and everyone else I have seen since, stepped back.*

The banishing of a leper seems harsh, unnecessary. The Ancient East hasn't been the only culture to isolate their wounded, however. We may not build colonies or cover our mouths in their presence, but we certainly build walls and duck our eyes. And a person needn't have leprosy to feel quarantined.

One of my sadder memories involves my fourth-grade friend Jerry.[1] He and a half-dozen of us were an ever-present, inseparable fixture on the playground. One day I called his house to see if we could play. The phone was answered by a cursing, drunken voice telling me Jerry could not come over that day or any day. I told my friends what had happened. One of them explained that Jerry's father was an alcoholic. I don't know if I knew what the word meant, but I learned quickly. Jerry, the second baseman; Jerry, the kid with the red bike; Jerry, my friend on the corner was now "Jerry, the son of a drunk." Kids can be hard, and for some reason we were hard on Jerry. He was infected. Like the leper, he suffered from a condition he didn't create. Like the leper, he was put outside the village.

The divorced know this feeling. So do the handicapped. The unemployed have felt it, as have the less educated. Some shun unmarried moms. We keep our distance from the depressed and avoid the terminally ill. We have neighborhoods for immigrants, convalescent homes for the elderly, schools for the simple, centers for the addicted, and prisons for the criminals.

The rest simply try to get away from it all. Only God knows how many Jerrys are in voluntary exile—individuals living quiet, lonely lives infected by their fear of rejection and their memories of the last time they tried. They choose not to be touched at all rather than risk being hurt again.

Oh, how I repulsed those who saw me. Five years of leprosy had left my hands gnarled. Tips of my fingers were missing as were portions of an ear and my nose. At the sight of me, fathers grabbed their children. Mothers covered their faces. Children pointed and stared.

The rags on my body couldn't hide my sores. Nor could the wrap on my face hide the rage in my eyes. I didn't even try to hide it. How many nights did I shake my crippled fist at the silent sky? "What did I do to deserve this?" But never a reply.

Some think I sinned. Some think my parents sinned. I don't know. All I know is that I grew so tired of it all: sleeping in the colony, smelling the stench. I grew so tired of the damnable bell I was required to wear around my neck to warn people of my presence. As if I needed it. One glance and the announcements began, "Unclean! Unclean! Unclean!"

Several weeks ago I dared walk the road to my village. I had no intent of entering. Heaven knows I only wanted to look again upon my fields. Gaze again upon my home. And see, perchance, the face of my wife. I did not see her. But I saw some children playing in a pasture. I hid behind a tree and watched them scamper and run. Their faces were so joyful and their laughter so contagious that for a moment, for just a moment, I was no longer a leper. I was a farmer. I was a father. I was a man.

Infused with their happiness, I stepped out from behind the tree, straightened my back, breathed deeply . . . and they saw me. Before I could retreat, they saw me. And they screamed. And they scattered. One lingered, though, behind the others. One paused and looked in my direction. I don't know, and I can't say for sure, but I think, I really think, she was my daughter. And I don't know, I really can't say for sure. But I think she was looking for her father.

That look is what made me take the step I took today. Of course it was reckless. Of course it was risky. But what did I have to lose? He calls himself God's Son. Either he will hear my complaint and kill me or accept my demands and heal me. Those were my thoughts. I came to him as a defiant man. Moved not by faith but by a desperate anger. God had wrought this calamity on my body, and he would either fix it or end it.

But then I saw him, and when I saw him, I was changed. You must remember, I'm a farmer, not a poet, so I cannot find the words to describe what I saw. All I can say is that the Judean mornings are sometimes so fresh and the sunrises so glorious that to look at them is to forget the heat of the day before and the hurt of times past. When I looked at his face, I saw a Judean morning.

Before he spoke, I knew he cared. Somehow I knew he hated this disease as much as, no—more—than I hate it. My rage became trust, and my anger became hope.

From behind a rock, I watched him descend a hill. Throngs of people followed him. I waited until he was only paces from me, then I stepped out.

"Master!"

He stopped and looked in my direction as did dozens of others. A flood of fear swept across the crowd. Arms flew in front of faces. Chil-

dren ducked behind parents. "Unclean!" someone shouted. Again, I don't blame them. I was a huddled mass of death. But I scarcely heard them. I scarcely saw them. Their panic I'd seen a thousand times. His compassion, however, I'd never beheld. Everyone stepped back except him. He stepped toward me. Toward me.

Five years ago my wife had stepped toward me. She was the last to do so. Now he did. I did not move. I just spoke. "Lord, you can heal me if you will." Had he healed me with a word, I would have been thrilled. Had he cured me with a prayer, I would have rejoiced. But he wasn't satisfied with speaking to me. He drew near me. He touched me. Five years ago my wife had touched me. No one had touched me since. Until today.

"I will." His words were as tender as his touch. "Be healed!"

Energy flooded my body like water through a furrowed field. In an instant, in a moment, I felt warmth where there had been numbness. I felt strength where there had been atrophy. My back straightened, and my head lifted. Where I had been eye level with his belt, I now stood eye level with his face. His smiling face.

He cupped his hands on my cheeks and drew me so near I could feel the warmth of his breath and see the wetness in his eyes. "Don't tell anyone about this. But go and show yourself to the priest and offer the gift Moses commanded for people who are made well. This will show the people what I have done."

And so that is where I am going. I will show myself to my priest and embrace him. I will show myself to my wife, and I will embrace her. I will pick up my daughter, and I will embrace her. And I will never forget the one who dared to touch me. He could have healed me with a word. But he wanted to do more than heal me. He wanted to honor me,

to validate me, to christen me. Imagine that . . . unworthy of the touch
of a man, yet worthy of the touch of God.

THE POWER OF THE GODLY TOUCH

The touch did not heal the disease, you know. Matthew is careful to mention that it was the pronouncement and not the touch of Christ that cured the condition. "Jesus reached out his hand and touched the man and said, 'I will. Be healed!' And immediately the man was healed from his disease" (Matt. 8:3).

The infection was banished by a word from Jesus.

The loneliness, however, was treated by a touch from Jesus.

Oh, the power of a godly touch. Haven't you known it? The doctor who treated you, or the teacher who dried your tears? Was there a hand holding yours at a funeral? Another on your shoulder during a trial? A handshake of welcome at a new job? A pastoral prayer for healing? Haven't we known the power of a godly touch?

Can't we offer the same?

Many of you already do. Some of you have the master touch of the Physician himself. You use your hands to pray over the sick and minister to the weak. If you aren't touching them personally, your hands are writing letters, dialing phones, baking pies. You have learned the power of a touch.

But others of us tend to forget. Our hearts are good; it's just that our memories are bad. We forget how significant one touch can be. We fear saying the wrong thing or using the wrong tone or acting the wrong way. So rather than do it incorrectly, we do nothing at all.

Aren't we glad Jesus didn't make the same mistake? If your fear of doing the wrong thing prevents you from doing anything, keep in mind the perspective of the lepers of the world. They aren't picky. They aren't finicky. They're just lonely. They are yearning for a godly touch.

Jesus touched the untouchables of the world. Will you do the same?

*Do not merely listen to the word,
and so deceive yourselves. Do what it says.
Anyone who listens to the word but does
not do what it says is like a man who looks
at his face in a mirror and, after looking
at himself, goes away and immediately
forgets what he looks like.*

JAMES 1:22–24 NIV

HEARING GOD'S MUSIC

A Listening Heart

"Let he who has ears to hear, use them."

More than once Jesus said these words. Eight times in the Gospels and eight times in the Book of Revelation[1] we are reminded that it's not enough just to have ears—it's necessary to use them.

In one of his parables[2] Jesus compared our ears to soil. He told about a farmer who scattered seed (symbolic of the Word) in four different types of ground (symbolic of our ears). Some of our ears are like a hard road—unreceptive to the seed. Others have ears like rocky soil—we hear the Word but don't allow it to take root. Still others have ears akin to a weed patch—too overgrown, too thorny, with too much competition for the seed to have a chance. And then there are some who have ears that hear: well tilled, discriminate, and ready to hear God's voice.

Please note that in all four cases the seed is the same seed. The sower is the same sower. What's different is not the message or the messenger—it's the listener. And if the ratio in the story is significant, three-fourths of the world isn't listening to God's voice. Whether the cause be hard hearts, shallow lives, or anxious minds, 75 percent of us are missing the message.

It's not that we don't have ears; it's that we don't use them.

Scripture has always placed a premium on hearing God's voice. Indeed, the great command from God through Moses began with the words, "Hear, O Israel: the LORD our God is one LORD" (Deut. 6:4 KJV). Nehemiah and his men were commended because they were "attentive unto the book of the Law" (Neh. 8:3 KJV). "Happy are those who listen to me" is the promise of Proverbs 8:34. Jesus urges us to learn to listen like sheep. "The sheep recognize his voice. . . . they follow because they are familiar with [the shepherd's] voice. They won't follow a stranger's voice but will scatter because they aren't used to the sound of it" (John 10:3–5 MSG). Each of the seven churches in Revelation is addressed in the same manner: "He who has an ear, let him hear what the Spirit says to the churches."[3]

Our ears, unlike our eyes, do not have lids. They are to remain open, but how easily they close.

Denalyn and I were shopping for luggage sometime back. We found what we wanted in one store and told the salesclerk we were going to another store to compare prices. He asked me if I wanted to take his business card. I told him, "No, your name is easy to remember, Bob."

To which he replied, "My name is Joe."

I had heard the man, but I hadn't listened.

Pilate didn't listen either. He had the classic case of ears that didn't hear. Not only did his wife warn him, "Don't do anything to that man, because he is innocent" (Matt. 27:19), but the very Word of Life stood before Pilate in his chamber and proclaimed, "Everyone who belongs to the truth listens to me" (John 18:37). But Pilate had selective hearing. He allowed the voices of the people to dominate the voices of conscience and the carpenter. "Their voices prevailed" (Luke 23:23 RSV).

In the end Pilate inclined his ear to the crowd and away from the Christ and ignored the message of the Messiah. "Faith comes from hearing" (Rom. 10:17), and since Pilate didn't hear, he never found faith.

"Let he who has ears to hear, use them." How long has it been since you had your hearing checked? When God throws seed your way, what is the result? May I raise a question or two to test how well you hear God's voice?

HOW LONG HAS IT BEEN
SINCE YOU LET GOD HAVE YOU?

I mean really *have* you? How long since you gave him a portion of undiluted, uninterrupted time listening for his voice? Apparently Jesus did. He made a deliberate effort to spend time with God.

Spend much time reading about the listening life of Jesus and a distinct pattern emerges. He spent regular time with God, praying and listening. Mark says, "Very early in the morning, while it was still dark, Jesus got up, left the house and went off to a solitary place, where he prayed" (Mark 1:35 NIV). Luke tells us, "Jesus often withdrew to lonely places and prayed" (Luke 5:16 NIV).

Let me ask the obvious. If Jesus, the Son of God, the sinless Savior of humankind, thought it worthwhile to clear his calendar to pray, wouldn't we be wise to do the same?

Not only did he spend regular time with God in prayer, he spent regular time in God's Word. Of course we don't find Jesus pulling a leather-bound New Testament from his satchel and reading it. We do, however, see the stunning example of Jesus, in the throes of the wilderness temptation, using the Word of God to deal with Satan. Three times he is tempted, and each time he repels the attack with the phrase: "It is written in the Scriptures" (Luke 4:4,8,12), and then he quotes a verse. Jesus is so familiar with Scripture that he not only knows the verse, he knows how to use it.

And then there's the occasion when Jesus was asked to read in the synagogue. He is handed the book of Isaiah the prophet. He finds the passage, reads it, and declares, "While you heard these words just now, they were coming true!" (Luke 4:21). We are given the picture of a person who knows his way around in Scripture and can recognize its fulfillment. If Jesus thought it wise to grow familiar with the Bible, shouldn't we do the same?

If we are to be just like Jesus—if we are to have ears that hear God's voice—then we have just found two habits worth imitating: the habits of prayer and Bible reading. Consider these verses:

Base your happiness on your hope in Christ. When trials come endure them patiently; steadfastly maintain *the habit of prayer.* (Rom. 12:12 PHILLIPS, italics mine)

The man who looks into the perfect law, the law of liberty, and makes a habit of so doing, is not the man who hears and forgets. He puts that law into practice and he wins true happiness. (James 1:25 PHILLIPS)

If we are to be just like Jesus, we must have a regular time of talking to God and listening to his Word.

SURROGATE SPIRITUALITY

Wait a minute. Don't you do that. I know exactly what some of you are doing. You are tuning me out. *Lucado is talking about daily devotionals, eh? This is a good time for me to take a mental walk over to the fridge and see what we have to eat.*

I understand your reluctance. Some of us have tried to have a daily quiet time and have not been successful. Others of us have a hard time concentrating. And all of us are busy. So rather than spend time with God, listening for his voice, we'll let others spend time with him and then benefit from their experience. Let them tell us what God is saying. After all, isn't that why we pay preachers? Isn't that why we read Christian books? *These folks are good at daily devotions. I'll just learn from them.*

If that is your approach, if your spiritual experiences are secondhand and not firsthand, I'd like to challenge you with this thought: Do you do that with other parts of your life? I don't think so.

You don't do that with vacations. You don't say, "Vacations are such a hassle, packing bags and traveling. I'm going to send someone on vacation for me. When he returns, I'll hear all about it and be spared all the inconvenience." Would you do that? No! You want the experience firsthand. You want the sights firsthand, and you want to rest firsthand. Certain things no one can do for you.

You don't do that with romance. You don't say, "I'm in love with that wonderful person, but romance is such a hassle. I'm going to hire a surrogate lover to enjoy the romance in my place. I'll hear all about it and be spared the inconvenience." Who would do that? Perish the thought. You want the romance firsthand. You don't want to miss a word or a date, and you certainly don't want to miss the kiss, right? Certain things no one can do for you.

You don't let someone eat on your behalf, do you? You don't say, "Chewing is such a bother. My jaws grow so tired, and the variety of tastes is so overwhelming. I'm going to hire someone to chew my food, and I'll just swallow whatever he gives me." Would you do that? Yuck! Of course not! Certain things no one can do for you.

And one of those is spending time with God.

Listening to God is a firsthand experience. When he asks for your attention, God doesn't want you to send a substitute; he wants you. He invites *you* to vacation in his splendor. He invites *you* to feel the touch of his hand. He invites *you* to feast at his table. He wants to spend time with *you*. And with a little training, your time with God can be the highlight of your day.

A friend of mine married an opera soprano. She loves concerts. Her college years were spent in the music department, and her earliest memories are of keyboards and choir risers. He, on the other hand, leans more toward Monday Night Football and country music. He also loves his wife, so on occasion he attends an opera. The two sit side by side in the same auditorium, listening to the same music, with two completely different responses. He sleeps and she weeps.

I believe the difference is more than taste. It's training. She has spent hours learning to appreciate the art of music. He has spent none. Her ears are Geiger-counter sensitive. He can't differentiate between *staccato* and *legato*. But he is trying. Last time we talked about the concerts, he told me he is managing to stay awake. He may never have the same ear as his wife, but with time he is learning to listen and appreciate the music.

LEARNING TO LISTEN

I believe we can, too. Equipped with the right tools, we can learn to listen to God. What are those tools? Here are the ones I have found helpful.

A regular time and place. Select a slot on your schedule and a corner of your world, and claim it for God. For some it may be best to do this in the morning. "In the morning my prayer comes before you" (Ps. 88:13 NIV). Others prefer the evening and agree with David's prayer, "Let my . . . praise [be] like the evening sacrifice" (Ps. 141:2). Others prefer many encounters during the day. Apparently the author of Psalm 55 did. He wrote, "Evening, morning and noon I cry out" (v. 17 NIV).

Some sit under a tree, others in the kitchen. Maybe your commute to work or your lunch break would be appropriate. Find a time and place that seems right for you.

How much time should you take? As much as you need. Value quality over length. Your time with God should last long enough for you to say what you want and for God to say what he wants. Which leads us to a second tool you need—*an open Bible.*

God speaks to us through his Word. The first step in reading the Bible is to ask God to help you understand it. "But the Helper will teach you everything and will cause you to remember all that I told you. This Helper is the Holy Spirit whom the Father will send in my name" (John 14:26).

Before reading the Bible, pray. Don't go to Scripture looking for your own idea; go searching for God's. Read the Bible prayerfully. Also, read the Bible carefully. Jesus told us, "Search, and you will find" (Matt. 7:7). God commends those who "chew on Scripture day and night" (Ps. 1:2 MSG). The Bible is not a newspaper to be skimmed but rather a mine to be quarried. "Search for it like silver, and hunt for it like hidden treasure. Then you will understand respect for the LORD, and you will find that you know God" (Prov. 2:4–5).

Here is a practical point. Study the Bible a little at a time. God seems to send messages as he did his manna: one day's portion at a time. He provides "a command here, a command there. A rule here, a rule there. A little lesson here, a little lesson there" (Isa. 28:10). Choose depth over quantity. Read until a verse "hits" you, then stop and meditate on it. Copy the verse onto a sheet of paper, or write it in your journal, and reflect on it several times.

On the morning I wrote this, for example, my quiet time found me in Matthew 18. I was only four verses into the chapter when I read, *"The greatest person in the kingdom of heaven is the one who makes himself humble like this child."* I needed to go no further. I copied the words in my journal and have pondered them on and off during the day. Several times I asked God, "How can I be more childlike?" By the end of the day, I was reminded of my tendency to hurry and my proclivity to worry.

Will I learn what God intends? If I listen, I will.

Don't be discouraged if your reading reaps a small harvest. Some days a lesser portion is all we need. A little girl returned from her first day at school. Her mom asked, "Did you learn anything?" "I guess not," the girl responded. "I have to go back tomorrow and the next day and the next day . . ."

Such is the case with learning. And such is the case with Bible study. Understanding comes a little at a time over a lifetime.

There is a third tool for having a productive time with God. Not only do we need a regular time and an open Bible, we also need *a listening heart.* Don't forget the admonition from James: "The man who looks into the perfect law, the law of liberty, and makes a habit of so doing, is not the man who hears and forgets. He puts that law into practice and he wins true happiness" (James 1:25 PHILLIPS).

We know we are listening to God when what we read in the Bible is what others see in our lives. Perhaps you've heard the story of the not-so-bright fellow who saw an advertisement for a cruise. The sign in the travel agency window read "Cruise—$100 Cash."

I've got a hundred dollars, he thought. *And I'd like to go on a cruise.* So he entered the door and announced his desires. The fellow at the desk asked for the money, and the not-too-bright guy started counting it out. When he got to one hundred, he was whacked over the head and knocked out cold. He woke up in a barrel floating down a river. Another sucker in another barrel floated past and asked him, "Say, do they serve lunch on this cruise?"

The not-too-bright fellow answered, "They didn't last year."

It's one thing not to know. It's another to know and not learn. Paul urged his readers to put into practice what they had learned from him. "What you have learned and received and heard and seen in me, do" (Phil. 4:9 RSV).

If you want to be just like Jesus, let God have you. Spend time listening for him until you receive your lesson for the day—then apply it.

I have another question to check your hearing. Read it, and see how well you do.

HOW LONG SINCE
YOU LET GOD LOVE YOU?

My daughters are too old for this now, but when they were young—crib-size and diaper-laden—I would come home, shout their names, and watch them run to me with extended arms and squealing voices. For the next few moments we would speak the language of love. We'd roll on the floor, gobble bellies, and tickle tummies and laugh and play.

We delighted in each other's presence. They made no requests of me, with the exception of "Let's play, Daddy." And I made no demands of them, except, "Don't hit Daddy with the hammer."

My kids let me love them.

But suppose my daughters had approached me as we often approach God. "Hey, Dad, glad you're home. Here is what I want. More toys. More candy. And can we go to Disneyland this summer?"

"Whoa," I would have wanted to say. "I'm not a waiter, and this isn't a restaurant. I'm your father, and this is our house. Why don't you just climb up on Daddy's lap and let me tell you how much I love you?"

Ever thought God might want to do the same with you? *Oh, he wouldn't say that to me.* He wouldn't? Then to whom was he speaking when he said, "I have loved you with an everlasting love" (Jer. 31:3 NIV)? Was he playing games when he said, "Nothing . . . will ever be able to separate us from the love of God that is in Christ" (Rom. 8:39)? Buried in the seldom-quarried mines of the minor prophets is this jewel:

> The LORD your God is with you; the mighty One will save you. He will rejoice over you. You will rest in his love; he will sing and be joyful about you. (Zeph. 3:17)

Don't move too quickly through that verse. Read it again and prepare yourself for a surprise.

> The LORD your God is with you; the mighty One will save you. He will rejoice over you. You will rest in his love; he will sing and be joyful about you. (Zeph. 3:17)

Note who is active and who is passive. Who is singing, and who is resting? Who is rejoicing over his loved one, and who is being rejoiced over?

We tend to think we are the singers and God is the "singee." Most certainly that is often the case. But apparently there are times when God wishes we would just be still and (what a stunning thought!) let him sing over us.

I can see you squirming. You say you aren't worthy of such affection? Neither was Judas, but Jesus washed his feet. Neither was Peter, but Jesus fixed him breakfast. Neither were the Emmaus-bound disciples, but Jesus took time to sit at their table.

Besides, who are we to determine if we are worthy? Our job is simply to be still long enough to let him have us and let him love us.

DO YOU HEAR THE MUSIC?

I'm going to conclude by telling you a story you've heard before, though you've not heard it as I am going to tell it. But you have heard it. Surely you have, for you are in it. You are one of the characters. It is the story of the dancers who had no music.

Can you imagine how hard that would be? Dancing with no music? Day after day they came to the great hall just off the corner of Main and Broadway. They brought their wives. They brought their husbands. They brought their children and their hopes. They came to dance.

The hall was prepared for a dance. Streamers strung, punch bowls filled. Chairs were placed against the walls. People arrived and sat, knowing they had come to a dance but not knowing how to dance because they had no music. They had balloons; they had cake. They even had a stage on which the musicians could play, but they had no musicians.

One time a lanky fellow claimed to be a musician. He sure looked the part, what with his belly-length beard and fancy violin. All stood the day he stood before them and pulled the violin out of the case and placed it beneath his chin. *Now we will dance,* they thought, but they were wrong. For though he had a violin, his violin had no strings. The pushing and pulling of his bow sounded like the creaking of an unoiled door. Who can dance to a sound like that? So the dancers took their seats again.

Some tried to dance without the music. One wife convinced her husband to give it a try, so out on the floor they stepped, she dancing her way and he dancing his. Both efforts were commendable—but far from compatible. He danced some form of partnerless tango, while she was spinning like a ballerina. A few tried to follow their cue, but since there was no cue, they didn't know how to follow. The result was a dozen or so dancers with no music, going this way and that, bumping into each other and causing more than one observer to seek safety behind a chair.

Over time, however, those dancers grew weary, and everyone resumed the task of sitting and staring and wondering if anything was ever going to happen. And then one day it did.

Not everyone saw him enter. Only a few. Nothing about his appearance would compel your attention. His looks were common, but his music was not. He began to sing a song, soft and sweet, kind and compelling. His song took the chill out of the air and brought a summer-sunset glow to the heart.

And as he sang, people stood—a few at first, then many— and they began to dance. Together. Flowing to a music they had never heard before, they danced.

Some, however, remained seated. What kind of musician is this who never mounts the stage? Who brings no band? Who has no costume? Why, musicians don't just walk in off the street. They have an entourage, a reputation, a persona to project and protect. Why, this fellow scarcely mentioned his name!

"How can we know what you sing is actually music?" they challenged.

His reply was to the point: "Let the man who has ears to hear use them."

But the nondancers refused to hear. So they refused to dance. Many still refuse. The musician comes and sings. Some dance. Some don't. Some find music for life; others live in silence. To those who miss the music, the musician gives the same appeal: "Let the man who has ears to hear use them."

A regular time and place.
An open Bible.
An open heart.

Let God have you, and let God love you—and don't be surprised if your heart begins to hear music you've never heard and your feet learn to dance as never before.

*I will be in them and you
will be in me so that they will be
completely one. Then the world will know
that you sent me and that you loved
them just as much as you loved me.*

JOHN 17:23

CHAPTER FIVE

BEING LED BY AN UNSEEN HAND

A God-Intoxicated Heart

It's a wonderful day indeed when we stop working for God and begin working with God. (Go ahead, read the sentence again.)

For years I viewed God as a compassionate CEO and my role as a loyal sales representative. He had his office, and I had my territory. I could contact him as much as I wanted. He was always a phone or fax away. He encouraged me, rallied behind me, and supported me, but he didn't go with me. At least I didn't think he did. Then I read 2 Corinthians 6:1: We are "God's fellow workers" (NIV).

Fellow workers? Colaborers? God and I work together? Imagine the paradigm shift this truth creates. Rather than report to God, we work *with* God. Rather than check in with him and then leave, we check in with him and then follow. We are always in the presence of God. We never leave church. There is never a nonsacred moment! His presence never diminishes. Our awareness of his presence may falter, but the reality of his presence never changes.

This leads me to a great question. If God is perpetually present, is it possible to enjoy unceasing communion with him? In the last chapter we discussed the importance of setting aside daily time to spend with God. Let's take the thought a step further. A giant step further. What if our daily communion never ceased? Would it be possible to live—*minute by minute*—in the presence of God? Is such intimacy even possible? One man who wrestled with these questions wrote:

> Can we have that contact with God all the time? All the time awake, fall asleep in His arms, and awaken in His presence? Can we attain that? Can we do His will all the time? Can we think His thoughts all the time? . . . Can I bring the Lord back in my mind-flow every few seconds so that God shall always be in my mind? I choose to make the rest of my life an experiment in answering this question.[1]

The words are found in the journal of Frank Laubach. Born in the United States in 1884, he was a missionary to the illiterate, teaching them to read so they could know the beauty of the Scriptures. What fascinates me about this man, however, is not his teaching. I'm fascinated by his listening. Dissatisfied with his spiritual life, at the age of forty-five Laubach resolved to live in "continuous inner conversation with God and in perfect responsiveness to His will."[2]

He chronicled this experiment, begun on January 30, 1930, in his journal. Laubach's words have inspired me so much, I've included some key passages here. As you read them, keep in mind that they were not penned by a monk in a monastery but by a busy, dedicated instructor. By the time he died in 1970, Laubach and his techniques of education were known on almost every continent. He was widely respected and widely traveled. The desire of his heart was not recognition, however, but unbroken communion with the Father.

> JANUARY 26, 1930: I am feeling God in each movement, by an act of will—willing that He shall direct these fingers that now strike this typewriter—willing that He shall pour through my steps as I walk.

> MARCH 1, 1930: This sense of being led by an unseen hand which takes mine while another hand reaches ahead and prepares the way, grows upon me daily. . . . sometimes it requires a long time early in the morning. I determine not to get out of bed until that mind set upon the Lord is settled.

> APRIL 18, 1930: I have tasted a thrill in fellowship with God which has made anything discordant with God disgusting. This afternoon the possession of God has caught me up with such sheer joy that I thought I never had known anything like it. God was so close and so amazingly lovely that I felt like melting all over with a strange

blissful contentment. Having had this experience, which comes to me now several times a week, the thrill of filth repels me, for I know its power to drag me from God. And after an hour of close friendship with God my soul feels clean, as new fallen snow.

MAY 14, 1930: Oh, this thing of keeping in constant touch with God, of making Him the object of my thought and the companion of my conversations, is the most amazing thing I ever ran across. It is working. I cannot do it even half of a day—not yet, but I believe I shall be doing it some day for the entire day. It is a matter of acquiring a new habit of thought.

MAY 24, 1930: This concentration upon God is strenuous, but everything else has ceased to be so. I think more clearly, I forget less frequently. Things which I did with a strain before, I now do easily and with no effort whatever. I worry about nothing, and lose no sleep. I walk on air a good part of the time. Even the mirror reveals a new light in my eyes and face. I no longer feel in a hurry about anything. Everything goes right. Each minute I meet calmly as though it were not important. Nothing can go wrong excepting one thing. That is that God may slip from my mind.

JUNE 1, 1930: Ah, God, what a new nearness this brings for Thee and me, to realize that Thou alone canst understand me, for Thou alone knowest all! Thou art no longer a stranger, God! Thou art the only being in the universe who is not partly a stranger! Thou art all the way inside with me—here. . . . I mean to struggle tonight and tomorrow as never before, not once to dismiss thee. For when I lose Thee for an hour I lose. The thing Thou wouldst do can only be done when Thou hast full sway all the time.

Last Monday was the most completely successful day of my life to date, so far as giving my day in complete and continuous surrender to God is concerned. . . . I remember how as I looked at people with a love God gave, they looked back and acted as though they wanted to go with me. I felt then that for a day I saw a little of that marvelous pull that Jesus had as He walked along the road day after day "God-intoxicated" and radiant with the endless communion of His soul with God.[3]

What do you think of Frank Laubach's adventure? How would you answer his questions? *Can we have that contact with God all the time? All the time awake, fall asleep in His arms, and awaken in His presence?* Can we attain *that*?

Is such a goal realistic? Within reach? Or do you think the idea of constant fellowship with God is somewhat fanatical, even extreme? Whatever your opinion of Laubach's adventure, you have to agree with his observation that Jesus enjoyed unbroken communion with God. And if we are to be just like Jesus, you and I will strive to do the same.

GOD'S TRANSLATOR

Jesus' relationship with God went far deeper than a daily appointment. Our Savior was always aware of his father's presence. Listen to his words:

> The Son can do nothing on his own, but only what he sees the Father doing; for whatever the Father does, the Son does likewise. (John 5:19 NRSV)

> I can do nothing on my own. As I hear, I judge. (John 5:30 NRSV)

> I am in the Father and the Father is in me. (John 14:11 NRSV)

Clearly, Jesus didn't act unless he saw his father act. He didn't judge until he heard his father judge. No act or deed occurred without his father's guidance. His words have the ring of a translator.

There were a few occasions in Brazil when I served as a translator for an English speaker. He stood before the audience, complete with the message. I stood at his side, equipped with the language. My job was to convey his story to the listeners. I did my best to allow his words to come through me. I was not at liberty to embellish or subtract. When the speaker gestured, I gestured. As his volume increased, so did mine. When he got quiet, I did, too.

When he walked this earth, Jesus was "translating" God all the time. When God got louder, Jesus got louder. When God gestured, Jesus gestured. He was so in sync with the Father that he could declare, "I am in the Father and the Father is in me" (John 14:11 NRSV). It was as if he heard a voice others were missing.

I witnessed something similar to this on an airplane once. I kept hearing outbursts of laughter. The flight was turbulent and bumpy, hardly a reason for humor. But some fellow behind me was cracking up. No one else, just him. Finally I turned to see what was so funny. He was wearing headphones and apparently listening to a comedian. Because he could hear what I couldn't, he acted differently than I did.

The same was true with Jesus. Because he could hear what others couldn't, he acted differently than they did. Remember when everyone was troubled about the man born blind? Jesus wasn't. Somehow he knew that the blindness would reveal God's power (John 9:3). Remember when everyone was distraught about Lazarus's illness? Jesus wasn't. Rather than hurry to his friend's bedside, he said, "This sickness will not end in death. It is for the glory of God, to bring glory to the son of God" (John 11:4). It was as if Jesus could hear what no one else could. How could a relationship be more intimate? Jesus had unbroken communion with his father.

Do you suppose the Father desires the same for us? Absolutely. Paul says we have been "predestined to be conformed to the image of his Son" (Rom. 8:29 NRSV). Let me remind you: God loves you just the way you are, but he refuses to leave you that way. He wants you to be just like Jesus. God desires the same abiding intimacy with you that he had with his son.

PICTURES OF INTIMACY

God draws several pictures to describe the relationship he envisions. One is of a vine and a branch.

> I am the vine, and you are the branches. If any remain in me and I remain in them, they produce much fruit. But without me they can do nothing. . . . If you remain in me and follow my teachings, you can ask anything you want, and it will be given to you. (John 15:5,7)

God wants to be as close to us as a branch is to a vine. One is an extension of the other. It's impossible to tell where one starts and the other ends. The branch isn't connected only at the moment of bearing fruit. The gardener doesn't keep the branches in a box and then, on the day he wants grapes, glue them to the vine. No, the branch constantly draws nutrition from the vine. Separation means certain death.

God also uses the temple to depict the intimacy he desires. "Don't you know," Paul writes, "that your body is the temple of the Holy Spirit, who lives in you and was given to you by God?" (1 Cor. 6:19 TEV). Think with me about the temple for a moment. Was God a visitor or a resident in Solomon's temple? Would you describe his presence as occasional or permanent? You know the answer. God didn't come and go, appear and disappear. He was a permanent presence, always available.

What incredibly good news for us! We are NEVER away from God! He is NEVER away from us—not even for a moment! God doesn't come to us on Sunday mornings and then exit on Sunday afternoons. He remains within us, continually present in our lives.

The biblical analogy of marriage is the third picture of this encouraging truth. Aren't we the bride of Christ (Rev. 21:2)? Aren't we united with him (Rom. 6:5 RSV)? Haven't we made vows to him, and hasn't he made vows to us?

What does our marriage to Jesus imply about his desire to commune with us? For one thing, the communication never stops. In a happy home the husband doesn't talk to the wife only when he wants something from her. He doesn't pop in just when he wants a good meal or a clean shirt or a little romance. If he does, the home is not a home—it's a brothel that serves food and cleans clothes.

Healthy marriages have a sense of "remaining." The husband remains in the wife, and she remains in him. There is a tenderness, an honesty, an ongoing communication. The same is true in our relationship with God. Sometimes we go to him with our joys, and sometimes we go with our hurts, but we always go. And as we go, the more we go, the more we become like him. Paul says we are being changed from "glory to glory" (2 Cor. 3:18 KJV).

People who live long lives together eventually begin to sound alike, to talk alike, even to think alike. As we walk with God, we take on his thoughts, his principles, his attitudes. We take on his heart.

And just as in marriage, communion with God is no burden. Indeed, it is a delight. "How lovely is your dwelling place, O LORD Almighty! My soul yearns, even faints, for the courts of the LORD; my heart and my flesh cry out for the living God" (Ps. 84:1–2 NIV). The level of communication is so sweet nothing compares with it. Laubach wrote:

> It is my business to look into the very face of God until I ache with bliss. . . . Now I like the Lord's presence so much that when for a half hour or so He slips out of mind—as He does many times a day—I feel as though I had deserted Him, and as though I had lost something very precious in my life. (March 3, 1931; May 14, 1930)[4]

Can we consider one last analogy from the Bible? How about the sheep with the shepherd? Many times Scripture calls us the flock of God. "We are his people, the sheep he tends" (Ps. 100:3). We needn't know much about sheep to know that the shepherd never leaves the flock. If we see a flock coming down the path, we know a shepherd is nearby. If we see a Christian ahead, we can know the same. The Good Shepherd never leaves his sheep. "Even though I walk through a very dark valley, I will not be afraid, because you are with me" (Ps. 23:4).

God is as near to you as the vine is to the branch, as present within you as God was in the temple, as intimate with you as a husband with a wife, and as devoted to you as a shepherd to his sheep.

God desires to be as close to you as he was to Christ—
so close that he can literally speak through you and
all you need do is translate;

so close that tuning in to him is like putting on headphones;
>   so close that when others sense the storm and worry,
>   you hear his voice and smile.

Here is how King David described this most intimate of all relationships:

> I'm an open book to you;
>   even from a distance, you know what I'm thinking.
> You know when I leave and when I get back;
>   I'm never out of your sight.
> You know everything I'm going to say
>   before I start the first sentence.
> I look behind me and you're there,
>   then up ahead and you're there, too—
>   your reassuring presence, coming and going.
> This is too much, too wonderful—
>   I can't take it all in! (Ps. 139:1–6 MSG)

David wasn't the only Bible writer to testify to the possibility of a constant sense of God's presence. Consider these staccato statements from the pen of Paul that urge us never to leave the side of our Lord.

> Pray without ceasing. (1 Thess. 5:17 KJV)

> Be constant in prayer. (Rom. 12:12 RSV)

> Pray in the Spirit at all times. (Eph. 6:18)

Continue steadfastly in prayer. (Col. 4:2 RSV)

In everything . . . let your requests be made known to God. (Phil. 4:6 NASB)

Does unceasing communion seem daunting, complicated? Are you thinking, *Life is difficult enough. Why add this?* If so, remind yourself that God is the burden-remover, not the burden-giver. God intends that unceasing prayer lighten— not heighten—our load.

The more we search the Bible, the more we realize that unbroken communion with God is the intent and not the exception. Within the reach of *every* Christian is the unending presence of God.

PRACTICING THE PRESENCE

How, then, do I live in God's presence? How do I detect his unseen hand on my shoulder and his inaudible voice in my ear? A sheep grows familiar with the voice of the shepherd. How can you and I grow familiar with the voice of God? Here are a few ideas:

Give God your waking thoughts. Before you face the day, face the Father. Before you step out of bed, step into his presence. I have a friend who makes it a habit to roll out of his bed onto his knees and begin his day in prayer. Personally, I don't get that far. With my head still on the pillow and my eyes still closed, I offer God the first seconds of my day. The prayer is not lengthy and far from formal. Depending on how much sleep I got, it may not even be intelligible. Often it's nothing more than "Thank you for a night's rest. I belong to you today."

C. S. Lewis wrote: "The moment you wake up each morning . . . [all] your wishes and hopes for the day rush at you like wild animals. And the first job of each morning consists in shoving them all back; in listening to that other voice, taking that other point of view, letting that other, larger, stronger, quieter life come flowing in."[5]

Here is how the psalmist began his day: "Every morning, I tell you what I need, and I wait for your answer" (Ps. 5:3). Which leads to the second idea:

Give God your waiting thoughts. Spend time with him in silence. The mature married couple has learned the treasure of shared silence; they don't need to fill the air with constant chatter. Just being together is sufficient. Try being silent with God. "Be still, and know that I am God" (Ps. 46:10 NIV). Awareness of God is a fruit of stillness before God.

Dan Rather once asked Mother Teresa. "What do you say to God when you pray?"

Mother Teresa answered quietly, "I listen."

Taken aback, Rather tried again, "Well, then, what does God say?"

Mother Teresa smiled, "He listens."[6]

Give God your whispering thoughts. Through the centuries Christians have learned the value of brief sentence prayers, prayers that can be whispered anywhere, in any setting. Laubach sought unbroken communion with God by asking him questions. Every two or three minutes he would pray, "Am I in your will, Lord?" "Am I pleasing you, Lord?"

In the nineteenth century an anonymous Russian monk set out to live in unceasing communion with God. In a book entitled *The Way of the Pilgrim,* he tells of how he learned to have one prayer constantly in his mind: "Lord Jesus Christ, Son of God, have mercy on me, a sinner." With time, the prayer became so internalized that he was constantly praying it, even while consciously occupied with something else.

Imagine considering every moment as a potential time of communion with God. By the time your life is over, you will have spent six months at stoplights, eight months opening junk mail, a year and a half looking for lost stuff (double that number in my case), and a whopping five years standing in various lines.[7] Why don't you give these moments to God? By giving God your whispering thoughts, the common becomes uncommon. Simple phrases such as "Thank you, Father," "Be sovereign in this hour, O Lord," "You are my resting place, Jesus" can turn a commute into a pilgrimage. You needn't leave your office or kneel in your kitchen. Just pray where you are. Let the kitchen become a cathedral or the classroom a chapel. Give God your whispering thoughts.

And last, *give God your waning thoughts.* At the end of the day, let your mind settle on him. Conclude the day as you began it: talking to God. Thank him for the good parts. Question him about the hard parts. Seek his mercy. Seek his strength. And as you close your eyes, take assurance in the promise: "He who watches over Israel will neither slumber nor sleep" (Ps. 121:4 NIV). If you fall asleep as you pray, don't worry. What better place to doze off than in the arms of your Father.

Our faces, then, are not covered.
We all show the Lord's glory, and we are
being changed to be like him. This change
in us brings ever greater glory, which
comes from the Lord, who is the Spirit.

2 CORINTHIANS 3:18

Sunlight poured from his face.

MATTHEW 17:2 MSG

CHAPTER SIX

A CHANGED FACE AND A SET OF WINGS

A Worship-Hungry Heart

People on a plane and people on a pew have a lot in common. All are on a journey. Most are well-behaved and presentable. Some doze, and others gaze out the window. Most, if not all, are satisfied with a predictable experience. For many, the mark of a good flight and the mark of a good worship assembly are the same. "Nice," we like to say. "It was a nice flight/It was a nice worship service." We exit the same way we enter, and we're happy to return next time.

A few, however, are not content with nice. They long for something more. The boy who just passed me did. I heard him before I saw him. I was already in my seat when he asked, "Will they really let me meet the pilot?" He was either lucky or shrewd because he made the request just as he entered the plane. The question floated into the cockpit, causing the pilot to lean out.

"Someone looking for me?" he asked.

The boy's hand shot up like he was answering his second-grade teacher's question. "I am!"

"Well, come on in."

With a nod from his mom, the youngster entered the cockpit's world of controls and gauges and emerged minutes later with eyes wide. "Wow!" he exclaimed. "I'm so glad to be on this plane!"

No one else's face showed such wonder. I should know. I paid attention. The boy's interest piqued mine, so I studied the faces of the other passengers but found no such enthusiasm. I mostly saw contentment: travelers content to be on the plane, content to be closer to their destination, content to be out of the airport, content to sit and stare and say little.

There were a few exceptions. The five or so mid-age women wearing straw hats and carrying beachbags weren't content; they were exuberant. They giggled all the way down the aisle. My bet is they were moms-set-free-from-kitchens-and-kids. The fellow in the blue suit across the aisle wasn't content; he was cranky. He opened his laptop and scowled at its screen the entire trip. Most of us, however, were happier than he and more contained than the ladies. Most of us were content. Content with a predictable, uneventful flight. Content with a "nice" flight.

And since that is what we sought, that is what we got. The boy, on the other hand, wanted more. He wanted to see the pilot. If asked to describe the flight, he wouldn't say "nice." He'd likely produce the plastic wings the pilot gave him and say, "I saw the man up front."

Do you see why I say that people on a plane and people on

a pew have a lot in common? Enter a church sanctuary and look at the faces. A few are giggly, a couple are cranky, but by and large we are content. Content to be there. Content to sit and look straight ahead and leave when the service is over. Content to enjoy an assembly with no surprises or turbulence. Content with a "nice" service. "Seek and you will find," Jesus promised.[1] And since a nice service is what we seek, a nice service is usually what we find.

A few, however, seek more. A few come with the childlike enthusiasm of the boy. And those few leave as he did, wide-eyed with the wonder of having stood in the presence of the pilot himself.

COME ASKING

The same thing happened to Jesus. The day Jesus went to worship, his very face was changed.

"You're telling me that Jesus went to worship?"

I am. The Bible speaks of a day when Jesus took time to stand with friends in the presence of God. Let's read about the day Jesus went to worship:

> Six days later, Jesus took Peter, James, and John, the brother of James, up on a high mountain by themselves. While they watched, Jesus' appearance was changed; his face became bright like the sun, and his clothes became white as light. Then Moses and Elijah appeared to them, talking with Jesus.

Peter said to Jesus, "Lord, it is good that we are here. If you want, I will put up three tents here—one for you, one for Moses, and one for Elijah."

While Peter was talking, a bright cloud covered them. A voice came from the cloud and said, "This is my Son, whom I love, and I am very pleased with him. Listen to him!" (Matt. 17:1–5)

The words of Matthew presuppose a decision on the part of Jesus to stand in the presence of God. The simple fact that he chose his companions and went up on a mountain suggests this was no spur-of-the-moment action. He didn't awaken one morning, look at the calendar and then at his watch, and say, "Oops, today is the day we go to the mountain." No, he had preparations to make. Ministry to people was suspended so ministry to his heart could occur. Since his chosen place of worship was some distance away, he had to select the right path and stay on the right road. By the time he was on the mountain, his heart was ready. Jesus prepared for worship.

Let me ask you, do you do the same? Do you prepare for worship? What paths do you take to lead you up the mountain? The question may seem foreign, but my hunch is, many of us simply wake up and show up. We're sadly casual when it comes to meeting God.

Would we be so lackadaisical with, oh, let's say, the president? Suppose you were granted a Sunday morning breakfast at the White House? How would you spend Saturday night? Would you get ready? Would you collect your thoughts? Would you think about your questions and requests? Of course you would. Should we prepare any less for an encounter with the Holy God?

Let me urge you to come to worship prepared to worship. Pray before you come so you will be ready to pray when you arrive. Sleep before you come so you'll stay alert when you arrive. Read the Word before you come so your heart will be soft when you worship. Come hungry. Come willing. Come expecting God to speak. Come asking, even as you walk through the door, "Can I see the pilot today?"

REFLECTING HIS GLORY

As you do, you'll discover the purpose of worship—to change the face of the worshiper. This is exactly what happened to Christ on the mountain. Jesus' appearance was changed: "His face became bright like the sun" (Matt. 17:2).

The connection between the face and worship is more than coincidental. Our face is the most public part of our bodies, covered less than any other area. It is also the most recognizable part of our bodies. We don't fill a school annual with photos of people's feet but rather with photos of faces. God desires to take our faces, this exposed and memorable part of our bodies, and use them to reflect his goodness. Paul writes: "Our faces, then, are not covered. We all show the Lord's glory, and we are being changed to be like him. This change in us brings ever greater glory, which comes from the Lord, who is the Spirit" (2 Cor. 3:18).

God invites us to see his face so he can change ours. He uses our uncovered faces to display his glory. The transformation isn't easy. The sculptor of Mount Rushmore faced a lesser challenge than does God. But our Lord is up to the task. He loves to change the faces of his children. By his fingers, wrinkles of worry are rubbed away. Shadows of shame and doubt become portraits of grace and trust. He relaxes clenched jaws and smoothes furrowed brows. His touch can remove the bags of exhaustion from beneath the eyes and turn tears of despair into tears of peace.

How? Through worship.

We'd expect something more complicated, more demanding. A forty-day fast or the memorization of Leviticus perhaps. No. God's plan is simpler. He changes our faces through worship.

Exactly what is worship? I like King David's definition. "Oh magnify the LORD with me, and let us exalt His name together" (Ps. 34:3 NASB). Worship is the act of magnifying God. Enlarging our vision of him. Stepping into the cockpit to see where he sits and observe how he works. Of course, his size doesn't change, but our perception of him does. As we draw nearer, he seems larger. Isn't that what we need? A *big* view of God? Don't we have *big* problems, *big* worries, *big* questions? Of course we do. Hence we need a big view of God.

Worship offers that. How can we sing, "Holy, Holy, Holy" and not have our vision expanded? Or what about the lines from "It Is Well with My Soul"?

> My sin—O the bliss of this glorious thought,
> My sin—not in part but the whole,
> Is nailed to the cross and I bear it no more,
> Praise the Lord, praise the Lord, O my soul![2]

Can we sing those words and not have our countenance illuminated?

A vibrant, shining face is the mark of one who has stood in God's presence. After speaking to God, Moses had to cover his face with a veil (Exod. 34:33–35). After seeing heaven, Stephen's face glowed like that of an angel (Acts 6:15; 7:55–56).

God is in the business of changing the face of the world.

Let me be very clear. This change is his job, not ours. Our goal is not to make our faces radiant. Not even Jesus did that. Matthew says, "Jesus' appearance was changed" not "Jesus changed his appearance." Moses didn't even know his face was shining (Exod. 34:29). Our goal is not to conjure up some fake, frozen expression. Our goal is simply to stand before God with a prepared and willing heart and then let God do his work.

And he does. He wipes away the tears. He mops away the perspiration. He softens our furrowed brows. He touches our cheeks. He changes our faces as we worship.

But there's more. Not only does God change the face of those who worship, he changes those who watch us worship.

EVANGELISTIC WORSHIP

Remember the boy who went to see the pilot? His passion stirred me. I wanted to see the pilot, too. (And I wouldn't have refused the plastic wings.)

The same dynamic occurs when we come to worship with a heart of worship. Paul told the Corinthian church to worship in such a clear way that if an unbeliever entered, "he would find

. . . the secrets of his heart revealed; and . . . would fall down on his face and worship God, declaring that God is indeed among you" (1 Cor. 14:24–25 TJB).

David cites the evangelistic power of honest worship: "He put a new song in my mouth, a song of praise to our God. Many people will see this and worship him. Then they will trust the LORD" (Ps. 40:3).

Your heartfelt worship is a missionary appeal. Let unbelievers hear the passion of your voice or see the sincerity in your face, and they may be changed. Peter was. When Peter saw the worship of Jesus, he said, "Lord, it is good that we are here. If you want, I will put up three tents here—one for you, one for Moses, and one for Elijah" (Matt. 17:4).

Mark says Peter spoke out of fear (9:6). Luke says Peter spoke out of ignorance (9:33). But whatever the reason, at least Peter spoke. He wanted to do something for God. He didn't understand that God wants hearts and not tents, but at least he was moved to give something.

Why? Because he saw the transfigured face of Christ. The same happens in churches today. When people see us giving heartfelt praise to God—when they hear our worship—they are intrigued. They want to see the pilot! Sparks from our fire tend to ignite dry hearts.

I experienced something similar in Brazil. Our house was only blocks away from the largest soccer stadium in the world. At least once a week Maracana stadium would be packed with screaming soccer fans. Initially I was not numbered among them, but their enthusiasm was contagious. I wanted to see what they were so excited about. By the time I left Rio, I was a soccer convert and could shout with the rest of them.

Seekers may not understand all that happens in a house of worship. They may not understand the meaning of a song or the significance of the communion, but they know joy when they see it. And when they see your face changed, they may want to see God's face.

By the way, wouldn't the opposite be equally true? What happens when a seeker sees boredom on your face? Others are worshiping and you are scowling? Others are in his presence, but you are in your own little world? Others are seeking God's face while you are seeking the face of your wristwatch?

As long as I'm getting personal, may I come a step closer? Parents, what are your children learning from your worship? Do they see the same excitement as when you go to a basketball game? Do they see you prepare for worship as you do for a vacation? Do they see you hungry to arrive, seeking the face of the Father? Or do they see you content to leave the way you came?

They are watching. Believe me. They are watching.

Do you come to church with a worship-hungry heart? Our Savior did.

May I urge you to be just like Jesus? Prepare your heart for worship. Let God change your face through worship. Demonstrate the power of worship. Above all, seek the face of the pilot. The boy did. Because he sought the pilot, he left with a changed face and a set of wings. The same can happen to you.

I ask—ask the God of our Master,
Jesus Christ, the God of glory—to make
you intelligent and discerning in knowing
him personally, your eyes focused and clear,
so that you can see exactly what it is
he is calling you to do.

EPHESIANS 1:17–18 MSG

CHAPTER SEVEN

GOLF GAMES
AND CELERY STICKS

A Focused Heart

The golf game was tied with four holes to go. As we stood on the tee box, I spotted the next green. "Sure seems like a long way off," I commented. No one spoke. "Sure is a narrow fairway," I said as I teed up my ball. Again, no response. "How do they expect us to hit over those trees?" Still no answer.

The silence didn't disturb me. Years of ruthless competition against fellow ministers on municipal courses has taught me to be wary of their tricks. I knew exactly what they were doing. Intimidated by my impressive streak of bogeys, they resolved to psych me out (after all, we were playing for a soda). So I stepped up to the ball and took a swing. There is no other way to describe what happened next—*I hit a great drive.* A high arching fade over the crop of trees to my left. I could hear the other guys groan. I assumed they were jealous. After watching their drives, I knew they were. None of them even made it close to the trees. Rather than hit left, they each hit right and ended up miles from the green. That's when I should have suspected something, but I didn't.

They walked down their side of the fairway, and I walked down mine. But rather than find my ball sitting up on thick fairway grass, I discovered it hidden in weeds and rocks and surrounded by trees. "This *is* a tough hole," I muttered to myself. Nevertheless, I was up for the challenge. I studied the shot and selected a strategy, took out a club, and—forgive me but I must say it again—*I hit a great shot.* You would have thought my ball was radar controlled: narrowly missing one branch, sweeping around another, heading toward the green like a jackrabbit dashing for supper. Only the steep hill kept it from rolling onto the putting surface.

I'd learned from televised tournaments how to act in such moments. I froze my follow-through just long enough for the photographers to take their pictures, then I gave my club a twirl. With one hand I waved to the crowd, with the other I handed my club to my caddie. Of course, in my case there was no photographer or caddie, and there was no crowd. Not even my buddies were watching. They were all on the other side of the fairway, looking in the other direction. A bit miffed that my skill had gone unnoticed, I shouldered my clubs and started walking to the green.

Again, it should have occurred to me that something was wrong. The tally of curious events should've gotten my attention. No one commenting on the difficulty of the hole. No one complimenting my drive. Everyone else hitting to the right while I hit to the left. A perfect drive landing in the rough. My splendid approach shot, unseen. It should have occurred to me, but it didn't. Only as I neared the green did anything seem unusual. Some players were already putting! Players I didn't know. Players whom I'd never seen before. Players who, I assumed, were either horribly slow or lost. I looked around for my group only to find them also on the green—on a *different* green.

That's when it hit me. I'd played the wrong hole! I had picked out the wrong target. I had thought we were playing to the green on the left when we were supposed to play to the green on the right! All of a sudden everything made sense. My buddies hit to the right because they were supposed to. The groan I heard after my drive was one of pity, not admiration. No wonder the hole seemed hard—I was playing in the wrong direction. How discouraging. Golf is tough enough as it is. It's even tougher when you're headed the wrong way.

THE HEART ON TARGET

The same can be said about life. Life is tough enough as it is. It's even tougher when we're headed in the wrong direction.

One of the incredible abilities of Jesus was to stay on target. His life never got off track. Not once do we find him walking down the wrong side of the fairway. He had no money, no computers, no jets, no administrative assistants or staff; yet Jesus did what many of us fail to do. He kept his life on course.

As Jesus looked across the horizon of his future, he could see many targets. Many flags were flapping in the wind, each of which he could have pursued. He could have been a political revolutionary. He could have been a national leader. He could have been content to be a teacher and educate minds or to be a physician and heal bodies. But in the end he chose to be a Savior and save souls.

Anyone near Christ for any length of time heard it from Jesus himself. "The Son of Man came to find lost people and save them" (Luke 19:10). "The Son of Man did not come to be served. He came to serve others and to give his life as a ransom for many people" (Mark 10:45).

The heart of Christ was relentlessly focused on one task. The day he left the carpentry shop of Nazareth he had one ultimate aim—the cross of Calvary. He was so focused that his final words were, "It is finished" (John 19:30).

How could Jesus say he was finished? There were still the hungry to feed, the sick to heal, the untaught to instruct, and the unloved to love. How could he say he was finished? Simple. He had completed his designated task. His commission was fulfilled. The painter could set aside his brush, the sculptor lay down his chisel, the writer put away his pen. The job was done.

Wouldn't you love to be able to say the same? Wouldn't you love to look back on your life and know you had done what you were called to do?

DISTRACTED HEARTS

Our lives tend to be so scattered. Intrigued by one trend only until the next comes along. Suckers for the latest craze or quick fix. This project, then another. Lives with no strategy, no goal, no defining priority. Playing the holes out of order. Erratic. Hesitant. Living life with the hiccups. We are easily distracted by the small things and forget the big things. I saw an example of this the other day in the grocery store.

There is one section in the supermarket where I am a seasoned veteran: the sample section. I'm never one to pass up a snack. Last Saturday I went to the back of the store where the samplers tend to linger. Bingo! There were two sample givers awaiting hungry sample takers. One had a skillet of sausage and the other a plate full of cream-cheese-covered celery. You'll be proud to know I opted for the celery. I wanted the sausage, but I knew the celery was better for me.

Unfortunately, the celery lady never saw me. She was too busy straightening her sticks. I walked past her, and she never looked up. The sausage lady, however, saw me coming and extended the plate. I declined and made another circle past the celery lady. Same response. She never saw me. She was too busy getting her plate in order. So I made another loop past the sausage lady. Once again the offer came, and once again—with admirable resolve, I might add—I resisted. I was committed to doing the right thing.

So was the celery lady. She was determined to get every celery stick just so on her plate. But she cared more about the appearance of her product than the distribution. I stopped. I coughed. I cleared my throat. I did everything but sing a song. Still no response. The sausage lady, however, was waiting on me with sizzling sausage. I gave in; I ate the sausage.

The celery lady made the same mistake I had made on the golf course. She got off target. She was so occupied with the small matters (i.e., celery organization) that she forget her assignment (i.e., to help needy, hungry, pitiful shoppers like me).

How do we keep from making the same mistake in life? God wants us to be just like Jesus and have focused hearts. How do I select the right flag and stay on target? Consulting the map would be a good start. I would have saved myself a lot of hassle that day had I taken enough time to look at the map on the scorecard. The course architect had drawn one. What's true on the golf course is true in life as well. The one who designed our course left us directions. By answering four simple questions, we can be more like Jesus; we can stay on course with our lives.

AM I FITTING INTO GOD'S PLAN?

Romans 8:28 says, "We know that all that happens to us is working for our good if we love God and are fitting into his plans" (TLB). The first step for focusing your heart is to ask this question: Am I fitting into God's plan?

God's plan is to save his children. "He does not want anyone to be destroyed but wants all to turn away from their sins" (2 Pet. 3:9 TEV).

If God's goal is the salvation of the world, then my goal should be the same. The details will differ from person to person, but the big picture is identical for all of us. "We're Christ's representatives. God uses us to persuade men and women" (2 Cor. 5:20 MSG). Regardless of what you don't know about

your future, one thing is certain: you are intended to contribute to the good plan of God, to tell others about the God
who loves them and longs to bring them home.

But exactly how are you to contribute? What is your specific
assignment? Let's seek the answer with a second question.

WHAT ARE MY LONGINGS?

This question may surprise you. Perhaps you thought your
longings had nothing to do with keeping your life on track. I
couldn't disagree more. Your heart is crucial. Psalm 37:4 says,
"Enjoy serving the LORD, and he will give you what you want."
When we submit to God's plans, we can trust our desires. Our
assignment is found at the intersection of God's plan and our
pleasures. *What do you love to do? What brings you joy? What gives
you a sense of satisfaction?*

Some long to feed the poor. Others enjoy leading the
church. Others relish singing or teaching or holding the hands
of the sick or counseling the confused. Each of us has been
made to serve God in a unique way.

"We are God's workmanship, created in Christ Jesus to do
good works, which God prepared in advance for us to do"
(Eph. 2:10 NIV).

"You made all the delicate, inner parts of my body, and knit
them together in my mother's womb. . . . Your workmanship is
marvelous. . . . You were there while I was being formed. . . .
You saw me before I was born and scheduled each day of my life
before I began to breathe" (Ps. 139:13–16 TLB).

You are a custom design; you are tailor-made. God prescribed your birth. Regardless of the circumstances that surrounded your arrival, you are not an accident. God planned you before you were born.

The longings of your heart, then, are not incidental; they are critical messages. The desires of your heart are not to be ignored; they are to be consulted. As the wind turns the weather vane, so God uses your passions to turn your life. God is too gracious to ask you to do something you hate.

Be careful, however. Don't consider your desires without considering your skills. Move quickly to the third question.

WHAT ARE MY ABILITIES?

There are some things we want to do but simply aren't equipped to accomplish. I, for example, have the desire to sing. Singing for others would give me wonderful satisfaction. The problem is, it wouldn't give the same satisfaction to my audience. I am what you might call a prison singer—I never have the key, and I'm always behind a few bars.

Paul gives good advice in Romans 12:3: "Have a sane estimate of your capabilities" (PHILLIPS).

In other words, be aware of your strengths. When you teach, do people listen? When you lead, do people follow? When you administer, do things improve? Where are you most productive? Identify your strengths, and then—this is important—major in them. Take a few irons out of the fire so this one can get hot. Failing to focus on our strengths may prevent us from accomplishing the unique tasks God has called us to do.

A lighthouse keeper who worked on a rocky stretch of coastline received oil once a month to keep his light burning. Not being far from a village, he had frequent guests. One night a woman needed oil to keep her family warm. Another night a father needed oil for his lamp. Then another needed oil to lubricate a wheel. All the requests seemed legitimate, so the lighthouse keeper tried to meet them all. Toward the end of the month, however, he ran out of oil, and his lighthouse went dark, causing several ships to crash on the coastline. The man was reproved by his superiors, "You were given the oil for one reason," they said, "to keep the light burning."[1]

We cannot meet every need in the world. We cannot please every person in the world. We cannot satisfy every request in the world. But some of us try. And in the end, we run out of fuel. Have a sane estimate of your abilities and stick to them.

One final question is needed.

AM I SERVING GOD NOW?

Upon reading this, you may start feeling restless. *Maybe I need to change jobs. Perhaps I should relocate. I guess Max is telling me I need to go to seminary* . . . No, not necessarily.

Again, Jesus is the ideal example. When do we get our first clue that he knows he is the Son of God? In the temple of Jerusalem. He is twelve years old. His parents are three days into the return trip to Nazareth before they notice he is missing.

They find him in the temple studying with the leaders. When they ask him for an explanation, he says, "Did you not know that I must be about My Father's business" (Luke 2:49 NKJV).

As a young boy, Jesus already senses the call of God. But what does he do next? Recruit apostles and preach sermons and perform miracles? No, he goes home to his folks and learns the family business.

That is exactly what you should do. Want to bring focus to your life? Do what Jesus did. Go home, love your family, and take care of business. *But Max, I want to be a missionary.* Your first mission field is under your roof. What makes you think they'll believe you overseas if they don't believe you across the hall?

But Max, I'm ready to do great things for God. Good, do them at work. Be a good employee. Show up on time with a good attitude. Don't complain or grumble, but "work as if you were doing it for the Lord, not for people" (Col. 3:23).

THE P.L.A.N.

Pretty simple plan, don't you think? It's even easy to remember. Perhaps you caught the acrostic:

> Am I fitting into God's **P**lan?
> What are my **L**ongings?
> What are my **A**bilities?
> Am I serving God **N**ow?

Why don't you take a few moments and evaluate your direction? Ask yourself the four questions. You may find that you are doing what I did: hitting some good shots but in the wrong direction. In my case it cost me three sodas. I lost so many strokes I never caught up.

The same needn't be said about you, however. God allows you to start fresh at any point in life. "From now on, then, you must live the rest of your earthly lives controlled by God's will and not by human desires" (1 Pet. 4:2 TEV).

Circle the words *from now on*. God will give you a fresh scorecard. Regardless of what has controlled you in the past, it's never too late to get your life on course and be a part of God's P.L.A.N.

So from now on,
there must be no more lies.
Speak the truth to one another.

EPHESIANS 4:25 TJB

CHAPTER EIGHT

NOTHING BUT THE TRUTH

An Honest Heart

A woman stands before judge and jury, places one hand on the Bible and the other in the air, and makes a pledge. For the next few minutes, with God as her helper, she will "tell the truth, the whole truth, and nothing but the truth."

She is a witness. Her job is not to expand upon nor dilute the truth. Her job is to tell the truth. Leave it to the legal counsel to interpret. Leave it to the jury to resolve. Leave it to the judge to apply. But the witness? The witness speaks the truth. Let her do more or less and she taints the outcome. But let her do that—let her tell the truth—and justice has a chance.

The Christian, too, is a witness. We, too, make a pledge. Like the witness in court, we are called to tell the truth. The bench may be absent and the judge unseen, but the Bible is present, the watching world is the jury, and we are the primary witnesses. We are subpoenaed by no less than Jesus himself: "You will be my *witnesses*—in Jerusalem, in all of Judea, in Samaria, and in every part of the world" (Acts 1:8, italics mine).

We are witnesses. And like witnesses in a court, we are called to testify, to tell what we have seen and heard. And we are to speak truthfully. Our task is not to whitewash nor bloat the truth. Our task is to tell the truth. Period.

There is, however, one difference between the witness in court and the witness for Christ. The witness in court eventually steps down from the witness chair, but the witness for Christ never does. Since the claims of Christ are always on trial, court is perpetually in session, and we remain under oath. For the Christian, deception is never an option. It wasn't an option for Jesus.

WHAT GOD CAN'T DO

One of the most astounding assessments of Christ is this summary: "He had done nothing wrong, and he had never lied" (Isa. 53:9). Jesus was staunchly honest. His every word accurate, his every sentence true. No cheating on tests. No altering the accounts. Not once did Jesus stretch the truth. Not once did he shade the truth. Not once did he avoid the truth. He simply told the truth. No deceit was found in his mouth.

And if God has his way with us, none will be found in ours. He longs for us to be just like Jesus. His plan, if you remember, is to shape us along the lines of his Son (Rom. 8:28). He seeks not to decrease or minimize our deception but to eliminate our deception. God is blunt about dishonesty: "No one who is dishonest will live in my house" (Ps. 101:7).

Our Master has a strict honor code. From Genesis to Revelation, the theme is the same: God loves the truth and hates deceit. In 1 Corinthians 6:9–10 Paul lists the type of people who will not inherit the kingdom of God. The covey he portrays is a ragged assortment of those who sin sexually, worship idols, take part in adultery, sell their bodies, get drunk, rob people, and—there it is—*lie about others.*

Such rigor may surprise you. *You mean my fibbing and flattering stir the same heavenly anger as adultery and aggravated assault?* Apparently so. God views fudging on income tax the same way he views kneeling before idols.

> The LORD hates those who tell lies but is pleased with those who keep their promises. (Prov. 12:22)
>
> The LORD hates . . . a lying tongue. (Prov. 6:16–17)
>
> [God] destroys liars . . . [and] hates those who kill and trick others. (Ps. 5:6)

Why? Why the hard line? Why the tough stance?

For one reason: dishonesty is absolutely contrary to the character of God. According to Hebrews 6:18, *it is impossible for God to lie.* It's not that God will not lie or that he has chosen not to lie—*he cannot lie.* For God to lie is for a dog to fly and a bird to bark. It simply cannot happen. The Book of Titus echoes the same three words as the Book of Hebrews: "God cannot lie" (Titus 1:2).

God always speaks truth. When he makes a covenant, he keeps it. When he makes a statement, he means it. And when he proclaims the truth, we can believe it. What he says is true. Even "if we are not faithful, [God] will still be faithful, because he cannot be false to himself" (2 Tim. 2:13).

Satan, on the other hand, finds it impossible to tell the truth. According to Jesus, the devil is "the father of lies" (John 8:44). If you'll remember, deceit was the first tool out of the devil's bag. In the Garden of Eden, Satan didn't discourage Eve. He didn't seduce her. He didn't sneak up on her. He just lied to her. "God says you'll die if you eat the fruit? You will not die" (see Gen. 3:1–4).

BIG FAT LIAR. But Eve was suckered, and the fruit was plucked, and it's not more than a few paragraphs before husband and son are following suit and the honesty of Eden seems a distant memory.

It still does. Daniel Webster was right when he observed, "There is nothing as powerful as the truth and often nothing as strange."

THE WAGES OF DECEIT

According to a *Psychology Today* survey, the devil is still spinning webs, and we are still plucking fruit.

- More people say they have cheated on their marriage partners than on their tax returns or expense accounts.

- More than half say that if their tax returns were audited, they would probably owe the government money.

- About one out of three people admits to deceiving a best friend about something within the last year; 96 percent of them feel guilty about it.

- Nearly half predict that if they scratched another car in the parking lot, they would drive away without leaving a note—although the vast majority (89 percent) agree that would be immoral.[1]

Perhaps the question shouldn't be "Why does God demand such honesty?" but rather "Why do we tolerate such dishonesty?" Never was Jeremiah more the prophet than when he announced: "The heart is deceitful above all things" (Jer. 17:9 NIV). How do we explain our dishonesty? What's the reason for our forked tongues and greasy promises? We don't need a survey to find the answer.

For one thing, we don't like the truth. Most of us can sympathize with the fellow who received a call from his wife just as she was about to fly home from Europe. "How's my cat?" she asked.

"Dead."

"Oh, honey, don't be so honest. Why didn't you break the news to me slowly? You've ruined my trip."

"What do you mean?"

"You could have told me he was on the roof. And when I called you from Paris, you could have told me he was acting sluggish. Then when I called from London, you could have said he was sick, and when I called you from New York, you could have said he was at the vet. Then, when I arrived home, you could have said he was dead."

The husband had never been exposed to such protocol but was willing to learn. "OK," he said. "I'll do better next time."

"By the way," she asked, "how's Mom?"

There was a long silence, then he replied, "Uh, she's on the roof."

The plain fact is we don't like the truth. Our credo is *You shall know the truth, and the truth shall make you squirm.* Our dislike for the truth began at the age of three when mom walked into our rooms and asked, "Did you hit your little brother?" We knew then and there that honesty had its consequences. So we learned to, uhhh, well, it's not *really* lying . . . we learned to cover things up.

"Did I hit baby brother? That all depends on how you interpret the word *hit*. I mean, sure I made contact with him, but would a jury consider it a 'hit'? Everything is relative, you know."

"Did I hit baby brother? Yes, Dad, I did. But it's not my fault. Had I been born with nonaggressive chromosomes, and had you not permitted me to watch television, it never would have happened. So, you can say I hit my brother, but the fault isn't mine. I'm a victim of nurture and nature."

The truth, we learn early, is not fun. We don't like the truth.

Not only do we not like the truth, *we don't trust the truth*. If we are brutally honest (which is advisable in a discussion on honesty), we'd have to admit that the truth seems inadequate to do what we need done.

We want our bosses to like us, so we flatter. We call it polishing the apple. God calls it a lie.

We want people to admire us, so we exaggerate. We call it stretching the truth. God calls it a lie.

We want people to respect us, so we live in houses we can't afford and charge bills we can't pay. We call it the American way. God calls it living a lie.

IF WE DON'T TELL THE TRUTH

Ananias and Sapphira represent just how much we humans do not trust the truth. They sold a piece of property and gave half the money to the church. They lied to Peter and the apostles, claiming that the land sold for the amount they gave. Their sin was not in holding back some of the money for themselves; it was in misrepresenting the truth. Their deceit resulted in their deaths. Luke writes: "The whole church and all the others who heard about these things were filled with fear" (Acts 5:11).

More than once I've heard people refer to this story with a nervous chuckle and say, "I'm glad God doesn't still strike people dead for lying." I'm not so sure he doesn't. It seems to me that the wages of deceit is still death. Not death of the body, perhaps, but the death of:

- *a marriage*—Falsehoods are termites in the trunk of the family tree.

- *a conscience*—The tragedy of the second lie is that it is always easier to tell than the first.

- *a career*—Just ask the student who got booted out for cheating or the employee who got fired for embezzlement if the lie wasn't fatal.

- *faith*—The language of faith and the language of falsehood have two different vocabularies. Those fluent in the language of falsehood find terms like *confession* and *repentance* hard to pronounce.

We could also list the deaths of intimacy, trust, peace, credibility, and self-respect. But perhaps the most tragic death that occurs from deceit is our witness. The court won't listen to the testimony of a perjured witness. Neither will the world. Do we think our coworkers will believe our words about Christ when they can't even believe our words about how we handled our expense account? Even more significantly, do we think God will use us as a witness if we won't tell the truth?

Every high school football team has a player whose assignment is to carry the play from the coach to the huddle. What if the player doesn't tell the truth? What if the coach calls for a pass but the courier says the coach called for a run? One thing is certain: the coach won't call on that player very long. God says if we are faithful with the small things, he'll trust us with the greater things (Matt. 25:21). Can he trust you with the small things?

FACING THE MUSIC

Many years ago a man conned his way into the orchestra of the emperor of China although he could not play a note. Whenever the group practiced or performed, he would hold his flute against his lips, pretending to play but not making a sound. He received a modest salary and enjoyed a comfortable living.

Then one day the emperor requested a solo from each musician. The flutist got nervous. There wasn't enough time to learn the instrument. He pretended to be sick, but the royal physician wasn't fooled. On the day of his solo performance, the impostor took poison and killed himself. The explanation of his suicide led to a phrase that found its way into the English language: "He refused to face the music."[2]

The cure for deceit is simply this: face the music. Tell the truth. Some of us are living in deceit. Some of us are walking in the shadows. The lies of Ananias and Sapphira resulted in death; so have ours. Some of us have buried a marriage, parts of a conscience, and even parts of our faith—all because we won't tell the truth.

Are you in a dilemma, wondering if you should tell the truth or not? The question to ask in such moments is, Will God bless my deceit? Will he, who hates lies, bless a strategy built on lies? Will the Lord, who loves the truth, bless the business of falsehoods? Will God honor the career of the manipulator? Will God come to the aid of the cheater? Will God bless my dishonesty?

I don't think so either.

Examine your heart. Ask yourself some tough questions.

Am I being completely honest with my spouse and children? Are my relationships marked by candor? What about my work or school environment? Am I honest in my dealings? Am I a trustworthy student? An honest taxpayer? A reliable witness at work?

Do you tell the truth . . . always?

If not, start today. Don't wait until tomorrow. The ripple of today's lie is tomorrow's wave and next year's flood. Start today. Be just like Jesus. Tell the truth, the whole truth, and nothing but the truth.

Be self-controlled and alert.
Your enemy the devil prowls around like a
roaring lion looking for someone to devour.
Resist him, standing firm in the faith.

1 PETER 5:8–9 NIV

CHAPTER NINE

THE GREENHOUSE
OF THE MIND

A Pure Heart

Suppose you come to visit me one day and find me working in my green-house. (Neither my house nor thumb is green, but let's pretend.) I explain to you that the greenhouse was a gift from my father. He used state-of-the-art equipment to create the ideal structure for growth. The atmosphere is perfect. The lighting exact. The temperature is suited for flowers, fruit, or anything I want, and what I want is flowers and fruit.

I ask you to join me as I collect some seeds to plant. You've always thought I was a bit crazy, but what I do next removes all doubt. You watch me walk into a field and strip seeds off of weeds. Crab grass seeds, dandelion seeds, grass burr seeds. I fill a bag with a variety of weed seeds and return to the greenhouse.

You can't believe what you've just seen. "I thought you wanted a greenhouse full of flowers and fruit."

"I do."

"Then don't you think you ought to plant flower seeds and fruit seeds?"

"Do you have any idea how much those seeds cost? Besides, you have to drive all the way to the garden center to get them. No thanks, I'm taking the cheap and easy route."

You walk away mumbling something about one brick short of a load.

THE GREENHOUSE OF THE HEART

Everybody knows you harvest what you sow. You reap what you plant. Yet strangely, what we know when we develop land, we tend to forget when we cultivate our hearts.

Think for a moment of your heart as a greenhouse. The similarities come quickly. It, too, is a magnificent gift from your father. It, too, is perfectly suited for growing. And your heart, like a greenhouse, has to be managed.

Consider for a moment your thoughts as seed. Some thoughts become flowers. Others become weeds. Sow seeds of hope and enjoy optimism. Sow seeds of doubt and expect insecurity. "People harvest only what they plant" (Gal. 6:7).

The proof is everywhere you look. Ever wonder why some people have the Teflon capacity to resist negativism and remain patient, optimistic, and forgiving? Could it be that they have diligently sown seeds of goodness and are enjoying the harvest?

Ever wonder why others have such a sour outlook? Such a gloomy attitude? You would, too, if your heart were a greenhouse of weeds and thorns.

Perhaps you've heard the joke about the man who came home one day to a cranky wife. Arriving at 6:30 in the evening, he spent an hour trying to cheer her up. Nothing worked. Finally he said, "Let's start over and pretend I'm just getting home." He stepped outside, and when he opened the door, she said, "It's 7:30, and you're just now getting home from work?"

The wife was reaping the harvest of a few weedy thoughts. Let's pause and make an important application. If the heart is a greenhouse and our thoughts are seeds, shouldn't we be careful about what we sow? Shouldn't we be selective about the seeds we allow to come into the greenhouse? Shouldn't there be a sentry at the door? Isn't guarding the heart a strategic task? According to the Bible it is: "Above all else, guard your heart, for it is the wellspring of life" (Prov. 4:23 NIV). Or as another translation reads: "Be careful what you think, because your thoughts run your life."

What a true statement! Test the principle, and see if you don't agree.

Two drivers are stuck in the same traffic jam. One person stews in anger, thinking, *My schedule is messed up.* The other sighs in relief, *Good chance to slow down.*

Two mothers face the same tragedy. One is destroyed: *I'll never get over this.* The other is despondent but determined: *God will get me through.*

Two executives face the same success. One pats himself on the back and grows cocky. The other gives the credit to God and grows grateful.

Two husbands commit the same failure. One bitterly assumes

God's limit of grace has been crossed. The other gratefully assumes a new depth of God's grace has been discovered.

"Above all else, guard your heart, for it is the wellspring of life."

Let's look at it from another angle. Suppose I ask you to take care of my house while I'm out of town. You pledge to keep everything in great shape. But when I return, I find the place in shambles. The carpet is torn, walls are smeared, furniture is broken. Your explanation is not impressive: some bikers came by and needed a place to stay. Then the rugby team called, looking for a place for their party. And of course there was the fraternity—they wanted a place to hold their initiation ceremony. As the owner, I have one question: "Don't you know how to say no? This is not your house. You don't have the right to let in everyone who wants to enter."

Ever think God wants to say the same to us?

GUARDING OUR HEARTS

You've got to admit some of our hearts are trashed out. Let any riffraff knock on the door, and we throw it open. Anger shows up, and we let him in. Revenge needs a place to stay, so we have him pull up a chair. Pity wants to have a party, so we show him the kitchen. Lust rings the bell, and we change the sheets on the bed. Don't we know how to say no?

Many don't. For most of us, thought management is, well, unthought of. We think much about time management, weight management, personnel management, even scalp management.

But what about thought management? Shouldn't we be as concerned about managing our thoughts as we are managing anything else? Jesus was. Like a trained soldier at the gate of a city, he stood watch over his mind. He stubbornly guarded the gateway of his heart. Many thoughts were denied entrance. Need a few examples?

How about arrogance? On one occasion the people determined to make Jesus their king. What an attractive thought. Most of us would delight in the notion of royalty. Even if we refused the crown, we would enjoy considering the invitation. Not Jesus. "Jesus saw that in their enthusiasm, they were about to grab him and make him king, so he slipped off and went back up the mountain to be by himself" (John 6:15 MSG).

Another dramatic example occurred in a conversation Jesus had with Peter. Upon hearing Jesus announce his impending death on the cross, the impetuous apostle objected. "Impossible, Master! That can never be!" (Matt. 16:22 MSG). Apparently, Peter was about to question the necessity of Calvary. But he never had a chance. Christ blocked the doorway. He sent both the messenger and the author of the heresy scurrying: "Peter, get out of my way. Satan, get lost. You have no idea how God works" (Matt. 16:23 MSG).

And how about the time Jesus was mocked? Have you ever had people laugh at you? Jesus did, too. Responding to an appeal to heal a sick girl, he entered her house only to be told she was dead. His response? "The child is not dead but sleeping." The response of the people in the house? "They laughed at him." Just like all of us, Jesus had to face a moment of humiliation. But unlike most of us, he refused to receive it. Note his decisive response: "he put them all outside" (Mark 5:39–40 RSV). The mockery was not allowed in the house of the girl nor in the mind of Christ.

Jesus guarded his heart. If he did, shouldn't we do the same? Most certainly! "Be careful what you think, because your thoughts run your life" (Prov. 4:23). Jesus wants your heart to be fertile and fruitful. He wants you to have a heart like his. That is God's goal for you. He wants you to "think and act like Christ Jesus" (Phil. 2:5). But how? The answer is surprisingly simple. We can be transformed if we make one decision: *I will submit my thoughts to the authority of Jesus.*

It's easy to overlook a significant claim made by Christ at the conclusion of Matthew's gospel. "All authority in heaven and on earth has been given to me" (Matt. 28:18 NIV). Jesus claims to be the CEO of heaven and earth. He has the ultimate say on everything, especially our thoughts. He has more authority, for example, than your parents. Your parents may say you are no good, but Jesus says you are valuable, and he has authority over parents. He even has more authority over you than you do. You may tell yourself that you are too bad to be forgiven, but Jesus has a different opinion. If you give him authority over you, then your guilty thoughts are no longer allowed.

Jesus also has authority over your ideas. Suppose you have an idea that you want to rob a grocery store. Jesus, however, has made it clear that stealing is wrong. If you have given him authority over your ideas, then the idea of stealing cannot remain in your thoughts.

See what I mean by authority? To have a pure heart, we must submit all thoughts to the authority of Christ. If we are willing to do that, he will change us to be like him. Here is how it works.

GUARD AT THE DOORWAY

Let's return to the image of the greenhouse. Your heart is a fertile greenhouse ready to produce good fruit. Your mind is the doorway to your heart—the strategic place where you determine which seeds are sown and which seeds are discarded. The Holy Spirit is ready to help you manage and filter the thoughts that try to enter. He can help you guard your heart.

He stands with you on the threshold. A thought approaches, a questionable thought. Do you throw open the door and let it enter? Of course not. You "fight to capture every thought until it acknowledges the authority of Christ" (2 Cor. 10:5 PHILLIPS). You don't leave the door unguarded. You stand equipped with handcuffs and leg irons, ready to capture any thought not fit to enter.

For the sake of discussion, let's say a thought regarding your personal value approaches. With all the cockiness of a neighborhood bully, the thought swaggers up to the door and says, "You're a loser. All your life you've been a loser. You've blown relationships and jobs and ambitions. You might as well write the word *bum* on your résumé, for that is what you are."

The ordinary person would throw open the door and let the thought in. Like a seed from a weed, it would find fertile soil and take root and bear thorns of inferiority. The average person would say, "You're right. I'm a bum. Come on in."

But as a Christian, you aren't your average person. You are led by the Spirit. So rather than let the thought in, you take it captive. You handcuff it and march it down the street to the courthouse where you present the thought before the judgment seat of Christ.

"Jesus, this thought says I'm a bum and a loser and that I'll never amount to anything. What do you think?"

See what you are doing? You are submitting the thought to the authority of Jesus. If Jesus agrees with the thought, then let it in. If not, kick it out. In this case Jesus disagrees.

How do know if Jesus agrees or disagrees? You open your Bible. What does God think about you? Ephesians 2:10 is a good place to check: "For we are God's workmanship, created in Christ Jesus to do good works, which God prepared in advance for us to do" (NIV). Or how about Romans 8:1: "There is now no condemnation for those who are in Christ Jesus" (NIV)?

Obviously any thought that says you are inferior or insignificant does not pass the test—and does not gain entrance. You have the right to give the bully a firm kick in the pants and watch him run.

Let's take another example. The first thought was a bully; this next thought is a groupie. She comes not to tell you how bad you are but how good you are. She rushes to the doorway and gushes, "You are so good. You are so wonderful. The world is so lucky to have you," and on and on the groupie grovels.

Typically this is the type of thought you'd welcome. But you don't do things the typical way. You guard your heart. You walk in the Spirit. And you take every thought captive. So once again you go to Jesus. You submit this thought to the authority of Christ. As you unsheathe the sword of the Spirit, his Word, you learn that pride doesn't please God.

"Don't cherish exaggerated ideas of yourself or your importance" (Rom. 12:3 PHILLIPS).

"The cross of our Lord Jesus Christ is my only reason for bragging" (Gal. 6:14).

As much as you'd like to welcome this thought of conceit into the greenhouse, you can't. You only allow what Christ allows.

One more example. This time the thought is not one of criticism or flattery but one of temptation. If you're a fellow, the thought is dressed in flashy red. If you're a female, the thought is the hunk you've always wanted. There is the brush of the hand, the fragrance in the air, and the invitation. "Come on, it's all right. We're consenting adults."

What do you do? Well, if you aren't under the authority of Christ, you throw open the door. But if you have the mind of Christ, you step back and say, "Not so fast. You'll have to get permission from my big brother." So you take this steamy act before Jesus and ask, "Yes or no?"

Nowhere does he answer more clearly than in 1 Corinthians 6 and 7: "We must not pursue the kind of sex that avoids commitment and intimacy, leaving us more lonely than ever. . . . Is it a good thing to have sexual relations? Certainly—but only within a certain context. It's good for a man to have a wife, and for a woman to have a husband. Sexual drives are strong, but marriage is strong enough to contain them" (6:18; 7:1–2 MSG).

Now armed with the opinion of Christ and the sword of the Spirit, what do you do? Well, if the tempter is not your spouse, close the door. If the invitation is from your spouse, then HUBBA HUBBA HUBBA.

The point is this. Guard the doorway of your heart. Submit your thoughts to the authority of Christ. The more selective you are about seeds, the more delighted you will be with the crop.

Let your hope keep you joyful,
be patient in your troubles,
and pray at all times.

ROMANS 12:12 TEV

CHAPTER TEN

FINDING GOLD
IN THE GARBAGE

A Hope-Filled Heart

William Rathje likes garbage. This Harvard-educated researcher is convinced we can learn a lot from the trash dumps of the world. Archaeologists have always examined trash to study a society. Rathje does the same; he just eliminates the wait. The Garbage Project, as he calls his organization, travels across the continent, excavating landfills and documenting our eating habits, dress styles, and economic levels.[1] Rathje is able to find meaning in our garbage.

His organization documented that the average household wastes 10 percent to 15 percent of its solid food. The average American produces half a pound of trash per day, and the largest landfill in America, located near New York City, has enough trash to fill the Panama Canal. According to Rathje, trash decomposes more slowly than we thought it did. He found a whole steak from 1973 and readable newspapers from the Truman presidency. Rathje learns a lot by looking at our junk.

Reading about Rathje made me wonder, *What is it like to be a "garbologist"?* When he gives a speech, is the address referred to as "trash talk"? Are his staff meetings designated as "rubbish reviews"? Are his business trips called "junkets"? When he day-dreams about his work, does his wife tell him to get his mind out of the garbage?

Though I prefer to leave the dirty work to Rathje, his attitude toward trash intrigues me. What if we learned to do the same? Suppose we changed the way we view the garbage that comes our way? After all, don't you endure your share of rubbish? Snarled traffic. Computer foul-ups. Postponed vacations.

And then there are the days that a Dumpster couldn't hold all the garbage we face: hospital bills, divorce papers, pay cuts, and betrayals. What do you do when an entire truck of sorrow is dumped on you?

On Rathje's office wall is a framed headline he found in a paper: "Gold in Garbage." This garbologist finds treasure in trash. Jesus did the same. What everyone else perceived as calamity, he saw as opportunity. And because he saw what others didn't, he found what others missed.

Early in his ministry Jesus said this about our vision: "Your eyes are windows into your body. If you open your eyes wide in wonder and belief, your body fills up with light. If you live squinty-eyed in greed and distrust, your body is a dank cellar" (Matt. 6:22–23 MSG).

In other words, how we look at life determines how we live

life. But Jesus did much more than articulate this principle, he modeled it.

THE DARKEST NIGHT IN HISTORY

On the night before his death, a veritable landfill of woes tumbled in on Jesus. Somewhere between the Gethsemane prayer and the mock trial is what has to be the darkest scene in the history of the human drama. Though the entire episode couldn't have totaled more than five minutes, the event had enough badness to fill a thousand Dumpsters. Except for Christ, not one person did one good thing. Search the scene for an ounce of courage or a speck of character, and you won't find it. What you will find is a compost heap of deceit and betrayal. Yet in it all, Jesus saw reason to hope. And in his outlook, we find an example to follow.

"Get up, we must go. Look, here comes the man who has turned against me."

While Jesus was still speaking, Judas, one of the twelve apostles, came up. With him were many people carrying swords and clubs who had been sent from the leading priests and the older Jewish leaders of the people. Judas had planned to give them a signal, saying, "The man I kiss is Jesus. Arrest him." At once Judas went to Jesus and said, "Greetings, Teacher!" and kissed him.

Jesus answered, "Friend, do what you came to do."

Then the people came and grabbed Jesus and arrested

him. When that happened, one of Jesus' followers reached for his sword and pulled it out. He struck the servant of the high priest and cut off his ear.

Jesus said to the man, "Put your sword back in its place. All who use swords will be killed with swords. Surely you know I could ask my Father, and he would give me more than twelve armies of angels. But it must happen this way to bring about what the Scriptures say."

Then Jesus said to the crowd, "You came to get me with swords and clubs as if I were a criminal. Every day I sat in the Temple teaching, and you did not arrest me there. But all these things have happened so that it will come about as the prophets wrote." Then all of Jesus' followers left him and ran away (Matt. 26:46–56).

Had a reporter been assigned to cover the arrest, his head-line might have read:

A DARK NIGHT FOR JESUS
Galilean Preacher Abandoned by Friends

Last Friday they welcomed him with palm leaves. Last night they arrested him with swords. The world of Jesus of Nazareth turned sour as he was apprehended by a crowd of soldiers and angry citizens in a garden just out-side the city walls. Only a week since his triumphant entry, his popularity has taken a fatal plunge. Even his fol-lowers refuse to claim him. The disciples who took pride in being seen with him earlier in the week took flight from him last night. With the public crying for his death and the disciples denying any involvement, the future of this celebrated teacher appears bleak, and the impact of his mission appears limited.

The darkest night of Jesus' life was marked by one crisis after another. In just a moment we will see what Jesus saw, but first let's consider what an observer would have witnessed in the Garden of Gethsemane.

First he would have seen *unanswered prayer*. Jesus had just offered an anguished appeal to God. "My Father, if it is possible, do not give me this cup of suffering. But do what you want, not what I want" (26:39). This was no calm, serene hour of prayer. Matthew says that Jesus was "very sad and troubled" (26:37). The Master "fell to the ground" (26:39) and cried out to God. Luke tells us that Jesus was "full of pain" and that "his sweat was like drops of blood falling to the ground" (Luke 22:44).

Never has earth offered such an urgent request. And never has heaven offered more deafening silence. The prayer of Jesus was unanswered. *Jesus* and *unanswered prayer* in the same phrase? Isn't that an oxymoron? Would the son of Henry have no Ford or the child of Bill Gates own no computer? Would God, the one who owns the cattle on a thousand hills, keep something from his own son? He did that night. Consequently, Jesus had to deal with the dilemma of unanswered prayer. And that was just the beginning. Look who showed up next:

"With [Judas] were many people carrying swords and clubs who had been sent from the leading priests and the older Jewish leaders of the people. . . . Then the people came and grabbed Jesus and arrested him" (Matt. 26:47,51).

Judas arrived with an angry crowd. Again, from the perspective of an observer, this crowd represents another crisis. Not only did Jesus have to face unanswered prayer, he also had to deal with *unfruitful service*. The very people he came to save had now come to arrest him.

Let me give you a fact that may alter your impression of that night. Perhaps you envision Judas leading a dozen or so soldiers who are carrying two or three lanterns. Matthew tells us, however, that "many people" came to arrest Jesus. John is even more specific. The term he employs is the Greek word *speira* or a "group of soldiers" (John 18:3). At minimum, *speira* depicts a group of two hundred soldiers. It can describe a detachment as large as nineteen hundred![2]

Equipped with John's description, we'd be more accurate to imagine a river of several hundred troops entering the garden. Add to that figure untold watchers whom Matthew simply calls "the crowd," and you have a mob of people.

Surely in a group this size there is one person who will defend Jesus. He came to the aid of so many. All those sermons. All those miracles. Now they will bear fruit. And so we wait for the one person who will declare, "Jesus is an innocent man!" But no one does. Not one person speaks out on his behalf. The people he came to save have turned against him.

We can almost forgive the crowd. Their contact with Jesus

was too brief, too casual. Perhaps they didn't know better. But the disciples did. They knew better. They knew *him* better. But do they defend Jesus? Hardly. The most bitter pill Jesus had to swallow was the *unbelievable betrayal* by the disciples.

Judas wasn't the only turncoat. Matthew is admirably honest when he confesses, "All of Jesus' followers left him and ran away" (26:56).

For such a short word, *all* sure packs some pain. "*All* of Jesus' followers . . . ran away." John did. Matthew did. Simon did. Thomas did. They all did. We don't have to go far to find the last time this word was used. Note the verse just a few lines before our text: "But Peter said, 'I will never say that I don't know you! I will even die with you!' And *all* the other followers said the same thing" (26:35, italics mine).

All pledged loyalty, and yet *all* ran. From the outside looking in, all we see is betrayal. The disciples have left him. The people have rejected him. And God hasn't heard him. Never has so much trash been dumped on one being. Stack all the disloyalties of deadbeat dads and cheating wives and prodigal kids and dishonest workers in one pile, and you begin to see what Jesus had to face that night. From a human point of view, Jesus' world has collapsed. No answer from heaven, no help from the people, no loyalty from his friends.

Jesus, neck deep in rubbish. That's how I would have described the scene. That's how a reporter would have described it. That's how a witness would have portrayed it. But that's not how Jesus saw it. He saw something else entirely. He wasn't oblivious to the trash; he just wasn't limited to it. Somehow he was able to see good in the bad, the purpose in the pain, and God's presence in the problem.

We could use a little of Jesus' 20/20 vision, couldn't we? You and I live in a trashy world. Unwanted garbage comes our way on a regular basis. We, too, have unanswered prayers and unfruitful dreams and unbelievable betrayals, do we not? Haven't you been handed a trash sack of mishaps and heartaches? Sure you have. May I ask, what are you going to do with it?

SEEING WHAT JESUS SEES

You have several options. You could hide it. You could take the trash bag and cram it under your coat or stick it under your dress and pretend it isn't there. But you and I know you won't fool anyone. Besides, sooner or later it will start to stink. Or you could disguise it. Paint it green, put it on the front lawn, and tell everybody it is a tree. Again, no one will be fooled, and pretty soon it's going to reek. So what will you do? If you follow the example of Christ, you will learn to see tough times differently. Remember, God loves you just the way you are, but he refuses to leave you that way. He wants you to have a hope-filled heart . . . just like Jesus.

Here is what Christ did.

He found good in the bad. It would be hard to find someone worse than Judas. Some say he was a good man with a backfired strategy. I don't buy that. The Bible says, "Judas . . . was a thief. He was the one who kept the money box, and he often stole from it" (John 12:6). The man was a crook. Somehow he was able to live in the presence of God and experience the miracles of Christ and remain unchanged. In the end he decided he'd rather have money than a friend, so he sold Jesus for thirty pieces of silver. I'm sorry, but every human life is worth more than thirty pieces of silver. Judas was a scoundrel, a cheat, and a bum. How could anyone see him any other way?

I don't know, but Jesus did. Only inches from the face of his betrayer, Jesus looked at him and said, "Friend, do what you came to do" (Matt. 26:50). What Jesus saw in Judas as worthy of being called a friend, I can't imagine. But I do know that Jesus doesn't lie, and in that moment he saw something good in a very bad man.

It would help if we did the same. How can we? Again Jesus gives us guidance. He didn't place all the blame on Judas. He saw another presence that night: "this is . . . the time when darkness rules" (Luke 22:53). In no way was Judas innocent, but neither was Judas acting alone. Your attackers aren't acting alone either. "Our fight is not against people on earth but against the rulers and authorities and the powers of this world's darkness, against the spiritual powers of evil in the heavenly world" (Eph. 6:12).

Those who betray us are victims of a fallen world. We needn't place all the blame on them. Jesus found enough good in the face of Judas to call him friend, and he can help us do the same with those who hurt us.

Not only did Jesus find good in the bad, *he found purpose in the pain.* Of the ninety-eight words Jesus spoke at his arrest, thirty refer to the purpose of God.

"It must happen this way to bring about what the Scriptures say" (Matt. 26:54).

"All these things have happened so that it will come about as the prophets wrote" (v. 56).

Jesus chose to see his immediate struggle as a necessary part of a greater plan. He viewed the Gethsemane conflict as an important but singular act in the grand manuscript of God's drama.

I witnessed something similar on a recent trip. My daughter Andrea and I were flying to St. Louis. Because of storms, the flight was delayed and then diverted to another city where we sat on the runway waiting for the rain clouds to pass. As I was glancing at my watch and drumming my fingers, wondering when we would arrive, the fellow across the aisle tapped me on the arm and asked if he could borrow my Bible. I handed it to him. He turned to a young girl in the adjacent seat, opened the Bible, and the two read the Scriptures for the remainder of the trip.

After some time, the sky cleared, and we resumed our journey. We were landing in St. Louis when he returned the Bible to me and explained in a low voice that this was the girl's first flight. She'd recently joined the military and was leaving home for the first time. He asked her if she believed in Christ, and she said she wanted to but didn't know how. That's when he borrowed my Bible and told her about Jesus. By the time we landed, she told him she believed in Jesus as the Son of God.

I've since wondered about that event. Did God bring the storm so the girl could hear the gospel? Did God delay our arrival so she'd have ample time to learn about Jesus? I wouldn't put it past him. That is how Jesus chose to view the storm that came his way: necessary turbulence in the plan of God. Where others saw gray skies, Jesus saw a divine order. His suffering was necessary to fulfill prophecy, and his sacrifice was necessary to fulfill the law.

Wouldn't you love to have a hope-filled heart? Wouldn't you love to see the world through the eyes of Jesus? Where we see unanswered prayer, Jesus saw answered prayer. Where we see the absence of God, Jesus saw the plan of God. Note especially verse 53: "Surely you know I could ask my Father, and he would give me more than twelve armies of angels." Of all the treasures Jesus saw in the trash, this is most significant. He saw his father. He saw his father's presence in the problem. Twelve armies of angels were within his sight.

Sure, Max, but Jesus was God. He could see the unseen. He had eyes for heaven and a vision for the supernatural. I can't see the way he saw.

Not yet maybe, but don't underestimate God's power. He can change the way you look at life.

Need proof? How about the example of Elisha and his servant? The two were in Dothan when an angry king sent his army to destroy them.

> Elisha's servant got up early, and when he went out, he saw an army with horses and chariots all around the city. The servant said to Elisha, "Oh, my master, what can we do?"
>
> Elisha said, "Don't be afraid. The army that fights for us is larger than the one against us."

Then Elisha prayed, "LORD, open my servant's eyes, and let him see."

The LORD opened the eyes of the young man, and he saw that the mountain was full of horses and chariots of fire all around Elisha. (2 Kings 6:15–17)

By God's power, the servant saw the angels. Who is to say the same can't happen for you?

God never promises to remove us from our struggles. He does promise, however, to change the way we look at them. The apostle Paul dedicates a paragraph to listing trash bags: troubles, problems, sufferings, hunger, nakedness, danger, and violent death. These are the very Dumpsters of difficulty we hope to escape. Paul, however, states their value. "In all these things we have full victory through God" (Rom. 8:35–37). We'd prefer another preposition. We'd opt for *"apart* from all these things," or *"away* from all these things," or even, *"without* all these things." But Paul says, *"in"* all these things. The solution is not to avoid trouble but to change the way we see our troubles.

God can correct your vision.

He asks, "Who gives a person sight?" then answers, "It is I, the LORD" (Exod. 4:11). God let Balaam see the angel and Elisha see the army and Jacob see the ladder and Saul see the Savior. More than one have made the request of the blind man, "Teacher, I want to see" (Mark 10:51). And more than one have walked away with clear vision. Who is to say God won't do the same for you?

Sing to the LORD a new song;
sing to the LORD, all the earth.
Sing to the LORD and praise his name;
every day tell how he saves us.

PSALM 96:1–2

Rejoice that your names
are written in heaven.

LUKE 10:20 NIV

CHAPTER ELEVEN

WHEN HEAVEN CELEBRATES

A Rejoicing Heart

My family did something thoughtful for me last night. They had a party in my honor—a surprise birthday party. Early last week I told Denalyn not to plan anything except a nice, family evening at a restaurant. She listened only to the restaurant part. I was unaware that half a dozen families were going to join us.

In fact, I tried to talk her into staying at home. "Let's have the dinner on another night," I volunteered. Andrea had been sick. Jenna had homework, and I'd spent the afternoon watching football games and felt lazy. Not really in a mood to get up and clean up and go out. I thought I'd have no problem convincing the girls to postpone the dinner. Boy was I surprised! They wouldn't think of it. Each of my objections was met with a united front and a unanimous defense. My family made it clear—we were going out to eat.

Not only that, we were leaving on time. I consented and set about getting ready. But to their dismay, I moved too slowly. We were a study in contrasts. My attitude was *why hurry?* My daughters' attitude was *hurry up!* I was ho-hum. They were gung-ho. I was content to stay. They were anxious to leave. To be honest, I was bewildered by their actions. They were being uncharacteristically prompt. Curiously enthused. Why the big deal? I mean, I enjoy a night out as much as the next guy, but Sara giggled all the way to the restaurant.

Only when we arrived did their actions make sense. One step inside the door and I understood their enthusiasm. SURPRISE! No wonder they were acting differently. They knew what I didn't. They had seen what I hadn't. They'd already seen the table and stacked the gifts and smelled the cake. Since they knew about the party, they did everything necessary to see that I didn't miss it.

Jesus does the same for us. He knows about THE PARTY. In one of the greatest chapters in the Bible, Luke 15, he tells three stories. Each story speaks of something lost and of something found. A lost sheep. A lost coin. And a lost son. And at the end of each one, Jesus describes a party, a celebration. The shepherd throws the party for the lost-now-found sheep. The housewife throws a party because of the lost-now-found coin. And the father throws a party in honor of his lost-now-found son.

Three parables, each with a party. Three stories, each with the appearance of the same word: *happy*. Regarding the shepherd who found the lost sheep, Jesus says: "And when he finds it, he *happily* puts it on his shoulders and goes home" (vv. 5–6, italics mine). When the housewife finds her lost coin, she announces, "Be *happy* with me because I have found the coin that I lost" (v. 9, italics mine). And the father of the prodigal son explains to the reluctant older brother, "We had to celebrate and be *happy* because your brother was dead, but now he is alive. He was lost, but now he is found" (v. 32, italics mine).

The point is clear. Jesus is happiest when the lost are found. For him, no moment compares to the moment of salvation. For my daughter the rejoicing began when I got dressed and in the car and on the road to the party. The same occurs in heaven. Let one child consent to be dressed in righteousness and begin the journey home and heaven pours the punch, strings the streamers, and throws the confetti. "There is joy in the presence of the angels of God when one sinner changes his heart and life" (v. 10).

A century ago this verse caused Charles Spurgeon to write:

> There are Christmas days in heaven where Christ's high mass is kept, and Christ is not glorified because He was born in a manger but because he is born in a broken heart. And these are days when the shepherd brings home the lost sheep upon His shoulders, when the church has swept her house and found the lost piece of money, for then are these friends and neighbors called together, and they rejoice with joy unspeakable and full of glory over one sinner who repents.[1]

How do we explain such joy? Why such a stir? You've got to admit the excitement is a bit curious. We aren't talking about a nation of people or even a city of souls; we're talking about joy "when *one* sinner changes his heart and life." How could one person create that much excitement?

Who would imagine that our actions have such an impact on heaven? We can live and die and leave no more than an obituary. Our greatest actions on earth go largely unnoticed and unrecorded. Dare we think that God is paying attention?

According to this verse, he is. According to Jesus our decisions have a thermostatic impact on the unseen world. Our actions on the keyboard of earth trigger hammers on the piano strings of heaven. Our obedience pulls the ropes which ring the bells in heaven's belfries. Let a child call and the ear of the Father inclines. Let a sister weep and tears begin to flow from above. Let a saint die and the gate is opened. And, most important, let a sinner repent, and every other activity ceases, and every heavenly being celebrates.

Remarkable, this response to our conversion. Heaven throws no party over our other achievements. When we graduate from school or open our business or have a baby, as far as we know, the celestial bubbly stays in the refrigerator. Why the big deal over conversion?

We don't always share such enthusiasm, do we? When you hear of a soul saved, do you drop everything and celebrate? Is your good day made better or your bad day salvaged? We may be pleased—but exuberant? Do our chests burst with joy? Do we feel an urge to call out the band and cut the cake and have a party? When a soul is saved, the heart of Jesus becomes the night sky on the Fourth of July, radiant with explosions of cheer.

Can the same be said about us? Perhaps this is one area where our hearts could use some attention.

GOD'S MAGNUM OPUS

Why do Jesus and his angels rejoice over one repenting sinner? Can they see something we can't? Do they know something we don't? Absolutely. They know what heaven holds. They've seen the table, and they've heard the music, and they can't wait to see your face when you arrive. Better still, they can't wait to see you.

When you arrive and enter the party, something wonderful will happen. A final transformation will occur. You will be just like Jesus. Drink deeply from 1 John 3:2: "We have not yet been shown what we will be in the future. But we know that when Christ comes again, *we will be like him*" (italics mine).

Of all the blessings of heaven, one of the greatest will be you! You will be God's magnum opus, his work of art. The angels will gasp. God's work will be completed. At last, you will have a heart like his.

You will love with a perfect love.

You will worship with a radiant face.

You'll hear each word God speaks.

Your heart will be pure, your words will be like jewels, your thoughts will be like treasures.

You will be just like Jesus. You will, at long last, have a heart like his. Envision the heart of Jesus and you'll be envisioning your own. Guiltless. Fearless. Thrilled and joyous. Tirelessly worshiping. Flawlessly discerning. As the mountain stream is pristine and endless, so will be your heart. *You will be like him.*

And if that were not enough, everyone else will be like him as well. "Heaven is the perfect place for people made perfect."[2] Heaven is populated by those who let God change them. Arguments will cease, for jealousy won't exist. Suspicions won't surface, for there will be no secrets. Every sin is gone. Every insecurity is forgotten. Every fear is past. Pure wheat. No weeds. Pure gold. No alloy. Pure love. No lust. Pure hope. No fear. No wonder the angels rejoice when one sinner repents; they know another work of art will soon grace the gallery of God. They know what heaven holds.

There is yet another reason for the celebration. Part of the excitement is from our arrival. The other part is from our deliverance. Jesus rejoices that we are headed to heaven, but he equally rejoices that we are saved from hell.

WHAT WE'RE SAVED FROM

One phrase summarizes the horror of hell. "God isn't there."

Think for a moment about this question: What if God weren't here on earth? You think people can be cruel now, imagine us without the presence of God. You think we are brutal to each other now, imagine the world without the Holy Spirit. You think there is loneliness and despair and guilt now, imagine life without the touch of Jesus. No forgiveness. No hope. No acts of kindness. No words of love. No more food given in his name. No more songs sung to his praise. No more deeds done in his honor. If God took away his angels, his grace, his promise of eternity, and his servants, what would the world be like?

In a word, hell. No one to comfort you and no music to soothe you. A world where poets don't write of love and minstrels don't sing of hope, for love and hope were passengers on the last ship. The final vessel has departed, and the anthem of hell has only two words: "if only."

According to Jesus hell knows only one sound, the "weeping and gnashing of teeth" (Matt. 22:13 NIV). From hell comes a woeful, unending moan as its inhabitants realize the opportunity they have missed. What they would give for one more chance. But that chance is gone (Heb. 9:27).

POSSIBLE GODS AND GODDESSES

Can you see now why the angels rejoice when one sinner repents? Jesus knows what awaits the saved. He also knows what awaits the condemned. Can you see why we should rejoice as well? How can we? How can our hearts be changed so we rejoice like Jesus rejoices?

Ask God to help you have his eternal view of the world. His view of humanity is starkly simple. From his perspective every person is either:

- entering through the small gate or the wide gate (Matt. 7:13–14)

- traveling the narrow road or the wide road (Matt. 7:13–14)

- building on rock or sand (Matt. 7:24–27)

- wise or foolish (Matt. 25:2)

- prepared or unprepared (Matt. 24:45–51)

- fruitful or fruitless (Matt. 25:14–27)

- heaven called or hell bound (Mark 16:15–16)

At the sinking of the RMS *Titanic,* over twenty-two hundred people were cast into the frigid waters of the Atlantic. On shore the names of the passengers were posted in two simple columns—saved and lost.[3] God's list is equally simple.

Our ledger, however, is cluttered with unnecessary columns. Is he rich? Is she pretty? What work does he do? What color is her skin? Does she have a college degree? These matters are irrelevant to God. As he shapes us more and more to be like Jesus, they become irrelevant to us as well. "Our knowledge of men can no longer be based on their outward lives" (2 Cor. 5:16 PHILLIPS).

To have a heart like his is to look into the faces of the saved and rejoice! They are just one grave away from being just like Jesus. To have a heart like his is to look into the faces of the lost and pray. For unless they turn, they are one grave away from torment.

C. S. Lewis stated it this way:

It is a serious thing to live in a society of possible gods and goddesses, to remember that the dullest and most uninteresting person you talk to may one day be a creature which, if you saw it now, you would be strongly tempted to worship, or else a horror and a corruption such as now you meet only in a nightmare. All day long we are, in some degree, helping each other to one or the other of these destinations.[4]

And so my challenge to you is simple. Ask God to help you have his eternal view of the world. Every person you meet has been given an invitation to dinner. When one says yes, celebrate! And when one acts sluggish as I did last night, do what my daughters did. Stir him up and urge him to get ready. It's almost time for the party, and you don't want him to miss it.

*Let us run the race that is
before us and never give up.*

HEBREWS 12:1

CHAPTER TWELVE

FINISHING STRONG

An Enduring Heart

On one of my shelves is a book on power abs. The cover shows a closeup of a fellow flexing his flat belly. His gut has more ripples and ridges than a pond on a windy day. Inspired, I bought the book, read the routine, and did the sit-ups . . . for a week.

Not far from the power-abs book is a tape series on speed reading. This purchase was Denalyn's idea, but when I read the ad, I was equally enthused. The course promises to do for my mind what *Power Abs* promised to do for my gut—turn it into steel. The back-cover copy promises that mastering this six-week series will enable you to read twice as fast and retain twice the amount. All you have to do is listen to the tapes—which I intend to do . . . someday.

And then there is my bottle of essential minerals. Thirty-two ounces of pure health. One swallow a day and I'll ingest my quota of calcium, chloride, magnesium, sodium, and sixty-six other vital earthly elements. (There's even a trace of iron, which is good since I missed my shot at the iron abs and the steel-trap mind.) The enthusiast who sold me the minerals convinced me that thirty dollars was a small price to pay for good health. I agree. I just keep forgetting to take them.

Don't get me wrong. Not everything in my life is incomplete. (This book is finished . . . well, almost.) But I confess, I don't always finish what I start. Chances are I'm not alone. Any unfinished projects under your roof? Perhaps an exercise machine whose primary function thus far has been to hold towels? Or an unopened do-it-yourself pottery course? How about a half-finished patio deck or a half-dug pool or a half-planted garden? And let's not even touch the topic of diets and weight loss, OK?

You know as well as I, it's one thing to start something. It's something else entirely to complete it. You may think I'm going to talk to you about the importance of finishing everything. Could be you are bracing yourself for a bit of chastising.

If so, relax. "Don't start what you can't finish" is not one of my points. And I'm not going to say anything about what is used to pave the road to hell. To be honest, I don't believe you should finish everything you start. (Every student with homework just perked up.) There are certain quests better left undone, some projects wisely abandoned. (Though I wouldn't list homework as one of those.)

We can become so obsessed with completion that we become blind to effectiveness. Just because a project is on the table, doesn't mean it can't be returned to the shelf. No, my desire is not to convince you to finish everything. My desire is to encourage you to finish the *right* thing. Certain races are optional—like washboard abs and speed reading. Other races are essential—like the race of faith. Consider this admonition from the author of Hebrews: "Let us run the race that is before us and never give up" (Heb. 12:1).

THE RACE

Had golf existed in the New Testament era, I'm sure the writers would have spoken of mulligans and foot wedges, but it didn't, so they wrote about running. The word *race* is from the Greek *agon,* from which we get the word *agony.* The Christian's race is not a jog but rather a demanding and grueling, sometimes agonizing race. It takes a massive effort to finish strong.

Likely you've noticed that many don't? Surely you've observed there are many on the side of the trail? They used to be running. There was a time when they kept the pace. But then weariness set in. They didn't think the run would be this tough. Or they were discouraged by a bump and daunted by a fellow runner. Whatever the reason, they don't run anymore. They may be Christians. They may come to church. They may put a buck in the plate and warm a pew, but their hearts aren't in the race. They retired before their time. Unless something changes, their best work will have been their first work, and they will finish with a whimper.

By contrast, Jesus' best work was his final work, and his strongest step was his last step. Our Master is the classic example of one who endured. The writer of Hebrews goes on to say that Jesus "held on while wicked people were doing evil things to him" (v. 3). The Bible says Jesus "held on," implying that Jesus could have "let go." The runner could have given up, sat down, gone home. He could have quit the race. But he didn't. "He held on while wicked people were doing evil things to him."

THE RESISTANCE

Have you ever thought about the evil things done to Christ? Can you think of times when Jesus could have given up? How about his time of temptation? You and I know what it is like to endure a moment of temptation or an hour of temptation, even a day of temptation. But *forty* days? That is what Jesus faced. "The Spirit led Jesus into the desert where the devil tempted Jesus for forty days" (Luke 4:1–2).

We imagine the wilderness temptation as three isolated events scattered over a forty-day period. Would that it had been. In reality, Jesus' time of testing was nonstop; "the devil tempted Jesus for forty days." Satan got on Jesus like a shirt and refused to leave. Every step, whispering in his ear. Every turn of the path, sowing doubt. Was Jesus impacted by the devil? Apparently so. Luke doesn't say that Satan *tried* to tempt Jesus. The verse doesn't read, the devil *attempted* to tempt Jesus. No the passage is clear: "the devil *tempted* Jesus." Jesus was *tempted,* he was *tested.* Tempted to change sides? Tempted to go home? Tempted to settle for a kingdom on earth? I don't know, but I know he was tempted. A war raged within. Stress stormed without. And since he was tempted, he could have quit the race. But he didn't. He kept on running.

Temptation didn't stop him, nor did accusations. Can you imagine what it would be like to run in a race and be criticized by the bystanders?

Some years ago I entered a five-K race. Nothing serious, just a jog through the neighborhood to raise funds for a charity. Not being the wisest of runners, I started off at an impossible pace. Within a mile I was sucking air. At the right time, however, the spectators encouraged me. Sympathetic onlookers urged me on. One compassionate lady passed out cups of water, another sprayed us down with a hose. I had never seen these people, but that didn't matter. I needed a voice of encouragement, and they gave it. Bolstered by their assurance, I kept going.

What if in the toughest steps of the race, I had heard words of accusation and not encouragement? And what if the accusations came not from strangers I could dismiss but from my neighbors and family?

How would you like somebody to yell these words at you as you ran:

"Hey, liar! Why don't you do something honest with your life?" (see John 7:12).

"Here comes the foreigner. Why don't you go home where you belong?" (see John 8:48).

"Since when do they let children of the devil enter the race?" (see John 8:48).

That's what happened to Jesus. His own family called him a lunatic. His neighbors treated him even worse. When Jesus returned to his hometown, they tried to throw him off a cliff (Luke 4:29). But Jesus didn't quit running. Temptations didn't deter him. Accusations didn't defeat him. Nor did shame dishearten him.

I invite you to think carefully about the supreme test Jesus faced in the race. Hebrews 12:2 offers this intriguing statement: "[Jesus] accepted the shame as if it were nothing."

Shame is a feeling of disgrace, embarrassment, humiliation. Forgive me for stirring the memory, but don't you have a shameful moment in your history? Can you imagine the horror you would feel if everyone knew about it? What if a videotape of that event were played before your family and friends? How would you feel?

That is exactly what Jesus felt. *Why?* you ask. *He never did anything worthy of shame.* No, but we did. And since on the cross God made him become sin (2 Cor. 5:21), Jesus was covered with shame. He was shamed before his family. Stripped naked before his own mother and loved ones. Shamed before his fellow men. Forced to carry a cross until the weight caused him to stumble. Shamed before his church. The pastors and elders of his day mocked him, calling him names. Shamed before the city of Jerusalem. Condemned to die a criminal's death. Parents likely pointed to him from a distance and told their children, "That's what they do to evil men."

But the shame before men didn't compare with the shame Jesus felt before his father. Our individual shame seems too much to bear. Can you imagine bearing the collective shame of all humanity? One wave of shame after another was dumped on Jesus. Though he never cheated, he was convicted as a cheat. Though he never stole, heaven regarded him as a thief.

up cigars, but I have found something even sweeter. It involves two phases.

The first is a quiet moment before God. The moment the manuscript is in the mail, I find a secluded spot and stop. I don't say much, and, at least so far, neither does God. The purpose is not to talk as much as it is to relish. To delight in the sweet satisfaction of a completed task. Does a finer feeling exist? The runner feels the tape against his chest. It is finished. How sweet is the wine at the end of the journey. So for a few moments, God and I savor it together. We place the flag on the peak of Everest and enjoy the view.

Then (this really sounds mundane), I eat. I tend to skip meals during the homestretch, so I'm hungry. One year it was a Mexican dinner on the San Antonio River. Another it was room service and a basketball game. Last year I had catfish at a roadside café. Sometimes Denalyn joins me; other times I eat alone. The food may vary, and the company may change, but one rule remains constant. Throughout the meal I allow myself only one thought. *I am finished.* Planning future projects is not permitted. Consideration of tomorrow's tasks is not allowed. I indulge myself in a make-believe world and pretend that my life's work is complete.

And during that meal, in a minute way, I understand where Jesus found his strength. He lifted his eyes beyond the horizon and saw the table. He focused on the feast. And what he saw gave him strength to finish—and finish strong.

Such a moment awaits us. In a world oblivious to power abs and speed reading, we'll take our place at the table. In an hour that has no end, we will rest. Surrounded by saints and engulfed by Jesus himself, the work will, indeed, be finished. The final harvest will have been gathered, we will be seated, and Christ will christen the meal with these words: "Well done, good and faithful servant" (Matt. 25:23 KJV).

And in that moment, the race will have been worth it.

*May he enlighten the eyes of your mind
so that you can see what hope his call
holds for you, what rich glories he has
promised the saints will inherit.*

EPHESIANS 1:18 NIV

FIXING YOUR EYES ON JESUS

There are times when we see. And there are times when we *see.* Let me show you what I mean:

Everything changes the morning you see the "for sale" sign on your neighbor's boat. His deluxe bass boat. The bass boat you've coveted for three summers. All of a sudden nothing else matters. A gravitational tug pulls your car to the curb. You sigh as you behold your dream glistening in the sun. You run your fingers along the edge, pausing only to wipe the drool from your shirt. As you gaze, you are transported to Lake Tamapwantee, and it's just you and the glassy waters and your bass boat.

Or perhaps the following paragraph describes you better:

Everything changes the day you see him enter the English lit classroom. Just enough swagger to be cool. Just enough smarts to be classy. Not walking so fast as to be nervous, nor so slow as to be cocky. You've seen him before, but only in your dreams. Now he's really here. And you can't take your eyes off him. By the time class is over, you've memorized every curl and lash. And by the time this day is over, you resolve he's going to be yours.

There are times when we see. And then there are times when we *see*. There are times when we observe, and there are times when we memorize. There are times when we notice, and there are times when we study. Most of us know what it means to see a new boat or a new boy . . . but do we know what it's like to see Jesus? Do we know what it's like to "fix our eyes on Jesus" (Heb. 12:2 NIV)?

We've spent the last twelve chapters looking at what it means to be just like Jesus. The world has never known a heart so pure, a character so flawless. His spiritual hearing was so keen he never missed a heavenly whisper. His mercy so abundant he never missed a chance to forgive. No lie left his lips, no distraction marred his vision. He touched when others recoiled. He endured when others quit. Jesus is the ultimate model for every person. And what we have done in these pages is precisely what God invites you to do with the rest of your life. He urges you to fix your eyes upon Jesus. Heaven invites you to set the lens of your heart on the heart of the Savior and make him the object of your life. For that reason, I want us to close our time together with this question: What does it mean to *see* Jesus?

The shepherds can tell us. For them it wasn't enough to see the angels. You'd think it would have been. Night sky shattered with light. Stillness erupting with song. Simple shepherds roused from their sleep and raised to their feet by a choir of angels: "Glory to God in the highest!" Never had these men seen such splendor.

But it wasn't enough to see the angels. The shepherds wanted to see the one who sent the angels. Since they wouldn't be satisfied until they saw him, you can trace the long line of Jesus-seekers to a person of the pasture who said, "Let's go. . . . Let's *see*" (Luke 2:15, italics mine).

Not far behind the shepherds was a man named Simeon. Luke tells us Simeon was a good man who served in the temple during the time of Christ's birth. Luke also tells us, "Simeon had been told by the Holy Spirit that he would not die before he saw the Christ promised by the Lord" (Luke 2:26). This prophecy was fulfilled only a few days after the shepherds saw Jesus. Somehow Simeon knew that the blanketed bundle he saw in Mary's arms was the Almighty God. And for Simeon, seeing Jesus was enough. Now he was ready to die. Some don't want to die until they've seen the world. Simeon's dream was not so timid. He didn't want to die until he had seen the maker of the world. He had to see Jesus.

He prayed: "God, you can now release your servant; release me in peace as you promised. With *my own eyes* I've seen your salvation" (Luke 2:29–30 MSG, italics mine).

The Magi had the same desire. Like Simeon, they wanted to see Jesus. Like the shepherds, they were not satisfied with what they saw in the night sky. Not that the star wasn't spectacular. Not that the star wasn't historical. To be a witness of the blazing orb was a privilege, but for the Magi, it wasn't enough. It wasn't enough to see the light over Bethlehem; they had to see the Light of Bethlehem. It was him they came to see.

And they succeeded! They all succeeded. More remarkable than their diligence was Jesus' willingness. Jesus wanted to be seen! Whether they came from the pasture or the palace, whether they lived in the temple or among the sheep, whether their gift was of gold or honest surprise . . . they were welcomed. Search for one example of one person who desired to see the infant Jesus and was turned away. You won't find it.

You will find examples of those who didn't seek him. Those, like King Herod, who were content with less. Those, like the religious leaders, who preferred to read about him than to see him. The ratio between those who missed him and those who sought him is thousands to one. But the ratio between those who sought him and those who found him was one to one. *All who sought him found him.* Long before the words were written, this promise was proven: "God . . . rewards those who truly want to find him" (Heb. 11:6).

The examples continue. Consider John and Andrew. They, too, were rewarded. For them it wasn't enough to listen to John the Baptist. Most would have been content to serve in the shadow of the world's most famous evangelist. Could there be a better teacher? Only one. And when John and Andrew saw him, they left John the Baptist and followed Jesus. Note the request they made.

"Rabbi," they asked, "where are you staying?" (John 1:38). Pretty bold request. They didn't ask Jesus to give them a minute or an opinion or a message or a miracle. They asked for his address. They wanted to hang out with him. They wanted to know him. They wanted to know what caused his head to turn and his heart to burn and his soul to yearn. They wanted to study his eyes and follow his steps. They wanted to see him. They wanted to know what made him laugh and if he ever got tired. And most of all, they wanted to know, *Could Jesus be who John said he was—and if he is, what on earth is God doing on the earth?* You can't answer such a question by talking to his cousin; you've got to talk to the man himself.

Jesus' answer to the disciples? "Come and see" (v. 39). He didn't say, "Come and glance," or "Come and peek." He said, "Come and see." Bring your bifocals and binoculars. This is no time for side-glances or occasional peeks. "Let us fix our eyes on Jesus, the author and perfecter of our faith" (Heb. 12:2 NIV).

The fisherman fixes his eyes on the boat. The girl fixes her eyes on the boy. The disciple fixes his eyes on the Savior.

That's what Matthew did. Matthew, if you remember, was converted at work. According to his résumé, he was a revenue consultant for the government. According to his neighbors, he was a crook. He kept a tax booth and a hand extended at the street corner. That's where he was the day he saw Jesus. "Follow me," the Master said, and Matthew did. And in the very next verse we find Jesus sitting at Matthew's dining room table. "Jesus was having dinner at Matthew's house" (Matt. 9:10).

A curbside conversion couldn't satisfy his heart, so Matthew took Jesus home. Something happens over a dinner table that doesn't happen over an office desk. Take off the tie, heat up the grill, break out the sodas, and spend the evening with the suspender of the stars. "You know, Jesus, forgive me for asking but I've always wanted to know . . ."

Again, though the giving of the invitation is impressive, the acceptance is more so. Didn't matter to Jesus that Matthew was a thief. Didn't matter to Jesus that Matthew had built a split-level house with the proceeds of extortion. What did matter was that Matthew wanted to know Jesus, and since God "rewards those who truly want to find him" (Heb. 11:6), Matthew was rewarded with the presence of Christ in his home.

Of course, it only made sense that Jesus spend time with Matthew. After all, Matthew was a top draft pick, shoulder-tapped to write the first book of the New Testament. Jesus hangs out with only the big guys like Matthew and Andrew and John. Right?

May I counter that opinion with an example? Zacchaeus was far from a big guy. He was small, so small he couldn't see over the crowd that lined the street the day Jesus came to Jericho. Of course the crowd might have let him elbow up to the front, except that he, like Matthew, was a tax collector. But he, like Matthew, had a hunger in his heart to see Jesus.

It wasn't enough to stand at the back of the crowd. It wasn't enough to peer through a cardboard telescope. It wasn't enough to listen to someone else describe the parade of the Messiah. Zacchaeus wanted to see Jesus with his own eyes.

So he went out on a limb. Clad in a three-piece Armani suit and brand-new Italian loafers, he shimmied up a tree in hopes of seeing Christ.

I wonder if you would be willing to do the same. Would you go out on a limb to see Jesus? Not everyone would. In the same Bible where we read about Zacchaeus crawling across the limb, we read about a young ruler. Unlike Zacchaeus, the crowd parted to make room for him. He was the . . . ahem . . . *rich, young ruler*. Upon learning that Jesus was in the area, he called for the limo and cruised across town and approached the carpenter. Please note the question he had for Jesus: "Teacher, what good thing must I do to have life forever?" (Matt. 19:16).

Bottom line sort of fellow, this ruler. No time for formalities or conversations. "Let's get right to the issue. Your schedule is busy; so is mine. Tell me how I can get saved, and I'll leave you alone."

There was nothing wrong with his question, but there was a problem with his heart. Contrast his desire with that of Zacchaeus, "Can I make it up that tree?"

Or John and Andrew, "Where are you staying?"
Or Matthew, "Can you spend the evening?"
Or Simeon, "Can I stay alive until I see him?"
Or the Magi, "Saddle up the camels. We aren't stopping until we find him."
Or the shepherd, "Let's go. . . . Let's see."

See the difference? The rich, young ruler wanted medicine. The others wanted the Physician. The ruler wanted an answer to the quiz. They wanted the teacher. He was in a hurry. They had all the time in the world. He settled for a cup of coffee at the drive-through window. They wouldn't settle for anything less than a full-course meal at the banquet table. They wanted more than salvation. They wanted the Savior. They wanted to see Jesus.

They were earnest in their search. One translation renders Hebrews 11:6: "God . . . rewards those who *earnestly* seek him" (NIV, italics mine).

Another reads: "God rewards those who *search* for him" (PHILLIPS, italics mine).

And another: "God . . . rewards those who *sincerely look* for him" (TLB, italics mine).

I like the King James translation: "He is a rewarder of them that *diligently* seek him" (italics mine).

Diligently—what a great word. Be diligent in your search. Be hungry in your quest, relentless in your pilgrimage. Let this book be but one of dozens you read about Jesus and this hour be but one of hundreds in which you seek him. Step away from the puny pursuits of possessions and positions, and seek your king.

Don't be satisfied with angels. Don't be content with stars in the sky. Seek him out as the shepherds did. Long for him as Simeon did. Worship him as the wise men did. Do as John and Andrew did: ask for his address. Do as Matthew: invite Jesus into your house. Imitate Zacchaeus. Risk whatever it takes to see Christ.

God rewards those who seek *him*. Not those who seek doctrine or religion or systems or creeds. Many settle for these lesser passions, but the reward goes to those who settle for nothing less than Jesus himself. And what is the reward? What awaits those who seek Jesus? Nothing short of the heart of Jesus. "And as the Spirit of the Lord works within us, we become more and more like him" (2 Cor. 3:18 TLB).

Can you think of a greater gift than to be like Jesus? Christ felt no guilt; God wants to banish yours. Jesus had no bad habits; God wants to remove yours. Jesus had no fear of death; God wants you to be fearless. Jesus had kindness for the diseased and mercy for the rebellious and courage for the challenges. God wants you to have the same.

He loves you just the way you are, but he refuses to leave you that way. He wants you to be just like Jesus.

CHAPTER 1: A HEART LIKE HIS

1. Adapted from Max Lucado, *A Gentle Thunder* (Dallas: Word Publishing, 1995), 46.

2. David Jeremiah audiotape: *The God of the Impossible,* TPR02.

CHAPTER 2: LOVING THE
PEOPLE YOU ARE STUCK WITH

1. Max Lucado, Ph.D. of Etymological Contortionism, *Max's Manual of Medical Terms* (Nonsense, Tex.: One Page Publishing, 1998), vol. 1, ch. 1, p. 1, sentence 1.

CHAPTER 3: THE TOUCH OF GOD

1. Not his actual name.

CHAPTER 4: HEARING GOD'S MUSIC

1. Matt. 11:15, 13:9, 13:43; Mark 4:9, 4:23, 8:18; Luke 8:8, 14:35; Rev. 2:7, 2:11, 2:17, 2:29, 3:6, 3:13, 3:22, 13:9.

2. Mark 4:1–20.

3. Rev. 2:7, 2:11, 2:17, 2:29, 3:6, 3:13, 3:22.

CHAPTER 5:
BEING LED BY AN UNSEEN HAND

1. Brother Lawrence and Frank Laubach, *Practicing His Presence,* (Goleta, CA: Christian Books, 1973.) Used by kind permission of Dr. Robert S. Laubach and Gene Edwards.

2. Ibid.

3. Ibid.

4. Ibid.

5. As quoted in Timothy Jones, *The Art of Prayer* (New York: Ballantine Books, 1997), 133.

6. Ibid., 140.

7. Charles R. Swindoll, *The Finishing Touch* (Dallas: Word Publishing, 1994), 292.

CHAPTER 6:
A CHANGED FACE AND A SET OF WINGS

1. Matt. 7:7 NIV.

2. Horatio G. Spafford, "It Is Well with My Soul."

CHAPTER 7:
GOLF GAMES AND CELERY STICKS

1. John Maxwell, *Developing the Leader within You* (Nashville: Thomas Nelson, 1993), 29.

CHAPTER 8: NOTHING BUT THE TRUTH

1. James Hassett, "But That Would Be Wrong," *Psychology Today,* November 1981, 34–41.

2. Paul Lee Tan, *Encyclopedia of 7700 Illustrations* (Rockville, Md.: Assurance Publishers, 1979), 562–63.

CHAPTER 10: FINDING GOLD IN THE GARBAGE

1. Jim Morrison, "Slightly Rotted Gold," *American Way Magazine,* 1 April 1992, 32–35.

2. William Barclay, *The Gospel of John,* vol. 2 (Philadelphia: The Westminster Press, 1975), 222.

CHAPTER 11: WHEN HEAVEN CELEBRATES

1. Charles Spurgeon's sermon entitled "The Sympathy of Two Worlds," quoted in John MacArthur, *The Glory of Heaven* (Wheaton, IL: Crossway Books, 1996), 246.

2. Ibid., 118.

3. James Ryle, unpublished manuscript. Used by permission.

4. C. S. Lewis, *The Weight of Glory* (New York: Macmillan, 1949), 14–15.

STUDY GUIDE

————— ✦❧✦❧✦ —————

ONE

A HEART LIKE HIS

Finding the Heart of Jesus

1. What would change in your life if Jesus really did become you?

   A. Who would be surprised at the "new you"? Why?

   B. Would you have "fences to mend"? If so, to whom do they belong?

2. Since God wants you to have a heart like his ("a new person, made to be like God," says Ephesians 4:23–24), give yourself a checkup:

   A. What's your heart condition today?

   B. What would happen during a spiritual "stress test"? Would the results differ, depending on what was happening in your life from day to day? Explain.

   C. What specific actions would you have to take to develop a heart like Jesus'?

3. God wants you to be like him, but he does love you just the way you are. Describe the "you" that God loves.

—————

A. What are your gifts, talents, abilities, concerns, cares, quirks, faults, needs, desires?

B. How would any of those be different if you had "a heart like his"? Which parts of you would be "tweaked"?

4. Jesus' thoughts, actions, and entire self reflected his intimate relationship with his father. As a result, his heart was supremely spiritual.

A. Describe a "spiritual heart."

B. Describe any differences between your heart and that of Christ.

5. As Max points out, we've "tapped into" God's power, but not enough of us use it to its full extent.

A. Describe your "power usage." How much of his light do you use at work? At home? In your community?

B. What can you learn from reflecting on the heart of Christ?

Probing the Mind of Jesus

1. Read Philippians 2:5–13.

A. We are to have the same attitude as Christ, to "think and act like Christ Jesus." How difficult is this for you? What is difficult about it? Explain.

B. How much effort are you willing to expend to comply with the directive of this passage? What kind of effort?

C. What about your heart needs the most attention?

2. Ephesians 4:20–32 deals with some specific no-no's for those Christians who want to live as "children of light."

   A. Which part of your "old self" gives you the most trouble?

   B. What can you determine today to do about this?

3. Jesus was sinless—his words and actions were always pure. Read 1 John 3:1–10.

   A. How does it make you feel to know you have an example like this? Is it intimidating or comforting to you? Explain.

   B. Jesus has given his sinless self to you and is waiting to remake you into someone just like himself. How can you use this thought to motivate you to become like him? Does it? Explain.

Becoming the Hands of Jesus

1. Write down Colossians 3:10 on a card and post it where you will see it every day. Memorize it and thank God for loving you enough to change you into someone like him!

2. Spend a few minutes imagining yourself handling a particular prickly situation, one that you usually struggle with. Now imagine how you could handle it with "a heart like his." Then pray that God will enable you to handle an actual situation just as you did in your imagination. The next time it occurs, write in a journal what happened, and see how God will answer your honest prayers!

TWO

LOVING THE PEOPLE
YOU ARE STUCK WITH

A Forgiving Heart

Finding the Heart of Jesus

1. Consider "the claustrophobia that comes with commitment."

   A. Have you experienced commitment claustrophobia?

   B. Where do you encounter this—with a spouse, child, employee, or someone else? Explain.

   C. Have you ever felt fearful or frustrated because of the permanence involved in commitment? If so, describe your reaction.

   D. If you feel "stuck" with someone right now (with a major case of stuckititus), do you feel most like fleeing, fighting, or forgiving? Explain.

   E. How would you feel if you knew that person felt the same way about you? Do you think anyone does? If so, explain.

2. Jesus was able to love people who were even hard to like.

   A. Name some folks you find hard to like. Why is this?

   B. Name some folks who may find you hard to like. Why is this?

3. Jesus knew no one "expected" him to do the work of the lowliest servant when he washed the feet of the disciples as described in John 13. Remember he was fully aware that they would desert him in his greatest hour of need—yet he served them with a heart bursting with love.

   A. If footwashing were still a custom today, would you be willing to serve one of the people you named in study question 1 or 2 above in such a way? Explain.

   B. Think of someone who "washed your feet" when you didn't deserve it. What were the circumstances?

4. As you shift your gaze away from your "problem person" and onto Jesus, what happens to your ability to forgive that person?

   A. Name the sins for which Christ has had to forgive you this day alone. Are any of them "repeats"? Explain.

   B. Realizing all the clean-up duty Jesus has had to perform on you, how willing are you to do the same for others? How do you respond to those who continually, repeatedly, cause you the same problems?

5. Max reminds us there was only one man in that Passover Supper room worthy of having his feet washed, and that was the footwasher himself. The one who should have been served chose to become the servant.

   A. Name several relationships you could improve by doing some unexpected footwashing.

B. How could you "wash" someone's "feet"? How do you think it would be received? Explain.

C. Do any of the people involved sit at your supper table? If so, is this kind of footwashing easier or harder? Why?

Probing the Mind of Jesus

1. Meditate on Colossians 3:12–17.

    A. Insert people's names where appropriate in this passage ("Bear with _____, and forgive whatever grievances you may have against _____.")

    B. Now repeat this exercise, asking God to help someone bear with you.

2. Put yourself into the scene described in John 13:1–17.

    A. You're sitting there, waiting. And waiting. Just where is that wretched servant anyway? Then your Master, of all people, gets up to do the work. How do you feel, watching while he is working? What are you thinking?

    B. If you were at this scene and knew what Judas was about to do, would you have washed his feet as Jesus did? Explain.

3. Ephesians 4:32 says, "Be kind and loving [or compassionate] to each other, and forgive each other just as God forgave you in Christ." Read the next verse (Eph. 5:1).

A. How grimy did God get when he reached down to clean you up? How grimy are you willing to get in order to be an "imitator of God"?

B. Ephesians 5:2 continues, "And live a life of love, just as Christ loved us and gave himself up for us as a fragrant offering and sacrifice to God." With God's help, what kind of changes do you need to make in order to make your life a sweet-smelling sacrifice? Explain.

C. Is there a Judas in your life? Can you do for him what Jesus did for his Judas?

Becoming the Hands of Jesus

1. Thank God for his daily mercy and forgiveness. Express your gratitude for his limitless grace. Meditate on the biblical truth that he remembers your sins no more, but they are as far from him as "the east is from the west"!

2. The wronged wife in the story at the end of this chapter was merciful to her husband. She forgave and was willing to let go of her hurt. She said, "Let's move on." Think of a person who has wounded you. Determine today that you will start this same process. Ask God to help you bathe his/her feet in his love, and deliberately forget the hurt. Spend time in prayer about this person and the situation. Ask God to help you know how to forgive the hurt and love the person just as Jesus does.

THREE

THE TOUCH OF GOD
A Compassionate Heart

Finding the Heart of Jesus

1. Remember some instances when "God's very hands" ministered to you. How did this make you feel?

2. Do you think you have the "hands of heaven"? Explain. Do you make it a practice to seek out opportunities to care for others with those hands?

3. Have you ever "quarantined" someone from your life?

   A. If so, what was/is the situation? Why did you make the exclusion?

   B. What would cause you to include him/her once again?

4. Though Jesus' words cured the leper's disease, Max points out that only Christ's loving touch banished the man's loneliness.

   A. Describe some periods in your life when no words came, but a touch said it all.

   B. Is talking about "godly touching" easier than actually doing it? Explain.

   C. Do you find it easy or difficult to receive such a touch? Why?

5. Make a list of ways to "touch" someone emotionally without physically touching them (Here's a start: cards, visits, etc.)

Probing the Mind of Jesus

1. Read again the story of the cleansed leper from Matthew 8:1–4. Read also Mark 1:40–45 and Luke 5:12–16. All three writers mention the touch of Jesus, as well as his healing words.

    A. Why do you think Jesus thought it was important to physically touch the man?

    B. Would the story have been diminished without the touch? Explain.

2. The Mark account states that the cleansed leper, though having been warned not to tell the story to anyone, instead went out and began to talk freely.

    A. Why did Jesus command the man to be silent?

    B. What happened when the man spoke out?

    C. Would you have been able to keep quiet if such a marvelous thing had happened to you? Explain.

3. The niv rendering of Colossians 3:12 states that we are to "clothe [ourselves] with compassion and kindness." Dressing is a deliberate act; we intentionally do it and it never "just happens." But as we do it every day, it becomes a natural act.

A. Think of someone who has a compassionate spirit? How is this spirit expressed through his/her actions, speech, demeanor?

B. With the Lord's help, how can you work at better showing compassion?

Becoming the Hands of Jesus

1. Spend a few minutes thanking the Lord for those who have taken the time to show you compassion or kindness when you needed it most. Bring them by name before the Lord. Then tell them personally, through a note or phone call, what their ministry to you has meant.

2. Ask God to show you someone who needs that special "godly touch." Chances are you already know who it is. If you sense some resistance on your part ("Not him/her! Not me—I can't!"), ask the Lord to make your hands into his and surrender them to him. Then follow as he leads you.

FOUR

HEARING GOD'S MUSIC
A Listening Heart

Finding the Heart of Jesus

1. Scripture often reminds us that it's not enough to have ears—we must use them. The problem is, we often don't.

A. We are to "listen like sheep" who follow their master's well-known voice. How do you try to hear God's voice on a regular basis?

B. How can you become so familiar with the Master that you'd know "a stranger's voice" immediately? How can you recognize false teaching when you hear it?

2. Jesus made it a habit to pray. Max says Christ "cleared his calendar" in order to speak with his father.

A. Describe your own prayer life. Do days ever go by when you realize you've totally neglected this privilege? How did those days go for you?

B. What would happen to your marriage/family/friendship/work relationships if your communication with the people in them was the same as that between you and your Savior?

3. Jesus was intimately familiar with Scripture.

A. Christ knew the Bible and how to use it. How's your scripture memory?

B. How easy is it for you to locate a specific verse?

C. Do you understand most Scripture well enough to apply it effectively? Explain.

D. How are you at explaining Scripture to others, especially those who don't yet know Christ?

4. If we want to be like Jesus, we need to let God have us.

A. Do you really want to be "had"? Explain.

B. How can you surrender your entire life, your whole being, to him? Be specific.

C. When is the best time for you to spend the necessary time listening for him in Bible study and prayer, until you have received your lesson for each day? Do you take advantage of this time?

5. The Bible says we are worthy because of what Christ did for us; we did nothing to deserve such a lofty status. Because of this, he wants us to open our hearts completely to him.

A. How do you react to such undeserved affection? Why?

B. What happens between you and God when you open your heart to him?

Probing the Mind of Jesus

1. Read the parable of the sower in Mark 4:1–20.

A. Give yourself a checkup: Which seed describes you best? Why?

B. What kind of changes might be needed to make you into seed sown on good soil, producing a crop a hundred times over?

2. John 10:1–18 describes the relationship between a shepherd and his sheep, as well as that between the Lord and his people. The passage says sheep will "run away" from strangers

because they do not recognize them. They are so attuned to their master that they want no other, and the master is so in love with his sheep he will die for them.

    A. What benefits do sheep receive by sticking close to their master?

    B. What dangers lurk if they choose to wander away?

    C. Do you think sheep fret over their "worthiness"? Explain.

    D. What parallels can you draw between sheep and people?

3. If we want to be like Jesus, we must have a regular time of talking to God and listening to his Word.

    A. Romans 12 contains a list of "do's" for those who wish to live in harmony with the Lord and with others. Why are we to do these things? How are we to do them?

    B. How can you make your prayer times worshipful?

    C. Define "being faithful in prayer."

    D. Is it possible to be faithful in prayer without spending time in the Word? Explain.

Becoming the Hands of Jesus

1. Living in the communications age, we are inundated with so much information that we can become overloaded. Newspapers, magazines, television, and the Internet all scream for our attention. Challenge yourself this week to spend as many or more hours reading the Bible as you do with your paper or TV. Then record the difference it makes in your life.

2. If you don't already do so, keep a journal of your journey with the Lord. For one month, record the passages you study and the amount of time you spend with him in prayer as a result. Track the positive changes you find in your relationship with the Lord as well as with others.

FIVE

BEING LED BY AN UNSEEN HAND
A God-Intoxicated Heart

Finding the Heart of Jesus

1. We are always in the presence of God.

   A. Does the statement above comfort you or tire you? Why?

   B. What does the reality of God's continuous presence mean to you as you go about your everyday activities?

2. God wants us to enjoy the same intimacy with him that he has with his Son.

   A. Do you like intimacy or do you prefer standing a bit apart, keeping your "space"? Explain.

   B. How do you try to keep parts of yourself hidden from others? What would you like to keep hidden from God?

3. God is never away from us.

   A. Have you ever found yourself feeling especially close to God on Sunday morning but miles away by Tuesday afternoon? If so, describe this experience. Why do you think this happens?

   B. God is absolutely committed to us and provides a model for us. What is your level of commitment—to your spouse, your children, your church, etc.? Are they secure in the knowledge you'll never leave and you'll always be there for them? How have you conveyed to them your commitment?

4. In the Christian's "marriage to Jesus," the communication never stops.

   A. When you talk to God, what do you mention first? Does the giving of praise and honor regularly come before the litany of requests? If not, why not?

   B. How long would a friendship last if the only communication between two people was the asking of favors? Would you long for something else, for something deeper? Explain.

   C. Is God the first person to whom you talk when something great happens to you? Is he the last when you have a problem? Explain.

5. Consider every moment in your life a potential time of communion with God.

A. Do you know anyone else besides God who would really want to hear from you all the time?

B. How is your sense of worth affected by knowing God will never leave you? Does this change your worship of him?

Probing the Mind of Jesus

1. First Corinthians 6:1 names believers as God's "fellow workers," or to put it more commonly, God's "coworkers."

    A. What would happen to your everyday work ethic if you truly believed yourself to be working right alongside the one true God? Would you work harder? Would you do your best at everything with God at the next work-station? Explain.

    B. Should life itself be easier to handle, knowing the Almighty is going through it right along with you? If so, how?

2. Read John 5:16–30.

    A. Jesus said the Son did "nothing by himself"; what the Father did, the Son did. Can the same be said of you? Why? What causes you to run ahead of God? What areas of your life do you try to handle without God's help?

    B. Jesus also didn't attempt to please himself but his father (v. 30). Who are you most trying to please? Your spouse? Your parents? The neighbors?

3. God's word picture of a vine and its branches in John 15:1–8 describes the relationship he desires with his people. He wants to be completely connected to us.

   A. How does your desire for intimacy with God compare to that of Frank Laubach, who felt lost after just a half-hour without thinking of him?

   B. List some practical ways your life would change if you were this connected.

   C. Jesus talks of pruning the branches that bear fruit so they will become even more fruitful. Describe a time you felt the effects of his pruning knife. What kind of fruit was borne afterward? Do you desire even bigger, better fruit, even if you must be pruned again and again? Explain.

Becoming the Hands of Jesus

1. Ask the Lord for two special verses: one to meditate on when you awake and one for the evening as you retire. Do it faithfully for at least a solid week. Use those bookends to begin directing your whole day toward a totally God-centered life.

2. God already knows what you're thinking, wanting, and doing. Realize that he wants to hear from you, so begin talking to him as if he were on the car seat beside you in the morning, standing in the line at the bank, or sitting at

the next desk. He's not interested in flowery phrases or pious sounding words—he just wants you.

SIX

A CHANGED FACE AND A SET OF WINGS
A Worship-Hungry Heart

Finding the Heart of Jesus

1. Describe a time you met a famous person or attended a very important event. Did you buy a new dress or suit? Were you thinking about it for days beforehand? How important was the famous person or the event compared to a meeting with Jesus?

2. How do you define worship? What is involved?

   A. Why do you worship?

   B. Is worship more or less important to you today than when you first came to know the Lord?

3. Jesus prepared himself for worship, yet we're often casual when it comes to meeting God.

   A. Think about a typical Sunday morning before you leave for church. Be honest with yourself. Do tempers flare? Are you rushing around? Describe the day.

B. What could you do to improve the situation, even beginning the night before? What keeps you from implementing these changes?

4. God changes our faces through worship.

A. How can you give more conscious thought to the words you're singing, praying, or hearing?

B. What happens to your face as you leave the service and head to your work week?

C. Would anyone know by looking at you on Tuesday that you'd been with the Master on Sunday? How?

5. God changes those who watch us worship.

A. What aspects of your worship are designed to attract people who don't know Christ?

B. How often during the service do you take time to pray for any unsaved people who might be sitting alongside you?

Probing the Mind of Jesus

1. Read Matthew 17:1–9.

A. Do you think the disciples understood the purpose of their worship trip to the mountain?

B. How do you think they were affected by their experience? (Read 1 Peter 1:16–18.)

C. Why do you suppose Christ told them to tell no one about it?

2. Second Corinthians 3:12–18 contrasts Moses' wearing a veil to mask God's glory with the believer's privilege of an unveiled face.

   A. How do we sometimes present "veiled faces" or hearts as we worship? Why do we do this?

   B. How can you best "reflect God's glory" this week? At home? At work? With friends?

3. Read Psalm 34 silently to yourself, then read it aloud.

   A. How "big" does God seem to you in this passage? What words would you use to describe God and his glory?

   B. Read through the passage again and count the number of reasons there are to praise God.

   C. Now look at your face in a mirror. Do you see God's reflection? Explain.

Becoming the Hands of Jesus

1. If Sunday mornings before church are a problem at your house, sit down with your family and talk it through. See if anyone else has been concerned. Determine to make physical, practical preparations the night before (find that lost shoe, make clothing decisions, etc.). Take time for a meeting with the Lord at home before you meet him at

church. And remember: he is reachable in the car on the way, too!

2. Whether you're the "official greeter" at your church or not, consider making this your mission opportunity next Sunday. Instead of waiting for visitors to make themselves known, put God's smile on your face, and purposefully seek them out.

S E V E N

GOLF GAMES AND CELERY STICKS
A Focused Heart

Finding the Heart of Jesus

1. One of the incredible traits of Jesus was his ability to stay on target.

   A. How on track is your life? Explain.

   B. Where do you want to go in your life? Name some specific goals you have.

2. Our lives tend to be scattered.

   A. In what way(s) does this statement reflect your life?

   B. What are your priorities?

   C. Are you easily distracted by the small things and forgetful about the big things? Explain.

3. God wants us to have focused hearts, to stay on target, to fit into God's plan.

   A. What is God's plan concerning you?

   B. How do your plans compare with those of God? Explain.

4. When we submit to God's plans, we can trust our desires.

   A. If whatever you desired came to be, do you think it would be good for you? Explain.

   B. How can you commit yourself to whatever God wants for you, even if it might be different from what you desire?

5. In Romans 12:3 Paul advises that we should "have a sane estimate of [our] capabilities."

   A. You are probably aware of your weaknesses, but what are your strengths?

   B. How are you using those strengths to serve and honor God? Have you thanked him for them?

Probing the Mind of Jesus

1. Read Mark 10:42–45.

   A. What kind of ruler was Jesus describing in verse 42?

   B. How should the behavior of "those who want to be great" differ from the actions of others?

   C. How do you think things would have changed if Jesus had chosen to "be served" instead of to serve?

2. Compare Mark 10:45 with Luke 19:10.

    A. Do these two verses say the same thing? Why or why not?

    B. Would you consider one or both to be Christ's "mission statement"? Explain.

3. Romans 8:28 has often been quoted and misquoted.

    A. How does this verse function when so-called "bad things" happen to us?

    B. Do you think God "plans" the "bad things" or that he just allows them? Is it the same thing?

    C. Continue reading from verse 28 to the end of the chapter. Describe how these verses relate to the "bad things" in your life.

4. God wants to use us to bring about his plan. (Read 2 Corinthians 5:17–21).

    A. What are you doing to serve as Christ's representative or ambassador?

    B. What tools do you have to prepare you for this work? How are you using them?

5. Spend some time in Psalm 37.

    A. How much time do you spend fretting over "evil men"? Are you ever worried they won't "get theirs"? Explain.

    B. What does God say will happen to them?

    C. What should you be doing instead of worrying about retribution?

D. When your heart and God's come together, what happens to your desires?

Becoming the Hands of Jesus

1. Both Psalm 139:14 and Ephesians 2:10 declare God's marvelous workmanship in you. Do you believe them? Take a few moments to write down the specific things about you that illustrate that statement. Dedicate those qualities to the Lord and determine to start using them for him today.

2. When you were little did anyone ask, "What do you want to be when you grow up?" How did your answer then compare with today? As you've grown up in the Lord, what do you want to be, to do, for him? Spend some time in prayer and then compose a personal life mission statement, with which you can serve and honor God.

EIGHT

NOTHING BUT THE TRUTH
An Honest Heart

Finding the Heart of Jesus

1. The Christian is a witness.

   A. What's the difference between a witness in court and a witness for Christ?

B. We know there's a penalty for perjury in court. Is there one for the Christian? Explain.

2. Jesus didn't lie, cheat, or stretch the truth.

A. How do you measure up to God's standard in this area?

B. Do you think there's a difference between "regular" lies and "white" ones? Explain.

C. Once you realize you've been dishonest, what do you do about it? Does it depend on how big the lie was? Explain.

3. God is as angry about lying as he is about such things as adultery and aggravated assault.

A. Do you agree with this viewpoint? Explain.

B. How can you strive to live out God's honor code? What do you do when you fall short?

4. God always speaks the truth. The Bible says he "cannot lie."

A. In what circumstances are you most tempted to lie?

B. Do others consider you to be an honest person? Would your assessment and theirs differ?

C. How do you feel about lying or evading the truth a little in order to spare the feelings of others?

5. There are times when the truth is difficult.

A. Name some situations in which we are more comfortable with a lie than the truth.

B. How is it possible to lie without using words?

C. We know there are consequences to lying. Have you ever been caught in a lie? What happened? How did you feel? What did you learn from these consequences?

Probing the Mind of Jesus

1. Read Ephesians 4:17–32. Paul admonishes his readers to get rid of their former way of life and display a "new attitude of the mind."

   A. Since Christians are members of one body, is it worse to be dishonest with a fellow believer than with one who is not? Explain.

   B. How can you be dishonest with yourself?

   C. Do you agree that lying should be placed in the same category with anger, theft, foul language, etc.? Do you "rank" sins, considering some worse than others? Explain.

2. Spend some time in Psalm 101.

   A. What do you do when others are "slandering [their] neighbor in secret"?

   B. What kind of company do you keep? Do you tolerate liars?

3. Titus 1:2 and 2 Timothy 2:13 remind us that we can always believe God.

A. How should this truth affect our everyday lives? Does it? Explain.

B. Which of God's promises are most precious to you? Why?

C. When you promise something, can you be relied upon? Explain.

4. Think about the story of Ananias and Sapphira in Acts 5.

A. Why do you think this couple lied about the price of the land? Why didn't they tell Peter they were just giving a portion of what they received?

B. Do you think Ananias and Sapphira ever thought they would be found out? Why or why not?

C. What was it about this lie that angered Peter?

D. How do you feel about the harsh punishment God meted out? How would their witness for Christ in the community have been affected had they not been so judged? What happened to the witness of the church after their deaths?

Becoming the Hands of Jesus

1. In a concordance, look up the words *lie, lies, lying.* Then look up words like *truth* and *honest* or *honesty.* How do you think the number of references to these words corresponds to God's concern in these matters?

2. From one of the verses you found in the listings above, claim one as your own. Write it on the flyleaf of your Bible. Repeat it each day. Ask God to help you be more like him in the area of honesty.

NINE

THE GREENHOUSE OF THE MIND
A Pure Heart

Finding the Heart of Jesus

1. How can you manage your heart "as a greenhouse"? How can you let the analogy get personal?

   A. What kind of "seeds" are you allowing to grow?

   B. What weeds do you see? How can you keep them from flourishing? How do they sometimes crowd out the flowers?

   C. Would you classify yourself as usually optimistic or negative? Explain. How does your optimism or negativism affect those around you?

2. There should be a sentry at the door of our hearts.

   A. Where do your thoughts usually go when you allow them to wander?

B. How can you immediately recognize "wrong thoughts"? How could you do so more easily?

3. We need to submit our thoughts to the authority of Jesus.

   A. If your thoughts were written down on paper and submitted to Christ before you thought them, how many of them would he "red pencil"? Would you be surprised, or would you have known the results beforehand?

   B. If your thoughts were broadcast to those around you, would you be embarrassed? Would they be disappointed? Sad? Hurt? Surprised?

4. The Bible is the "check point" for our questionable thoughts.

   A. In your study of Scripture, what validation can you find for an inferiority complex? A prideful spirit? Conceit? Impure sexual desires?

   B. Some people think the Bible is just a book of no's whose aim is to squelch free-spiritedness. What happens to us when we follow our own "free-spirit" instead of God's Word?

Probing the Mind of Jesus

1. In 1 Peter 5:8–9 the devil is compared to a "roaring lion."

   A. In what circumstances do you most often feel you're going to be "devoured" in your thought life?

B. How can you put up a good resistance to the devil? How can you increase your levels of self-control and alertness?

2. Read Galatians 6:7–10.

A. God recognizes that we become weary in our struggles with sin (v. 9). Once you realize the need to keep your thought life under control (to plant the right seeds), what do you do if you're tempted to give in to spiritual fatigue?

B. What are the benefits that can be reaped from a God-centered thought life?

3. Proverbs 4:20–23 admonishes us to pay close attention to what God says.

A. We are to keep his words not only in our sight but in our hearts. What is the difference between these two?

B. The heart is compared to a "wellspring" of life. Look up the word "wellspring" in a dictionary. Why do you think that word is used in verse 23?

C. You've heard the expression "You are what you eat." Do you believe you are also what you think? Give some examples.

4. In 2 Corinthians 10:3–5 Paul reminds us that though we live in the world, we are not to act as if we are part of the

world (v. 3). He recognizes that life is a fight and reminds us we have been given "divine power" (v. 4) to help win the battle.

A. Verse 5 tells us to "capture" our thoughts, making them obedient to Christ. How can we do this? What are we to do with these thoughts, once we've captured them?

B. How can you tell your wrong, impure, ungodly thoughts no and refuse them readmittance? In what way can this be like a battle?

Becoming the Hands of Jesus

1. Think about a plot of fertile ground for a moment. Is more work involved in the planting stage or the weeding stage? What happens to the crop if the latter is neglected? What market exists for the sale of weeds? Would anyone ever plant weed seeds on purpose? Translate those questions into an evaluation of your thought life. Decide today to plant roses and, with God's help, keep the thistles out.

2. Plant a seed, literally. Use the right soil. Water it. Make sure it gets the correct amount of water and sunshine. Put it where you can see it. Nurture it. Watch it grow. Consider it to be an outward expression of what you are doing inwardly with the garden of your heart.

TEN

FINDING GOLD IN THE GARBAGE
A Hope-Filled Heart

Finding the Heart of Jesus

1. How do you view the "garbage" that comes your way?

    A. Do you think you've had more or less troubles and sorrow than the average person? Explain.

    B. What next "bad thing" are you worried about that might be lurking around the corner?

    C. Why do you think we hang on to the pain and the hurt rather than look for the good in our troubles?

2. How we look at life determines how we live it.

    A. The saying goes "When life gives you lemons, make lemonade." Have you had to make lemonade out of your life circumstances?

    B. Describe someone you know who's good at this. How do you feel when you're around this person? What can you learn from him or her?

3. We need to see our troubles as Jesus sees them.

    A. Analyze your feelings about any unanswered prayers, unfruitful dreams, or unbelievable betrayals. Are they recent, or have you been hanging on to the resulting hurts for a long while? Explain.

B. How can you see these things as Jesus does?

4. Jesus found good in the bad, purpose in the pain.

   A. Do you think this is realistically possible in every situation? Explain. What would you say to someone who thought this was a "Pollyanna" view of life?

   B. Describe a time you found good in the bad, purpose in the pain. Did you have this attitude while you were going through the difficulty, or did these insights come later? Explain.

5. Jesus can change the way you look at life.

   A. How do we often underestimate the power of God?

   B. How would your life change if you consistently believed that God's power is the same today as it was in the days of Elisha?

Probing the Mind of Jesus

1. Romans 12:9–16 tells us that troubles are a part of life for everyone; no one is exempt.

   A. How should we respond to evil? How are we to behave when afflicted? How is this possible?

   B. Why does God allow us to go through these troubles? What do you think is to be gained by them?

C. Do you someday expect to find out God's purpose in your suffering? What if you never do?

2. Compare your spiritual eyesight to that described in Matthew 6:22–23.

   A. Describe someone you know who prefers to live in the darkness rather than the light. Do you enjoy being around this person? Explain.

   B. What's God's opinion about this?

3. Read about Jesus' betrayal in Matthew 26:46–52.

   A. Even after Judas betrayed him, Jesus called him "friend." Have you ever felt betrayed by a "friend." If so, is this person still your friend? Explain.

   B. In so-called righteous indignation, one of Jesus' companions sliced off the ear of the high priest's servant. Luke records that Jesus responded with a healing touch. How can we respond in such a way when we are hurt? What keeps us from responding like this?

4. In Matthew 26:53, Jesus reminds the mob that came for him that he could be rescued from their clutches immediately if he so desired.

   A. In what way can your own difficult situations be easier to handle, knowing that God could get you out of them if he chose to do so? Can they ever be made more difficult because of this knowledge? Explain.

   B. How do you respond when God chooses not to change your circumstances? Do you still believe God is present in the problem? Explain.

Becoming the Hands of Jesus

1. Borrow some eyeglasses from a person with an acute vision problem. Put them up to your eyes. Look at a tree, a flower, the face of the person next to you. Now look at these same objects with your normal vision (with or without glasses). What was the difference? Were things distorted the first time? Were they blurry? It's much easier to see all the detail when you view something in the correct way, isn't it? When viewed through the perfect, all-seeing eyes of God, everything that happens to us makes sense!

2. Think about your friends, especially a friendship that went sour. Did that person hurt you, betray you in a way that still smarts whenever you think of it? Ask the Lord to soften your heart, to forgive him/her. Give your grudge to God and ask him to heal your wounds. Make it a point to pray for your friend by name on a regular basis and look for ways to begin the process of restoration.

ELEVEN

WHEN HEAVEN CELEBRATES
A Rejoicing Heart

Finding the Heart of Jesus

1. Jesus knows about the "party"!

A. What is this party? Are you sure you're going to it? How do you know?

B. What did God do to make sure you don't miss the party? What situations did he use? Who were the people involved?

2. Jesus is happiest when the lost are found.

A. Describe a time when you were separated from your parent, "lost" in a store when you were a child. How did you feel the moment you discovered you were alone? Panic? Fear?

B. What do you think your parents thought during their search for you? Was there joy when you were found? If so, describe it.

C. Compare this incident with how God must feel when a sinner repents and comes home to Christ.

3. When you get to the "party," you will be like Jesus. Everyone else will be, too.

A. Which aspects of Jesus' character do you most desire for yourself?

B. Which aspects of his character will you appreciate most in others?

C. How can you love these people right now, while we're all getting ready?

4. Jesus rejoices that we are saved from hell.

A. Describe what you know about hell. Do you believe it's a real place? Why or why not? Read some scriptures that talk about it.

B. How do you rejoice that you're on your way to heaven? Do you ever thank him that you will miss hell? Explain.

5. You can have God's eternal view of the world.

A. Which things that you hold dear to your heart become insignificant when you come to hold God's eternal view of the world?

B. If this viewpoint dominated more of your thinking, how would you spend your time differently?

C. When you hold this view, what happens to your perception of people?

Probing the Mind of Jesus

1. The Psalms are a great place for praise. Read Psalm 96, paying special attention to verses 1 and 2.

A. What does it mean that "all the earth" should sing? Why songs?

B. How and how often do you praise God for your own salvation? How do you respond to other people's salvation stories?

2. Read the three parables of Jesus in Luke 15.

A. Much time and effort was spent in looking for the lost

sheep and the lost coin. What does that say about the lost ones' worth to their owners?

B. Neighbors and friends were called to help rejoice when the lost ones were found. Why was that?

C. The older son in the third story resented the party given for his prodigal brother; he didn't consider his brother worthy of that attention. Do you ever feel someone is "too bad" to be saved, that he/she should not be allowed at the "party" to be held in heaven? Explain. Apart from the grace of God, do you deserve to go?

3. Luke 15:10 speaks of the worth of a single person to God.

A. What should this verse do to our feelings of worthlessness?

B. How should this verse influence your desire to tell others of the salvation that's available in Christ? Does it have this effect with you? Explain.

4. In Matthew 22:13, hell is described as a place "outside," in the dark, where there will be "wailing and gnashing of teeth," with no way out.

A. If this is true, then why do people speak so lightly of that place?

B. Do you think it's important to emphasize the horrors of hell to unbelievers? Explain.

5. Second Corinthians 5:11–16 speaks of a compelling need to tell others of Christ's great gift of salvation.

A. Is it your main purpose in life to bring others to the "party"? How many people have you introduced to Christ so far?

B. Think of someone you know who needs the Lord. How might you be used to introduce this person to Christ? Are you asking God to give you a new heart of love for them? If not, why not?

Becoming the Hands of Jesus

1. Using a concordance or other study tool, search the Scriptures to make a list of all the blessings of heaven. Across the page, write down all the horrors of hell. Then praise God for blessing you with the things in the first list and rescuing you from those in the second.

2. Look through the pages of your favorite hymnal. Find those songs that have to do with heaven. Sing one right now!

TWELVE

FINISHING STRONG
An Enduring Heart

Finding the Heart of Jesus

1. Learn to finish the right things.

A. How much time do you spend on non-essentials?

B. How do you determine what a non-essential is?

2. Finishing strong in the Christian's race takes a massive effort.

A. At the beginning of your relationship with Christ, were your expectations of the Christian life any different from the reality you have experienced? If so, explain.

B. Do you think Christians sometimes paint a "too rosy" picture of what life is like after the salvation experience? Describe any examples you can think of.

C. Would people say you are a stronger believer today than yesterday? Why or why not?

D. What have been your primary joys as a Christian? Your difficulties?

3. By focusing on the reward ahead, Jesus had the strength to endure the shame of the whole world.

A. What does it mean to be focused? How focused are you?

B. What kinds of things most often get in the way of a sharp focus? How can you deal with these more effectively? What keeps you from dealing with them?

4. Jesus looked beyond the horizon, saw the table set before him, and focused on the feast.

A. If you could have your own feast right now, what would be on the table? Who would be the guests?

B. What do you think that "heavenly feast" will be like?

Probing the Mind of Jesus

1. Spend some time pondering Ephesians 1:15–23.

   A. In verse 18 Paul prays that the eyes of our hearts (our minds) may be "enlightened." Why do you think he says that? What kinds of things have been right in front of you that you still haven't seen?

   B. Describe an inheritance that either you or someone you're close to has received. Try to describe any of the "rich glories" that will be the Christian's inheritance.

   C. How much of God's "incomparably great power" (v. 19) have you experienced? Describe your experiences. What more is left to experience?

2. The Christian race is discussed at length in Hebrews 12.

   A. Why does Paul call the Christian life a "race" instead of a walk, a jog, or some other activity?

   B. What kinds of things hinder you from racing effectively? Do you know anyone who has quit? If so, why did it happen?

   C. How can we continue to joyfully look toward the end? How do we sometimes lose sight of the goal?

   D. Why are you in the race? How can you overcome the urge to stop, rest, and take it easy?

3. The forty-day temptation of Jesus is described in Luke 4:1–13.

A. Jesus ate nothing during this time of temptation and naturally became very hungry. When you are under physical distress, is it harder to keep spiritually focused? Explain. What do you do to compensate?

B. Each time the devil tries to get at Jesus, he responds by using Scripture correctly. How can his example help you in your personal struggles? What strategies can you adopt?

C. The devil attempted to get Christ's eyes off his father, to doubt the love and concern he knew was there. How does Satan use the same tactics with us? How can we respond? How have you responded in the past to such attacks? What happened?

4. Read the parable of the talents in Matthew 25:14–30.

A. With what specific "talents" have you been entrusted? Name them.

B. Do you think the man with five talents had more responsibility than the ones with two or one? Why or why not? If you believe you have just one talent, do you ever spend time wishing God had gifted you with five instead? Explain. How are you using the one you have?

C. Since the one-talent servant knew what his master was like and what he'd expect on his return, why do you suppose he neglected his duty? Do we do this as well? Explain.

D. Compare the master's responses between the more gifted and least gifted servants. In whose place can you most easily put yourself? Why?

E. If you came to the end of your race as a Christian right this minute, would you expect to hear the Master's words as spoken in verse 23? Explain.

Becoming the Hands of Jesus

1. If you are physically able, challenge yourself to a footrace. Set a goal—say, the house at the end of the block—and start running. When you get winded, keep huffing. When you want to quit, don't stop. Make yourself do it. Reward yourself when you get home—try some time alone with a good book. Then make the analogy between your physical exercise and the race we've just been discussing. What do you learn?

2. Take inventory of the projects that surround you, the things that take up the most of your time. Who or what do they benefit? What would happen if you discontinued your involvement? Sort and filter. Resolve to include only those things that prod you on to your goal.

MORE INSPIRATIONAL BOOKS FROM
❧ MAX LUCADO ❧

THE GREAT HOUSE OF GOD

God's greatest desire is to be your dwelling place—the home for your heart. Using the Lord's Prayer as a floor plan for *The Great House of God*, Max Lucado introduces us to a God who desires his children to draw close to Him—indeed, to live with Him. Warm your heart by the fire in the living room. Nourish your spirit in the kitchen. Step into the hallway and find forgiveness. No house is more complete, no foundation more solid. So come into the house built just for you…the great house of God.

IN THE GRIP OF GRACE

Can anything separate us from the love of God? Can you drift too far? Wait too long? Out-sin the love of God? The answer is found in one of life's sweetest words—*grace*. In his most theologically challenging book yet, Max Lucado shows how you can't fall beyond God's love. "God doesn't condone our sin, nor does He compromise His standard. Rather than dismiss our sin, He assumes our sin and incredibly, incredibly sentences Himself. God is still holy. Sin is still sin. And we are redeemed."

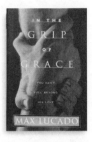

A GENTLE THUNDER

How far do you want God to go in getting your attention? Don't answer too quickly. What if God moved you to another land? (as He did Abraham.) What if He called you out of retirement? (Remember Moses?) How about the voice of an angel or the bowel of a fish (Gideon and Jonah.) God does what it takes to get our attention. That's the message of this book: the relentless pursuit of God. Searching, wrestling, pulling us back to Him, over and over again. Softly shouting, gently thundering…whatever it takes to get us home safely.

WHEN GOD WHISPERS YOUR NAME

Do you find it hard to believe that the One who made everything keeps your name in His heart and on His lips? In fact, did you realize that your name is written on the hand of God (Is. 49:16)? Perhaps you've never seen your name honored. And you can't remember when you heard it spoken with kindness. If you're struggling to find your way, Lucado offers the inspiration to believe that God has already bought the ticket-with your name on it. This book affirms that God can move you along on your journey with power from beyond.

HE STILL MOVES STONES

Why does the Bible contain so many stories of hurting people? Though their situations vary, their conditions don't. They have nowhere to turn. Yet before their eyes stands a never-say-die Galilean who majors in stepping in when everyone else steps out. Lucado reminds us that the purpose of these portraits isn't to tell us what Jesus *did*—but rather to remind us what Jesus still *does*. He comes to do what you can't. He comes to move the stones you can't budge. He still moves stones.

THE APPLAUSE OF HEAVEN

It is what you always dreamed but never expected. It's having God as your dad, your biggest fan, and your best friend. It is having the King of kings in your cheering section. It is hearing the applause of heaven. Max Lucado believes that the Beatitudes provide what we need to discover the joy of God. Much more than a how-to book on happiness, *The Applause of Heaven* is an encounter with the Source of joy. Read it and see that the Joy of God is within your reach.

IN THE EYE OF THE STORM

Come face-to-face with Jesus when He experienced more stress than any other day of his life aside from his crucifixion. Before the morning became evening, he has reason to weep, run, shout, curse, praise, and doubt. His life went from calm to chaos within a matter of moments. If you know what it means to be caught in life's storms…if you've ever ridden the roller coaster of sorrow and celebration… if you've ever wondered if God in heaven can relate to you on earth, then this book will encourage and inspire you.

LET THE JOURNEY BEGIN

Here's the perfect book for anyone facing a new beginning…from a college graduate to a new Christian. Combining insights from Max Lucado with full-color original art, this gift book addresses topics such as "Setting Your Compass in the Right Direction," "When God Says No," "God's Signature Makes You Special'" and "Mountains You Weren't Made To Climb." Only by anchoring these truths firmly in our hearts will we be ready for whatever lies ahead. *Let the Journey Begin* provides God's roadmap for all our new beginnings!

GOD'S INSPIRATIONAL PROMISE BOOK

This unique gift book combines God's promises found in Scripture with heartwarming passages from Max Lucado's most popular writings. The result is a one-of-a-kind promise book that will continually draw you closer to the comfort and hope of God. Each topical reading features God's Scripture promises on one page accompanied by a message from Max on the opposite page. More than ninety readings are included, addressing topics such as God's Grace, Being a Godly Parent, Sin, Salvation, Reading God's Word, and Heaven.

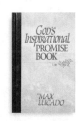

COSMIC CHRISTMAS

Was the birth of Jesus a quietly profound event? Or could it have included heavenly battles, angel armies, and a scheming Satan? Come along as Lucado takes us on a journey into his imagination — pulling back the curtain as we see what might have taken place one *Cosmic Christmas*.

THE CHRISTMAS CROSS

The Christmas Cross is a story about finding your way home for the holidays, told in the context of one man's journey in a small Texas town. Unique interactive elements inside this book — including envelopes with pullout letters and surprises — makes this a one-of-a-kind Christmas treasure.

THE INSPIRATIONAL BIBLE

Imagine studying the Bible with Max Lucado. He see the Bible as "stories of real people, real problems, real joy, and a real Savior." Edited by Max Lucado, *The Inspirational Bible* includes:

• 700 "Life Lessons" that apply Scriptural truths to everyday life

• Dramatic introductions to each book of the Bible writtten by Lucado

• 48 color pages that address topics from Forgiveness to Victory.

"LIFE LESSONS" BIBLE STUDY GUIDES

Max Lucado is your tour guide as you journey through both Old and New Testaments books in this exciting series. Each of the sixteen Bible Study Guides are ideal for either small group or individual study, and includes features like: "How To Study The Bible," inspirational quotes by Max and other popular authors, stirring introductions to the book of the Bible, thought-provoking questions, room for journaling and personal thoughts, and a closing prayer from Max Lucado.

WHEN
CHRIST
COMES

WHEN CHRIST COMES

The Beginning of
the Very Best

Max Lucado

WORD PUBLISHING

NASHVILLE

A Thomas Nelson Company

WHEN CHRIST COMES

Unless otherwise indicated, Scripture quotations used in this book are from the Holy Bible, New Century Version, copyright © 1987, 1988, 1991 by Word Publishing, Nashville, Tennessee 37214. Used by permission.

Other Scripture references are from the following sources:

The Contemporary English Version (CEV), © 1991 by The American Bible Society. Used by permission.

The Living Bible (TLB), copyright © 1971 by Tyndale House Publishers, Wheaton, Illinois. Used by permission.

The Message (MSG), copyright © 1993. Used by permission of NavPress Publishing Group.

The New King James Version (NKJV), copyright © 1979, 1980, 1982, Thomas Nelson, Inc., Publishers.

J. B. Phillips: The New Testament in Modern English, Revised Edition (PHILLIPS), copyright © J. B. Phillips 1958, 1960, 1972. Used by permission of Macmillan Publishing Co., Inc.

New American Standard Bible (NASB), copyright © 1960, 1977 by the Lockman Foundation.

The Revised Standard Version of the Bible (RSV), copyright © 1946, 1952, 1971, 1973 by the Division of Christian Education of the National Council of the Churches of Christ in the USA. Used by permission.

The Jerusalem Bible (TJB), copyright © 1968 by Darton, Longman, & Todd, Ltd., and Doubleday & Co., Inc.

The New Revised Standard Version of the Bible (NRSV), copyright © 1989 by the Division of Christian Education of the National Council of the Churches of Christ in the USA.

The Good News Bible: The Bible in Today's English Version (TEV), copyright © 1976 by the American Bible Society.

The Holy Bible, New International Version (NIV), copyright © 1973, 1978, 1984, International Bible Society. Used by permission of Zondervan Bible Publishers.

The New English Bible (NEB), copyright © 1961, 1970 by the Delegates of the Oxford University Press and the Syndics of the Cambridge University Press, 1961, 1970. Reprinted by permission.

The Holy Bible, New Living Translation (NLT), copyright © 1996. Used by permission of Tyndale House Publishers, Inc., Wheaton, Illinois. All rights reserved.

Library of Congress Cataloging-in-Publication Data

Lucado, Max.
    When Christ comes / Max Lucado.
        p.   cm.
    ISBN 0-8499-1298-9
    1. Second Advent. I. Title.
    BT886.L79 1999
    236'.9—dc21
                                                                          99-30283
                                                                          CIP

Printed in the United States of America
99 00 01 02 03 04 BVG 9 8 7 6 5 4 3

To my mother

Thelma Lucado

You gave more than birth——you gave yourself.

And I love you.

Contents

1. "You Do the Trusting; I'll Do the Taking"
When Will He Come?

Thoughts of the Second Coming unsettle me. Life with no end? Space with no bounds? And what about Armageddon, the lake of fire, the mark of the beast? Am I supposed to understand all this? Am I supposed to feel good about all this?

2. Waiting Forwardly
A Day to Anticipate

Some Christians are so obsessed with the last days that they are oblivious to these days. Others are just the opposite. They'll tell you Jesus is coming. But they live like he never will. One is too panicky, the other too patient. Isn't there a balance?

ACKNOWLEDGMENTS

Years ago I heard a cute, likely apocryphal story about Mark Twain. A Sunday school teacher told the author that his name had surfaced in Bible class. One of her young students was attempting to quote the names of the books in the New Testament. He began by saying, "Matthew, Mark Twain, Luke, and John."

"What do you think of that, Mr. Twain?" she inquired.

"Well," he replied, "it's been a long time since I've been in finer company."

I can say the same. Through the course of writing this book, I've enjoyed the company of some of God's finest children. And to a few of them, I offer a word of gratitude.

To my editor, Liz Heaney—How many books have we done now? More than a dozen, right? Each one hopefully better than the one before. Each one certainly more fun than the one before.

Thanks for being such a friend and not chuckling too loud at my mistakes.

To my assistant, Karen Hill—Somehow you do it all. Run the office. Run interference. Run to my aid when I'm in trouble. But, in the process, you never run out of laughter or energy. You are one of a kind. Thank you so, so, so much.

To Steve and Cheryl Green, Austin, Caroline, and Claire—As sure as the sun shines and sets, you are faithful friends. Thanks for being Jesus to our family.

To Steve Halliday—Thanks for another thoughtful study guide that stretches the mind and challenges the heart.

To the Word family—No author could entrust himself to a finer team.

To the Oak Hills congregation—What a year it has been! New location. New facility. New schedule. I'm so glad you didn't opt for a new preacher. We live in a time of answered prayer. For the privilege of sharing God's Word with you each week, I am eternally grateful.

To the Oak Hills elders—For your diligent pastoral care of the church, for your brotherly love for my family, for your ceaseless prayers for my work, I thank you.

To the (growing) Oak Hills staff—You are the finest, and I'm proud to be on the team.

To Victor and Tara McCracken—Thanks for a summer full of study. Welcome to San Antonio.

To Becky Rayburn, our office angel—What a blessing you are!

To my daughters, Jenna, Andrea, and Sara—One in high school, one in middle school, and one in elementary school, but all in my heart. I love you dearly.

And to my wife, Denalyn—To show me his grace, God gave me the cross. To show me his extravagance, God gave me you.

And to you, the reader—As your guide for the next few pages, I'll do my best to do my job: speaking up when I have something to offer and shutting up when I don't. And at any point, if you feel like closing the book and chatting with the real Author, please do.

I'll still be here when you return.

WHEN CHRIST COMES

....

You are in your car driving home. Thoughts wander to the game you want to see or meal you want to eat, when suddenly a sound unlike any you've ever heard fills the air. The sound is high above you. A trumpet? A choir? A choir of trumpets? You don't know, but you want to know. So you pull over, get out of your car, and look up. As you do, you see you aren't the only curious one. The roadside has become a parking lot. Car doors are open, and people are staring at the sky. Shoppers are racing out of the grocery store. The Little League baseball game across the street has come to a halt. Players and parents are searching the clouds.

And what they see, and what you see, has never before been seen.

As if the sky were a curtain, the drapes of the atmosphere part. A brilliant light spills onto the earth. There are no shadows. None. From whence came the light begins to tumble a river of color—spiking crystals of every hue ever seen and a million more never seen. Riding on the flow is an endless fleet of angels. They pass through the curtains one myriad at a time, until they occupy every square inch of the sky. North. South. East. West. Thousands of silvery wings rise and fall in unison, and over the sound of the trumpets, you can hear the cherubim and seraphim chanting, "Holy, holy, holy."

The final flank of angels is followed by twenty-four silver-bearded elders and a multitude of souls who join the angels in worship. Presently the movement stops and the trumpets are silent, leaving only the triumphant triplet: "Holy, holy, holy." Between each word is a pause. With each word, a profound reverence. You hear your voice join in the chorus. You don't know why you say the words, but you know you must.

Suddenly, the heavens are quiet. All is quiet. The angels turn, you turn, the entire world turns—and there he is. Jesus. Through waves of light you see the silhouetted figure of Christ the King. He is atop a great stallion, and the stallion is atop a billowing cloud. He opens his mouth, and you are surrounded by his declaration: "I am the Alpha and the Omega."

The angels bow their heads. The elders remove their crowns. And before you is a figure so consuming that you know, instantly you know: Nothing else matters. Forget stock markets and school reports. Sales meetings and football games. Nothing is newsworthy. All that mattered, matters no more, for Christ has come. . . .

I wonder how those words make you feel. Wouldn't it be interesting to sit in a circle and listen to people's reactions? If a cluster of us summarized our emotions regarding the return of Christ in one word—what words would we hear? What word would you use?

Discomfort? Likely a popular choice. You've been told your mistakes will be revealed. You've been told your secrets will be made known. Books will be opened, and names will be read. You know

God is holy. You know you are not. How could the thought of his return bring anything but discomfort?

Besides, there are all those phrases—"the mark of the beast," "the Antichrist," and "the battle of Armageddon." And what about "the wars and rumors of wars"? And what was that the fellow said on TV? "Avoid all phone numbers with the digits 666." And that magazine article disclosing the new senator as the Antichrist? Discomforting, to say the least.

Or perhaps discomfort is not your word of choice. *Denial* might be more accurate. (Or maybe it's by denial that you deal with the discomfort?) Ambiguity is not a pleasant roommate. We prefer answers and explanations, and the end of time seems short on both. Consequently, you opt not to think about it. Why consider what you can't explain? If he comes, fine. If not, fine. But I'm going to bed. I have to work tomorrow.

Or how about this word—*disappointment?* This one may surprise you, unless you've felt it; then you'll relate. Who would feel disappointment at the thought of Christ's coming? A mother-to-be might—she wants to hold her baby. An engaged couple might—they want to be married. A soldier stationed overseas might—he wants to go home before he goes home.

This trio is just a sampling of the many emotions stirred by the thought of Christ's return. Others might be *obsessed.* (These are the folks with the charts and codes and you-better-believe-it prophecies.) *Panic.* ("Sell everything and head to the hills!")

I wonder what God would want us to feel. It's not hard to find the answer. Jesus said it plainly in John 14: "Don't let your hearts be troubled. Trust in God, and trust in me. . . . I will come back and take you to be with me" (vv. 1, 3). It's a simple scenario. The Father has gone away for a while. But he will return. And until then, he wants his children to be at peace.

I want the same for my three daughters.

I left them last night so I could get away and finish this book. With a kiss and a hug, I walked out the door and promised to return. Did I want to leave them? No. But this book needed some work, and the publisher needed a manuscript, so here I am—in a hideaway—pounding a computer keyboard. We have accepted the fact that a time of separation is necessary to finish the job.

While we are apart, do I want them to feel discomfort? Do I want them dreading my return? No.

What about denial? Would I be pleased to hear that they have removed my picture from the mantel and my plate from the table and are refusing to discuss my arrival? I don't think so.

How about disappointment? "Oh, I hope Daddy doesn't come before Friday night—I really want to go to that slumber party." Am I such a fuddy-dud dad that my coming will spoil the fun?

Well, perhaps I am. But God isn't. And, if he has his way with us, thoughts of his return won't disappoint his children. He, too, is away from his family. He, too, has promised to return. He isn't writing a book, but he is writing history. My daughters don't understand all the intricacies of my task; we don't understand all the details of his. But our job in the meantime? Trust. Soon the final chapter will be crafted and he'll appear at the door. But until then Jesus says: "Don't let your hearts be troubled. Trust in God, and trust in me."

This is the desire of God. It's also the aim of this book.

No book can answer all the questions. And no reader will agree with all my suggestions. (Some of you were only a few lines into the opening description of the return before you stubbed an opinion on a sentence.) But perhaps God will use this book to encourage you to be at peace about his coming.

Would you like to discuss the end of time and feel better because of it? Could you use some comforting words regarding the return of Christ? If so, I think I've found some.

Let's talk.

Chapter 1

"You Do the Trusting;
I'll Do the Taking"

When Will He Come?

Don't let your hearts be troubled. Trust in God, and trust in me. . . .
I will come back and take you to be with me.
John 14:1, 3

Parenting is packed with challenges. Who among us has answers to the questions children ask?

"Why can't I have another puppy?"

"But you got married when you were eighteen. Why can't I?"

"Daddy, what is Viagra?"

Such questions would cause a sage to stammer. They pale, however, compared to one a child asks on a trip. In a comprehensive survey conducted by Lucado and Friends (I interviewed a couple of people in the hallway), I determined the most dreaded question in parentdom. What is the single query hated most by moms and dads? It's the one posed by the five-year-old on the trip, "How much farther?"

Give us the dilemmas of geometry and sexuality, just don't make a parent answer the question, "How much farther?"

It's an impossible question. How do you speak of time and distance to someone who doesn't understand time and distance? The novice parent assumes the facts will suffice, "Two hundred and fifty miles." But what do miles mean to a pre-K kid? Nothing! You might as well have spoken Yiddish! So the child asks, "What is two hundred and fifty miles?" At this point you're tempted to get technical and explain that one mile equals 5280 feet, so two hundred and fifty miles equals one million three hundred thousand feet. But four words into the sentence, and the child tunes you out. He sits quietly until you are quiet and then asks, "How much farther?"

The world of a youngster is delightfully free of mile markers and alarm clocks. You can speak of minutes and kilometers, but a child has no hooks for those hats. So what do you do? Most parents get creative. When our girls were toddlers, they loved to watch *The Little Mermaid*. So Denalyn and I used the movie as an economy of scale. "About as long as it takes you to watch *The Little Mermaid* three times."

And for a few minutes that seemed to help. But sooner or later, they ask again. And sooner or later, we say what all parents eventually say, "Just trust me. You enjoy the trip and don't worry about the details. I'll make sure we get home OK."

And we mean it. We don't want our kids to sweat the details. So we make a deal with them, "We'll do the taking. You do the trusting."

Sound familiar? It might. Jesus has said the same to us. Just prior to his crucifixion, he told his disciples that he would be leaving them. "Where I am going you cannot follow now, but you will follow later" (John 13:36).

Such a statement was bound to stir some questions. Peter spoke for the others and asked, "Lord, why can't I follow you now?" (v. 37).

See if Jesus' reply doesn't reflect the tenderness of a parent to a child: "Don't let your hearts be troubled. Trust in God, and trust in me. There are many rooms in my Father's house; I would not tell you this if it were not true. I am going there to prepare a place for you. . . . I will come back and take you to be with me so that you may be where I am going" (John 14:1–3).

Reduce the paragraph to a sentence and it might read: "You do the trusting and I'll do the taking." A healthy reminder when it comes to anticipating the return of Christ. For many, the verb *trust* is not easily associated with his coming.

Our pre-K minds are ill-equipped to handle the thoughts of eternity. When it comes to a world with no boundaries of space and time, we don't have the hooks for those hats. Consequently, our Lord takes the posture of a parent, "You do the trusting and I'll do the taking." This is precisely his message in these warm words of John 14. Let's ponder them for a bit.

All of his words can be reduced to two: *Trust me.* "Don't let your hearts be troubled. Trust in God, and trust in me" (v. 1).

Don't be troubled by the return of Christ. Don't be anxious about things you cannot comprehend. Issues like the millennium and the Antichrist are intended to challenge and stretch us, but not overwhelm and certainly not divide us. For the Christian, the return of Christ is not a riddle to be solved or a code to be broken, but rather a day to be anticipated.

Jesus wants us to trust him. He doesn't want us to be troubled, so he reassures us with these truths.

I have ample space for you. "There are many rooms in my Father's house" (v. 2). Why does Jesus refer to "many rooms"? Why does our Master make a point of mentioning the size of the house? You can answer that question as you think of the many times in life you've heard the opposite. Haven't there been occasions when you've been told: "We have no room for you here"?

Have you heard it in the workplace? "Sorry, I don't have room for you in my business."

Have you heard it in sports? "We don't have room for you on this team."

From someone you love? "I don't have room for you in my heart."

From a bigot? "We don't have room for your type in here."

Most sadly, have you heard it from a church? "You've made too many mistakes. We don't have room for you here."

Some of the saddest words on earth are: "We don't have room for you."

Jesus knew the sound of those words. He was still in Mary's womb when the innkeeper said, "We don't have room for you."

When the residents of his hometown tried to stone him, were they not saying the same? "We don't have room for prophets in this town."

When the religious leaders accused him of blasphemy, weren't they shunning him? "We don't have room for a self-proclaimed Messiah in this country."

And when he was hung on the cross, wasn't the message one of utter rejection? "We don't have room for you in this world."

Even today Jesus is given the same treatment. He goes from heart to heart, asking if he might enter. But more often than not, he hears the words of the Bethlehem innkeeper: "Sorry. Too crowded. I don't have room for you here."

But every so often, he is welcomed. Someone throws open the door of his or her heart and invites him to stay. And to that person Jesus gives this great promise: "Do not let your heart be troubled. Trust in God. And trust in me. In my Father's house are many rooms."

"I have ample space for you," he says. What a delightful promise he makes us! We make room for him in our hearts, and he makes room for us in his house. His house has ample space.

His house has a second blessing:

I have a prepared place for you. "I am going there to prepare a place for you" (v. 2). A few years back I spent a week speaking at a church in California. The members of the congregation were incredible hosts and hostesses. All my meals were lined up, each at a different house, each house with a full table and at each table wonderful conversation. But after a few meals, I noticed something strange. All we ate was salad. I like salad as much as the next guy, but I prefer it as a warmup to the main act. But everywhere I went, it was the main act. No meat. No dessert. Just salads.

At first I thought it was a California thing. But finally I had to ask. The answer confused me. "We were told that you eat nothing but salads." Well, I quickly corrected them, and wondered how they had heard such a preposterous distortion. As we traced the trail back, we determined that a miscommunication had occurred between our office and theirs.

The hosts meant well, but their information was bad. I'm happy to say that we corrected the problem and enjoyed some good meat.

I'm even happier to say Jesus won't make the same mistake with you.

He is doing for you what my California friends did for me. He is preparing a place. There is a difference, however. He knows exactly what you need. You needn't worry about getting bored or tired or weary with seeing the same people or singing the same songs. And you certainly needn't worry about sitting down to meal after meal of salad.

He is preparing the perfect place for you. I love John MacArthur's definition of eternal life, "Heaven is the perfect place for people made perfect." [1]

Trust the promises of Christ. "I have ample space for you; I have a prepared place for you."

And one last commitment from Jesus:

I'm not kidding. "I will come back and take you to be with me so that you may be where I am going" (v. 3). Can you detect a slight shift of tone in the last verse? The first sentences are couched in warmth. "Don't be troubled." "Trust God." "There are many rooms." There is kindness in these words. But then the tone changes. Just slightly. The kindness continues but is now spiked with conviction. "I will come back. . . ."

George Tulloch displayed similar determination. In 1996 he led an expedition to the spot where the *Titanic* sank in 1912. He and his crew recovered numerous artifacts, everything from eyeglasses to jewelry to dishware. In his search, Tulloch realized that a large piece of the hull had broken from the ship and was resting not far from the vessel. Tulloch immediately saw the opportunity at hand. Here was a chance to rescue part of the ship itself.

The team set out to raise the twenty-ton piece of iron and place it onto the boat. They were successful in lifting it to the surface, but a storm blew in and the ropes broke and the Atlantic reclaimed her treasure. Tulloch was forced to retreat and regroup. But before he left, he did something curious. He descended into the deep and, with the robotic arm of his submarine, attached a strip of metal to a section of the hull. On the metal he'd written these words, "I will come back, George Tulloch."[2]

At first glance, his action is humorous. I mean, it's not like he has to worry about a lot of people stealing his piece of iron. For one thing, it's two and one-half miles below the surface of the Atlantic. For another, well, it's a piece of junk. We wonder why anyone would be so attracted to it.

Of course one might say the same about you and me. Why would God go to such efforts to reclaim us? What good are we to him? He must have his reasons because two thousand years ago, he entered the murky waters of our world in search of his children. And on all who will allow him to do so, he lays his claim and tags his name. "I will come back," he says.

George Tulloch did. Two years later he returned and rescued the piece of iron.

Jesus will as well. We don't know when he will come for us. We don't know how he will come for us. And, we really don't even know why he would come for us. Oh, we have our ideas and opinions. But most of what we have is faith. Faith that he has ample space and a prepared place and, at the right time, he will come so that we can be where he is.

He will do the taking. It's up to us to do the trusting.

Chapter 2

WAITING FORWARDLY

A Day to Anticipate

So what kind of people should you be? You should live
holy lives and serve God, as you wait for and look
forward to the coming of the day of God.
2 Peter 3:11–12

Funny how Scripture remembers different people. Abraham is remembered trusting. Envision Moses, and you envision a person leading. Paul's place in Scripture was carved by his writing and John is known for his loving. But Simeon is remembered, interestingly enough, not for leading nor preaching nor loving, but rather for looking.

"Now in Jerusalem there was a man named Simeon. He was an upright and devout man; he *looked forward* to Israel's comforting and the Holy Spirit rested on him" (Luke 2:25 TJB, emphasis mine).

Let's take a look at Simeon, the man who knew how to wait for the arrival of Christ. The way he waited for the first coming is a model for how we should wait for the Second Coming.

Our brief encounter with Simeon occurs eight days after the birth of Jesus. Joseph and Mary have brought their son to the temple. It's the day of a sacrifice, the day of circumcision, the day of dedication. But for Simeon, it's the day of celebration.

Let's imagine a white-headed, wizened fellow working his way down the streets of Jerusalem. People in the market call his name and he waves but doesn't stop. Neighbors greet him and he returns the greeting but doesn't pause. Friends chat on the corner and he smiles but doesn't stop. He has a place to be and he hasn't time to lose.

Verse 27 contains this curious statement: "Prompted by the Spirit he came to the Temple." Simeon apparently had no plans to go to the temple. God, however, thought otherwise. We don't know how the prompting came—a call from a neighbor, an invitation from his wife, a nudging within the heart—we don't know. But somehow Simeon knew to clear his calendar and put away his golf clubs. "I think I'll go to church," he announced.

On this side of the event, we understand the prompting. Whether Simeon understood or not, we don't know. We do know, however, that this wasn't the first time God tapped him on the shoulder. At least one other time in his life, he had received a message from God.

"The Holy Spirit had revealed to him that he would not die until he had seen him—God's anointed King" (v. 26 TLB).

You've got to wonder what a message like that would do to a person. What does it do to you if you know you will someday see God? We know what it did to Simeon.

He was "constantly expecting the Messiah" (v. 25 TLB).

He was "living in expectation of the salvation of Israel" (v. 25 PHILLIPS).

He "watched and waited for the restoration of Israel" (v. 25 NEB).

Simeon is a man on tiptoe, wide-eyed and watching for the one who will come to save Israel.

Maybe you know what it's like to look for someone who has come for you. I do. When I travel somewhere to speak, I often don't know who will pick me up at the airport. Someone has been sent, but I don't know the person. Hence, I exit the plane searching the faces for a face I've never seen. But though I've never seen the person, I know I'll find him. He may have my name on a sign, or my book in his hand, or just a puzzled expression on his face. Were you to ask me how I will recognize the one who has come for me, I would say, "I don't know, I just know I will."

I bet Simeon would have said the same. "How will you know the king, Simeon?" "I don't know. I just know I will." And so he searches. Like Colombo after clues, he searches. Studying each passing face. Staring into the eyes of strangers. He's looking for someone.

The Greek language, rich as it is with terms, has a stable full of verbs which mean "to look." One means to "look up," another "look away;" one is used to "look upon" and another "looking in." To "look at something intently" requires one word and to "look over someone carefully" mandates another.

Of all the forms of *look*, the one which best captures what it means to "look for the coming" is the term used to describe the action of Simeon: *prosdechomai*. *Dechomai* meaning "to wait." *Pros* meaning "forward." Combine them and you have the graphic picture of one "waiting forwardly." The grammar is poor, but the image is great. Simeon was waiting; not demanding, not hurrying, he was waiting.

At the same time, he was waiting *forwardly*. Patiently vigilant.

Calmly expectant. Eyes open. Arms extended. Searching the crowd for the right face, and hoping the face appears today.

Such was the lifestyle of Simeon, and such can be ours. Haven't we, like Simeon, been told of the coming Christ? Aren't we, like Simeon, heirs of a promise? Are we not prompted by the same Spirit? Are we not longing to see the same face?

Absolutely. In fact, the very same verb is used later in Luke to describe the posture of the waiting servant:

> Be dressed, ready for service, and have your lamps shining. Be like servants who are waiting [*prosdechomai*] for their master to come home from a wedding party. When he comes and knocks, the servants immediately open the door for him. They will be blessed when their master comes home, because he sees that they were watching for him. I tell you the truth, the master will dress himself to serve and tell the servants to sit at the table, and he will serve them. (Luke 12:35–37)

Please note the posture of the servants: ready and waiting. Please note the action of the master. He is so thrilled that his attendants are watching for him that he takes the form of a servant and serves them! They sit at the feast and are cared for by the master! Why? Why are they honored in such a way? The master loves to find people looking for his return. The master rewards those who "wait forwardly."

Both words are crucial.

First, we must *wait*. Paul says "we are hoping for something we do not have yet, and we are waiting for it patiently" (Rom. 8:25).

Simeon is our model. He was not so consumed with the "not yet" that he ignored the "right now." Luke says Simeon was a "good man and godly" (2:25). Peter urges us to follow suit.

"The day of the Lord will come like a thief. The skies will disappear with a loud noise. Everything in them will be destroyed by fire, and the earth and everything in it will be burned up. In that way everything will be destroyed. So what kind of people should you be?" (2 Pet. 3:10–11).

Great question. What kind of people should we be? Peter tells us: "You should live holy lives and serve God, as you wait for and *[here is that word again]* look forward to the coming of the day of God" (vv. 11–12).

Hope of the future is not a license for irresponsibility in the present. Let us wait forwardly, but let us wait.

But for most of us, waiting is not our problem Or, maybe I should state, waiting *is* our problem. We are so good at waiting that we don't wait *forwardly*. We forget to look. We are so patient that we become complacent. We are too content. We seldom search the skies. We rarely run to the temple. We seldom, if ever, allow the Holy Spirit to interrupt our plans and lead us to worship so that we might see Jesus.

It is to those of us who are strong in waiting and weak in watching that our Lord was speaking when he said, "No one knows when that day or time will be, not the angels in heaven, not even the Son. Only the Father knows. . . . So always be ready, because you don't know the day your Lord will come. . . . The Son of Man will come at a time you don't expect him" (Matt. 24:36, 42, 44).

Simeon reminds us to "wait forwardly." Patiently vigilant. But not so patient that we lose our vigilance. Nor so vigilant that we lose our patience.

In the end, the prayer of Simeon was answered. "Simeon took the baby in his arms and thanked God; 'Now, Lord, you can let me, your servant, die in peace, as you said'" (Luke 2:28–29).

One look into the face of Jesus, and Simeon knew it was time to go home. And one look into the face of our Savior, and we will know the same.

Chapter 3

THE CRADLE OF HOPE

A Day of Proof and Promise

Christ rose first; then when Christ comes back,
all his people will become alive again.
1 Corinthians 15:23 TLB

The 1989 Armenian earthquake needed only four minutes to flatten the nation and kill thirty thousand people. Moments after the deadly tremor ceased, a father raced to an elementary school to save his son. When he arrived, he saw that the building had been leveled. Looking at the mass of stones and rubble, he remembered a promise he had made to his child: "No matter what happens, I'll always be there for you." Driven by his own promise, he found the area closest to his son's room and began to pull back the rocks. Other parents arrived and began sobbing for their children. "It's too late," they told the man. "You know they are dead. You can't help." Even a police officer encouraged him to give up.

But the father refused. For eight hours, then sixteen, then thirty-two, thirty-six hours he dug. His hands were raw and his energy gone, but he refused to quit. Finally, after thirty-eight wrenching hours, he pulled back a boulder and heard his son's voice. He called his boy's name, "Arman! Arman!" And a voice answered him, "Dad, it's me!" Then the boy added these priceless words, "I told the other kids not to worry. I told them if you were alive, you'd save me, and when you saved me, they'd be saved, too. Because you promised, 'No matter what, I'll always be there for you.'" [1]

God has made the same promise to us. "I will come back . . . ," he assures us. Yes, the rocks will tumble. Yes, the ground will shake. But the child of God needn't fear—for the Father has promised to take us to be with him.

But dare we believe the promise? Dare we trust his loyalty? Isn't there a cautious part of us that wonders how reliable these words may be?

Perhaps you have no doubts. If so, you might want to skip this chapter. Others of us, however, could use a reminder. How can we know he will do what he said? How can we believe he will move the rocks and set us free?

Because he's already done it once.

Let's revisit the moment, shall we? Let's sit on the floor, feel the darkness, and be swallowed in the silence as we gaze with the eyes of our hearts where the eyes of our face could never see.

Let's go to the tomb, for Jesus lies in the tomb.

Still. Cold. Stiff. Death has claimed its greatest trophy. He is not asleep in the tomb or resting in the tomb or comatose in the tomb; he is dead in the tomb. No air in his lungs. No thoughts in his brain. No feeling in his limbs. His body is as lifeless as the stone slab upon which he has been laid.

The executioners made sure of it. When Pilate learned that Jesus was dead, he asked the soldiers if they were certain. They were. Had they seen the Nazarene twitch, had they heard even one moan, they would have broken his legs to speed his end. But there was no need. The thrust of a spear removed all doubt. The Romans knew their job. And their job was finished. They pried loose the nails, lowered his body, and gave it to Joseph and Nicodemus.

Joseph of Arimathea. Nicodemus the Pharisee. They sat in seats of power and bore positions of influence. Men of means and men of clout. But they would've traded it all for one breath out of the body of Jesus. He had answered the prayer of their hearts, the prayer for the Messiah. As much as the soldiers wanted him dead, even more these men wanted him alive.

As they sponged the blood from his beard, don't you know they listened for his breath? As they wrapped the cloth around his hands, don't you know they hoped for a pulse? Don't you know they searched for life?

But they didn't find it.

So they do with him what they were expected to do with a dead man. They wrap his body in clean linen and place it in a tomb. Joseph's tomb. Roman guards are stationed to guard the corpse. And a Roman seal is set on the rock of the tomb. For three days, no one gets close to the grave.

But then, Sunday arrives. And with Sunday comes light—a light within the tomb. A bright light? A soft light? Flashing? Hovering? We don't know. But there was a light. For he is the light. And with the light came life. Just as the darkness was banished, now the decay is reversed. Heaven blows and Jesus breathes. His chest expands.

Waxy lips open. Wooden fingers lift. Heart valves swish and hinged joints bend.

And, as we envision the moment, we stand in awe.

We stand in awe not just because of what we see, but because of what we know. We know that we, too, will die. We know that we, too, will be buried. Our lungs, like his, will empty. Our hands, like his, will stiffen. But the rising of his body and the rolling of the stone give birth to a mighty belief: "What we believe is this: If we get included in Christ's sin-conquering death, we also get included in his life-saving resurrection. We know that when Jesus was raised from the dead it was a signal of the end of death-as-the-end. Never again will death have the last word. When Jesus died, he took sin down with him, but alive he brings God down to us" (Rom. 6:5–9 MSG).

To the Thessalonians Paul stated: "Since Jesus died and broke loose from the grave, God will most certainly bring back to life those who die in Jesus" (1 Thess. 4:14 MSG).

And to the Corinthians he affirmed: "All who are related to Christ will rise again. Each, however, in his own turn: Christ rose first; then when Christ comes back, all his people will become alive again" (1 Cor. 15:22–23 TLB).

For Paul and any follower of Christ, the promise is simply this: The resurrection of Jesus is proof and preview of our own.

But can we trust the promise? Is the resurrection a reality? Are the claims of the empty tomb true? This is not only a good question. It is *the* question. For as Paul wrote, "If Christ has not been raised, then your faith has nothing to it; you are still guilty of your sins" (1 Cor. 15:17). In other words, if Christ has been raised, then his followers will join him; but if not, then his followers are fools. The resurrection, then, is the keystone in the arch of the Christian faith. If it be solid, the doorway is trustworthy. Dislodge it and the doorway crumbles.

However, the keystone is not easily budged, for if Jesus is not in the tomb, where is he?

Some speculate he never even died. He was only thought to be dead, but he was actually unconscious. Then he awoke and walked out of the grave. But honestly, how likely is this theory? Jesus endures torturous whippings, thirst and dehydration, nails in his hands and feet, and most of all, a spear in his side. Could a man survive such treatment? And even if he did, could he single-handedly roll back a huge rock from the tomb and then overpower Roman guards and escape? Hardly. Dismiss any thought of Jesus not being dead.

Others accuse the disciples of stealing the body in order to fake the resurrection. They say that Jesus' followers—ordinary tax collectors and fishermen—overcame the sophisticated and well-armed Roman soldiers and detained them long enough to roll back the sealed stone and unwrap the body and escape. Hardly seems plausible, but even if it were, even if the disciples did steal the body, how do we explain their martyrdom? Many of them died for the faith. They died for their belief in the resurrected Lord. Would they fake the resurrection and then die for a hoax? I don't think so. We have to agree with John R. W. Stott, who wrote, "Hypocrites and martyrs are not made of the same stuff."[2]

Some go so far as to claim that the Jews stole the body. Is it possible that Jesus' enemies took the corpse? Perhaps. But why would they? They want the body in the tomb. And we ask just as quickly, if they did steal the body, why didn't they produce it? Display it? Place the carpenter's corpse on a funeral bier and parade it through Jerusalem, and the movement of Jesus would have sizzled like a torch in a lake. But they didn't produce the body. Why? Because they didn't have it.

Christ's death was real. The disciples didn't take his body. The Jews didn't take it. So where is it? Well, during the last two thousand years, millions have opted to accept the simple explanation the angel gave to Mary Magdalene. When she came to visit the grave and found it empty, she was told: "He is not here. He has risen from the dead as he said he would" (Matt. 28:6).

For three days Jesus' body decayed. It did not rest, mind you. It decayed. The cheeks sank and the skin paled. But after three days the process was reversed. There was a stirring, a stirring deep within the grave . . . and the living Christ stepped forth.[3]

And the moment he stepped forth, everything changed. As Paul stated: "When Jesus was raised from the dead it was a signal of the end of death-as-the-end" (Rom. 6:5–6 MSG).

Don't you love that sentence? "It was the signal of the end of death-as-the-end." The resurrection is an exploding flare announcing to all sincere seekers that it is safe to believe. Safe to believe in ultimate justice. Safe to believe in eternal bodies. Safe to believe in heaven as our estate and the earth as its porch. Safe to believe in a time when questions won't keep us awake and pain won't keep us down. Safe to believe in open graves and endless days and genuine praise.

Because we can accept the resurrection story, it is safe to accept the rest of the story.

Because of the resurrection, everything changes.

Death changes. It used to be the end; now it is the beginning.

The cemetery changes. People once went there to say good-bye; now they go to say, "We'll be together again."

Even the coffin changes. The casket is no longer a box where we hide bodies, but rather a cocoon in which the body is kept until God sets it free to fly.

And someday, according to Christ, he will set us free. He will come back. "I will come back and take you to be with me" (John 14:3). And to prove that he was serious about his promise, the stone was rolled and his body was raised.

For he knows that someday this world will shake again. In the blink of an eye, as fast as the lightning flashes from the east to the west, he will come back. And everyone will see him—you will, I will. Bodies will push back the dirt and break the surface of the sea. The earth will tremble, the sky will roar, and those who do not know him will shudder. But in that hour you will not fear, because you know him.

For you, like the boy in Armenia, have heard the promise of your Father. You know that he has moved the stone—not the stone of the Armenian earthquake, but the stone of the Arimathean's grave. And in the moment he removed the stone, he also removed all reason for doubt. And we, like the boy, can believe the words of our Father: "I will come back and take you to be with me so that you may be where I am" (John 14:3).

Chapter 4

INTO THE WARM ARMS OF GOD

A Day of Happy Reunions

He'll come down from heaven and the dead in Christ will rise—
they'll go first. Then the rest of us who are still alive at the time will
be caught up with them into the clouds to meet the Master. Oh, we'll
be walking on air! And then there will be one huge family reunion
with the Master. So reassure one another with these words.
1 Thessalonians 4:16–18 MSG

If you ever need to be reminded of the frailty of humankind, I have a scene for you to witness. The next time you think people have grown too stoic and self-sufficient, I have a place for you to go. Should you ever worry that hearts are too hard and tears too rare, let me take you to the place where the knees of men buckle and the tears of women flow. Let me take you to a school, and let's watch the parents as they leave their children in class for the very first time.

It's a traumatic event. Long after the school bell has rung and class has begun, adults linger in the parking lot, offering words of comfort and forming support groups. Even though the parents know the school is good, that education is right, and that they'll see their youngster in four short hours, still, they don't want to say good-bye.

We don't like to say good-bye to those we love.

But what is experienced at schools in August is a picnic compared to what is experienced in a cemetery at death. It is one thing to leave loved ones in familiar surroundings. But it is something else entirely to release them into a world we do not know and cannot describe.

We don't like to say good-bye to those we love.

But we have to. Try as we might to avoid it, as reluctant as we are to discuss it, death is a very real part of life. Each one of us must release the hand of one we love into the hand of one we have not seen.

Can you remember the first time death forced you to say good-bye? Most of us can. I can. One day when I was in the third grade, I came home from school surprised to see my father's truck in the driveway. I found him in his bathroom shaving. "Your Uncle Buck died today," he said. His announcement made me feel sad. I liked my uncle. I didn't know him well, but I liked him. The news also made me curious.

At the funeral I heard words like *departed, passed on, gone ahead.* These were unfamiliar terms. I wondered, *Departed to where? Passed on to what? Gone ahead for how long?*

Of course, I've learned since that I'm not the only one with questions about death. Listen in on any discussion about the return of Christ, and someone will inquire, "But what about those who have already died? What happens to Christians between their death and Jesus' return?"

Apparently the church in Thessalonica asked such a question. Listen to Paul's words to them: "We want you to be quite certain, brothers, about those who have died, to make sure that you do not grieve about them, like the other people who have no hope" (1 Thess. 4:13 TJB).

The Thessalonian church had buried her share of loved ones. And Paul wants the members who remain to be at peace regarding the ones who have gone ahead. Many of you have buried loved ones as well. And just as God spoke to them, he speaks to you.

If you'll celebrate a marriage anniversary alone this year, he speaks to you.

If your child made it to heaven before making it to kindergarten, he speaks to you.

If you lost a loved one in violence, if you learned more than you want to know about disease, if your dreams were buried as they lowered the casket, God speaks to you.

He speaks to all of us who have stood or will stand in the soft dirt near an open grave. And to us he gives this confident word: "I want you to know what happens to a Christian when he dies so that when it happens, you will not be full of sorrow, as those are who have no hope. For since we believe that Jesus died and then came back to life again, we can also believe that when Jesus returns, God will bring back with him all the Christians who have died" (1 Thess. 4:13–14 TLB).

God transforms our hopeless grief into hope-filled grief. How? By telling us that we will see our loved ones again.

Bob Russell is a friend of mine who preaches in Kentucky. His father passed away recently. The funeral was held on a cold, blustery, Pennsylvania day. The snow-covered roads precluded the funeral procession, so the director told Bob, "I'll take your dad's body to the grave." Bob couldn't bear the thought of missing his father's burial, so he and his brother and their sons piled into a four-wheel drive vehicle and followed the hearse. Here is how he described the event:

> We plowed through ten inches of snow into the cemetery, got about fifty yards from my dad's grave, with the wind blowing about twenty-five miles per hour, and the six of us lugged that casket down to the gravesite. . . . We watched the body lowered into the grave and we turned to leave. I felt something was undone, so I said, "I'd like for us to have a prayer." The six of us huddled together and I prayed, "Lord, this is such a cold, lonely place. . . ." And then I got too choked up to pray anymore. I kept battling to get my composure, and finally I just whispered, "But I thank you, for we know to be absent from the body is to be safe in your warm arms."[1]

Isn't that what we want to believe? Just as a parent needs to know that his or her child is safe at school, we long to know that our loved ones are safe in death. We long for the reassurance that the soul goes immediately to be with God. But dare we believe it? Can we believe it? According to the Bible we can.

Scripture is surprisingly quiet about this phase of our lives. When speaking about the period between the death of the body and the resurrection of the body, the Bible doesn't shout; it just whispers. But at the confluence of these whispers, a firm voice is heard. This authoritative voice assures us that, at death, the Christian immediately enters into the presence of God and enjoys conscious fellowship with the Father and with those who have gone before.

Where do I get such ideas? Listen to some of the whispers:

> For me to live is Christ and to die is gain. If I am to go on living in the body, this will mean fruitful labor for me. Yet what shall I choose? I do not know! I am torn between the two: I desire to depart and be with Christ, which is better by far. (Phil. 1:21–23 NIV)

The language here suggests an immediate departure of the soul after death. The details of the grammar are a bit tedious but led one scholar to suggest: "What Paul is saying here is that the moment he departs or dies, that very moment he is with the Christ."[2]

Another clue comes from the letter Paul wrote to the Corinthians. Perhaps you've heard the phrase "to be absent from the body is to be at home with the Lord"? Paul used it first: "We really want to be away from the body and be at home with the Lord" (2 Cor. 5:8).

At the Second Coming of Christ, our bodies will be resurrected. But obviously Paul is not speaking of that in this verse. Otherwise he would not have used the phrase "away from the body." Paul is describing a phase after our death and prior to the resurrection of our bodies. During this time we will be "at home with the Lord."

Isn't this the promise that Jesus gave the thief on the cross? Earlier the thief had rebuked Jesus. Now he repents and asks for mercy. "Remember me when you come into your kingdom" (Luke 23:42). Likely, the thief is praying that he be remembered in some distant time in the future when the kingdom comes. He didn't expect an immediate answer. But he received one: "I tell you the truth, today you will be with me in paradise" (v. 43). The primary message of this passage is God's unlimited and surprising grace. But a secondary message is the immediate translation of the saved into the presence of God. The soul of the believer journeys home, while the body of the believer awaits the resurrection.

As Stephen was being martyred, he saw "heaven open and the Son of Man standing at God's right side" (Acts 7:56). As he was near death he prayed, "Lord Jesus, receive my spirit" (v. 59). It is safe to assume that Jesus did exactly that. Though the body of Stephen was dead, his spirit was alive. Though his body was buried, his spirit was in the presence of Jesus himself.

Some don't agree with this thought. They propose an intermediate period of purgation, a "holding tank" in which we are punished for our sins. This "purgatory" is the place where, for an undetermined length of time, we receive what our sins deserve so that we can rightly receive what God has prepared.

But two things trouble me about this teaching. For one, none of us can endure what our sins deserve. For another, Jesus already has. The Bible teaches that the wages of sin is death, not purgatory (see Rom. 6:23). The Bible also teaches that Jesus became our purgatory and took our punishment: "When he had brought about the purgation of sins, he took his seat at the right hand of Majesty on high" (Heb. 1:3 NEB). There is no purgatory because purgatory occurred at Calvary.

Others feel that while the body is buried, the soul is asleep. They come by their conviction honestly enough. Seven different times in two different epistles, Paul uses the term *sleep* to refer to death (see 1 Cor. 11:30; 15:6, 18, 20; 1 Thess. 4:13–15). One could certainly deduce that the time spent between death and the return of Christ is spent sleeping. (And, if such is the case, who would complain? We could certainly use the rest!)

But there is one problem. The Bible refers to some who have already died, and they are anything but asleep. Their bodies are sleeping, but their souls are wide awake. Revelation 6:9–11 refers to the souls of martyrs who cry out for justice on the earth. Matthew 17:3 speaks of Moses and Elijah, who appeared on the Mount of Transfiguration with Jesus. Even Samuel, who came back from the grave, was described wearing a robe and having the appearance of a god (1 Sam. 28:13–14). And what about the cloud of witnesses who surround us (Heb. 12:1)? Couldn't these be the heroes of our faith and the loved ones of our lives who have gone before?

I think so. I think Bob's prayer was accurate. When it is cold on earth, we can take comfort in knowing that our loved ones are in the warm arms of God.

We don't like to say good-bye to those whom we love. Whether it be at a school or a cemetery, separation is tough. It is right for us to weep, but there is no need for us to despair. They had pain here. They have no pain there. They struggled here. They have no struggles there. You and I might wonder why God took them home. But they don't. They understand. They are, at this very moment, at peace in the presence of God.

I had been ministering in San Antonio for less than a year when one of our members asked me to speak at the funeral of his mother. Her name was Ida Glossbrenner, but her friends called her Polly.

As the son and I planned the service, he told me a fascinating story about the final words his mother spoke. Mrs. Glossbrenner was unresponsive for the last few hours of her life. She never spoke a word. But moments before her death, she opened her eyes and stated in a clear voice, "My name is Ida Glossbrenner, but my friends call me Polly."

Meaningless words of hallucination? Perhaps. Or, perhaps more. Perhaps Ida was, well, maybe she was at the schoolhouse doors of heaven. Her body behind her. Her soul in the presence of God. And maybe she was getting acquainted.

I don't know. But I do know this. When it is cold on earth, we can take comfort in knowing that our loved ones are in the warm arms of God. And when Christ comes, we will hold them, too.

Chapter 5

THE BRAND-NEW YOU

A Day of Rejuvenation

There is an order to this resurrection: Christ was raised first; then,
when Christ comes back, all his people will be raised.
1 Corinthians 15:23 nlt

Suppose you were walking past my farm one day and saw me in the field crying. (I don't have a farm nor am I prone to sitting in fields, but play along with me.) There I sit, disconsolate at the head of a furrowed row. Concerned, you approach me and ask what is wrong. I look up from beneath my John Deere tractor hat and extend a palm full of seeds in your direction. "My heart breaks for the seeds," I weep. "My heart breaks for the seeds."

"What?"

Between sobs I explain, "The seeds will be placed in the ground and covered with dirt. They will decay, and we will never see them again."

As I weep, you are stunned. You look around for a turnip truck off which you are confident I tumbled. Finally, you explain to me a basic principle of farming: Out of the decay of the seed comes the birth of a plant.

You put a finger in my face and kindly remind me: "Do not bemoan the burial of the seed. Don't you know that you will soon witness a mighty miracle of God? Given time and tender care, this tiny kernel will break from its prison of soil and blossom into a plant far beyond its dreams."

Well, maybe you aren't that dramatic, but those are your thoughts. Any farmer who grieves over the burial of a seed needs a reminder: A time of planting is not a time of grief. Any person who anguishes over the burial of a body may need the same. We may need the reminder Paul gave the Corinthians. "There is an order to this resurrection: Christ was raised first; then, when Christ comes back, all his people will be raised" (1 Cor. 15:23 NLT).

In the last chapter we looked at what happens to the Christian between the death of the body and the return of our Savior. In this phase, Scripture assures us that our souls are living, but our body is buried. This is an intermediate period in which we are "away from this body and . . . at home with the Lord" (2 Cor. 5:8).

Upon death, our souls will journey immediately to the presence of God while we await the resurrection of our bodies. And when will this resurrection occur? You guessed it. When Christ comes. "When Christ comes again, those who belong to him will be raised to life, and then the end will come" (1 Cor. 15:23–24).

This kind of verse stirs a classroom of questions: What does Paul mean, "those who belong to him will be raised to life"? What will be raised? My body? If so, why *this* body? I don't like my body. Why don't we start over on a new model?

Come with me back to the farm, and let's look for some answers.

If you were impressed with my seed allegory, I'd better be honest. I stole the idea from the apostle Paul. The fifteenth chapter of his letter to the Corinthians is the definitive essay on our resurrection. We won't study the entire chapter, but we will isolate a few verses and make a few points.

He writes: "But someone may ask, 'How are the dead raised? What kind of body will they have?' Foolish person! When you sow a seed, it must die in the ground before it can live and grow. And when you sow it, it does not have the same 'body' it will have later. What you sow is only a bare seed, maybe wheat or something else. But God gives it a body that he has planned for it" (1 Cor. 15:35–38).

In other words: You can't have a new body without the death of the old body.[1] Or, as Paul says, "When you sow a seed, it must die in the ground before it can live and grow" (v. 35).

A friend told me that Paul's parallel between seeds sown and bodies buried reminded her of a remark made by her youngest son. He was a first grader, and his class was studying plants about the same time the family attended a funeral of a loved one. One day, as they were driving past a cemetery, the two events came together in one statement. "Hey, Mom," he volunteered, pointing toward the graveyard. "That's where they plant people."

The apostle Paul would have liked that. In fact, Paul would like us to change the way we think about the burial process. The graveside service is not a burial, but a planting. The grave is not a hole in the ground, but a fertile furrow. The cemetery is not the resting place, but rather the transformation place.

Most assume that death has no purpose. It is to people what the black hole is to space—a mysterious, inexplicable, distasteful, all-consuming power. Avoid it at all costs. And so we do! We do all we can to live and not die. God, however, says we must die in order to live. When you sow a seed, it must die in the ground before it can grow (v. 35). What we see as the ultimate tragedy, he sees as the ultimate triumph.

And when a Christian dies, it's not a time to despair, but a time to trust. Just as the seed is buried and the material wrapping decomposes, so our fleshly body will be buried and will decompose. But just as the buried seed sprouts new life, so our body will blossom into a new body. As Jesus said, "Unless a grain of wheat falls into the earth and dies, it remains a single grain of wheat; but if it dies, it brings a good harvest" (John 12:24 PHILLIPS).

If you'll permit a sudden shift of metaphors, let me jump from plants and a farm to dinner and dessert. Don't we love to be enticed by dessert? Don't we love to hear the cook say, "As soon as you are finished, I have a surprise for you." God says something similar regarding our body. "Let's finish with the one you have, and then I have a surprise."

What is this surprise? What is this new body I will receive? Again, our seed analogy helps. Paul wrote, "When you sow it [the seed], it does not have the same 'body' it will have later" (1 Cor. 15:37). Meaning, we can't envision the new body by looking at the old body.

I think you'll appreciate the way Eugene Peterson paraphrases this text:

There are no diagrams for this kind of thing. We do have a parallel experience in gardening. You plant a "dead" seed; soon there is a flourishing plant. There is no visual likeness between seed and plant. You could never guess what a tomato would look like by looking at a tomato seed. What we plant in the soil and what grows out of it doesn't look anything alike. The dead body that we bury in the ground and the resurrection body that comes from it will be dramatically different. (1 Cor. 15:37 MSG)

Paul's point is clear. You can't envision the glory of the plant by staring at the seed, nor can you garner a glimpse of your future body by studying the present one. All we know is that this body will be changed.

"Come on, Paul, just give us a clue. Just a hint. Can't you tell us a little more about our new bodies?"

Apparently he knew we would ask, for the apostle stays on the subject for a few more paragraphs and provides one final point: You may not be able to envision it, but one thing's for sure: You are going to love your new body.

Paul outlines three ways God will transform our bodies. Our bodies will be changed from:

1. Corruption to incorruption—"The body is sown in corruption, it is raised in incorruption" (v. 42 NKJV).
2. Dishonor to glory—"It is sown in dishonor, it is raised in glory" (v. 43 NKJV).

3. Weakness to power—"It is sown in weakness, it is raised in power" (v. 43 NKJV).

Corruption. Dishonor. Weakness. Three unflattering words used to describe our bodies. But who would argue with them?

Julius Schniewind didn't. He was a highly regarded European Bible scholar. In the final weeks of his life, he battled a painful kidney disease. His biographer tells how, one night, after the professor had led a Bible study, he was putting on his coat to go home. As he did, the severe pain in his side caused him to groan aloud the Greek phrase "*Soma tapeinōseōs, soma tapeinōseōs.*" The student of Scripture was quoting the words of Paul, "For our citizenship is in heaven, from which we also eagerly wait for the Savior, the Lord Jesus Christ, who will transform our lowly body [*soma tapeinōseōs*]" (Phil. 3:20–21 NKJV).[2]

You and I don't go about mumbling Greek phrases, but we do know what it is like to live in a lowly body. In fact, some of you know all too well. Out of curiosity I made a list of the news I've heard in the last twenty-four hours concerning failing health. Here is what has come my way:

- A professor was diagnosed with Parkinson's disease.
- A middle-aged man is concerned about his test results. We learn tomorrow if he has cancer.
- A friend's father is scheduled for eye surgery.
- Another friend had a stroke.
- A minister died after four decades of preaching.

Can you relate? You probably can. In fact, I wonder if God wants to use the next few lines to speak directly to you. Your body is so tired, so worn. Joints ache and muscles fatigue. You understand why Paul described the body as a tent. "We groan in this tent," he wrote (2 Cor. 5:2). Your tent used to be sturdy and strong, but the seasons have passed and the storms have raged, and this old canvas has some bare spots. Chilled by the cold, bowed by the wind, your tent is not as strong as it used to be.

Or, then again, maybe your "tent," your body, never has been strong. Your sight never has been crisp, your hearing never has been clear. Your walk never has been sturdy; your heart never has been steady. You've watched others take for granted the health you've never had. Wheelchairs, doctor visits, hospital rooms, needles, stethoscopes—if you never saw another one for the rest of your life, you'd be happy. You'd give anything, yes, anything, for one full day in a strong, healthy body.

If that describes you, let God speak to your heart for just a moment. The purpose of this book is to use the return of Christ to encourage the heart. Few people need encouragement more than the physically afflicted. And few verses encourage more than Philippians 3:20–21. We read verse 20 a few paragraphs ago; you'll relish verse 21: "He will take these dying bodies of ours and change them into glorious bodies like his own" (Phil. 3:21 TLB).

Let's sample a couple of other versions of this verse:

"He will transfigure these wretched bodies of ours into copies of his glorious body" (TJB).

"He will transfigure the body belonging to our humble state, and give it a form like that of his own resplendent body" (NEB).

Regardless of the wording, the promise is the same. Your body will be changed. You will not receive a different body; you will receive a renewed body. Just as God can make an oak out of a kernel or a tulip out of a bulb, he makes a "new" body out of the old one. A body without corruption. A body without weakness. A body without dishonor. A body identical to the body of Jesus.

My friend Joni Eareckson Tada makes this same point. Rendered a quadriplegic by a teenage diving accident, the last two decades have been spent in discomfort. She, more than most, knows the meaning of living in a lowly body. At the same time, she more than most, knows the hope of a resurrected body. Listen to her words:

> Somewhere in my broken, paralyzed body is the seed of what I shall become. The paralysis makes what I am to become all the more grand when you contrast atrophied, useless legs against splendorous resurrected legs. I'm convinced that if there are mirrors in heaven (and why not?), the image I'll see will be unmistakably "Joni," although a much better, brighter Joni. So much so, that it's not worth comparing. . . . I will bear the likeness of Jesus, the man from heaven.[3]

Would you like a sneak preview of your new body? We have one by looking at the resurrected body of our Lord. After his resurrection, Jesus spent forty days in the presence of people. The resurrected Christ was not in a disembodied, purely spiritual state. On the contrary, he had a body—a touchable, visible body.

Just ask Thomas. Thomas said he wouldn't believe in the resurrection unless "I . . . put my finger where the nails were and put my hand into his side" (John 20:25). The response of Christ? He appeared to Thomas and said, "Put your finger here, and look at my hands. Put your hand here in my side. Stop being an unbeliever and believe" (v. 27).

Jesus didn't come as a mist or a wind or a ghostly specter. He came in a body. A body that maintained a substantial connection with the body he originally had. A body that had flesh and bones. For did he not tell his followers, "A spirit has not flesh and bones as you see that I have" (Luke 24:39 RSV)?

Jesus' resurrected body, then, was a real body, real enough to walk on the road to Emmaus, real enough to appear in the form of a gardener, real enough to eat breakfast with the disciples at Galilee. Jesus had a real body.[4]

At the same time, this body was not a clone of his earthly body. Mark tells us that Jesus "appeared in another form" (Mark 16:12 RSV). While he was the same, he was different. So different that Mary Magdalene, his disciples on the sea, and his disciples on the path to Emmaus did not recognize him. Though he invited Thomas to touch his body, he passed through a closed door to be in Thomas's presence.[5]

So what do we know about the resurrected body of Jesus? It was unlike any the world had ever seen.

What do we know about our resurrected bodies? They will be unlike any we have ever imagined.

Will we look so different that we aren't instantly recognized? Perhaps. (We may need nametags.) Will we be walking through walls? Chances are we'll be doing much more

Will we still bear the scars from the pain of life? The marks of war. The disfigurements of disease. The wounds of violence. Will these remain on our bodies? That is a very good question. Jesus, at least for forty days, kept his. Will we keep ours? On this issue, we have only opinions, but my opinion is that we won't. Peter tells us that "by his wounds you have been healed" (1 Pet. 2:24 NIV). In heaven's accounting, only one wound is worthy to be remembered. And that is the wound of Jesus. Our wounds will be no more.

God is going to renew your body and make it like his. What difference should this make in the way you live?

Your body, in some form, will last forever. Respect it.

You will live forever in this body. It will be different, mind you. What is now crooked will be straightened. What is now faulty will be fixed. Your body will be different, but you won't have a different body. You will have this one. Does that change the view you have of it? I hope so.

God has a high regard for your body. You should as well. Respect it. I did not say worship it. But I did say respect it. It is, after all, the temple of God (see 1 Cor. 6:19). Be careful how you feed it, use it, and maintain it. You wouldn't want anyone trashing your home; God doesn't want anyone trashing his. After all, it is his, isn't it? A little jogging and dieting to the glory of God wouldn't hurt most of us. Your body, in some form, will last forever. Respect it.

I have one final thought.

Your pain will NOT last forever. Believe it.

Are your joints arthritic? They won't be in heaven.

Is your heart weak? It will be strong in heaven.

Has cancer corrupted your system? There is no cancer in heaven.

Are your thoughts disjointed? Your memory failing? Your new body will have a new mind.

Does this body seem closer to death than ever before? It should. It is. And unless Christ comes first, your body will be buried. Like a seed is placed in the ground, so your body will be placed in a tomb. And for a season, your soul will be in heaven while your body is in the grave. But the seed buried in the earth will blossom in heaven. Your soul and body will reunite, and you will be like Jesus.

Chapter 6

A New Wardrobe

A Day of Redemption

Live in him so that when Christ comes back, we can be
without fear and not be ashamed in his presence.
1 John 2:28

I make no claims to being a good golfer, but I readily confess to being a golf addict. If you know of a twelve-step program for the condition, sign me up. "Hi, I'm Max. I'm a golfaholic." I love to play golf, watch golf, and, on good nights, I even dream golf.

Knowing this will help you appreciate the extreme joy I felt when I was invited to attend the Masters Golf Tournament. A pass to the Masters is the golfer's Holy Grail. Tickets are as scarce as birdies on my scorecard. So, I was thrilled. The invitation came via pro golfer Scott Simpson. Each player is given a certain number of passes, and Scott offered Denalyn and me two of his. (If there was ever any question about Scott's place in heaven, that gesture erased the doubt.)

So off we went to Augusta National Country Club in Augusta, Georgia, where golf heritage hangs like moss from the trees. There you find the green where Nicklaus sank *the* putt. The fringe where

Mize holed *the* chip. The fairway where Saranson hit *the* approach shot. I was a kid in a candy store. And, like a kid, I couldn't get enough. It wasn't enough to see the course and walk the grounds, I wanted to see the locker room. That's where the clubs of Hogan and Azinger are displayed. That's where the players hang out. And that's where I wanted to be.

But they wouldn't let me. A guard stopped me at the entrance. I showed him my pass, but he shook his head. I told him I knew Scott, but that didn't matter. I promised to send his eldest child through college, but he didn't budge. "Only caddies and players," he explained. Well, he knew I wasn't a player. He also knew I wasn't a caddie. Caddies at the Masters are required to wear white coveralls. My clothing was a dead giveaway. So I left, figuring I'd never see the clubhouse. I had made it all the way to the door but was denied entrance.

Many, many people fear the same will happen to them. Not at Augusta, but in heaven. They fear being turned away at the door. A legitimate fear, don't you think? We're talking about a pivotal moment. To be turned away from seeing golf history is one thing, but to be refused admission into heaven is quite another.

That is why some people don't want to discuss the return of Christ. It makes them nervous. They may be God-fearing and church-attending but still nervous. Is there a solution for this fear? Need you spend the rest of your life wondering if you will be turned away at the door? Yes, there is a solution and, no, you don't have to worry. According to the Bible, it is possible to "know beyond the shadow of a doubt that you have eternal life" (1 John 5:13 MSG). How? How can any of us know for sure?

Curiously, it all has to do with the clothing we wear.

Jesus explained the matter in one of his parables. He tells the story of a king who plans a wedding party for his son. Invitations are given, but the people "refused to come" (Matt. 22:3). The king is patient and offers another invitation. This time the servants of the king are mistreated and killed. The king is furious. The murderers are punished and the city is destroyed and the invitation is re-extended, this time, to everyone.

The application of the parable is not complicated. God invited Israel, his chosen ones, to be his children. But they refused. Not only did they refuse, they killed his servants and crucified his son. The consequence was the judgment of God. Jerusalem was burned and the people were scattered.

As the parable continues, the king offers yet another invitation. This time the wedding was opened to everyone—"good and bad," or Jews and Gentiles. Here is where we non-Jews appear in the parable. We are the beneficiaries of a wide invitation. And someday, when Christ comes, we will stand at the entryway to the king's castle. But the story doesn't end there. Standing at the doorway is not enough. A certain wardrobe is required. The parable ends with a chilling paragraph.

Let's pick up the story at the end of verse 10:

> "And the wedding hall was filled with guests. When the king came in to see the guests, he saw a man who was not dressed for a wedding. The king said, 'Friend, how were you allowed to come in here? You are not dressed for a wedding.' But the man said nothing. So the king told some servants, 'Tie this

man's hands and feet. Throw him out into the darkness, where people will cry and grind their teeth with pain.'" (Matt. 22:10–13)

Jesus loved surprise endings, and this one surprises . . . and frightens. Here is a man who was at the right place, surrounded by the right people, but dressed in the wrong garment. And because he wore the wrong clothing, he was cast from the presence of the king.

"Wrong clothes? Max, are you telling me that Jesus cares what clothes we wear?"

Apparently so. In fact, the Bible tells us exactly the wardrobe God desires.

"But clothe yourselves with the Lord Jesus Christ and forget about satisfying your sinful self" (Rom. 13:14).

"You were all baptized into Christ, and so you were all clothed with Christ. This means that you are all children of God through faith in Christ Jesus" (Gal. 3:26–27).

This clothing has nothing to do with dresses and jeans and suits. God's concern is with our spiritual garment. He offers a heavenly robe that only heaven can see and only heaven can give. Listen to the words of Isaiah: "The LORD makes me very happy; all that I am rejoices in my God. He has covered me with clothes of salvation and wrapped me with a coat of goodness" (Isa. 61:10).

Remember the words of the father when the prodigal son returned? He wanted his son to have new sandals, a new ring, and what else? New clothes. "Bring the best clothes and put them on him" (Luke 15:22). No son of his was going to be seen in shabby, muddy rags. The father wanted the son to have the best clothing available.

Your Father wants you to have the same.

Again, this discussion of clothing has nothing to do with what the store sells you. It has everything to do with what God gives you when you give your life to him. Let me explain.

When a person becomes a follower of Christ, when sins are confessed and the grace of Jesus is accepted, a wonderful miracle of the soul occurs. The person is placed "in" Christ. The apostle Paul described himself as "a man in Christ" (2 Cor. 12:2). When he described his colleagues, he called them "fellow workers in Christ Jesus" (Rom 16:3 NIV). The greatest promise is extended, not to the wealthy or educated, but to those who are "in Christ." "Therefore there is now no condemnation for those who are *in Christ Jesus*" (Rom. 8:1 NIV, emphasis mine). John urges us to "live in him so that when Christ comes back, we can be without fear and not ashamed in his presence" (1 John 2:28).

What does it mean to be "in Christ"? The clothing illustration is a good one. Why do we wear clothes? There are parts of our body we want to hide.

The same can be true with our spiritual lives. Do we want God to see everything about us? No. If he did, we would be fearful and ashamed. How could we ever hope to go to heaven with all our mistakes showing? "The true life," Paul says, "is a hidden one in God, through Christ" (Col. 3:3 PHILLIPS).

Let's take this a step further. Let's imagine how a person who isn't wearing the clothing of Christ appears in the eyes of heaven. For the sake of discussion, envision a decent human being . . . we'll call him Danny Decent. Danny, from our perspective, does every-thing right. He pays his taxes, pays his bills, pays attention to his family, and pays respect to his superiors. He is a good person. In fact, were we to dress him, we would dress him in white.

But heaven sees Danny differently. God sees what you and I miss. For as Mr. Decent walks through life, he makes mistakes. And every time he sins, a stain appears on his clothing. For example, he stretched the truth when he spoke to his boss yesterday. He was stained. He fudged, ever so slightly, on his expense report. Another stain. The other guys were gossiping about the new employee and, rather than walk away, he chimed in. Still another. From our per-spective, these aren't big deals. But our perspective doesn't matter. God's does. And what God sees is a man wrapped in mistakes.

Unless something happens, Danny will be the man in the parable, the one without the wedding garment. The wedding garment, you see, is the righteousness of Christ. And if Danny faces Christ wear-ing his own decency instead of Christ's goodness, he will hear what the man in the parable heard. "'You are not dressed for a wedding.' . . . So the king told some servants, 'Tie this man's hands and feet. Throw him out into the darkness, where people will cry and grind their teeth with pain'" (Matt. 22:12–13).

What happens if Danny changes his clothes? What if he agrees with Isaiah, who said, "Our righteous acts are like filthy rags" (Isa. 64:6 NIV)? Suppose he goes to Christ and prays, "Lord, take away these rags. Clothe me in your grace." Suppose he confesses the prayer of this hymn: "Weary, come to Thee for rest, naked come to Thee for dress."[1]

If he does, here is what happens. Jesus, in an act visible only to the eyes of heaven, removes the robe of stains and replaces it with his robe of righteousness. As a result, Danny is clothed in Christ. And, as a result, Danny is dressed for the wedding.

To quote another hymn: "Dressed in His righteousness alone, faultless to stand before the throne."[2]

God has only one requirement for entrance into heaven: that we be clothed in Christ.

Listen to how Jesus describes the inhabitants of heaven: "They will walk with me and wear white clothes, because they are worthy. Those who win the victory will be dressed in white clothes like them. And I will not erase their names from the book of life, but I will say they belong to me before my Father and before his angels" (Rev. 3:4–5).

Listen to the description of the elders: "Around the throne there were twenty-four other thrones with twenty-four elders sitting on them. They were dressed in white and had golden crowns on their heads" (Rev. 4:4).

And what is the clothing of the angels? "The armies of heaven, dressed in fine linen, white and clean, were following him on white horses" (Rev. 19:14).

All are dressed in white. The saints. The elders. The armies. How would you suppose Jesus is dressed? In white?

You'd think so. Of all the people worthy to wear a spotless robe, Christ is. But according to the Bible he doesn't. "Then I saw heaven opened, and there before me was a white horse. The rider on the horse is called Faithful and True, and he is right when he judges and makes war. His eyes are like burning fire, and on his head are many crowns. He has a name written on him, which no one but himself knows. He is dressed in a robe dipped in blood, and his name is the Word of God" (Rev. 19:11–13).

Why is Christ's robe not white? Why is his cloak not spotless? Why is his garment dipped in blood? Let me answer by reminding you what Jesus did for you and me. Paul says simply, "He changed places with us" (Gal. 3:13).

He did more than remove our coat; he put on our coat. And he wore our coat of sin to the cross. As he died, his blood flowed over our sins. They were cleansed by his blood. And because of this, when Christ comes, we have no fear of being turned away at the door.

Speaking of being turned away at the door, did I fail to tell you the rest of the Masters Golf Tournament story? I'm sure you are dying to hear whether or not I made it into the locker room. Well, wouldn't you know it, I did.

The day prior to the tournament, the golfers play an exhibition round on a par-three course. It is customary for the golfers to give their caddie the afternoon off and invite a friend or family member to take his place. Well, Scott invited me to be his caddie. "Of course, you'll have to wear the white overalls," he explained.

And, of course, I didn't mind. *Snicker.*

That afternoon, when the round was over, I made my way to the clubhouse. And through the same door, walking past the same guard, I stepped into golfer's inner sanctum. What made the difference? One day I was turned away, the next I was welcomed. Why the change?

Simple, I was wearing the right clothes.

Chapter 7

LOOK WHO'S IN THE WINNER'S CIRCLE!

A Day of Rewards

When the master comes and finds the servant
doing his work, the servant will be blessed.
Matthew 24:46

It's Sunday, September 27, 1998. Even though the St. Louis Cardinals have no hope of making the Major League Baseball play-offs, the ballpark is packed. It was packed three weeks earlier when Mark McGwire tied Roger Maris's home run record with a 430-foot shot off the stadium club window. It was packed the next day when 46,100 fans, as well as half of the human race, watched him break the record with a clothesline shot over the left field fence.

And it is packed today. Since Friday, McGwire has hit not one or two home runs, but three. For thirty-seven years, no one could hit more than sixty-one homers in one season; now the St. Louis slugger has hit sixty-eight. And he isn't finished. Number sixty-nine lands in the left field seats. It takes two curtain calls to silence the crowd. Home run number seventy comes in the seventh inning. The fans are on their feet before he comes to bat; they stay on their feet long after he crosses the plate.

They cheer the home run. They cheer the new record. They cheer the fellow who caught the ball. They cheer the season. And they cheer something else.

I'm speculating now. But I really believe that they—and we—cheered something else. We cheered because he did what we wanted to do. Wasn't there a time when you wanted to be where Mark McGwire was? Think a little. Scroll back a bit. Wasn't there a younger, more idealistic you who dreamed of hitting the big ball? Or winning the Pulitzer? Or singing on Broadway? Or commanding a fleet? Or receiving the Nobel Peace Prize? Or clutching an Oscar?

Wasn't there a time when you stepped up to the plate with a bat on your shoulder and stars in your eyes? Just a few years and Little League would become the big leagues and watch out Babe, watch out Mickey, watch out Roger—here I come!

But most of us don't make it. Bats are traded for calculators or stethoscopes or computers. And, with only slight regret, we set about the task of making a living. We understand. Not everyone can be a Mark McGwire. For every million who aspire, only one achieves. The vast majority of us don't hit the big ball, don't feel the ticker tape, don't wear the gold medal, don't give the valedictory address.

And that's OK. We understand that in the economy of earth, there are a limited number of crowns.

The economy of heaven, however, is refreshingly different. Heavenly rewards are not limited to a chosen few, but "to all those who have waited with love for him to come again" (2 Tim. 4:8). The three-letter word *all* is a gem. The winner's circle isn't reserved for a handful of the elite, but for a heaven full of God's children who "will receive the crown of life that God has promised to those who love him" (James 1:12 NIV).

From the mouth of Jesus, we hear a similar promise: The saved of Christ will receive their reward. "When the master comes and finds the servant doing his work, the servant will be blessed" (Matt. 24:46).

The promise is echoed in the epistles: "The Lord will reward everyone for whatever good he does, whether he is slave or free" (Eph. 6:8 NIV).

And in the beatitudes: "Rejoice and be glad, because great is your reward in heaven" (Matt. 5:12 NIV).

For all we don't know about the next life, this much is certain. The day Christ comes will be a day of reward. Those who went unknown on earth will be known in heaven. Those who never heard the cheers of men will hear the cheers of angels. Those who missed the blessing of a father will hear the blessing of their heavenly Father. The small will be great. The forgotten will be remembered. The unnoticed will be crowned and the faithful will be honored. What McGwire heard in the shadow of the St. Louis Arch will be nothing compared to what you will hear in the presence of God. McGwire received a Corvette. You'll receive a crown—not just one crown, but three. Would you enjoy a preview?

The crown of life. "Blessed is the man who perseveres under trial, because when he has stood the test, he will receive the crown of life that God has promised to those who love him" (James 1:12 NIV).

To help you appreciate eternity, consider this rule of thumb: Heaven will be wonderful, not only because of what is present, but because of what is absent. Say that again? I'll be glad to. *Heaven will be wonderful, not only because of what is present, but because of what is absent.*

As the apostle John took notes on what he saw in heaven, he was careful to mention what was absent. Remember his famous list of "no mores"? God "will wipe away every tear from their eyes, and there will be no more death, sadness, crying, or pain, because all the old ways are gone" (Rev. 21:4).

Did you catch the first "no more"? *There will be no more death.* Can you imagine a world with no death, only life? If you can, you can imagine heaven. For citizens of heaven wear the crown of life.

What have you done today to avoid death? Likely a lot. You've popped pills, pumped pecks, passed on the pie, and pursued the polyunsaturates. (Please pardon the perpetuity of p's in this paragraph.) Why? Why the effort? Because you are worried about staying alive. That won't be a worry in heaven.

In fact, you won't be worrying at all. Some of you moms worry about your kids getting hurt. You won't worry in heaven. In heaven we'll feel no pain. Some of you fellows worry about getting old. You won't in heaven. We'll all be ceaselessly strong. You travelers worry about the plane crashing. You won't in heaven. Heaven has no planes that I know of. If it does, they don't crash. But if they crash, no one dies. So you don't have to worry.

Last summer I hurt my back. The injury was nothing serious, but enough to wake me up. I needed to get in better shape. So I set out on an exercise regimen that was, if I say so myself, pretty strict. In time the back muscles were strengthened, my weight was down, and I was feeling pretty strong. I was beginning to field calls from professional football teams, weightlifting magazines, and modeling agencies, when I came very close to losing it all. A lady ran a red light and nearly hit me. We avoided the collision and kept going, but it was close. My sculpted physique could have been hurt! As I was driving away, this goofy thought popped in my head: *Is that my reward for all my exercise? I mean, I run, eat right, lift weights, and, through no fault of my own, it could be gone in a second.*

Isn't that the way life goes? We are frail creatures. Of course, my experience is small compared to the loss of others. Consider the mother who gives birth only to be rewarded with a stillborn child. Consider the man who works hard to retire, only to have retirement cut short by cancer. Consider the high-school athlete who trains hard, only to be injured. We are not made of steel, we are made of dust. And this life is not crowned with life, it is crowned with death.

The next life, however, is different. Jesus urged the Christians in Smyrna to "be faithful, even if you have to die, and I will give you the crown of life" (Rev. 2:10).

Let me suggest another crown we'll receive in heaven.

The crown of righteousness. "I have done my best in the race, I have run the full distance, and I have kept the faith. And now there is waiting for me the victory prize of being put right with God, which the Lord, the righteous Judge, will give me on that Day— and not only to me, but to all those who wait with love for him to appear" (2 Tim. 4:7–8 TEV).

The word *righteousness* defines itself. It means, simply, to be in a right relationship with God. The apostle Paul looks toward the day when he is crowned in righteousness. Now, the careful Bible student might raise a question here. Aren't we already righteous? Didn't I just read a chapter that stated that we are clothed in righteousness when we become Christians? Yes, you did.

Then why do we also receive a crown of righteousness? What happens in heaven that hasn't happened on earth? That is a good question and can be answered by using a favorite analogy of the apostle Paul, the analogy of adoption.

While we lived in Rio de Janeiro, we met several American families who came to Brazil to adopt children. They would spend days, sometimes weeks, immersed in a different language and a strange culture. They fought the red tape and paid the large fees, all with the hope of taking a child to the United States.

In some cases the adoption was completed before the child was born. For financial reasons, the couple would often have to return to the U.S. while awaiting the birth of their child. Think about their position: The papers have been signed, the money has been given, but the child is not yet born. They must wait until the birth before they can return to Brazil and claim the child.

Hasn't God done the same for us? He entered our culture, battled the resistance, and paid the unspeakable price which adoption required. Legally we are his. He owns us. We have every legal privilege accorded to a child. We are just waiting for him to return. We are, as Paul said, "waiting for God to finish making us his own children" (Rom. 8:23).

We are in a right relationship now; we are clothed with Christ. But when Jesus comes, the relationship will be made even "righter."

(I know that's not a word.) Our wardrobe will be complete. We will be crowned with righteousness. We will be rightly related to God.

Think about what that means. What prevents people from being rightly related to God? Sin. And if heaven promises a right relationship with God, what is missing in heaven? You got it, baby. Sin. Heaven will be sin-free. Both death and sin will be things of the past.

Is this a big deal? I think so. Earlier we tried to imagine a world with no death; let's do the same with sin. Can you imagine a world minus sin? Have you done anything recently because of sin?

At the very least, you've complained. You've worried. You've grumbled. You've hoarded when you should have shared. You've turned away when you should have helped. You've second-guessed, and you've covered up. But you won't do that in heaven.

Because of sin, you've snapped at the ones you love and argued with the ones you cherish. You have felt ashamed, guilty, bitter. You have ulcers, sleepless nights, cloudy days, and a pain in the neck. But you won't have those in heaven.

Because of sin, the young are abused and the elderly forgotten. Because of sin, God is cursed and drugs are worshiped. Because of sin, the poor have less and the affluent want more. Because of sin, babies have no daddies and husbands have no wives. But in heaven, sin will have no power; in fact, sin will have no presence. There will be no sin.

Sin has sired a thousand heartaches and broken a million promises. Your addiction can be traced back to sin. Your mistrust can be traced back to sin. Bigotry, robbery, adultery—all because of sin. But in heaven, all of this will end.

Can you imagine a world without sin? If so, you can imagine heaven.

Let me make this promise more practical. Some time ago a friend asked a very honest question about eternity. It had to do with his ex-wife. She is now a Christian and he is now a Christian. But things are still icy between them. He wondered how he would feel when he saw her in heaven.

I told him he would feel great. I told him he would be thrilled to see her. Why? Well, what causes tension between people? In a word, *sin*. If there is no sin, there is no tension. None. No tension between ex and ex, between black and white, between abused and abuser, even between the murdered and the repentant murderer.

The beautiful prophecy of Isaiah 11 will come true: "Then wolves will live in peace with lambs, and leopards will lie down to rest with goats. Calves, lions, and young bulls will eat together, and a little child will lead them" (Isa. 11:6).

Almost a millennium later John made a similar promise. Heaven will be great, he said, not just because of what is present, but because of what is missing. God "will wipe away every tear from their eyes, and there will be no more death, sadness, crying, or pain, because all the old ways are gone" (Rev. 21:4).

John's list could have gone on forever. Since heaven has no sin or death there will be no more _____. You fill in the blank. No more aspirin. Chemotherapy. Wheelchairs. Divorce. Jail cells or broken hearts. Crippled limbs or car wrecks.

To be crowned in life means no more death. To be crowned in righteousness means no more sin. And to be crowned in glory means no more defeat.

Let's look at this last crown.

The crown of glory. "And when the Chief Shepherd appears, you will receive the crown of glory that will never fade away" (1 Pet. 5:4 NIV).

It's worthy of note that Mark McGwire almost gave up. He almost quit baseball in high school so he could play golf. But he didn't. Something pulled him back. A few years into his career, he almost quit again. Neither his marriage nor the season was anything to write home about. He told his wife he was going to quit, but something made him return. Then there were the foot injuries. From '92 to '95 he endured multiple surgeries and missed two-thirds of the games. He told his parents he was going to quit. But something made him stay.

What made him stay? A dream. Somewhere he got the idea that he could do it. Long before his name was mentioned in the same breath with Ruth and Maris, long before he was called the St. Louis slugger or Big Mac, long before the fans thought he could, he thought he could. He dreamed of beating the record. He set his eyes on the prize, and he didn't give up.

May I close with a special word to a special group? Some of you have never won a prize in your life. Oh, maybe you were quartermaster in your Boy Scout troop or in charge of sodas at the homeroom Christmas party, but that's about it. You've never won much. You've watched the Mark McGwires of this world carry home the trophies and walk away with the ribbons. All you have are "almosts" and "what ifs."

If that hits home, then you'll cherish this promise: "And when the Chief Shepherd appears, you will receive the crown of glory that will never fade away" (1 Pet. 5:4 NIV).

Your day is coming. What the world has overlooked, your Father has remembered, and sooner than you can imagine, you will be blessed by him. Look at this promise from the pen of Paul: "God will praise each one of them" (1 Cor. 4:5).

What an incredible sentence. *God will praise each one of them.* Not "the best of them" nor " a few of them" nor "the achievers among them," but "God will praise each one of them."

You won't be left out. God will see to that. In fact, God himself will give the praise. When it comes to giving recognition, God does not delegate the job. Michael doesn't hand out the crowns. Gabriel doesn't speak on behalf of the throne. God himself does the honors. God himself will praise his children.

And what's more, the praise is personal! Paul says, "God will praise each one of them" (1 Cor. 4:5). Awards aren't given a nation at a time, a church at a time, or a generation at a time. The crowns are given one at a time. God himself will look you in the eye and bless you with the words, "Well done, good and faithful servant! You have been faithful with a few things; I will put you in charge of many things. Come and share your master's happiness!" (Matt. 25:23 NIV).

With that in mind, let me urge you to stay strong. Don't give up. Don't look back. Let Jesus speak to your heart as he says, "Hold on to what you have, so that no one will take your crown" (Rev. 3:11 NIV).

Chapter 8

YOU'D DO IT ALL AGAIN

A Day of Sweet Surprises

You are our hope, our joy, and the crown we will take
pride in when our Lord Jesus Christ comes.
1 *Thessalonians 2:19*

Oskar Schindler had his share of less-than-noteworthy character-istics. He was a womanizer and a heavy drinker. He bribed officials and was a member of the German Nazi Party. But buried in the dark of his heart was a diamond of compassion for the condemned Jews of Krakow, Poland.

The ones Hitler sought to kill, Schindler sought to save. He couldn't save them all, but he could save a few, and so he did what he could. What began as a factory for profit became a haven for eleven hundred fortunate souls whose names found their way onto his list—Schindler's list.

If you saw the movie by the same name, you'll remember how the story ends. With the defeat of the Nazis came the reversal of roles. Now Schindler would be hunted and the prisoners would be free. Oskar Schindler prepares to slip into the night. As he walks to his car, his factory workers line both sides of the road. They have come to thank the man who saved them. One of the Jews presents Schindler with a letter signed by each person, documenting his deed. He is also given a ring, formed out of the gold extracted from a worker's tooth. On it is carved a verse from the Talmud, "He who saves a single life saves the world entire."

In that moment, in the brisk air of the Polish night, Schindler is surrounded by the liberated. Row after row of faces. Husbands with wives. Parents with children. They know what Schindler did for them. They will never forget.

What thoughts raced through Schindler's mind in that moment? What emotions surface when a person finds himself face to face with lives he's changed?

Someday you'll find out. Schindler saw the faces of the delivered; you will, too. Schindler heard the gratitude of the redeemed; you'll hear the same. He stood in a community of rescued souls; the same is reserved for you.

When will this occur? It will occur when Christ comes. The promise of 1 Thessalonians 2:19 isn't limited to the apostle Paul. I'll explain. "You are our hope, our joy, and the crown we will take pride in when our Lord Jesus Christ comes" (1 Thess. 2:19).

It's been about six months since Paul left Thessalonica. He, Timothy, and Silas spent three fruitful weeks in the city. The result of their stay was a nucleus of believers. Luke provides a one-sentence profile of the church when he writes: "Some of them [the Jews] were convinced and joined Paul and Silas, along with many of the Greeks who worshiped God and many of the important women" (Acts 17:4).

An eclectic group attended the first church service: Some were Jews, some were Greeks, some were influential females, but all were convinced that Jesus was the Messiah. And in a short time, all paid a price for their belief. Literally. The young believers were dragged into the presence of the city leaders and forced to post bond for their own release. That night they helped Paul, Timothy, and Silas sneak out of the city.

Paul moves on, but part of his heart is still in Thessalonica. The little church is so young, so fragile, but oh-so-special. Just the thought of them makes him proud. He longs to see them again. "We always thank God for all of you and mention you when we pray" (1 Thess. 1:2). He dreams of the day he might see them again and, even more, dreams of the day they see Christ together.

Note what he says to them: "You are our hope, our joy, and the crown we will take pride in when our Lord Jesus Christ comes" (1 Thess. 2:19). The verse conjures up an image akin to the one of Schindler and the survivors. An encounter between those freed and the one who led them to freedom. A moment in which those saved can meet the one who led them to salvation.

In this case Paul will meet with the Thessalonians. He will search the sea of faces for his friends. They will find him, and he will find them. And, in the presence of Christ, they will enjoy an eternal reunion.

Try to imagine doing the same. Think about the day Christ comes. There you are in the great circle of the redeemed. Your body has been made new—no more pain or problems. Your mind has been made new—what you once understood in part, you now understand clearly. You feel no fear, no danger, no sorrow.

Though you are one of a throng, it's as if you and Jesus are all alone.

And he asks you this question. I'm speculating now, but I wonder if Christ might say these words to you: "I'm so proud that you let me use you. Because of you, others are here today. Would you like to meet them?"

Chances are you'd be surprised at such a statement. It's one thing for the Apostle Paul to hear such words. He was an apostle. We can imagine a foreign missionary or famous evangelist hearing these words—but us?

Most of us wonder what influence we have. (Which is good, for if we knew, we might grow arrogant.) Most of us can relate to the words of Matthew 25, "Master what are you talking about?" (v. 37 MSG).

At that point Jesus might—again, these are wild speculations—but Jesus might turn to the crowd and invite them. With his hand on your shoulder, he announces, "Do we have any here who were influenced by this child of mine?" One by one, they begin to step out and walk forward.

The first is your neighbor, a crusty old sort who lived next door. To be frank, you didn't expect to see him. "You never knew I was watching," he explains, "but I was. And because of you, I am here."

And then comes a cluster of people, a half-dozen or so. One speaks for the others and says, "You helped out with the youth devotional when we were kids. You didn't open your mouth much, but you opened your house. We became Christians in your living room."

The line continues. A coworker noticed how you controlled

your temper. A receptionist remarks how you greeted her each morning.

Someone you don't even remember reminds you of the time you saw her in the hospital. You came to visit a friend in the next bed, but on the way out you stopped and spoke a word of hope with this stranger who looked lonely.

You are most amazed by the people from other countries. After all, you never even traveled to Asia or Africa or Latin America, but look! Cambodians, Nigerians, Colombians. How did you influence them? Christ reminds you of the missionaries who came your way. Your friends said you had a soft spot for them. You always gave money. "I can't go, but I can send," you'd say. Now you understand; you didn't have a soft spot. You had the Holy Spirit. And because you were obedient to the Spirit, Utan from Cambodia wants to say thanks. So does Kinsley from Nigeria and Maria from Colombia.

It's not long before you and your Savior are encircled by the delightful collection of souls you've touched. Some you know, most you don't, but for each you feel the same. You feel what Paul felt for the Thessalonians: pride. You understand what he meant when he said: "You are our hope, our joy, and the crown we will take pride in when our Lord Jesus Christ comes" (1 Thess. 2:19).

Not a haughty, look-what-I've-done pride. But rather an awestruck joy which declares, "I'm so proud of your faith."

But Jesus isn't finished. He loves to save the best for last, and I can't help but imagine him doing the same in heaven. You've seen the neighbors, the coworkers, the people you hardly knew, the foreigners you never knew, but there is one more group. And Jesus parts the crowd so you will see them.

Your family.

Your spouse is the first to embrace you. There were times when you wondered if either of you would make it. But now you hear the words whispered in your ear, "Thanks for not giving up on me."

Then your parents. No longer frail like you last saw them, but robust and renewed. "We're proud of you," they say. Next come your children. Children for whom you cared and over whom you prayed. They thank you; over and over they thank you. They know how hard it was, and how hard you tried, and they thank you.

And then some faces you don't recognize. You have to be told—these are grandchildren and great-grandchildren and descendants you never saw until today. They, like the others, thank you for an inherited legacy of faith.

They thank you.

Will such a moment occur? I don't know. If it does, you can be certain of two things. First, its grandeur and glory will far outstrip any description these words can carry. "No one has ever imagined what God has prepared for those who love him" (1 Cor 2:9). And that "no one" certainly includes this one.

Second, if such a moment of reunion occurs, you can be certain you won't regret any sacrifice you made for the kingdom. The hours of service for Christ? You won't regret them. The money you gave? You'd give it a thousand times over. The times you helped the poor and loved the lost? You'd do it again.

Oskar Schindler would have. Earlier we wondered about Schindler's final thoughts. We wondered how he felt, surrounded by the people he had saved. His last appearance in the movie gives us a good idea. There, in the presence of the survivors, he tucks the letter away in his coat. He accepts the ring, and looks from face to face. For the first time, he shows emotion. He leans toward Isaac Stern, the factory foreman, and says something in a voice so low, Stern asks him to repeat it. He does. "I could have done more," he says, gesturing toward a car he could have sold. "That would have released ten prisoners." The gold pin on his lapel would have bribed an official to release two more. In that moment, Schindler's life is reduced to one value. Profit is forgotten. The factory doesn't matter. All the tears and tragedy of the nightmare are distilled into one truth. People. Only one thing counts—people.

I suggest you'll feel the same. Oh, you won't feel the regrets. Heaven knows no regret. Our God is too kind to let us face the opportunities we missed. But he is happy to let us see the ones we seized. In that moment, when you see the people God let you love, I dare say, you'd do it all again in a heartbeat.

You'd change the diapers, fix the cars, prepare the lessons, repair the roofs. One look into the faces of the ones you love, and you'd do it all again.

In a heartbeat . . . a heavenly heartbeat.

Chapter 9

THE LAST DAY OF EVIL

A Day of Reckoning

Satan, who tricked them [God's people], was thrown into the lake of burning sulfur with the beast and the false prophet. There they will be punished day and night forever and ever.

Revelation 20:10

My theater career peaked when I was nine years old. I was a proud member of the Odessa Boys Choir, a collection of thirty West Texas pre-puberty kids whose primary task was to sing at ladies' luncheons and Lion's Club meetings. We always wore green blazers and black slacks and marched onto the risers singing, "Hey, Look Me Over." Lawrence Welk would have been proud.

Our big break came during my second year in the choir. The local junior college drama department needed some youngsters to be the Munchkins in their production of *The Wizard of Oz*. Would we be interested? *Interested* was not the word. We were thrilled. So long Women's Wednesday Auxiliary. Hell-o-o-o-o-o, Broadway!

But our little Munchkin feet never touched the stage until the dress rehearsal. We rehearsed in a different time and place. We in the choir learned our part independently of the junior college cast.

We never saw Dorothy. We never heard about the Scarecrow, and we certainly knew nothing about the Wizard.

This was significant because I was unacquainted with the plot. You assumed that everyone knew the Yellow Brick Road story? Not me. As I was growing up, *The Wizard of Oz* was on television once a year, always on a Sunday night. The rest of my friends, the rest of the school—yea verily, the rest of the free world got to stay home and watch *The Wizard of Oz*. But did I? No, siree. Not me. No way. We had church on Sunday nights and I had to go listen to some dumb preacher. . . . (Oops, sorry. Guess I tapped into some repressed childhood anger.)

Suffice it to say, I had heard of *The Wizard of Oz* but had never seen it. So I didn't know the story. On the day of the dress rehearsal, I was woefully misinformed. Since we'd practiced away from the cast, I thought we (the Odessa Boys Choir) were the cast. Oh, I'd heard the director speak of supporting characters, but I assumed that they were minor and we were major. The city of Odessa, Texas, in other words, was turning out *en masse* to see we Munchkins. And not just we Munchkins, but especially "me Munchkin."

You see, I'm trying to find a way to say this humbly (it is hard)— I was a special Munchkin. I was a part of the "Lullaby Guild." Some of you connoisseurs of fine movies remember there were two choruses within the larger chorus of Munchkins. There was the "Lollipop Guild" and the "Lullaby Guild." With great talent we, the other three Munchkins and myself, stepped forth at the appropriate time, presented the Kansas farm girl with a gift, and sang, "On behalf of the Lullaby Guild, we wish to welcome you to Munchkin Land."

Prior to dress rehearsal, our practice never went any further. Consequently, I knew of nothing more. I assumed that the play ended with my presentation of the gift. Many nights I fell asleep envisioning Dorothy swooning at my feet and the crowd calling for more of Max the Munchkin. Agents would call, Hollywood would beckon, Broadway would beg. My career would be launched.

Imagine, then, my chagrin when I learned the truth. Finally, we were on the real stage with the real cast. We sang our Lullaby Guild song, but rather than practice curtain calls, the director patted our heads and hurried us out of the way with, "Nice job, little Munchkins." I was stunned. "You mean there is more to the show than me?" There was, and I was about to see it.

Out of a puff of smoke came the cackle of a wicked witch. She ran from stage right to stage left, cape flying and wand waving. I went from hurt to horrified! Talk about stage fright. They didn't have to tell me to act afraid. Who said anything about a witch?! I didn't know anything about a witch!

I would have, of course, if I had known the story.

By the way, we can make the same mistake in life that I made on stage. If we aren't acquainted with the end of the script, we can grow fearful in the play. That's why it's wise to ponder the last act.

The presence of Satan is one reason some people fear the return of Christ. Understandably so. Terms such as "Armageddon," "lake of fire," and the "scarlet beast" are enough to unnerve the stoutest heart. And certainly those who do not know God have reason to be anxious. But those dressed in Christ? No. They need only read the manuscript's final reference to the devil. "Satan, who tricked them [God's people], was thrown into the lake of burning sulfur with the beast and the false prophet. There they will be punished day and night forever and ever" (Rev. 20:10).

God hasn't kept the ending a secret. He wants us to see the big picture. He wants us to know that he wins. And he also wants us to know that the evil we witness on the stage of life is not as mighty as we might think.

Many passages teach these truths, but my favorite is a couple of verses recorded by Luke. Jesus speaks the words on the night before his death. He is in the upper room with his followers. They are shocked to hear his prophecy that one of them will betray the Master. Their defensiveness leads to an argument, and the argument leads Jesus to exhort them to servanthood.

Then in an abrupt shift, Jesus turns to Simon Peter and makes this intriguing statement: "Simon, Simon, Satan has asked to test all of you as a farmer sifts his wheat. I have prayed that you will not lose your faith! Help your brothers be stronger when you come back to me" (Luke 22:31–32).

This passage gives us a glimpse into an unseen world. It raises many questions, but it also affords many assurances, the chief of which is the chain of command. God is clearly in control, and the devil is on a short leash. Did you notice the verb that followed Satan's name? *Ask.* "Satan has asked. . . ."

The devil didn't demand, resolve, or decide. He asked. Just as he requested permission to tempt Job, he requested permission to tempt Simon Peter. Sort of recasts our image of the old snake, doesn't it? Instead of the mighty Darth Vader of Gloom, a better caricature is a skinny, back-alley punk who acts tough, but ducks fast when God flexes. "Uh, uh . . . I'd . . . uh . . . like to do a number on Peter—that is, if you don't mind." The chain of command is clear. Satan does nothing outside of God's domain, and God uses Satan to advance the cause of his kingdom.[1]

Why don't we ask someone who knows?

Julie Lindsey was working the late shift at a hotel just south of Montgomery, Alabama. Her part-time employment helped pay her college bills as she finished school. She was a devout believer. But her belief was tested the night two men held a gun to her head and forced her into their truck. She was robbed, repeatedly raped, and left handcuffed to a tree. It was two o'clock in the morning before she was rescued.

The nightmare nearly destroyed her. She couldn't function, the hotel fired her, and she dropped out of school. In her words, she was "shattered, lost, and bewildered."

This is one of the pieces that doesn't fit the puzzle. How does such a tragedy have a place in God's plan? In time, Julie learned the answer to that question. Listen to her words:

> After this experience, I spent a great deal of time thinking about God....I searched and I prayed for understanding. I longed to be healed....My spirit and faith were sorely tested; my spiritual journey in the months that followed was painful, but also wonderful.
>
> God allowed me to profit from an awful and devastating event. So many good things are in my life now. I have wonderful friends—most of whom I would never have met or known were it not for this experience. I have a job that allows me to work with and serve crime victims. I have a deeper

relationship with God. I am spiritually wiser and more mature. I have been blessed beyond what I can tell in these pages, and I am very grateful. Romans 8:28 came alive in my life: "All things work together for good for those who love God and are called according to his purpose. . . ." Now I ask you, who won?[2]

Julie now has a ministry speaking to groups about God's mercy and healing. Can't you imagine the devil groaning with each message? What he intended for evil, God used for good. Satan unknowingly advanced the cause of the Kingdom. Rather than destroy a disciple, he strengthened a disciple.

Think about that the next time evil flaunts its cape and races across your stage. Remember, the final act has already been scripted. And the day Christ comes will be the end of evil.

In the meantime—while we wait for Christ's return—we can be encouraged because:

Jesus is praying for us. This is no ho-hum warning Peter hears from the lips of Jesus. "Simon, Simon, Satan has asked to test all of you as a farmer sifts his wheat" (Luke 22:31). Loose translation? "Satan is going to slap your faith like a farmer slaps wheat on the threshing floor." You'd expect Jesus' next words to be, "So get out of town!" Or "Duck!" or "Put it in high gear before it's too late!"

But Jesus shows no panic. He is surprisingly casual. "I have prayed that you will not lose your faith! Help your brothers be stronger when you come back to me" (v. 32).

Can you hear the calmness in his voice? Forgive me, but I almost detect the accent of a streetwise, tattooed, leather-jacketed guy from Brooklyn: "Yo, Peter, Satan wanted to kill you, but you don't need to worry. I told him to go easy."

The sum of the matter is simple: Jesus has spoken and Satan has listened. The devil may land a punch or two. He may even win a few rounds, but he never wins the fight. Why? Because Jesus takes up for you. You'll love the way this truth appears in Hebrews: "But because Jesus lives forever, he will never stop serving as priest. So he is able always to save those who come to God through him because he always lives, asking God to help them" (Heb. 7:24–25).

Here's how it reads in other translations:

"He always lives to intercede for them" (NIV).

"He is always living to plead on their behalf" (NEB).

"He's . . . always on the job to speak up for them" (MSG).

Paul says the same thing in Romans: "The Spirit himself speaks to God for us, even begs God for us . . ." (Rom. 8:26). And then in verse 34, "The One who died for us—who was raised to life for us!—is in the presence of God at this very moment sticking up for us" (MSG).

Jesus, at this very moment, is protecting you. You may feel like a Munchkin on stage with a wicked witch, but don't worry. Evil must pass through Christ before it can touch you. And God will "never let you be pushed past your limit; he'll always be there to help you come through it" (1 Cor. 10:13 MSG).

"The Lord knows how to rescue godly men from trials" (2 Pet. 2:9 NIV), and he will rescue you. He will rescue us all on the day Christ comes.

We can be encouraged because Jesus is praying for us. We can also be encouraged because:

We will prevail. "When you come back to me . . ." are the words Jesus uses with Peter. Not "*if* you come back to me," or "at the *possibility* you'll come back to me," but "*when* you come back to me." Jesus has absolutely no insecurity, and neither should we. What Jesus did with Peter is what I wish someone had done with me, the Munchkin. He read him the rest of the script.

Suppose you had been present during that dress rehearsal of *The Wizard of Oz*. Suppose you'd seen a wide-eyed, red-headed kid hiding from the witch. And suppose you felt sorry for him. What would you have done? How would you have made him feel better?

Simple, you would have told him the rest of the story. "Sure, Max, the witch stirs up some trouble. Yes, Dorothy and the guys have their problems. But in the end, the witch melts like wax and everyone gets home safely."

Isn't that what God has told us about Satan? Read again the words of John: "The Devil who deceived them [God's people] will be hurled into Lake Fire and Brimstone, joining the Beast and False Prophet, the three in torment around the clock for ages without end" (Rev. 20:10 MSG).

God has kept no secrets. He has told us that, while on this yellow brick road, we will experience trouble. Disease will afflict bodies. Divorce will break hearts. Death will make widows and devastation will destroy countries. We should not expect any less. But just because the devil shows up and cackles, we needn't panic. "In [this] world you will have tribulation," Jesus promises, "but be of good cheer, I have overcome the world" (John 16:33 NKJV).

Our Master speaks of an accomplished deed. "I *have* overcome the world." It is finished. The battle is over. Be alert. But don't be alarmed. The witch has no power. The manuscript has been published. The book has been bound. Satan is loosed for a season, but the season is oh-so-brief. The devil knows this. "He is filled with fury, because he knows that his time is short" (Rev. 12:12 NIV). Just a few more scenes, just a few more turns in the road, and his end will come.

And we Munchkins will be there to see it.

Chapter 10

ITEMIZED GRACE

A Day of Permanent Pardon

In those days before the flood, people were eating and drinking,
marrying and giving their children to be married, until the day
Noah entered the boat. They knew nothing about what was
happening until the flood came and destroyed them.
It will be the same when the Son of Man comes.
Matthew 24:38–39

Denalyn and I recently spent half a Saturday watching our daughter Andrea play in a middle-school volleyball tournament. The first game was at eight o'clock and the second at eleven o'clock. In between the two contests, one of the parents invited the rest of us parents to eat breakfast at her restaurant. Not "a" restaurant, but "her" restaurant. Not wanting to miss a free meal, a dozen or so of us piled into our cars and off we went.

The food was served cafeteria style, so we all stood in line. All, that is, except our hostess. She stood next to the cash register. Being the owner, she wanted to make sure we didn't pay for our food. The attendant totaled the bill and rang up the charge, but we never gave a penny. As each of us took our turn before the register, our generous friend would tell the attendant, "I know him, he's with me. His bill is covered." Ah, the joy of knowing the right person.

Consider what happened that morning. The kindness of our hostess was magnified. Every time a debt was pardoned, her generosity was revealed. Also, those who knew the hostess were rewarded. Our trays were full and soon were our bellies. Why? Well, we simply accepted her invitation. And, those who did not know her had to pay the price. Though her generosity was abundant, it was not universal.

It may seem odd to hear someone analyze a breakfast invitation. Either I am hinting for another breakfast, or I am about to make a point. Actually, I'm going to make a point (though breakfast sounds good). What we saw that Saturday morning is a sampling of what we will all see when Christ comes.

The day Christ comes will be a day of judgment. This judgment will be marked by three accomplishments.

First, God's grace will be revealed. Our host will receive all the credit and attention.

Second, rewards for his servants will be unveiled. Those who accepted his invitation will be uniquely honored.

And third, those who do not know him will pay a price. A severe, terrible price. Jesus refers to this price in Matthew 24: 38–39: "In those days before the flood, people were eating and drinking, marrying and giving their children to be married, until the day Noah entered the boat. They knew nothing about what was happening until the flood came and destroyed them. It will be the same when the Son of Man comes."

As Jesus sought for a way to explain his return, he hearkened back to the flood of Noah. Parallels are obvious. A message of judgment was proclaimed then. It is proclaimed still. People didn't listen then. They refuse to listen today. Noah was sent to save the faithful. Christ was sent to do the same. A flood of water came then. A flood of fire will come next. Noah built a safe place out of wood. Jesus made a safe place with the cross. Those who believed hid in the ark. Those who believe are hidden in Christ.

Most important, what God did in Noah's generation, he will do at Christ's return. He will pronounce a universal, irreversible judgment. A judgment in which grace is revealed, rewards are unveiled, and the impenitent are punished. As you read the story of Noah, you won't find the word *judgment*. But you will find ample evidence of one.

The era of Noah was a sad one. "People on earth did what God said was evil, and violence was everywhere" (Gen. 6:11). Such rebellion broke the heart of God. "His heart was filled with pain" (Gen. 6:6). He sent a flood, a mighty purging flood, upon the earth. The skies rained for forty days. "The water rose so much that even the highest mountains under the sky were covered by it. It continued to rise until it was more than twenty feet above the mountains" (Gen. 7:19–20). Only Noah, his family, and the animals on the ark escaped. Everyone else perished. God didn't slam the gavel on the bench, but he did close the door of the ark. According to Jesus: "It will be the same when the Son of Man comes" (Matt. 24:39). And so a judgment was rendered.

Talk about a thought that stirs anxiety! Just the term *judgment day* conjures up images of tiny people at the base of a huge bench. On the top of the bench is a book and behind the bench is God and from God comes a voice of judgment—Guilty! *Gulp.* We are supposed to encourage each other with these words? How can the judgment stir anything except panic? For the unprepared, it can't. But for the follower of Jesus who understands the judgment—the hour is not to be dreaded. In fact, once we understand it, we can anticipate it.

Let's deal with some fundamental questions, and I'll show you what I mean.

Who will be judged? Everyone who has ever lived. According to Matthew 25:32, "Before him [the Son of Man] will be gathered all the nations" (RSV). In 2 Corinthians 5:10 Paul writes, "for we must all appear before the judgment seat of Christ" (NIV). Just as the whole earth was judged in the days of Noah, all humanity will be judged on the day Christ comes.

This stirs a hornet's nest of dilemmas, not the least of which is: What of those who never heard of Christ? What of those who lived before the time of Christ or who never heard his gospel? Will they be judged as well? Yes, but by a different standard.

Men will be judged on the basis of the light they had, not on the basis of a light they never saw. The person in the remote jungle who never heard of Jesus is judged differently than the person who is only a broadcast or open Bible away from the gospel.

Jesus explains as much with his harsh criticism of the cities Chorazin and Bethsaida:

> In the towns where Jesus had worked most of his miracles, the people refused to turn to God. So Jesus was upset with them and said: "You people of Chorazin are in for trouble! You

people of Bethsaida are in for trouble too! If the miracles that took place in your towns had happened in Tyre and Sidon, the people there would have turned to God long ago. They would have dressed in sackcloth and put ashes on their heads. I tell you that on the day of judgment the people of Tyre and Sidon will get off easier than you will." (Matt. 11:20–22 CEV)

The phrase "get off easier" is a revealing one. Not everyone will be judged by the same standard. The greater our privilege, the greater our responsibilities. Chorazin and Bethsaida saw much, so much was expected of them. The gospel was clearly presented to them, yet they clearly rejected it. "The saddest road to hell is that which runs under the pulpit, past the Bible and through the midst of warnings and invitations."[1]

On the other hand, Tyre and Sidon saw less, so less was expected. They, to use the words of Christ, will "get off easier" than others. The principle? God's judgment is based upon humanity's response to the message received. He will never hold us accountable for what he doesn't tell us.

At the same time, he will never let us die without telling us something. Even those who never heard of Christ are given a message about the character of God. "The heavens declare the glory of God; the skies proclaim the work of his hands. Day after day they pour forth speech; night after night, they display knowledge. There is no speech or language where their voice is not heard" (Ps. 19:1–3 NIV).

Nature is God's first missionary. Where there is no Bible, there are sparkling stars. Where there are no preachers, there are springtimes. Where there is no testament of Scripture, there is the testament of changing seasons and breath-stealing sunsets. If a person has nothing but nature, then nature is enough to reveal something about God. As Paul says: "The basic reality of God is plain enough. Open your eyes and there it is! By taking a long and thoughtful look at what God has created, people have always been able to see what their eyes can't see: eternal power, for instance and the mystery of his divine being" (Rom. 1:20 MSG).

Paul goes on to say, "God's law is not something alien, imposed on us from without, but woven into the very fabric of our creation. There is something deep within them that echoes God's yes and no, right and wrong. Their response to God's yes and no will become public knowledge on the day God makes his final decision about every man and woman. The Message from God that I proclaim through Jesus Christ takes into account all these differences" (Rom. 2:15–16 MSG).

We do not know how God will take the differences into account, but he will. If you and I, in our sinful state, are concerned about it, we can be sure that God in his holiness has already settled it. We can trust the witnesses who cry from heaven: "Yes, Lord God All-Powerful, your judgments are honest and fair" (Rev. 16:7 CEV).

Having established who will be judged, let's ask another question.

What will be judged? Simply put: all things that we have done in this present life. Again 2 Corinthians 5:10 is clear: "For we must all appear before the judgment seat of Christ, that each one may receive what is due him for the things done while in the body, whether good or bad" (NIV). This includes deeds, words, and thoughts. Isn't that the understanding of Revelation 20:12? "The dead were judged by what they had done, which was written in the books." Similar statements are found elsewhere.

"God will bring every deed into judgment, including every hidden thing, whether it is good or evil" (Eccles. 12:14 NIV).

"On the day of judgment, men will render account for every careless word they utter" (Matt. 12:36 RSV).

Jesus summarizes the matter in Luke 12:2: "Everything that is hidden will be shown, and everything that is secret will be made known."

Even for the believer? Will we be judged as well? Hebrews 10:30 states as much: "The Lord will judge his people."(NIV) The apostle Paul concurs: "For we will all stand before God's judgment seat. . . . So, then, each of us will give an account of himself to God" (Rom. 14:10, 12 NIV).

Did I detect an eyebrow arching? Why would a Christian be judged? Not a bad question. Let's make it our third.

Why will Christians be judged? Don't we have a new wardrobe? Aren't we clothed in the righteousness of Christ? Haven't our sins been cast as far as the east is from the west? They have. And we can stand firmly on this underpinning truth: "Therefore there is now no condemnation for those who are in Christ Jesus" (Rom. 8:1 NIV). Because we are clothed in Christ, we can be without fear on the day God judges us.

But if we are clothed in Christ, why do we need a judgment at all?

I can find at least two answers. First, so our rewards can be unveiled, and second, so that God's grace can be revealed.

Let's talk for a moment about rewards. Salvation is the result of grace. Without exception, no man or woman has ever done one work to enhance the finished work of the cross. Our service does not earn our salvation. Our service does, however, impact our rewards. As one writer stated, "We are accepted into heaven on the basis of faith alone, but we are adorned in heaven on the basis of the fruits of our faith."[2]

If this strikes you as strange, you aren't alone. Scripture offers just enough teaching to convince us of rewards, but not enough to answer our questions about them. In what form do they come? How are they dispensed? We aren't told. We are simply assured they exist. In addition to the crowns of life, righteousness, and glory, Scripture indicates that there are other rewards.

Some of the clearest writing on the topic is found in 1 Corinthians 3:10–15. In these verses, Paul envisions two lives. Both are built on the foundation of Christ; that is to say, both are saved. One, however, adds to that foundation with valuable works of gold, silver, and jewels. The other is content to take the cheap route and makes no substantive contribution to the kingdom. His work is comprised of flammable wood, grass, and straw.

On the day of judgment, the nature of each work will be revealed. Paul writes: "That Day will appear with fire, and the fire will test everyone's work to show what sort of work it was. If the building that has been put on the foundation still stands, the builder will get a reward. But if the building is burned up, the builder will suffer loss. The builder will be saved, but it will be as one who escaped from a fire" (1 Cor. 3:13–15).

Please note: Both builders will be saved, but only one will be rewarded. And that reward will be on the basis of works. Exactly what forms the rewards will take, we do not know. I was once counseled to maintain a "reverent agnosticism" on the question. Translated: be peacefully ignorant.

My feeling is that the rewards will come in the form of added responsibility, not added privilege. Such is the indication from Matthew 25:21: "Well done, good and faithful servant; you were faithful over a few things, I will make you ruler over many things. Enter into the joy of your lord" (NKJV). The worker appears to be given more duty rather than more relaxation. But again, we don't know for sure.

What we do know is this: We are saved by grace, and we are rewarded according to deeds. Anything beyond that is speculation. In fact, any speculation beyond that is dangerous lest we grow competitive.

But won't we be competitive in heaven? Won't the distribution of awards create jealousy for some and arrogance for others? No, it won't. In our sinless state our focus will finally be off of ourselves and onto Jesus Christ. We will gladly adopt the attitude Christ commands in Luke 17:10: "So you also, when you have done everything you were told to do, should say 'We are unworthy servants; we have only done what was our duty'" (NIV).

Still the question remains, why must our deeds be exposed? According to Jesus, "Everything that is hidden will be shown, and everything that is secret will be made known" (Luke 12:2). Is Jesus saying that all secrets will be revealed? The secrets of sinners and saints alike? He is, but—and this is essential—the sins of the saved will be revealed as *forgiven* sins. Our transgressions will be announced as *pardoned* transgressions. That is the second reason believers will be judged. The first, so our acts can be rewarded and second, so that God's grace can be revealed.

You've probably heard the story of the couple who resorted to do-it-yourself marriage counseling. They resolved to make a list of each other's faults and then read them aloud. Sounds like a constructive evening, don't you think? So she made hers and he made his. The wife gave her list of complaints to the husband and he read them aloud. "You snore, you eat in bed, you get home too late and up too early. . . ." After finishing, the husband did the same. He gave her his list. But when she looked at the paper, she began to smile. He, too, had written his grievances, but next to each he had written, "I forgive this."

The result was a tabulated list of grace.

You'll receive such a list on judgment day. Remember the primary purpose of judgment: to reveal the grace of the Father. As your sins are announced, God's grace is magnified.

Imagine the event. You are before the judgment seat of Christ. The book is opened and the reading begins—each sin, each deceit, each occasion of destruction and greed. But as soon as the infraction is read, grace is proclaimed.

Disrespected parents at age thirteen.
Shaded the truth at age fifteen.
Gossiped at age twenty-six.
Lusted at age thirty.
Disregarded the leading of the Spirit at age forty.
Disobeyed God's word at age fifty-two.

The result? God's merciful verdict will echo through the universe. For the first time in history, we will understand the depth of his goodness. Itemized grace. Catalogued kindness. Registered forgiveness. We will stand in awe as one sin after another is proclaimed, and then pardoned. Jealousies revealed, then removed. Infidelities announced, then cleansed. Lies exposed, then erased.

The devil will shrink back in defeat. The angels will step forward in awe. And we saints will stand tall in God's grace. As we see how much he has forgiven us, we will see how much he loves us. And we will worship him. We will join in the song of the saints: "You are worthy to take the scroll and to open its seals, because you were killed, and with the blood of your death you bought people for God from every tribe, language, people, and nation" (Rev. 5:9).

What a triumph this will be for our Master!

Perhaps you're thinking, *It will be triumph for him, but humiliation for me.* No, it won't. Scripture promises, "The one who trusts in him will never be put to shame" (1 Pet. 2:6 NIV). But how can this be? If the hidden is known and the secret is shown, won't I be embarrassed beyond recovery? No, you won't. Here is why.

Shame is a child of self-centeredness. Heaven's occupants are not self-centered, they are Christ-centered. You will be in your sinless state. The sinless don't protect a reputation or project an image. You won't be ashamed. You'll be happy to let God do in heaven what he did on earth—be honored in your weaknesses.

Heads bowed in shame? No. Heads bowed in worship? No doubt.

By the way, won't it feel good to have it all out in the open? No more games. No more make-believe. No more cover-ups. No more status seekers or ladder climbers. The result will be the first genuine community of forgiven people. Only one is worthy of the applause of heaven, and he's the one with the pierced hands and feet.

So don't worry about feeling shame. The believer has nothing to fear from the judgment. The unbeliever, however, has much to fear. Which takes us to our final question.

What is the destiny of those who don't know Christ? Remember the three purposes of judgment? God's grace will be revealed. His rewards will be unveiled. And those who do not know him will pay a price. A severe, terrible price.

Let's return to the story of the free meal at the restaurant. What would have happened if a stranger tried to horn in on the breakfast? No one did, but someone could have tried. He could have slipped in between the invited guests and acted like he was a part of the group. Would he have succeeded? Would he have fooled our hostess? No. She knew all her guests by name.

So does Christ. "The Lord knows those who belong to him" (2 Tim. 2:19). Just as our hostess stood next to the cash register, so our Savior will stand at the judgment seat. Just as she covered our debt, so Christ will forgive our sins. And just as she would have turned away the ones she did not know, Jesus will do the same. "I don't know this person," she would have said. "Get away from me, you who do evil. I never knew you," Jesus will declare (Matt. 7:23).

For that person, the day of judgment will be a day of shame. His sins will be revealed, but not as forgiven sins. Can you imagine the same list minus the proclamation of pardon? One deed after another until not even the sinner questions God's right to punish.

For those who never accepted God's mercy, judgment will be a day of wrath. It will be like it was in the days of Noah. But that is a topic for the next page.

Chapter 11

LOVE'S CAUTION

....

A Day of Ultimate Justice

The flood came and destroyed them. It will be
the same when the Son of Man comes.
Matthew 24:39

I did something different recently; I listened to the airline attendant as she gave her warnings. Typically, my nose is buried in a book or project, but a commercial plane had crashed the day before. Watching the newscasts of the event convinced me to pay attention. I realized that if this plane had trouble, I wouldn't know what to do.

So I listened. As she held up the seat belt, I buckled mine. As she described the oxygen mask, I looked up to see where it was stored. When she pointed toward the exit doors, I turned to find them. That's when I noticed what she notices on every flight. No one was listening! No one was paying attention. I was shocked. I seriously considered standing up and shouting, "You folks better listen up. One mishap and this plane becomes a flaming mausoleum. What this woman is telling you might save your life!"

I wondered what would happen if she used more drastic means.

What if she took a gasoline-drenched doll and set it on fire? What if the in-flight screen projected images of passengers racing to exit a blazing plane? What if she marched up and down the aisle, yanking away newspapers and snatching up magazines, demanding that the passengers listen if they want to survive this flaming inferno?

She would lose her job. But she'd make her point. And she'd also be doing the passengers a favor. Our Savior has done the same for us. He was motivated by more than duty, however. He was motivated by love. And love cautions the loved.

Christ's caution is clear: "In those days before the flood, people were eating and drinking, marrying and giving their children to be married, until the day Noah entered the boat. They knew nothing about what was happening until the flood came and destroyed them. It will be the same when the Son of Man comes" (Matt. 24:38–39).

As we pointed out in the last chapter, the parallels between the flood of Noah and the return of Christ come easily. People refused to listen then. Many refuse to listen still. God sent a safe place for the faithful then: an ark. God sends a safe place for the faithful today: his Son. A flood came then. A flood will come. The first was a flood of water. The next is a flood of vengeance. The first flood was irreversible. So is the second. Once the door is shut, it is shut forever. There was screaming on the day of the flood. There will be "weeping and gnashing of teeth" on the day of judgment (Matt. 25:30 NIV). Regarding the lost, the Bible says, "The smoke of their torment goes up for ever and ever; and they have no rest, day or night" (Rev. 14:11 RSV).

This is serious business. Hell is a serious topic. A topic we'd rather avoid. We agree with C. S. Lewis: "There is no doctrine which I would more willingly remove from Christianity than [hell], if it lay in my power. . . . I would pay any price to be able to say truthfully: 'All will be saved.'"[1]

Wouldn't we all? But dare we? Let's work with this for a moment.

Does hell serve a purpose? As much as we resist the idea, isn't the absence of hell even worse? Remove it from the Bible and, at the same time, remove any notion of a just God and a trustworthy Scripture. Let me explain.

If there is no hell, God is not just. If there is no punishment of sin, heaven is apathetic toward the rapists and pillagers and mass murderers of society. If there is no hell, God is blind toward the victims and has turned his back on those who pray for relief. If there is no wrath toward evil, then God is not love, for love hates that which is evil.

To say there is no hell is also to say God is a liar and his Scripture untrue. The Bible repeatedly and stoutly affirms the dualistic outcome of history. Some will be saved. Some will be lost. "Many of those who sleep in the dust of the earth shall awake, some to everlasting life, and some to shame and everlasting contempt" (Dan. 12:2 RSV). Paul agreed: "To those who by patience in well-doing seek for glory and honor and immortality, he will give eternal life; but for those who are factious and do not obey the truth, but obey wickedness, there will be wrath and fury" (Rom. 2:7–8 RSV).

People object to this point by gravitating to the teachings of Jesus. The idea of hell, they say, is an Old Testament idea. Curiously, the Old Testament is comparatively silent on the topic. The New

Testament is the primary storehouse of thoughts on hell. And Jesus is the primary teacher. No one spoke of eternal punishment more often or more clearly than Christ himself.

Think about these facts: Thirteen percent of the teachings of Christ are about judgment and hell. More than half of his parables relate to God's eternal judgment of sinners. Of the twelve times that the word *gehenna*—the strongest biblical word for hell—appears in Scripture, there is only one time in which Jesus was not the speaker.[2] No one spoke of hell more than Christ did. "Anyone who believes and is baptized will be saved, but anyone who does not believe will be punished" (Mark 16:16).

Are we to ignore these statements? Can we scissor them out of our Bibles? Only at the expense of a just God and a reliable Bible. Hell is a very real part of the economy of heaven.

Even now, before Christ comes, the presence of hell serves a powerful purpose. It functions somewhat like my dad's workshop. That is where he disciplined my brother and me. When my mom was angry, we got spankings. When my dad was angry, we got whippings. You can guess which one we preferred. All Dad had to say was, "Go to the workshop," and my bottom would begin to tingle. I don't know how you feel about corporal punishment. I don't mention the topic to discuss it. I mention it to explain the impact that the workshop had on my behavior.

You see, my father loved me. I knew he loved me. And most of the time, his love was enough. There were many bad things I didn't do because I knew he loved me. But there were a few times when love was not enough. The temptation was so strong, or the rebellion so fierce, that the thought of his love didn't slow me down. But the thought of his anger did. When love didn't compel me, fear corrected me. The thought of the workshop—and the weeping and gnashing of teeth therein—was just enough to straighten me out.

The application might be obvious. If not, let me make it so. Our heavenly Father loves his children. He really does. Most of the time, that love will be enough to make us follow him. But there will be times when it won't. The lure of lust will be so mighty, the magnet of greed so strong, the promise of power so seductive, that people will reject the love of God. In those moments, the Holy Spirit may mention "the workshop." He may remind us that "whatever a man sows, that he will also reap" (Gal. 6:7 RSV). And the reminder that there is a place of punishment may be just what we need to correct our behavior.

Jesus provides such a reminder in Luke 16.

What is hell like? Jesus is the only eyewitness of hell who has walked on earth. And his description stands as the most reliable and graphic ever written. Every single word in this story is significant. Every single word is sobering.

> There was a rich man who always dressed in the finest clothes and lived in luxury every day. And a very poor man named Lazarus, whose body was covered with sores, was laid at the rich man's gate. He wanted to eat only the small pieces of food that fell from the rich man's table. And the dogs would come and lick his sores. (Luke 16:19–21)

The story begins at a posh house in an exclusive neighborhood. The man who owns the house is extravagant. He wears the finest clothes. The Greek suggests he uses fabric that is literally worth its weight in gold. He eats sumptuously every day. In an era when most can afford meat once a week, his daily diet is exotic.

Botanical gardens sprawl within his gates. Gold and china sparkle upon his table. Ripe fruit from groomed orchards are a part of each meal. He lives, Jesus says, in luxury every day.

But outside his gate sits a beggar by the name of Lazarus. His body is covered with sores. Skin drapes from his bones. He's been laid at the gate. Someone too kind to ignore him, yet too powerless to help him, loaded the man in a wagon and deposited him in front of the house of the rich man. In those days the wealthy didn't use napkins after a meal; they would wipe their hands on chunks of bread. Lazarus asks only for the crumbs from this bread.

Heed the contrast. A nameless baron basking in leisure. A named beggar lying in misery. Between them a gate; a tall, spiked door. Inside a person feasts. Outside a person starves. And from above, a just God renders a verdict. The curtain of death falls. Both die. And as the stage lights are turned up on scene two, we gasp at the reversal of destiny.

"Later, Lazarus died, and the angels carried him to the arms of Abraham. The rich man died, too, and was buried. In the place of the dead, he was in much pain" (vv. 22–23).

The beggar, who had nothing but God, now has everything. The wealthy man, who had everything but God, now has nothing. The beggar, whose body probably had been cast into a garbage dump called Gehenna, is now honored with a seat near Abraham. The rich man, who'd been buried in a hewn tomb and anointed with priceless myrrh, is destined for the Gehenna of eternity. The pain of Lazarus has ended. The pain of the rich man has just begun.

If the story ceased here, we would be stunned. But the story goes on. Jesus now escorts us to the edge of hell and reveals its horrors. The rich man is in relentless torment. Five verses make four references to his pain.

"In the place of the dead he was in much pain" (v. 23).

"I am suffering in this fire!" (v. 24).

"Now he [Lazarus] is comforted here, and you are suffering" (v. 25).

"I [the rich man] have five brothers, and Lazarus could warn them so that they will not come to this place of pain" (v. 28).

Perhaps the last phrase is the most telling. The rich man defines his new home as a "place of pain." Every fiber of his being is tortured. And what's worse (yes, there is something worse), he can see the place of comfort which he will never know. He lifts up his eyes and sees the beggar who once lived at his gate. Now the rich man is the one begging.

"The rich man saw Abraham far away with Lazarus at his side. He called, 'Father Abraham, have mercy on me! Send Lazarus to dip his finger in water and cool my tongue, because I am suffering in this fire!'" (vv. 23–24).

Hell might be tolerable if its citizens were lobotomized. But such is not the case. The citizens are awake. They ask questions. They speak. They plead. Of all the horrors of hell, the worst must be the knowledge that the suffering will never cease. "These will go away into eternal punishment, but the righteous into eternal life" (Matt. 25:46 NASB).

The same adjective used to describe the length of heavenly life is used to describe the duration of punishment: *eternal*. Good people live "forever." Evil people are punished "forever."[3]

Revelation 14:11 is equally disturbing: "The smoke from their burning pain will rise forever and ever. There will be no rest, day or night, for those who worship the beast and his idol or who get the mark of his name."

We would love to believe that sinners will be given a second chance, that a few months or millenniums of purgatory will purify their souls, and ultimately all will be saved. But as attractive as this sounds, Scripture simply doesn't teach it. Abraham's response to the lost man's request affirms that the patience of God stops at the gate of hell. "Between us and you a great chasm has been fixed, so that those who want to go from here to you cannot, nor can anyone cross over from there to us" (Luke 16:26 NIV).

The term *fixed* originates in a Greek word which means "to set forth, to make fast." It literally means "to cement, to permanently establish." Paul uses the same word in Romans 16:25 when he boasts about Jesus, "who is able to establish you" (NIV).

Fascinating. The same power which establishes the saved in the kingdom, seals the fate of the lost. There will be no missionary journeys to hell and no holiday excursions to heaven. This is a hard teaching, and it gives rise to a hard question.

How could a loving God send people to hell? That's a commonly asked question. The question itself reveals a couple of misconceptions.

First, God does not *send* people to hell. He simply honors their choice. Hell is the ultimate expression of God's high regard for the dignity of man. He has never forced us to choose him, even when that means we would choose hell. As C. S. Lewis stated: "There are only two kinds of people in the end: those who say to God, 'Thy will be done' and those to whom God says, in the end, 'Thy will be done.' All that are in hell choose it."[4] In another book Lewis said it this way: "I willingly believe the damned are, in one sense, successful rebels to the end; that the doors of hell are locked on the inside."[5]

No, God does not "send" people to hell. Nor does he send "people" to hell. That is the second misconception.

The word *people* is neutral, implying innocence. Nowhere does Scripture teach that innocent people are condemned. People do not go to hell. Sinners do. The rebellious do. The self-centered do. So how could a loving God send people to hell? He doesn't. He simply honors the choice of sinners.

Jesus' story concludes with a surprising twist. We hear the rich man plead: "Please send Lazarus to my father's house. I have five brothers, and Lazarus could warn them so that they will not come to this place of pain" (Luke 16:27–28).

What is this? The rich man suddenly possessed with evangelistic fervor? The one who never knew God now prays for missionaries? Remarkable what one step into hell can do to your priorities. Those who know the horrors of hell will do whatever it takes to warn their friends.

Jesus, who understands the final flood of wrath, pleads with us to make any sacrifice to avoid it. "If your hand or your foot causes you to sin, cut it off and throw it away; it is better for you to enter life maimed or lame than with two hands or two feet to be thrown into the eternal fire" (Matt. 18:8–9 RSV).

This story is, without a doubt, the most disturbing story Jesus ever told. It's packed with words such as *torment*, *pain,* and *suffering*. It teaches concepts that are tough to swallow, concepts such as "conscious punishment" and "permanent banishment." But it also teaches a vital truth which is easily overlooked. This story teaches the unimaginable love of God.

"What? The love of God? Max, you and I read two different stories. The one I read spoke of punishment, hell, and eternal misery. How does that teach the love of God?"

Because God went there, for you. God spanned the chasm. God crossed the gulf. Why? So you won't have to.

Never forget that while on the cross, Jesus became sin. "Christ had no sin, but God made him become sin so that in Christ we could become right with God" (2 Cor. 5:21). Jesus became sin, the very object which God hates, the very object God punishes.

"The wages of sin is death," Paul stated in Romans 6:23 (NIV). The rich man is testimony to the verse. Lead a life of sin and earn an eternity of suffering. God punishes sin. Even when the sin is laid on his own son. That is exactly what occurred on the cross. "The LORD has laid on him the iniquity of us all" (Isa. 53:6 NIV).

And because he did, Jesus "took our suffering on him and felt our pain for us" (Isa. 53:4). What the rich man felt, Jesus felt. What you saw as you stared into the pit of hell, Jesus experienced. . . the pain, the anguish, the isolation, the loneliness. No wonder he cried out, "My God, my God, why have you rejected me?" (Mark 15:34).

Like the rich man, Jesus knew hell. But unlike the rich man, Jesus didn't stay there. "He [Jesus] too shared in their humanity so that by his death he might destroy him who holds the power of death—that is, the devil—and free those who all their lives were held in slavery by their fear of death" (Heb. 2:14–15 NIV).

Yes, hell's misery is deep, but not as deep as God's love.

So how do we apply this message? If you are saved, it should cause you to rejoice. You've been rescued. A glance into hell leads the believer to rejoice. But it also leads the believer to redouble his efforts to reach the lost. To understand hell is to pray more earnestly and to serve more diligently. Ours is a high-stakes mission.

And the lost? What is the meaning of this message for the unprepared? Heed the warnings and get ready. This plane won't fly forever. "Death is the destiny of every man; the living should take this to heart" (Eccles. 7:2 NIV).

Chapter 12

SEEING JESUS

A Day of Joyful Amazement

We know that when Christ comes again, we will be
like him, because we will see him as he really is.

1 John 3:2

Augustine once posed the following experiment. Imagine God saying to you, "I'll make a deal with you if you wish. I'll give you anything and everything you ask: pleasure, power, honor, wealth, freedom, even peace of mind and a good conscience. Nothing will be a sin; nothing will be forbidden; and nothing will be impossible to you. You will never be bored and you will never die. Only . . . you will never see my face."[1]

The first part of the proposition is appealing. Isn't there a part of us, a pleasure-loving part of us, that perks up at the thought of guiltless, endless delight? But then, just as we are about to raise our hands and volunteer, we hear the final phrase, "You will never see my face."

And we pause. *Never?* Never know the image of God? Never, ever behold the presence of Christ? At this point, tell me, doesn't the bargain begin to lose some of its appeal? Don't second thoughts begin to surface? And doesn't the test teach us something about our hearts? Doesn't the exercise reveal a deeper, better part of us that wants to see God?

For many it does.

For others, however, Augustine's exercise doesn't raise interest as much as it raises a question. An awkward question, one you may be hesitant to ask for fear of sounding naive or irreverent. Since you may feel that way, why don't I ask it for you? At the risk of putting words in your mouth, let me put words in your mouth. "Why the big deal?" you ask. "No disrespect intended. Of course I want to see Jesus. But to see him *forever!?* Will he be that amazing?"

According to Paul he will. "On the day when the Lord Jesus comes," he writes, "all the people who have believed will be amazed at Jesus" (2 Thess. 1:10).

Amazed at Jesus. Not amazed at angels or mansions or new bodies or new creations. Paul doesn't measure the joy of encountering the apostles or embracing our loved ones. If we will be amazed at these, which certainly we will, he does not say. What he does say is that we will be amazed at Jesus.

What we have only seen in our thoughts, we will see with our eyes. What we've struggled to imagine, we will be free to behold. What we've seen in a glimpse, we will then see in full view. And, according to Paul, we will be amazed.

What will be so amazing?

Of course I have no way of answering that question from personal experience. But I can lead you to someone who can. One Sunday morning many Sundays ago, a man named John saw Jesus.

And what he saw, he recorded, and what he recorded has tantalized seekers of Christ for two thousand years.

To envision John, we should imagine an old man with stooped shoulders and shuffling walk. The years have long past since he was a young disciple with Jesus in Galilee. His master has been crucified, and most of his friends are dead. And now, the Roman government has exiled him to the Island of Patmos. Let's imagine him on the beach. He has come here to worship. The wind stirs the cattails and the waves slap the sand, and John sees nothing but water—an ocean that separates him from his home. But no amount of water could separate him from Christ.

"On the Lord's day I was in the Spirit, and I heard a loud voice behind me that sounded like a trumpet. The voice said, 'Write what you see in a book and send it to the seven churches: to Ephesus, Smyrna, Pergamum, Thyatira, Sardis, Philadelphia, and Laodicea'" (Rev. 1:10–11).

John is about to see Jesus. Of course this isn't his first time to see his Savior.

You and I only read about the hands that fed the thousands. Not John. He saw them—knuckled fingers, callused palms. He saw them. You and I only read about the feet that found a path through the waves. Not John. John saw them—sandaled, ten-toed, and dirty. You and I only read about his eyes—his flashing eyes, his fiery eyes, his weeping eyes. Not so with John. John saw them. Gazing on the crowds, dancing with laughter, searching for souls. John had seen Jesus.

For three years he'd followed Christ. But this encounter was far different from any in Galilee. The image was so vivid, the impression so powerful, John was knocked out cold. "When I saw him I fell in a dead faint at his feet" (Rev. 1:17 TJB).

He describes the event like this:

> I turned to see who was talking to me. When I turned, I saw seven golden lampstands and someone among the lampstands who was "like a Son of Man." He was dressed in a long robe and had a gold band around his chest. His head and hair were white like wool, as white as snow, and his eyes were like flames of fire. His feet were like bronze that glows hot in a furnace, and his voice was like the noise of flooding water. He held seven stars in his right hand, and a sharp double-edged sword came out of his mouth. He looked like the sun shining at its brightest time. When I saw him, I fell down at his feet like a dead man. He put his right hand on me and said, "Do not be afraid." (Rev. 1:12–17)

If you are puzzled by what you just read, you aren't alone. The world of Revelation cannot be contained or explained, it can only be pondered. And John gives us a vision to ponder, a vision of Christ that comes at you from all angles. Swords and bronze feet and white hair and sunlight. What are we to make of such an image?

First of all, keep in mind that what John wrote is not what he saw. (Yes, you read that sentence correctly.) What John wrote is not what he saw. What he wrote is *like* what he saw. But what he saw was so otherworldly that he had no words to describe it.

Consequently, he stumbled into the storage closet of metaphors and returned with an armload of word pictures. Did you notice how often John used the word *like?* He describes hair like wool, eyes like fire, feet like bronze, a voice like the noise of flooding water, and then says Jesus looked like the sun shining at its brightest time. The implication is clear. The human tongue is inadequate to describe Christ. So in a breathless effort to tell us what he saw, John gives us symbols. Symbols originally intended for and understood by members of seven churches in Asia.

For us to comprehend the passage we must understand the symbols as the original readers understood them.

By the way, John's strategy is not strange. We do the same. If you open your newspaper to an editorial page and see a donkey talking to an elephant, you know the meaning. This isn't a cartoon about a zoo, it is a cartoon about politics. (On second thought, maybe it is a cartoon about a zoo!) But you know the symbolism behind the images. And in order for us to understand John's vision, we must do the same. And as we do, as we begin to interpret the pictures, we gain glimpses of what we will see when we see Christ. Let's give it a go.

When we see Christ, what will we see?

We will see the perfect priest. "He was dressed in a long robe and had a gold band around his chest" (v. 13). The first readers of this message knew the significance of the robe and band. Jesus is wearing the clothing of a priest. A priest presents people to God and God to people.

You have known other priests. There have been others in your life, whether clergy or not, who sought to bring you to God. But they, too, needed a priest. Some needed a priest more than you did. They, like you, were sinful. Not so with Jesus. "Jesus is the kind of high priest we need. He is holy, sinless, pure, not influenced by sinners, and he is raised above the heavens" (Heb. 7:26).

Jesus is the perfect priest.

He is also pure and purifying: "His head and hair were white like wool, as white as snow, and his eyes were like flames of fire" (Rev. 1:14).

What would a person look like if he had never sinned? If no worry wrinkled his brow and no anger shadowed his eyes? If no bitterness snarled his lips and no selfishness bowed his smile? If a person had never sinned, how would he appear? We'll know when we see Jesus. What John saw that Sunday on Patmos was absolutely spotless. He was reminded of the virgin wool of sheep and the untouched snow of winter.

And John was also reminded of fire. Others saw the burning bush, the burning altar, the fiery furnace, or the fiery chariots, but John saw the fiery eyes. And in those eyes he saw a purging blaze which will burn the bacteria of sin and purify the soul.

A priest; white-haired, snow-pure, and white-hot. (Already we see this is no pale Galilean.) The image continues.

When we see Jesus we will see absolute strength. "His feet were like bronze that glows hot in a furnace" (v. 15).

John's audience knew the value of this metal. Eugene Peterson helps those of us who don't by explaining:

> Bronze is a combination of iron and copper. Iron is strong but it rusts. Copper won't rust but it's pliable. Combine the two in bronze and the best quality of each is preserved, the strength of the iron and the endurance of the copper. The rule

of Christ is set on this base: the foundation of his power is tested by fire.[2]

Every power you have ever seen has decayed. The muscle men in the magazines, the automobiles on the racetrack, the armies in the history books. They had their strength and they had their day, but their day passed. But the strength of Jesus will never be surpassed. Never. When you see him, you will, for the first time, see true strength.

Up until this point, John has described what he saw. Now he tells what he heard. He shares the sound of Christ's voice. Not the words, but the sound, the tone, the timbre. The sound of a voice can be more important than the words of a voice. I can say, "I love you," but if I do so with a coerced grumble, you will not feel loved. Ever wonder how you would feel if Jesus spoke to you? John felt like he was near a waterfall: "His voice was like the noise of flooding water" (v. 15).

The sound of a river rushing through a forest is not a timid one. It is the backdrop against all other sounds. Even when nature sleeps, the river speaks. The same is true of Christ. In heaven his voice is always heard—a steady, soothing, commanding presence.

In his hands are the seven stars. "He held seven stars in his right hand" (v. 16). We later read that "the seven stars are the angels of the seven churches" (v. 20). With apologies to southpaws, the right hand in Scripture is the picture of readiness. Joseph was blessed with Jacob's right hand (Gen. 48:18), the Red Sea was divided when God stretched out his right hand (Exod. 15:12), the right hand of God sustains us (Ps. 18:35), and Jesus is at the right hand of God interceding (Rom. 8:34). The right hand is a picture of action. And what does John see in the right hand of Christ? The angels of the churches. Like a soldier readies his sword or a carpenter grips his hammer, Jesus secures the angels, ready to send them to protect his people.

How welcome is this reassurance! How good to know that the pure, fiery, bronzed-footed Son of Man has one priority: the protection of his church. He holds them in the palm of his right hand. And he directs them with the sword of his word: "And a sharp double-edged sword came out of his mouth" (v. 16).

The sound of his voice soothes the soul, but the truth of his voice pierces the soul. "God's word is alive and working and is sharper than a double-edged sword. It cuts all the way into us, where the soul and spirit are joined, to the center of our joints and bones. And it judges the thoughts and feelings in our hearts. Nothing in all the world can be hidden from God" (Heb. 4:12–13).

No more charades. No more games. No more half-truths. Heaven is an honest land. It is a land where the shadows are banished by the face of Christ. "His face was like the sun shining in all its brilliance" (Rev. 1:16 NIV).

What are we to do with such a picture? How are we to assimilate these images? Are we to combine them on a canvas and consider it a portrait of Jesus? I don't think so. I don't think the goal of this vision is to tell us what Jesus looks like, but rather who Jesus is:

The Perfect Priest.
The Only Pure One.
The Source of Strength.

The Sound of Love.

The Everlasting Light.

And what will happen when you see Jesus?

You will see unblemished purity and unbending strength. You will feel his unending presence and know his unbridled protection. And—all that he is, you will be, for you will be like Jesus. Wasn't that the promise of John? "We know that when Christ comes again, we will be like him, because we will see him as he really is" (1 John 3:2).

Since you'll be pure as snow, you will never sin again.

Since you will be as strong as bronze, you will never stumble again.

Since you'll dwell near the river, you will never feel lonely again.

Since the work of the priest will have been finished, you will never doubt again.

When Christ comes, you will dwell in the light of God. And you will see him as he really is.

Chapter 13

CROSSING THE THRESHOLD

A Day of Everlasting Celebration

I promised to give you to Christ, as your only
husband. I want to give you as his pure bride.
2 Corinthians 11:2

The story of the prince and his peasant bride. A more intriguing romance never occurred. His attraction to her is baffling. He, the stately prince. She, the common peasant. He, peerless. She, plain. Not ugly, but she can be. And often is. She tends to be sullen and sour, even cranky. Not the kind of soul you'd want to live with.

But according to the prince, she is the soul he can't live without. So he proposed to her. On the dusty floor of her peasant's cottage, he knelt, took her hand, and asked her to be his bride. Even the angels inclined an ear to hear her whisper, "Yes."

"I'll return for you soon," he promised.

"I will be waiting," she pledged.

No one thought it odd that the prince would leave. He is, after all, the son of the king. Surely he has some kingdom work to do.

What's odd is not his departure, but her behavior during his absence. She forgets she's engaged!

You'd think the wedding would be ever on her mind, but it isn't. You'd think the day would be on the tip of her tongue. But it's not. Some of her friends have never heard her speak of the event. Days pass—even weeks—and his return isn't mentioned. Why, there have been times, perish the thought, when she has been seen cavorting with the village men. Flirting. Whispering. In the bright of day. Dare we wonder about her activities in the dark of night?

Is she rebellious? Maybe. But mostly, she is just forgetful. She keeps forgetting that she is engaged. That's no excuse, you say. Why, his return should be her every thought! How could a peasant forget her prince? How could a bride forget her groom?

That's a good question. How could we? You see, the story of the prince and his peasant bride is not an ancient fable. It's not a tale about them, but rather a portrayal of us. Are we not the bride of Christ? Have we not been set apart "as a pure bride to one husband" (2 Cor. 11:2 NLT)? Did God not say to us, "I will make you my promised bride forever" (Hos. 2:19 NCV)?

We are engaged to our maker! We, the peasants, have heard the promise of the prince. He entered our village, took our hand, and stole our hearts. Why, even the angels inclined their ears to hear us say, "Yes."

And the same angels must be puzzled at our behavior. We don't always act like we are engaged, do we? Days will pass—even weeks—and we'll say nothing about our wedding. Why, some of those who know us well don't even know our prince is coming.

What's wrong? Are we rebellious? To a degree, but I think mostly we are just forgetful. Amnesic.

I stopped in a vitamin store last week. I asked a clerk to show me around. We passed a bottle on the shelf which looked familiar, a bottle of gingko. Just the week earlier my mom had told me she was taking gingko for her memory. I knew I had heard of the vitamin, but couldn't place where. Guess what I asked the clerk? I pointed to the bottle and said, "Help me remember what this is for." (He gave me a discount.)

To forget the purpose of gingko is one thing. But to forget our engagement to Christ is another. We need a reminder! May I offer an incentive?

You have captured God's heart.

I first witnessed the power of a marriage proposal in college. I shared a class with a girl who got engaged. I don't remember much about the class, except that the hour was early and the teacher was dull. (Doctors used to send insomniacs to his class for treatment.) I don't even remember the name of the girl. I do remember that she was shy and unsure of herself. She didn't stand out in the crowd and seemed to like it that way. No makeup. No dress-up. She was ordinary.

One day, however, that all began to change. Her hair changed. Her dress changed. Even her voice changed. She spoke. She spoke with confidence. What made the difference?

Simple. She was chosen. A young man she loved looked her squarely in the eye and said, "Come and spend forever with me." And she was changed. Empowered by his proposal. Validated by his love. His love for her convinced her that she was worth loving.

God's love can do the same for us. We, like the girl, feel so common. Insecurities stalk us. Self-doubt plagues us. But the marriage proposal of the prince can change all that.

Want a cure for insecurity? An elixir for self-doubt? Then meditate on these words intended for you:

> My sister, my bride, you have thrilled my heart; you have thrilled my heart with a glance of your eyes, with one sparkle from your necklace. Your love is so sweet, my sister, my bride. Your love is better than wine, and your perfume smells better than any spice. . . . My sister, my bride, you are like a garden locked up, like a walled-in spring, a closed-up fountain. (Song of Sol. 4:9–12)

Does such language strike you as strange? Do you find it odd to think of God as an enthralled lover? Do you feel awkward thinking of Jesus as a suitor intoxicated on love? If so, how else do you explain his actions? Did logic put God in a manger? Did common sense nail him to a cross? Did Jesus come to earth guided by a natural law of science? No, he came as a prince with his eye on the maiden, ready to battle even the dragon itself if that's what it took to win her hand.

And that is exactly what it took. It took a battle with the dragon of hell. He has "loved you with an everlasting love; [he has] drawn you with loving-kindness" (Jer. 31:3 NIV).

While writing this chapter, I received a phone call from a man wanting advice regarding his girlfriend. He didn't know what to do. Their work had them in different cities and their view of the relationship had them on two different pages. He was ready to get married; she was ready to give it some time. You should have heard the emotion in his voice. "I guess I can live without her," he said. "But I don't want to."

There is no doubt that Jesus can live without us, but he doesn't want to. He longs for his bride.

Have you ever noticed the way a groom looks at his bride during the wedding? I have. Perhaps it's my vantage point. As the minister of the wedding, I'm positioned next to the groom. Side by side we stand, he about to enter the marriage, I about to perform it. By the time we reach the altar, I've been with him for some time backstage as he tugged his collar and mopped his brow. His buddies reminded him that it's not too late to escape, and there's always a half-serious look in his eyes that he might. As the minister, I'm the one to give him the signal when it's our turn to step out of the wings up to the altar. He follows me into the chapel like a criminal walking to the gallows. But all that changes when she appears. And the look on his face is my favorite scene in the wedding.

Most miss it. Most miss it because they are looking at her. But when other eyes are on the bride, I sneak a peek at the groom. If the light is just so and the angle just right, I can see a tiny reflection in his eyes. Her reflection. And the sight of her reminds him why he is here. His jaw relaxes and his forced smile softens. He forgets he's wearing a tux. He forgets his sweat-soaked shirt. He forgets the bet he made that he wouldn't puke. When he sees her, any thought of escape becomes a joke again. For it's written all over his face, "Who could bear to live without this bride?"

And such are precisely the feelings of Jesus. Look long enough into the eyes of our Savior and, there, too, you will see a bride. Dressed in fine linen. Clothed in pure grace. From the wreath in her hair to the clouds at her feet, she is royal; she is the princess. She is the bride. His bride. Walking toward him, she is not yet with him. But he sees her, he awaits her, he longs for her.

"Who could bear to live without her?" you hear him whisper.

And who is that bride? Who is this beauty who occupies the heart of Jesus?

It is not nature. He loves his creation and creation groans to be with him, but he never called creation his bride.

It is not his angels. His angels are ever present to worship and serve him, but he never called the heavenly beings his bride.

Then who? Who is this bride about whom Jesus speaks and for whom Jesus longs? Who is this maiden who has captured the heart of God's son?

You are. You have captured the heart of God. "As a man rejoices over his new wife, so your God will rejoice over you" (Isa. 62:5).

The challenge is to remember that. To meditate on it. To focus on it. To allow his love to change the way you look at you.

Do you ever feel unnoticed? New clothes and styles may help for a while. But if you want permanent change, learn to see yourself as God sees you: "He has covered me with clothes of salvation and wrapped me with a coat of goodness, like a bridegroom dressed for his wedding, like a bride dressed in jewels" (Isa. 61:10).

Does your self-esteem ever sag? When it does, remember what you are worth. "You were bought, not with something that ruins like gold or silver, but with the precious blood of Christ, who was like a pure and perfect lamb" (1 Pet. 1:18–19).

Are you concerned whether the love will last? You needn't be. "It is not our love for God, it is God's love for us in sending his Son to be the way to take away our sins" (1 John 4:10).

Ever feel like you have nothing?

Just look at the gifts he has given you: He has sent his angels to care for you, his Holy Spirit to dwell in you, his church to encourage you, and his word to guide you. You have privileges only a fiancée could have. Anytime you speak, he listens; make a request and he responds. He will never let you be tempted too much or stumble too far. Let a tear appear on your cheek, and he is there to wipe it. Let a love sonnet appear on your lips, and he is there to hear it. As much as you want to see him, he wants to see you more.

He is building a house for you. And with every swing of the hammer and cut of the saw, he's dreaming of the day he carries you over the threshold. "There are many rooms in my Father's house; I would not tell you this if it were not true. I am going there to prepare a place for you. After I go and prepare a place for you, I will come back and take you to be with me so that you may be where I am" (John 14:2–3).

You have been chosen by Christ. You are released from your old life in your old house, and he has claimed you as his beloved. "Then where is he?" you might ask. "Why hasn't he come?"

There is only one answer. His bride is not ready. She is still being prepared.

Engaged people are obsessed with preparation. The right dress. The right weight. The right hair and the right tux. They want everything to be right. Why? So their fiancée will marry them? No. Just the opposite. They want to look their best *because* their fiancée is marrying them.

The same is true for us. We want to look our best for Christ. We want our hearts to be pure and our thoughts to be clean. We want our faces to shine with grace and our eyes to sparkle with love. We want to be prepared.

Why? In hopes that he will love us? No. Just the opposite. Because he already does.

You are spoken for. You are engaged, set apart, called out, a holy bride. Forbidden waters hold nothing for you. You have been chosen for his castle. Don't settle for one-night stands in the arms of a stranger.

Be obsessed with your wedding date. Guard against forgetfulness. Be intolerant of memory lapses. Write yourself notes. Memorize verses. Do whatever you need to do to remember. "Aim at what is in heaven . . . Think only about the things in heaven" (Col. 3:1–2). You are engaged to royalty, and your Prince is coming to take you home.

WITH AN EAR FOR THE TRUMPET

When it comes to animals, our house is a zoo. I wonder if other folks have the strange experiences we do. We had a bird enter through the chimney and get stuck in the bedroom. Another one knocked himself silly flying into a window. We forgot to feed a goldfish for a week—and he survived. We let a rabbit nibble on a backyard plant—and he didn't. It seems we have more than our share of animal episodes. In fact, sometimes I wonder if God sends them our way so that I will have ample illustrations.

Such was my thought last week with Fred. Fred is one of the two hamsters under the domain of our nine-year-old daughter, Sara. She was letting him run up and down the piano keyboard. I don't know what Denalyn would have thought about a hamster on her new piano, but she wasn't home. Besides, I was presiding over the affair in fine fatherly fashion, stretched out on the couch. The little fellow wasn't doing any harm—he seemed to be having fun. I know we were. Sara and I got a good giggle out of Fred's wind sprints. He brought new meaning to "tickling the ivories." But after several dashes, all three of us were a bit tired. So Sara set Fred where you place the sheet music. I closed my eyes and Sara, for just a moment, stepped away from the piano. Just a moment was all Fred needed to get into trouble.

To understand what happened next, you need to know that our piano is one of the horizontal versions. Had the piano been of the upright sort, Fred would have been safe. Had the lid been closed, Fred would have been safe. But the lid was open and Sara was distracted and I was dozing off when Fred decided to peer over the edge.

I opened my eyes just in time to see him tumble into a pool of piano strings and hammers. Sara and I both sprang into action, but it was too late. Our little friend was not only inside the instrument, he was under the strings. We could see his furry back rubbing against the wires as he ran back and forth looking for a way to escape.

Fred was trapped.

And we were stumped. How do you get a hamster out of a piano? We tried several approaches.

We tried nudging him. Wedging our fingers between the wires, we tried to coax him toward the opening. Didn't work. He ran the opposite direction and disappeared in a corner. We couldn't see him. We held a lamp over the piano and still couldn't see him. We tried flashlights and still couldn't see him. Coaxing didn't work.

So we tried calling him out of hiding. We used every voice possible.

The voice of a search party: "Fred, can you hear us?"

The voice of a friend: "Come on Fred, old buddy."

The voice of a mother: "Freddie-pooh, where are you?"

Even the voice of a drill sergeant: "Fred. Get out!"

Nothing worked. Coaxing didn't work. Calling didn't work. So we came up with another idea. How about a little piano music? We had to be careful; certain songs could be dangerous. A rousing rendition of John Philip Sousa might knock him out. So we were delicate, softly touching first this key, then that, then pausing to listen for the sound of little feet. We heard nothing. We played more and listened more. Still no luck. We tried some creative tunes. We thought "Three Blind Mice" might make him homesick. "I've Got You under My Strings" seemed appropriate. We even attempted a variation of "Pop, Goes the Hamster." But he didn't get the message. He refused to come out of his hiding place.

Only one alternative remained. We had to *(gulp!)* dismantle the piano. Some of you would not be intimidated by this task. I was. My hands are anything but handy. I have trouble opening a loaf of bread, much less opening a musical instrument. But Fred, the hamster, was in danger. Could we bear the thought of him stranded in the piano? Could we bear the smell of him stranded in the piano? So I grabbed my trusty Phillips screwdriver and began looking for a place to start.

I couldn't find one. The frame had no bolts. The keyboard had no screws. I figured out how to remove a pedal, but that wasn't much help.

So, once again, we were trapped. All of us were trapped. Fred hadn't come up for air, and we hadn't come up with a solution. All we could do was pray that he survive the night and call a piano tuner in the morning. I hadn't quite figured out what to say to the tuner, however. ("No, the piano sounds fine. But we have a hamster who really gets into his music.")

It was when we sat down to take a break that I wondered, *Do these things happen to other families? Or does God know that I need a conclusion for the book?*

If so, he certainly gave me a good one with Fred. We have a lot in common—you and I do—with Sara's pet. Like Fred, we took a fall. And, like Fred, we are trapped. Trapped, not by piano wires, but by guilt, anxiety, and pride. This is a foreign, fearful place. We were never meant to be here. Somehow we know, we were never meant to be this far from our Master's hand. We don't know how to get out.

But God does. He is not baffled. And he wants us to know that he will soon come and take us home. Isn't this the final declaration of the Bible? "I'm on my way! I'll be there soon!" (Rev. 22:20 MSG). But do we pay attention? Some do. But others of us, like Fred, are a bit slow to respond. Thankfully, God understands. And he gets creative.

He coaxes. Through the fingers of circumstance and situation, he tries to get us to look up. But we, like Fred, make a dash for the corner.

He calls for us. Sometimes whispering. Other times shouting. But we don't always answer.

So he provides some music. Divine fingers touch the keyboard of the universe. We are treated to regular symphonies of sunrises and sunsets. Soaring eagles and slapping waves. All intended to get our attention. But most stay in the corners.

God has even been known to do a little dismantling. Those times when our world seems to be falling apart? God's been known to pull out a Phillips and shake things up a bit—not because he doesn't love us. Just the opposite. He loves us dearly. And he will do whatever it takes to rescue his children.

Even if it means becoming one of us and entering our world.

I said it jokingly to the girls. After we had tried everything possible, I said, "Well, if one of us could become a hamster, we could go in and show Fred the way out."

Of course we couldn't even begin to do such a thing. But can you imagine if you could? Can you imagine becoming like Fred? Taking on a round belly, short legs, and whiskers? (Some of you think I just described your husband.) Leaving your great world for his cramped world? Why, we couldn't imagine such an act. But God could—and God did. And the journey from human to hamster is nothing compared to the span between heaven and earth. God became a baby. He entered a world, not of piano strings and hammers, but a world of problems and heartaches.

"The Word became human and lived here on earth among us. He was full of unfailing love and faithfulness" (John 1:14 NLT).

The operative word of the verse is *among*. He lived *among* us. He donned the costliest of robes: a human body. He made a throne out of a manger and a royal court out of some cows. He took a common name—Jesus—and made it holy. He took common people and made them the same. He could have lived over us or away from us. But he didn't. He lived *among* us.

He became a friend of the sinner and brother of the poor. He touched their sores and felt their tears and paid for their mistakes.

He entered a tomb and came out and pledged that we'd do the same. And to us all, and to all the frightened Freds of the world, he shared the same message. "Don't let your hearts be troubled. Trust in God, and trust in me. . . . I will come back and take you to be with me so that you may be where I am" (John 14:1, 3).

And how do we respond?

Some pretend he doesn't exist. They occupy themselves with a study of the piano and ask no questions about the Maestro.

Others hear him, but don't believe him. It's not easy to believe that God would go so far to take us home.

But then, a few decide to give it a try. They venture out of their corners and peek up through the opening. Each day they look toward the sky. They, like Simeon, "wait for" and "look forward to" the day Christ comes (2 Pet. 3:11). They know there is more to life than the belly of a piano, and they want to be ready when Christ comes.

Be numbered among the searchers, won't you? Live with an ear for the trumpet and an eye for the clouds. And when he calls your name, be ready.

Oh, you might wonder whatever happened to Fred. Well, he finally made his way back to the place where he fell in. He looked up. And when he did, Sara was there. He lifted his head just high enough so that she could reach in and lift him out.

Which is exactly what God will do for you. You will look up, and he will reach down and take you home . . .

when Christ comes.

ENDNOTES

CHAPTER 1: "YOU DO THE TRUSTING; I'LL DO THE TAKING"

1. John MacArthur, *The Glory of Heaven* (Wheaton, Ill.: Crossway Books, 1996), 118.

2. *Titanic Live,* broadcast on the Discovery Channel, 16 August 1998; *PrimeTime Live,* 13 August 1998.

CHAPTER 3: THE CRADLE OF HOPE

1. Jack Canfield and Mark Hansen, *Chicken Soup for the Soul* (Deerfield Beach, Fla.: Health Communications, 1993), 273–74.

2. John R. W. Stott, *Basic Christianity,* Downers Grove, Ill.: InterVarsity, 1971), 50.

3. Some resist the idea of the body of Jesus seeing decay in the grave. Acts 13:37 seems to indicate such: "But the One whom God raised from the dead did not see decay" (NIV). (See also Acts 2:27, 31). However, the original text employs the word *diaphthora,* which has a broader meaning than bodily decomposition. The word commonly means "destruction." The context of Luke's point is not the decay of the body, but the destruction of the body. Whereas David's body became "dust and ashes" (MSG), the body of Jesus did not see "destruction." Heaven interrupted and defeated the process.

   Besides, if the body of Jesus did not decay, then his death would have been different from ours. However, his death was like our death. He tasted "death for everyone" (Heb. 2:9 NIV). "He became obedient to death, even death on a cross" (Phil. 2:8 NIV). It would seem, then, that Jesus endured a death like ours so we could be promised a resurrection like his. Whether his body actually decayed, however, is a small discussion in light of the great truth of the ressurrection.

CHAPTER 4: INTO THE WARM ARMS OF GOD

1. Taken from Bob Russell, *Favorite Stories* (Louisville, Ky.: The Living Word Ministries), audiotape.

2. Anthony Hoekema, *The Bible and the Future* (Grand Rapids, Mich.: Eerdmans, 1979), 104. *Analysai* (to depart) is an aorist infinitive, depicting the momentary experience of death. Linked to *analysai* by a single article is the present infinitive, *einai* (to be). The single article ties the two infinitives together so that the actions depicted by the infinitives are two aspects of the same thing, like two sides of the same coin. Paul is saying here that the moment he departs or dies, that very moment, he will be with Christ.

CHAPTER 5: THE BRAND-NEW YOU

1. Unless, of course, you are alive when Christ returns, and then you will also get a new body. Paul says this in 1 Corinthians 15:51.

2. Hans-Joachim Kraus, *Charisma der Theologie,* as quoted in John Piper, *Future Grace* (Sisters, Oreg.: Multnomah Books, 1995), 370.

3. Joni Eareckson Tada, *Heaven:Your Real Home* (Grand Rapids, Mich.: Zondervan, 1995), 39.

4. Luke 24:13–35; John 20:10–18; John 21:12–14.

5. John 20:14, John 21:1–4; Luke 24:16; John 20:26.

CHAPTER 6: A NEW WARDROBE

1. David Danner, "Rock of Ages."

2. Edward Mote, "The Solid Rock."

CHAPTER 9: THE LAST DAY OF EVIL

1. I wrote about this more fully in *The Great House of God*. For a more in-depth treatment of this truth, see pages 143–55.

2. Joe Beam, *Seeing the Unseen* (West Monroe, La.: Howard, 1994), 230.

Chapter 10: Itemized Grace

1. J. C. Ryle as quoted by John Blanchard in *Whatever Happened to Hell?* (Wheaton, Ill.: Crossway Books, 1995), 184.

2. Donald Bloesch, *Essentials of Evangelical Theology* (San Francisco: Harper and Row, 1978), 229.

CHAPTER 11: LOVE'S CAUTION

1. C. S. Lewis, as quoted in Larry Dixon, *The Other Side of the Good News* (Wheaton, Ill.: Victor Books, 1992), 45.

2. For two contrasting views on the duration of hell, consider Blanchard, *Whatever Happened to Hell?* and Edward William Fudge, *The Fire That Consumes* (Carlisle, UK: The Paternoster Press, 1994).

3. Blanchard, *Whatever Happened to Hell?*, 130.

4. C. S. Lewis, *The Great Divorce* (New York: Macmillan, 1946), 66–67. As quoted in Blanchard, *Whatever Happened to Hell?*, 151.

5. C. S. Lewis, *The Problem of Pain* (New York: Macmillan, 1967), 127. As quoted in Blanchard, *Whatever Happened to Hell?*, 152.

Chapter 12: Seeing Jesus

1. Peter Kreeft, *Heaven: The Heart's Deepest Longing* (San Francisco: Ignatius Press, 1980), 49.

2. Eugene Peterson, *Reversed Thunder* (San Francisco: HarperSanFrancisco, 1988), 36–37.

WHEN CHRIST COMES

Study Guide

AS PREPARED BY STEVE HALLIDAY

WHEN CHRIST COMES

Looking Back

1. How do you respond to Max's description of Christ's return? How do you think you'd respond if you really saw the return of Christ?

2. What one word would you use to summarize your emotions regarding the return of Christ? Discomfort? Denial? Disappointment? Obsession? Joy?

3. What do you think Max meant when he wrote, "Some of you were only a few lines into the opening description of the return before you stubbed an opinion on a sentence"? Did *you* "stub an opinion"? If so, explain.

Looking Ahead

1. Read John 14:1–3. What was Jesus' main purpose in telling us about his return?

2. Read Matthew 24:30–31. How does Jesus picture his return?

Looking In

1. When was the last time you pondered the Lord's return? How did your thoughts affect the rest of your day?

2. As you're reading *When Christ Comes*, determine to do your own biblical study on Christ's return, especially focusing on the present-day effects of such a study.

1

"YOU DO THE TRUSTING; I'LL DO THE TAKING"

Looking Back

1. "We don't want our kids to sweat the details."

   A. Why don't we want our kids to sweat the details? What can happen when they *do* sweat the details?

   B. How does this idea apply to our relationship with God?

2. "'You do the trusting and I'll do the taking.' A healthy reminder when it comes to anticipating the return of Christ. For many, the verb *trust* is not easily associated with his coming."

   A. What does Max mean by "You do the trusting and I'll do the taking"?

   B. Why do so many people have trouble connecting "trust" with Christ's coming? Do *you* have such trouble? Explain.

3. "Don't be troubled by the return of Christ. Don't be anxious about things you cannot comprehend. Issues like the millennium and the Antichrist are intended to challenge and stretch us, but not overwhelm and certainly not divide us. For the Christian, the return of Christ is not a riddle to be solved or a code to be broken, but rather a day to be anticipated."

A. How can an issue that we can't fully comprehend still "challenge and stretch us"?

B. How can such issues "overwhelm" or "divide" us?

C. How can we make sure that such issues don't overwhelm or divide us?

4. Max outlines three truths that Jesus gave to keep us from being troubled:
   - "I have ample space for you."
   - "I have a prepared place for you."
   - "I'm not kidding."

A. What's important about each of these three truths? How can they help to keep us from being troubled?

B. Which of these truths is most significant to you personally? Why?

Looking Ahead
1. Read John 14:1–3.

A. On a day-by-day basis, how do you "trust in God"? What does this trust look like for you?

B. What is the primary reason for Christ's return, according to verse 3?

2. Read 1 Thessalonians 1:9–10.

A. What specific actions did the Thessalonians take once they came to Christ? How do they provide a pattern for us?

B. How do you actively wait for Christ to return?

3. Read Hebrews 10:23–25.

A. "The day" the writer mentions in verse 25 is the day Christ returns to earth. How does he say we are to act until then? How is our behavior related to Christ's return, in the writer's view?

Looking In

1. Do you find it easy or hard to trust God with the details of your life? Explain.

2. Determine this week to have a significant conversation with a fellow believer about the return of Christ. How can you encourage each other in your walk of faith by discussing Christ's return?

2
WAITING FORWARDLY

Looking Back

1. Max writes that Scripture characterizes Abraham as *trusting*, Moses as *leading*, Paul as *writing*, John as *loving*, and Simeon as *looking*.

   A. For the Christian, how are these traits significant?

   B. How do you think Scripture would characterize you?

2. "Simeon is a man on tiptoe; wide-eyed and watching for the one who will come to save Israel."

   A. Do you see this as a picture of active or passive looking? Explain.

   B. How would you describe your own waiting for the coming of Christ?

3. "The master loves to find people looking for his return. The master rewards those who 'wait forwardly.'"

   A. What does it mean to "wait forwardly"?

   B. Why do you think the master loves to find people anticipating his return?

4. "Hope of the future is not a license for irresponsibility in the present."

   A. What does Max mean by this statement?

   B. From your own experience, describe how someone's hope of the future prompted them to act irresponsibly in the present. What happened? How could it have been avoided?

Looking Ahead

1. Read 2 Peter 3:11–12.

   A. According to Peter, how should our hope of the future affect our lives? Is this principle at work in your own life? Explain.

   B. Peter says we can "speed" the coming of "the day of God." How?

2. Read Luke 2:25–35.

   A. What did Simeon say about Jesus in verses 29–32?

   B. How did Jesus' parents react to this in verse 33? Why?

   C. What did Simeon tell Mary about Jesus in verses 34–35? What events are predicted here?

3. Read Matthew 24:36–44.

    A. What is the primary admonition given to us in these verses? What are we to do now? How do we do this?

    B. What do these verses say about setting a date or time for Christ's return? How should we react when people do this? Explain.

Looking In

1. All of us have times during the week when we find ourselves waiting—in line at the checkout stand, in the mechanic's shop, in a doctor's office. Determine this week to use some of this "waiting time" to meditate on "waiting forwardly" for the return of Jesus. Then at the end of the week, tell someone about your experience. How has it affected the way you live?

2. Try to put yourself in Simeon's place. How has it felt to wait all those years for the Messiah? How has your waiting changed the way you live? How did it feel when you finally saw the Savior? How will you live from that time on? Now shift forward to the present again. How can you adopt some of the strategies pioneered by Simeon? What might happen if you did?

3

THE CRADLE OF HOPE

Looking Back

1. "No matter what happens, I'll always be there for you."

   A. Why did the son in this story believe his father's promise? What difference did it make to the son that he had this promise?

   B. Does God give us such a promise? Explain.

2. "Yes, the rocks will tumble. Yes, the ground will shake. But the child of God needn't fear—for the Father has promised to take us to be with him."

   A. How does such a promise give us practical help when the rocks tumble and the ground shakes?

   B. Describe a time in your life when the rocks tumbled and the ground shook—but the promise of Christ's return buoyed up your soul.

3. "For Paul and any follower of Christ, the promise is simply this: The resurrection of Jesus is proof and preview of our own."

   A. How is the resurrection of Christ "proof and preview" of our own resurrection?

B. How can this give us comfort in difficult times?

4. "In the blink of an eye, as fast as the lightning flashes from the east to the west, he will come back. And everyone will see him—you will, I will. Bodies will push back the dirt and break the surface of the sea. The earth will tremble, the sky will roar, and those who do not know him will shudder. But in that hour you will not fear, because you know him."

A. How would you feel if Christ were to come back this instant? Explain.

B. Max says those who don't know Christ at his return will "shudder," while those who know him "will not fear." Why the difference?

5. Max mentions three alternatives to the idea that Christ rose from the grave:
   - Jesus never actually died; he simply fainted on the cross.
   - Jesus' disciples stole his body from the tomb.
   - The Jews stole Jesus' body from the tomb.

A. How would you respond to each of these alternative theories? What problems does each have?

Looking Ahead

1. Read 1 Corinthians 15:22–23.

A. What two groups of people are described in this passage? To which group do you belong? How do you know?

B. Why does this passage depend on the truth of 1 Corinthians 15:17? What's the connection?

2. Read Romans 6:5–9.

A. What connection does the apostle Paul make between Christ's death and resurrection and our own?

B. How should this truth affect us in the here-and-now, according to Paul?

3. Read 1 Thessalonians 4:14.

A. What promise is given here? How is this promise designed to give us hope?

Looking In

1. After preparing yourself in prayer, determine this week to speak about Jesus' resurrection to someone who doesn't yet know Christ. What hope does his resurrection bring you? How can your friend benefit from this same hope?

2. Have a discussion this week with your children or other members of your family about the significance of the resurrection for daily living. How does it affect your life?

4

INTO THE WARM ARMS OF GOD

Looking Back

1. "Can you remember the first time death forced you to say good-bye?"

    A. Answer Max's question. Describe this time.

    B. Describe the most recent time death forced you to say good-bye. How was this different from the first time?

2. "Just as a parent needs to know that his or her child is safe at school, we long to know that our loved ones are safe in death."

    A. Do you agree with Max? Why or why not?

    B. How can loved ones be "safe in death"? What does this mean?

3. "When speaking about the period between the death of the body and the resurrection of the body, the Bible doesn't shout; it just whispers."

    A. Why do you think the Bible merely "whispers" about this period?

    B. What's the best way to react to this whisper?

4. "'What Paul is saying here is that the moment he departs or dies, that very moment he is with the Christ.'"

A. How can this truth give hope to terminally ill individuals?

B. How can this truth give hope to those loved ones who are left behind?

Looking Ahead

1. Read 1 Thessalonians 4:13–18.

A. According to verse 13, how do "the rest of men" grieve when they lose a loved one? Why do they grieve in this way?

B. Who is coming back with Jesus, according to Paul?

C. Which is the one group that will never taste death, according to verse 17?

2. Read Philippians 1:21–26.

A. What was Paul's internal struggle in this passage? How was he "torn"?

B. What did Paul expect would happen the moment he died? Explain.

3. Read Acts 7:54–60.

A. What did Stephen see before he died? Why did this fill him with hope? Why did it so anger the crowd?

B. What does it mean that Stephen "fell asleep"? Why use this terminology?

Looking In

1. Try an experiment for one week. Attempt to engage several people in conversation about death and dying. What kind of reactions do you get?

2. Spend some time this week thinking about your own funeral. What aspects of this event would be celebratory? What would you want to be said? Who would you want to be there? Why?

5

THE BRAND-NEW YOU

Looking Back

1. "Out of the decay of the seed comes the birth of a plant."

   A. Why is this principle from agriculture important to spiritual faith?

   B. How does this principle look backward and forward at the same time?

2. "The graveside service is not a burial, but a planting. The grave is not a hole in the ground, but a fertile furrow. The cemetery is not the resting place, but rather the transformation place."

   A. Explain what Max means by this statement.

   B. Do you normally think like this? Why or why not?

3. Max says God will transform our bodies in three ways, from:
   - Corruption to incorruption.
   - Dishonor to glory.
   - Weakness to power.

   A. What is involved with each of these three ways? What is the significance of each?

   B. How can we use this knowledge to transform the way we live now?

4. Max offers two complementary truths to end this chapter:
   - Your body, in some form, will last forever. Respect it.
   - Your pain will NOT last forever. Believe it.

   A. How do you "respect" your body? How can you disrespect it?

   B. How do we sometimes show that we have forgotten our pain will not last forever? How can we make sure that we won't forget this truth?

Looking Ahead

1. Read 1 Corinthians 15:20–26.

   A. In what way is Christ the "firstfruits" of those who have "fallen asleep"?

   B. What is the last "enemy" to be destroyed?

2. Read 1 Corinthians 15:35–44.

   A. How does Paul say our bodies are like a seed? How does this analogy help to explain our future bodies?

   B. Name some of the differences between our present bodies and our future bodies.

3. Read Philippians 3:20–21.

   A. How will our bodies be transformed?

   B. What will our new bodies be like?

   C. Who will accomplish this?

4. Read John 20:10–21:14; Luke 24:36–43.

   A. How was Jesus' resurrection body like his mortal body?

   B. How was Jesus' resurrection body unlike his mortal body?

   C. What significance does this hold for us?

Looking In

1. In a single sitting, read the accounts of Jesus' post-resurrection appearances found in each of the four Gospels. Try to put yourself in the disciples' place—how do you think you would have reacted to these appearances? What do you think these appearances did for the disciples' faith? What can they do for your own faith?

2. Spend some time daydreaming about the potential of your future glorified body. What about your present body will be better? What do you think it will be like to have such a strong, amazing body? What do you imagine you will do with it? At the conclusion of your daydreaming, spend some more time thanking God that this new body he speaks of in Scripture isn't merely a daydream, but will surely come into being. In you!

6

A NEW WARDROBE

Looking Back

1. "I had made it all the way to the door but was denied entrance."

   A. Why was Max denied entrance to the locker room at Augusta National Country Club?

   B. How do you think Max felt when he was denied entrance? How would you have felt?

2. "To be turned away from seeing golf history is one thing, but to be refused admission into heaven is quite another. That is why some people don't want to discuss the return of Christ. It makes them nervous. They may be God-fearing and church-attending but still nervous."

    A. Does discussing the return of Christ ever make you nervous? Explain.

    B. Do you ever worry that you will be refused entrance into heaven? Explain.

3. "God sees what you and I miss. For as Mr. Decent walks through life, he makes mistakes. And every time he sins, a stain appears on his clothing. For example, he stretched the truth when he spoke to his boss yesterday. He was stained. He fudged, ever so slightly, on his expense report. Another stain. The other guys were gossiping about the new employee and, rather than walk away, he chimed in. Still another. From our perspective, these aren't big deals. But our perspective doesn't matter. God's does. And what God sees is a man wrapped in mistakes."

    A. Is it easier to see other people's stains or our own? Explain.

    B. Do you think God sees a person "wrapped in mistakes" when he looks at you? Explain.

4. "He did more than remove our coat; he put on our coat. And he wore our coat of sin to the cross. As he died, his blood flowed over our sins. They were cleansed by his blood. And because of

this, when Christ comes, we have no fear of being turned away at the door."

A. What "coat" of ours did Christ put on? How was that "coat" made clean?

B. What kind of "coat" are you wearing right now? How do you know?

Looking Ahead

1. Read 1 John 2:28.

   A. To whom is this verse addressed? How is this significant?

   B. How can we make sure we are "unashamed" at the coming of Christ?

2. Read Matthew 22:1–14.

   A. Why did the first group of invited guests (verses 4–6) not come to the king's banquet?

   B. Describe the second group of guests who were invited to the king's banquet (verses 9–10).

   C. What is the significance of the man who was found at the banquet without wedding clothes (verses 11–13)? What is Jesus' point?

3. Read Romans 13:14 and Galatians 3:26–29.

   A. What sort of clothing is described here? What is its significance?

   B. How does one put on this sort of clothing? Have you put it on? Explain.

4. Read Galatians 3:13 and 2 Corinthians 5:21.

   A. In what way did Christ take our place?

   B. What was the purpose of this exchange?

Looking In

1. Sometimes we think the best way to make sure we are "unashamed" at the coming of Christ is to focus on cutting out of our lives all the things that might make us ashamed—and therefore end up concentrating on our sin rather than on Christ. For a couple of days, try this experiment instead: Consciously dwell on the idea that Christ could return at any moment. Think about him, not your sin—and then describe your experience in a personal journal.

2. Read a book that chronicles the ability of Jesus Christ to transform the lives of all kinds of people (like Max Lucado's *Just Like Jesus*). Then spend several minutes thanking God for what he is doing in your own life.

7

LOOK WHO'S IN THE WINNER'S CIRCLE!

Looking Back

1. "We cheered because he did what we wanted to do. Wasn't there a time when you wanted to be where Mark McGwire was? Think a little. Scroll back a bit. Wasn't there a younger, more idealistic you who dreamed of hitting the big ball? Or winning the Pulitzer? Or singing on Broadway? Or commanding a fleet? Or receiving the Nobel Peace Prize? Or clutching an Oscar?"

   A. If you're a baseball fan, how did you react to McGwire's amazing season?

   B. If you're not particularly a baseball fan, what dream did you once nurture as a younger person? Describe that dream.

2. "Heavenly rewards are not limited to a chosen few, but 'to all those who have waited with love for him to come again'" (2 Tim. 4:8).

   A. Why do you think God tells us in advance about rewards? How often do you think of heavenly rewards? Explain.

   B. Do you think a heavenly reward is waiting for you? Explain.

3. Max mentions three types of crowns:
    - The crown of life.
    - The crown of righteousness.
    - The crown of glory.

    A. What is the significance of each of these crowns?

    B. Which of these crowns means the most to you? Why?

4. "Heaven will be wonderful, not only because of what is present, but because of what is absent."

    A. How can something be wonderful because of what it lacks?

    B. What kind of things will heaven lack? How does this make you feel?

Looking Ahead

1. Read Matthew 24:42–47.

    A. Why does Jesus compare his return to a break-in by a thief? How are the two alike? How are they different?

    B. How do verses 42–44 define what a "faithful and wise" servant is?

    C. How will the Lord reward "faithful and wise" servants (verses 46–47)?

2. Read 2 Timothy 4:6–8.

   A. Describe Paul's circumstances when he penned these words. How did the ideas he wrote about encourage his own heart?

   B. What sort of crown is mentioned here? To whom is it given? Do you expect to receive this crown? Explain.

3. Read James 1:12.

   A. Describe the person James has in view in this verse. Why is this significant?

   B. What crown does James mention here? To whom is it given? Do you expect to receive this crown? Explain.

4. Read 1 Peter 5:1–4.

   A. Describe the person Peter has in view in this verse.

   B. What crown does Peter mention here? To whom is it given? Do you expect to receive this crown? Explain.

Looking In

1. Take a few moments to envision yourself in heaven's "winner's circle." Imagine that all of heaven is focused on you. What is God saying about your life on earth? What sort of rewards do you think you might receive? Now shift back to this moment in time. Do you need to make any changes in your life in order to receive the kind of rewards you'd like? If so, what? Ask God for the

strength to do what you really believe you need to do and thank him for the rewards he's already described for us.

2. Get a concordance and look up the words *reward* and *inheritance*. Consider only those verses that talk about our eternal reward. What did you learn in your study that you didn't know before? What effect did your study have on the way you live today?

8

YOU'D DO IT ALL AGAIN

Looking Back

1. "Schindler saw the faces of the delivered; you will, too. Schindler heard the gratitude of the redeemed; you'll hear the same. He stood in a community of rescued souls; the same is reserved for you."

A. Would it have been difficult to do what Schindler did? Explain.

B. What is difficult about trying to live a godly life here on earth? Explain.

C. How can focusing on others help us to keep moving forward in our spiritual walk?

2. "Most of us wonder what influence we have. (Which is good, for if we knew, we might grow arrogant.)"

A. Do you ever wonder what influence you have? Explain.

B. Why might we grow arrogant if we knew the whole story?

3. Max writes about "an awestruck joy which declares, 'I'm so proud of your faith.'"

A. What will prompt this kind of awestruck joy? What part can you play in it?

B. How is it possible to be "proud" of someone's faith? Isn't pride a sin?

4. Max says two things will happen in heaven if we find out how our faith has influenced that of others:

- The grandeur and glory of the moment will far outstrip any description.
- We won't regret any sacrifice we made for the kingdom.

A. How can you maximize your influence for the kingdom?

B. What kind of "sacrifices" is God calling you to make for the kingdom? How do you respond to these calls? Explain.

Looking Ahead
1. Read 1 Thessalonians 2:17–20.

A. What does Paul call the Christians in Thessalonica (verse 17)? How do you think he feels about them? Explain.

B. What three things does Paul call the Christians in Thessalonica in verse 19? How does Paul think he'll feel about them when Christ returns?

2. Read 1 Corinthians 1:9.

A. What does this verse tell us about the day Christ returns?

B. Compare this verse to Isaiah 64:4. How has Paul slightly changed the verse in 1 Corinthians? What significance do you think this might have?

3. Read Acts 17:1–10.

A. What do you learn about the birth of the church in Thessalonica?

B. What clues do you get from this text about the difficulties the Thessalonians faced in their newfound faith? How can their experience help and encourage us today?

Looking In

1. Sit down at a table, take a pad of paper and a pen or pencil, and try to list as many people as possible on whom you might have an influence. Family members? Friends? Church acquaintances? Store clerks? Gas station attendants? Paper boy? Neighbors? Then

try to think about the last time you saw these people. What kind of influence did you probably have on them? Could you have influenced them toward Christ?

2. Spend a significant amount of time asking God to help you be the influence for him that you really want to be. Ask him to give you insight into ways to be a strong influence, and ask him to show you what you might need to change to become the most effective influence you can be. Then thank him for hearing your prayer and allowing you to be an influence in your world for him.

9

THE LAST DAY OF EVIL

Looking Back

1. "If we aren't acquainted with the end of the script, we can grow fearful in the play. That's why it's wise to ponder the last act."
   A. What does Max mean by "the play"? How about "the end of the script"?

   B. How can we ponder "the last act"?

2. "God hasn't kept the ending a secret. He wants us to see the big picture. He wants us to know that he wins. And he also wants us to know that the evil we witness on the stage of life is not as mighty as we might think."

A. Is Satan frightening to you?

B. How does God "win" in the end? How do you encourage yourself to think about this ultimate divine victory?

3. Max gives us two reasons to be encouraged now despite whatever pain we might have to endure at the hands of evil:
   • Jesus is praying for us.
   • We will prevail.
   A. Speculate for a moment: What kind of prayers do you think Jesus is offering on your behalf? Why these prayers?

   B. In what way will we prevail? What will this look like? How does this make you feel? Explain.

Looking Ahead
1. Read Revelation 20:10.
   A. What is the ultimate destiny of the devil? How does this happen? Who ensures that it happens?

   B. Why would the apostle John tell us about this event? How can it help us today?

2. Read Luke 22:31–34.
   A. Why is it significant that Jesus said Satan "asked" to sift Peter as wheat?

B. What prayer did Jesus offer on Peter's behalf?

C. What confidence did Jesus have that his prayer would be answered?

D. Why is this conversation especially significant in light of what Jesus predicted in verse 34? How does verse 33 show that Peter's confidence was misplaced?

3. Read Hebrews 7:20–26 and Romans 8:26–27.
   A. What promises are given to us in these two passages?

   B. Why do you think we are given these promises? What is the point?

4. Read John 16:33.
   A. What promise does Jesus give us about life in this world?

   B. Why should we be encouraged even in difficult circumstances?

Looking In

1. Memorize Hebrews 7:25–26 and Romans 8:26–27. Write these verses on cards and put them where you can see them when you go about your daily tasks. Thank God that he has not left you alone, that his eye is constantly on you, and that Jesus himself prays for you and your needs.

2. If you have children, think of a creative way to emphasize for them the truth that Jesus prays for them constantly. Create a little story or craft that will teach them about God's continual love and care for them. And make sure that you believe whatever you tell them!

10

ITEMIZED GRACE

Looking Back

1. Max says the day of judgment at Christ's return will be marked by three accomplishments:
   - God's grace will be revealed.
   - Rewards for God's servants will be unveiled.
   - Those who do not know God will pay a price.

   A. How will God's grace be revealed at the second coming of Christ?

   B. How will God's rewards be unveiled?

   C. What kind of price will be paid by those who don't know God?

2. "What God did in Noah's generation, he will do at Christ's return. He will pronounce a universal, irreversible judgment. A

judgment in which grace is revealed, rewards are unveiled, and the impenitent are punished."

A. How will Christ's second coming be like what happened in Noah's day?

B. How can we, like Noah, prepare for that day?

3. Max asks four "fundamental questions" about Christ's judgment:
   - Who will be judged?
   - What will be judged?
   - Why will Christians be judged?
   - What is the destiny of those who don't know Christ?

A. What answer does Max give for each of these questions?

B. What do you think of the answers Max gives? Do you think he's right? Explain.

4. "God's merciful verdict will echo through the universe. For the first time in history, we will understand the depth of his goodness. Itemized grace. Catalogued kindness. Registered forgiveness. We will stand in awe as one sin after another is proclaimed, and then pardoned."

A. What does Max mean by "itemized grace"? How will this show God's goodness?

B. Are you ready for the day of judgment? Explain.

Looking Ahead

1. Read Genesis 6:5–14; 7:17–23.

   A. What do these passages teach us about God's response to sin?

   B. How do these passages prefigure what God will once again do in response to sin?

2. Read Matthew 24:31–46.

   A. What groups are judged as described in these passages?

   B. On what basis are they judged?

   C. What is the final outcome of this judgment for all groups concerned?

3. Read Romans 14:10–12.

   A. Which group is in view in these verses?

   B. On what basis are the members of this group judged?

4. Read 1 Corinthians 3:10–15.

   A. What kind of judgment will Christians undergo?

   B. What are the possible results of this judgment? What is not possible?

5. Read 2 Thessalonians 1:6–10.

   A. What is the destiny of those who don't know God?

   B. In your opinion, what is the worst part of this destiny? Explain.

Looking In

1. Compare 2 Timothy 2:19 with Titus 1:15–16. As you take inventory of your life, how can you increasingly demonstrate that you belong to Christ? How can you make sure that your life does not "deny" Christ? How can you help others to live the pure lives God intends for his people?

2. Over the course of a day, make a mental list of all the acts of grace God has shown to you in just the last year. Then at the end of the day, give thanks to God for each one of these graces he has brought to your mind.

11

LOVE'S CAUTION

Looking Back

1. Max quotes C. S. Lewis, who wrote: "There is no doctrine which I would more willingly remove from Christianity than [hell], if it lay in my power. . . . I would pay any price to be able to say truthfully: 'All will be saved.'"

A. Do you resonate with Lewis's comment? Explain.

B. Why cannot we truthfully say, "All will be saved"?

2. "If there is no hell, God is not just. If there is no punishment of sin, heaven is apathetic toward the rapists and pillagers and mass murderers of society."
   A. Why would God not be just if there were no hell?

   B. How does punishment of sin show heaven is not apathetic toward wickedness?

3. "The New Testament is the primary storehouse of thoughts on hell. And Jesus is the primary teacher. No one spoke of eternal punishment more often or more clearly than Christ himself."
   A. How are these facts significant? How do they make you feel? Why?

   B. Why do you think Jesus and the New Testament spoke so often of hell?

4. "When love didn't compel me, fear corrected me. The thought of the workshop—and the weeping and gnashing of teeth therein—was just enough to straighten me out."
   A. How is this kind of fear merely another face of love?

   B. How does Max's personal experience relate to what God tells us of hell?

5. "People do not go to hell. Sinners do. The rebellious do. The self-centered do. So how could a loving God send people to hell? He doesn't. He simply honors the choice of sinners."

   A. What do you think of Max's teaching above? Do you agree with him? Explain.

   B. If you have ever told a non-Christian something like this, what was the reaction? What happened?

Looking Ahead

1. Read Revelation 9:20–21; 11:10; 16:9–11,21; 14:9–11.

   A. How do the unredeemed react to God's judgments in these passages?

   B. How does God finally respond in Revelation 14:9–11?

2. Read Daniel 12:2 and Matthew 25:46.

   A. What two groups of people are mentioned in both of these texts?

   B. What are the respective destinies of these two groups?

   C. How long will these groups remain in their respective states?

3. Read Luke 16:19–31.

    A. What do you learn about hell in this passage?

    B. How do verses 27–28 show the insanity of saying, "I'll be OK in hell because that's where all my friends will be"?

4. Read Hebrews 2:14–18.

    A. Why did Jesus take on human flesh, according to this passage?

    B. What did Jesus accomplish by his death, according to this passage?

    C. What confidence can we have because Jesus did these things?

Looking In

1. Although it will not be a pleasant study, get a concordance and look up all the verses it lists under the words "hell" or "Hades." What do you discover in your study?

2. For one week, listen for the way people speak of the idea of "hell," whether at work, in the shopping mall, on TV, or in any movies you might see. What do people in this culture believe about hell? What phrases do they use that show an ignorance of its true nature? Why is this significant?

12
SEEING JESUS

Looking Back

1. "Imagine God saying to you, 'I'll make a deal with you if you wish. I'll give you anything and everything you ask: pleasure, power, honor, wealth, freedom, even peace of mind and a good conscience. Nothing will be a sin; nothing will be forbidden; and nothing will be impossible to you. You will never be bored and you will never die. Only . . . you will never see my face.'"

   A. How did you react when you first read this paragraph? Why?

   B. How do you think your best friends would react if they were given this choice? Explain. How would you react? Explain.

2. "Paul doesn't measure the joy of encountering the apostles or embracing our loved ones. If we will be amazed at these, which certainly we will, he does not say. What he does say is that we will be amazed at Jesus."

   A. Why will we be amazed at Jesus?

   B. What amazes you about Jesus right now?

3. "The human tongue is inadequate to describe Christ. So in a breathless effort to tell us what he saw, John gives us symbols."

   A. Why is the human tongue inadequate to describe Christ?

   B. If you had to suggest some other symbols to describe Christ, what symbols might you choose? Describe and explain them.

4. Max describes Christ as:
   - The Perfect Priest.
   - The Only Pure One.
   - The Source of Strength.
   - The Sound of Love.
   - The Everlasting Light.

   A. Explain the significance of each of these descriptions.

   B. Which of these descriptions means the most to you? Why?

Looking Ahead

1. Read 1 John 3:1–3.

   A. How great is the love of God? What epitomizes that love, according to verse 1?

   B. What will happen when we see Christ, according to verse 2? Why will this happen?

C. How is this knowledge supposed to affect us today, according to verse 3?

2. Read Revelation 1:10–18.

A. What picture of Christ do you get when you read this passage? Explain.

B. How did John react to this "unveiling" of Christ? Why was this appropriate?

C. How did Jesus respond to John's reaction? How does this show us his astonishing love?

3. Read Zechariah 12:10–13:1.

A. How does the prophet Zechariah picture the return of Christ?

B. How does "the house of David" react to his coming?

C. How does God respond in 13:1?

Looking In

1. Memorize Hebrews 12:2–3. Meditate on this question: How can pondering Jesus keep you from growing weary and losing heart?

2. We live in a day in which differing views of Christ's coming have divided some Christians. How can you make sure that your own view does not add to this discord? How can it, in fact, encourage others and bring about peace and hope?

13

CROSSING THE THRESHOLD

Looking Back

1. "Is she rebellious? Maybe. But mostly, she is just forgetful."

   A. How does the church sometimes "forget" about her fiancé, Christ?

   B. How can you make sure that you aren't one who forgets about Jesus?

2. "To forget the purpose of gingko is one thing. But to forget our engagement to Christ is another. We need a reminder! May I offer an incentive? *You have captured God's heart.*"

   A. How do we know that we have "captured God's heart"?

   B. How does it make you feel to know that you have captured God's heart?

   C. How are we to respond to this wonderful knowledge?

3. "Allow his love to change the way you look at you."

   A. How do you look at you right now?

   B. How can Christ's love change the way you look at you?

4. "You might ask, 'Why hasn't he come?' There is only one answer. His bride is not ready. She is still being prepared."

   A. How do you think the church is still being prepared for Christ?

   B. In what ways is Christ preparing you for his return?

5. "We want to look our best for Christ. We want our hearts to be pure and our thoughts to be clean. We want our faces to shine with grace and our eyes to sparkle with love. We want to be prepared. Why? In hopes that he will love us? No. Just the opposite. Because he already does."

   A. How does Christ's love for you cause you to seek personal purity?

   B. What word do you think best describes Christ's love for you? Why this word?

Looking Ahead

1. Read Ephesians 5:25–27.

   A. What is Christ's vision for his church, according to these verses?

B. How do you "fit into" this vision? Does this description "fit" you? Explain.

2. Read Revelation 21:2, 9–27.

A. How does John picture "the bride of the Lamb"? What image comes to mind when you read this passage?

B. List the characteristics of the city you find in this passage. What do you think these varied characteristics are meant to teach us about this "bride"?

3. Read 2 Corinthians 11:2–3.

A. What was Paul's goal regarding the church at Corinth?

B. How ought this to be the goal of all of us?

C. How can we ensure that this goal is accomplished? What must we avoid?

4. Read Jeremiah 31:3; Isaiah 62:5; 1 John 4:10.

A. How does God feel about us, according to these passages?

B. How should we respond to this knowledge? How can we practically encourage ourselves to do this?

Looking In

1. If you are married, get out your wedding album, sit down with

your spouse, and reminisce over the day of your wedding. Then take a few moments to discuss "the marriage supper of the Lamb" described in Revelation 19:6–9. How will the wonderful feelings of your own marriage be multiplied and intensified on that day in heaven with Christ?

2. The next time you attend a wedding, prepare yourself by reading Revelation 19:6–9. How do human weddings preview the marriage supper of the Lamb? How can both encourage us in our walk of faith?

WITH AN EAR FOR THE TRUMPET

Looking Back

1. "Like Fred, we took a fall. And, like Fred, we are trapped. Trapped, not by piano wires, but by guilt, anxiety, and pride."
   A. How do guilt, anxiety, and pride "trap" us?

   B. What kind of things tend to "trap" you? How can you be freed from them?

2. "God understands. And he gets creative. He coaxes. Through the fingers of circumstance and situation, he tries to get us to look up. But we, like Fred, make a dash for the corner."

A. How has God been creative in your own experience to rescue you?

B. In what ways do you "dash for the corner"? Why do you do this?

3. Max says we respond to God's overtures in several ways:
   - We pretend God doesn't exist.
   - We don't believe him.
   - We decide to give it a try.
   A. Which of these responses have characterized you at some point in your life?

   B. Which one, if any, characterizes you now? Explain.

4. "Fred finally made his way back to the place where he fell in. He looked up. And when he did, Sara was there. He lifted his head just high enough so that she could reach in and lift him out. Which is exactly what God will do for you. You will look up, and he will reach down and take you home . . . *when Christ comes.*"
   A. What comes to mind when you think of the word "home"?

   B. What are you most looking forward to about the day Christ comes?

Looking Ahead
1. Read Revelation 22:7,12–14,17,20.

A. What does the apostle John emphasize in these final few verses?

B. What would you do today if you knew Christ were coming back at seven o'clock tonight?

2. Read 1 Thessalonians 4:16–18.
   A. What three "sounds" are mentioned in this passage?

   B. What will happen after we hear these sounds?

   C. How does Paul expect that this truth will affect us right now?

3. Read Jude 24–25.
   A. How does Jude envision we will be presented to God?

   B. Who is responsible for this great event?

   C. What kind of response does this call forth from us?

4. Read 2 Peter 3:8–15.
   A. How does Peter counsel us to counter thoughts that suggest Christ is not coming back?

   B. What kind of people ought we to be, since Christ is coming back (verses 11, 14)?

   C. God's "patience" leads to what, according to verse 15?

Looking In

1. Memorize Jude 24–25 and encourage a good friend or family member to memorize it with you. Then take some time and discuss how its truth can help you both grow in faith.

2. Regardless of the time of year, get out a good recording of Handel's *Messiah* and listen to the "Hallelujah Chorus"—and remind yourself that "the King of kings and Lord of lords" is coming back to this earth . . . for *you!*

WHEN CHRIST COMES

Wouldn't it be refreshing to discuss the end of time and feel better because of it? Or to hear some truly comforting words regarding the return of Christ? As only master storyteller Max Lucado can do, he takes readers on an unforgettable journey to show what will happen on the glorious day *When Christ Comes*. For Christians, the return of Christ is not a riddle to be solved or a code to be broken, but rather a day to anticipate.

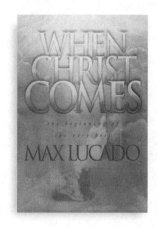

JUST LIKE JESUS

"What if, for one day, Jesus were to become you," asks master storyteller Max Lucado. "What if, for one day and night, Jesus lives your life with his heart? His priorities govern your actions. His passions drive your decisions. His love directs your behavior. What would you be like?" With this simple premise, Lucado tells how God loves you just the way you are but He refuses to leave you that way. The same one who saved your soul longs to remake your heart. His plan is nothing short of a total transformation. He wants you to be... *Just Like Jesus*.

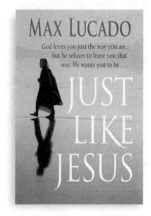

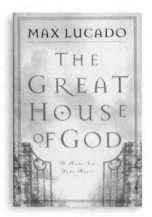

THE GREAT HOUSE OF GOD

God's greatest desire is to be your dwelling place—the home for your heart. Using the Lord's Prayer as a floor plan for *The Great House of God*, Max Lucado introduces us to a God who desires his children to draw close to Him—indeed, to live with Him. Warm your heart by the fire in the living room. Nourish your spirit in the kitchen. Step into the hallway and find forgiveness. No house is more complete, no foundation more solid. So come into the house built just for you...the great house of God.

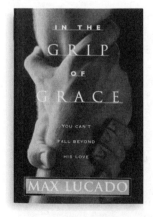

IN THE GRIP OF GRACE

Can anything separate us from the love of God? Can you drift too far? Wait too long? Out-sin the love of God? The answer is found in one of life's sweetest words—*grace*. In his most theologically challenging book yet, Max Lucado shows how you can't fall beyond God's love. "God doesn't condone our sin, nor does He compromise His standard. Rather than dismiss our sin, He assumes our sin and incredibly, incredibly sentences Himself. God is still holy. Sin is still sin. And we are redeemed."

A Gentle Thunder

How far do you want God to go in getting your attention? Don't answer too quickly. What if God moved you to another land? (as He did Abraham.) What if He called you out of retirement? (Remember Moses?) How about the voice of an angel or the bowel of a fish (Gideon and Jonah.) God does what it takes to get our attention. That's the message of this book: the relentless pursuit of God. Searching, wrestling, pulling us back to Him, over and over again. Softly shouting, gently thundering...whatever it takes to get us home safely.

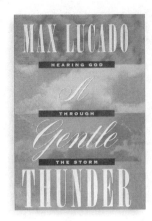

When God Whispers Your Name

Do you find it hard to believe that the One who made everything keeps your name in His heart and on His lips? In fact, did you realize that your name is written on the hand of God (Is. 49:16)? Perhaps you've never seen your name honored. And you can't remember when you heard it spoken with kindness. If you're struggling to find your way, Lucado offers the inspiration to believe that God has already bought the ticket-with your name on it. This book affirms that God can move you along on your journey with power from beyond.

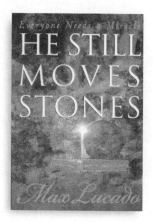

HE STILL MOVES STONES

Why does the Bible contain so many stories of hurting people? Though their situations vary, their conditions don't. They have nowhere to turn. Yet before their eyes stands a never-say-die Galilean who majors in stepping in when everyone else steps out. Lucado reminds us that the purpose of these portraits isn't to tell us what Jesus *did*—but rather to remind us what Jesus still *does*. He comes to do what you can't. He comes to move the stones you can't budge. He still moves stones.

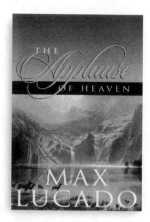

THE APPLAUSE OF HEAVEN

It is what you always dreamed but never expected. It's having God as your dad, your biggest fan, and your best friend. It is having the King of kings in your cheering section. It is hearing the applause of heaven. Max Lucado believes that the Beatitudes provide what we need to discover the joy of God. Much more than a how-to book on happiness, *The Applause of Heaven* is an encounter with the Source of joy. Read it and see that the Joy of God is within your reach.

IN THE EYE OF THE STORM

Come face-to-face with Jesus when He experienced more stress than any other day of his life aside from his crucifixion. Before the morning became evening, he has reason to weep, run, shout, curse, praise, and doubt. His life went from calm to chaos within a matter of moments. If you know what it means to be caught in life's storms…if you've ever ridden the roller coaster of sorrow and celebration… if you've ever wondered if God in heaven can relate to you on earth, then this book will encourage and inspire you.

COSMIC CHRISTMAS

Was the birth of Jesus a quietly profound event? Or could it have included heavenly battles, angel armies, and a scheming Satan? Come along as Lucado takes us on a journey into his imagination—pulling back the curtain as we see what might have taken place one *Cosmic Christmas*.

THE CHRISTMAS CROSS

The Christmas Cross is a story about finding your way home for the holidays, told in the context of one man's journey in a small Texas town. Unique interactive elements inside this book—including envelopes with pullout letters and surprises—makes this a one-of-a-kind Christmas treasure.

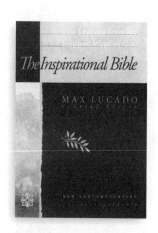

THE INSPIRATIONAL BIBLE

Imagine studying the Bible with Max Lucado. He see the Bible as "stories of real people, real problems, real joy, and a real Savior." Edited by Max Lucado, *The Inspirational Bible* includes:

- 700 "Life Lessons" that apply Scriptural truths to everyday life
- Dramatic introductions to each book of the Bible writtten by Lucado
- 48 color pages that address topics from Forgiveness to Victory.

"LIFE LESSONS" BIBLE STUDY GUIDES

Max Lucado is your tour guide as you journey through both Old and New Testaments books in this exciting series. Each of the sixteen Bible Study Guides are ideal for either small group or individual study, and includes features like: "How To Study The Bible," inspirational quotes by Max and other popular authors, stirring introductions to the book of the Bible, thought-provoking questions, room for journaling and personal thoughts, and a closing prayer from Max Lucado.

More Inspirational Books by Max Lucado

The Applause of Heaven

It is what you always dreamed but never expected. It's having God as your dad, your biggest fan, and your best friend. It is having the King of Kings in your cheering section. Max Lucado believes that the Beatitudes provide what we need to discover the joy of God. Much more than a how-to book on happiness, *The Applause of Heaven* is an encounter with the Source of joy.

The Christmas Cross

The Christmas Cross is a story about finding your way home for the holidays, told in the context of one man's journey in a small Texas town. Unique interactive elements inside this book—including envelopes with pullout letters and surprises—make this a one-of-a-kind Christmas treasure.

Cosmic Christmas

Was the birth of Jesus a quietly profound event? Or could it have included heavenly battles, angel armies, and a scheming Satan? Come along as Lucado takes us on a journey into his imagination—pulling back the curtain as we see what might have taken place one *Cosmic Christmas*.

A Gentle Thunder

How far would you want God to go in getting your attention? Don't answer too quickly. What if God called you out of retirement? (Remember Moses?) What if He moved you to another land (as He did with Abraham)? What if He used the voice of an angel or the bowels of a fish (as with Gideon and Jonah)? God does what it takes to get our attention. That's the message of this book: God's relentless pursuit of our hearts.

WORD PUBLISHING
www.wordpublishing.com

The Great House of God

Using the Lord's Prayer as a floor plan for *The Great House of God*, Max Lucado introduces us to a God who desires his children to draw close to him. Warm your heart by the fire in the living room. Nourish your spirit in the kitchen. Step into the hallway and find forgiveness. No house is more complete, no foundation more solid. So come into the house built just for you—*The Great House of God*.

He Chose the Nails

The wood. The thorns. The nails. In *He Chose the Nails*, Max Lucado examines the symbols surrounding Christ's crucifixion, revealing the claims of the cross and asserting that if they are true, then Christianity itself is true. Through the supporting evidence we see the cross as either the single biggest hoax of all time, or the hope of all humanity.

He Did This Just For You

Building on stories and illustrations from the book *He Chose the Nails* by Max Lucado, this riveting 64-page evangelistic book leads the readers through God's plan of salvation and offers an invitation to accept Christ. It's the perfect way to introduce the gospel to friends and acquaintances.

He Still Moves Stones

Why does the Bible contain so many stories of hurting people? Though their situations vary, their conditions don't. They have nowhere to turn. Yet before their eyes stands a never-say-die Galilean who majors in stepping in when everyone else steps out. Lucado reminds us that the purpose of these portraits isn't to tell us what Jesus *did*—but rather to remind us what Jesus still *does*.

WORD PUBLISHING
www.wordpublishing.com

THE MUSIC

Available Fall 1999

To locate the Christian bookstore nearest you
Call 1-800-991-7747

INTEGRITY
MUSIC.

In the Eye of the Storm

Come face-to-face with Jesus when He experienced more stress than any other day of his life aside from his crucifixion. Before morning became evening, he had reason to weep, run, shout, curse, praise, and doubt. If you know what it means to be caught in life's storms, if you've ever ridden the roller coaster of sorrow and celebration, or if you've ever wondered if God in heaven can relate to you on earth, then this book will encourage and inspire you.

In the Grip of Grace

Can anything separate us from the love of God? The answer is found in one of life's sweetest words—grace. Max Lucado shows how you can't fall beyond God's love. "God doesn't condone our sin, nor does He compromise His standard. Rather than dismiss our sin, He assumes our sin and incredibly, incredibly sentences Himself. God is still holy. Sin is still sin. And we are redeemed."

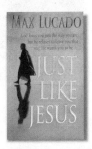

Just Like Jesus

"What if, for one day, Jesus became you?" asks master storyteller Max Lucado. With this simple premise, Lucado tells how God loves you just the way you are, but he refuses to leave you that way. He wants you to be—*Just Like Jesus.*

The Inspirational Bible
New Century Version

Imagine studying the Bible with Max Lucado. This beautifully designed Bible contains Lucado's dramatic introductions to each book and 48 special color pages which address topics from forgiveness to victory. Also, more than 1,000 "Life Lessons" offer insights from Max and other respected Christian leaders.

WORD PUBLISHING
www.wordpublishing.com

The "Life Lessons" Bible Study Series

Max Lucado is your tour guide as you journey through both Old and New Testament books in this exciting series. Each of the sixteen Bible Study Guides is ideal for either small group or individual study and includes features like: "How to Study the Bible," inspirational quotes by Max and other popular authors, stirring introductions to the books of the Bible, thought-provoking questions, room for journaling and personal thoughts, and a closing prayer.

When Christ Comes

Thoughts of the Second Coming are unsettling. Open graves and occupied clouds. Sin revealed and evil unveiled. Yet, for Max Lucado, the coming of Christ will be "the beginning of the very best." In *When Christ Comes*, Lucado shares how Christians can live in hope, confident in His comfort and peaceful in our preparations for His return.

When God Whispers Your Name

Do you find it hard to believe that the One who made everything keeps your name in His heart and on His lips? Did you realize that your name is written on the hand of God (Is. 49:16)? In this book, Lucado offers the inspiration to believe that God has already bought the ticket—with your name on it.

WORD PUBLISHING
www.wordpublishing.com